the atonement
debate

the atonement debate

papers from the london symposium
on the theology of atonement

including contributions from
steve chalke, chris wright, i. howard marshall & joel green

derek tidball, david hilborn & justin thacker
general editors

ZONDERVAN

ZONDERVAN.com/
AUTHORTRACKER
follow your favorite authors

ZONDERVAN

The Atonement Debate
Copyright © 2008 by Evangelical Alliance and London School of Theology

The Evangelical Alliance and London School of Theology assert their moral right to be identified as the authors of this work.

Requests for information should be addressed to:

Zondervan, *Grand Rapids, Michigan 49530*

Library of Congress Cataloging-in-Publication Data

London Symposium on the Theology of Atonement (2005 : London School of Theology)
   The atonement debate : papers from the London Symposium on the Theology of Atonement / Derek Tidball, David Hilborn, and Justin Thacker, general editors.
      p. cm.
   Includes bibliographical references.
   ISBN 978-0-310-27339-4 (softcover)
   1. Atonement—Congresses. I. Tidball, Derek. II. Hilborn, David. III. Thacker, Justin.
IV. Title.
BT265.3.L66 2005
232'.3—dc22   2007039307

Internet addresses (websites, blogs, etc.) and telephone numbers printed in this book are offered as a resource to you. These are not intended in any way to be or imply an endorsement on the part of Zondervan, nor do we vouch for the content of these sites and numbers for the life of this book.

Interior design by Matthew Van Zomeren
Printed in the United States of America

contents

abbreviations

AB	Anchor Bible
ABD	*Anchor Bible Dictionary.* Edited by D. N. Freedman. 6 vols. New York: Doubleday, 1992.
BDAG	W. Bauer, W. F. Arndt, F. W. Gingrich. *Greek-English Lexicon of the New Testament and Other Early Christian Literature.* 3rd ed. Revised and edited by F. W. Danker. Chicago and London: Univ. of Chicago Press, 2000.
BECNT	Baker Exegetical Commentary on the New Testament
CBQ	*Catholic Biblical Quarterly*
CurBS	*Currents in Research: Biblical Studies*
EQ	*Evangelical Quarterly*
ET	English translation
EuroJTh	*European Journal of Theology*
ExpTim	*Expository Times*
FRLANT	Forschungen zur Religion und Literatur des Alten und Neuen Testaments
HTS	Harvard Theological Studies
IBS	*Irish Biblical Studies*
ICC	International Critical Commentary
JETS	*Journal of the Evangelical Theological Society*
JSNTSup	Journal for the Study of the New Testament: Supplement Series
JSOTSup	Journal for the Study of the Old Testament: Supplement Series
JTS	*Journal of Theological Studies*
LSJ	H. G. Liddell and R. Scott, *A Greek-English Lexicon: With a Revised Supplement*, revised by H. S. Jones. Oxford: Clarendon, 1996.
LTPM	Louvain Theological and Pastoral Monographs
MNTC	Moffatt New Testament Commentary
MTP	*Metropolitan Tabernacle Pulpit*

NDT	*New Dictionary of Theology.* Edited by Sinclair B. Ferguson and David F. Wright. Leicester: IVP, 1998.
NIB	*The New Interpreter's Bible*
NICNT	New International Commentary on the New Testament
NICOT	New International Commentary on the Old Testament
NIDOTTE	*New International Dictionary of Old Testament Theology and Exegesis.* Edited by W. A. VanGemeren. 5 vols. Grand Rapids: Zondervan, 1997.
NIGTC	New International Greek Testament Commentary
NSBT	New Studies in Biblical Theology
NTOA	Novum Testamentum et Orbis Antiquus
SBLDS	Society of Biblical Literature Dissertation Series
SJLA	Studies in Judaism in Late Antiquity
SJT	*Scottish Journal of Theology*
SNTSMS	Society for New Testament Studies Monograph Series
TDOT	*Theological Dictionary of the Old Testament.* Edited by G. J. Botterweck and H. Ringgren. Translated by J. T. Willis, G. W. Bromiley, and D. E. Green. 8 vols. Grand Rapids: Eerdmans, 1974–97.
TOTC	Tyndale Old Testament Commentaries
TynBul	*Tyndale Bulletin*
WUNT	Wissenschaftliche Untersuchungen zum Neuen Testament

contributors

Steve Chalke founded Oasis Trust, London, in 1985.

Oliver D. Crisp is Lecturer in Theology at the University of Bristol, UK.

Joel B. Green is Professor of New Testament Interpretation at Asbury Seminary, Wilmore, Kentucky, USA.

Geoffrey Grogan is now retired and living in Scotland.

Sue Groom is Director of Deanery Licensed Ministers for Kensington.

David Hilborn is Director of Studies on the North Thames Ministerial Training Course. Prior to this he was Head of Theology at the Evangelical Alliance, UK.

Stephen R. Holmes is Lecturer in Theology at St Mary's College, University of St Andrews, Scotland.

Tony Lane is Professor of Historical Theology at London School of Theology.

Graham McFarlane lectures in systematic theology at London School of Theology.

I. Howard Marshall is Honorary Research Professor of New Testament, University of Aberdeen.

Rohintan K. Mody is an ordained minister of the Church of England.

Steve Motyer leads the Theology and Counselling Course at London School of Theology.

Lynnette J. Mullings is a pastor in the Wesleyan Holiness Church and Director of the Wesleyan Holiness Bible Institute.

Ian Randall is Senior Research Fellow at the International Baptist Theological Seminary, Prague.

Anna M. Robbins is Vice Principal of the London School of Theology and Lecturer in Ethics, Theology and Contemporary Culture.

Justin Thacker is Head of Theology at the Evangelical Alliance, UK.

Derek Tidball was Principal of the London School of Theology and is Chair of the Council of the Evangelical Alliance, UK.

David T. Williams is Deputy Head of Department, School of Theology and Religion, University of Fort Hare, South Africa.

Garry Williams is Academic Dean of Oak Hill Theological College, London.

Christopher J. H. Wright is International Director of the Langham Partnership International.

introduction

preface

derek tidball

In the midst of the London Symposium on the Theology of Atonement held at London School of Theology in July 2005, terrorist bombs struck at the heart of London's transport system, causing death and injury to many. The terrible events of 7/7 put in context the debate being held. On the one hand, they emphasised how important is the most crucial event of all time, that Jesus "was crucified under Pontius Pilate" for our fallen world, where evil stalks, and how central the message of the gospel is for the twenty-first century. On the other hand, they put some of the more abstruse points of conflict in perspective and underlined that some academic discussion can be a wasteful, not to say sinful, luxury.

The opening paper in this collection explains the reason for the calling of the symposium. While some evangelical theologians had expressed reservations about the way in which the penal substitutionary interpretation of the cross has often been communicated, it took the writing of a popular Christian leader to stoke the controversy and cause public debate. Part of the work of the Evangelical Alliance is to help different parts of the evangelical family to understand each other where controversy arises. So it was natural that EA should provide opportunities for those who, often passionately, differed from each other to talk and listen to one another. It was clear that a debate on the atonement hosted by EA in October 2004 was not an adequate forum to explore this issue. Hence a further opportunity was sought to consider the matter in greater depth. LST provided the academic context in which such a symposium could be held, and some two hundred participants gathered in July 2005 for further reflection and open engagement.

This book contains some of the papers given at the symposium. They have been reworked, in various degrees, since then. A few still bear the hallmarks of a spoken presentation. While we have sought to introduce coherence in style with regard to referencing and headings, the editors have not sought to impose a bland editorial conformity on the papers but rather have let the contributors speak for themselves. This inevitably leads to some unevenness and overlap. But few read such a book as this from cover to cover.

One presenter at the symposium requested us not to publish his paper, and another paper was left out of this present volume due to an administrative oversight. This has contributed to the *Christus Victor* theme not having as in-depth a focus as we would have wished. However, the issues are covered to some extent in other papers. Six papers have been added to make for a more rounded volume. These were offered for presentation at the symposium but could not be accommodated within the programme. These papers are those by Grogan, Crisp, David Williams, Lane, Randall and Tidball. Dr Simon Gathercole was to be at the symposium to present an exegetical paper on Romans 3:25–26 but was prevented from attending by the terrorist attacks. His paper was read for him by Professor Max Turner. It has subsequently been rewritten and augmented at Dr Gathercole's request by Rohintan Mody.

No attempt was made to produce an agreed statement at the end of the symposium. We believe the value of the symposium lay in the face-to-face interaction and in the papers, which now will enjoy wider circulation. Those who participated were self-selecting, and though a survey of opinions was conducted at the conclusion of our time together, it has no wider value than reflecting the views of those who remained until the end. A few stated that they had changed their position as a result of the debate. The final session consisted of a panel discussion, which included Alan Mann, the co-author of *The Lost Message of Jesus*. Those present will remember it as a significant time of healing of divisions.

All who took part in the symposium agree on three things: the central significance of the death of Christ to the Christian faith; the variety and richness of the way the New Testament interprets that death; and the urgent necessity to communicate the message of the cross in a way that is both faithful to the Bible's revelation and meaningful in the contemporary world. It is hoped that the publication of these papers will enable readers to explore the issues at stake in the debate about penal substitution more fully and, whatever their conclusion, to join with others with renewed energy in making known "Christ crucified".

chapter one

atonement, evangelicalism and the evangelical alliance

the present debate in context

david hilborn

> The Incarnation of the Son of God, His work of Atonement for the sinners of mankind, and His Mediatorial Intercession and Reign.
> — *Doctrinal Basis of Faith of the World's Evangelical Alliance, 1846*

> The substitutionary sacrifice of the incarnate Son of God as the sole all-sufficient ground of redemption from the guilt and power of sin, and from its eternal consequences.
> — *Evangelical Alliance (UK) Basis of Faith, 1970*

> The atoning sacrifice of Christ on the cross: dying in our place, paying the price of sin and defeating evil, so reconciling us with God.
> — *Evangelical Alliance (UK) Basis of Faith, 2005*

However it is defined, there is little doubt that the evangelical tradition is distinguished by a strong emphasis on the cross of Christ and on the atonement accomplished by Christ's death. Some might want to qualify David Bebbington's now familiar typology of evangelicalism, but it would be hard to deny his assertion that down the centuries, the "pre-eminent ground of agreement" between evangelicals has been "the cruciality of the cross".[1] Likewise, as Alister McGrath has expressed it, "Evangelicalism places an especial emphasis on the cross of Christ" and sees the atonement as establishing "the centrality of Christ to Christian worship and adoration".[2] Derek Tidball concurs, stressing that the atonement is "the central core of evangelical belief and preaching. Evangelicals make redemption the pivot of the faith. Where others place the doctrines of creation or of incarnation, evangelicals place the atonement. It is, quite simply, the heart of evangelicalism."[3]

As co-sponsors of the July 2005 symposium from which this volume is derived, both the Evangelical Alliance UK (EA) and the London School of Theology (LST) bear out such crucicentrism in their respective Bases of Faith. Both bodies have revised their doctrinal statements in recent times, but their formal theological commitments remain as atonement-centred as ever. At the heart of LST's Basis lies the affirmation that Jesus secured our salvation by "dying on the cross in our place", thus "representing us to God" and "redeeming us from the grip, guilt and punishment of sin".[4] When EA was formed in 1846, its Basis concisely asserted Christ's "work of Atonement for the sinners of mankind". When that original Basis was reworded in 1970, this brief statement was superseded by a clause which spelt out more explicitly how the atonement defines evangelical belief. That clause affirmed "the substitutionary sacrifice of the incarnate Son of God as the sole and all-sufficient ground of redemption from the guilt and power of sin, and from its eternal consequences". With comparable force, the present EA Basis affirms "the atoning sacrifice of Christ on the cross: dying in our place, paying the price of sin and defeating evil, so reconciling us to God".[5] Thus both EA and LST remain committed to the classical evangelical view that the atonement wrought by God in Christ on the cross stands at the heart of the gospel – that it critically authenticates Christian life and mission. Together, they look with Paul to "preach Christ crucified"; together, they seek "never to boast of anything except the cross of our Lord" (1 Cor. 1:23; Gal. 6:14).

For most evangelicals, the central importance of the cross as such is not in dispute. Indeed, the current controversies surrounding atonement theology in evangelicalism have more to do with *how* the cross operates at the heart of Christian faith, rather than whether it does so. There are multiple aspects to this "how" question, and many are covered elsewhere in this book. In particular, though, argument has centred on a theory or model of the atonement which has defined evangelical faith more than any other, but which has latterly been subject to mounting critique – not only from liberal theologians but also from several more radical representatives of the evangelical community. I am referring, of course, to "penal substitution". The particular dispute which prompted the joint EA-LST symposium was catalysed by the stark critique of penal substitution presented by Steve Chalke and Alan Mann in their book, *The Lost Message of Jesus* – a critique subsequently elaborated by Chalke in various articles, interviews and statements, and by Mann in his monograph *Atonement for a Sinless Society*.[6]

In sketching this background, it should be stressed that the chief purpose of the London symposium was not to subject Chalke, Mann and their work to a heresy trial. Some may regret that the intrinsic diversity of evangelicalism inevitably dilutes attempts to exercise pan-evangelical doctrinal discipline, and some may have remedies to suggest on this front. The symposium, however, was not the place to apply them. Through more than 160 years, the EA has occasionally urged certain of its members to resign over theological matters: T. R. Birks over hell and restitution in 1870; the Jesus Army over ecclesiology in the 1980s; Maurice Cerullo over prosperity teaching in the mid-1990s; and Courage Trust over their changed stance on homosexual practice at the turn of the millennium. Yet it has always been negotiated resignation rather than summary expulsion. Moreover, the problems have been as much to do with practice as belief.

Indeed, throughout the *Lost Message* controversy, Steve Chalke has clearly affirmed both past and present EA Bases of Faith. In such circumstances, what the original 1846 Basis called the "right to private judgement" must pertain, at least while the terms of the debate are clarified and the theological arguments carefully weighed. EA did not rush to operate as a thought police in this matter; it did not presume to make "windows into men's souls". Besides, as this volume confirms, intra-evangelical dispute on penal substitution is much older, wider and more momentous than any such narrow *ad hominem* targeting of Chalke or Mann would suggest. In fact, a key point in favour of holding the symposium at LST was that it would foster concentration on the broader issues at stake in the atonement debate, rather than on the personalities most immediately and most recently associated with that debate.

Having said all this, Alister McGrath is quite right to note that evangelicalism *on the ground* is one of the most personality-driven of all Christian traditions.[7] As the Alliance's head of theology at the time of the London symposium, my work was funded by a charitable body which for the most part operated not in scholarly arenas but through local evangelical congregations, parachurch organisations, and networks. In these contexts, it can take some time for doctrinal debates to filter through from the academy. They tend to remain relatively obscure until a high-profile preacher, evangelist or church leader popularises them – and in Britain few evangelical personalities enjoy as high a profile as Steve Chalke MBE. Hence, when he decided to question penal substitution in *The Lost Message of Jesus*, an issue which had barely registered in EA's postbags and inboxes for decades swiftly galvanised the evangelical community. As a personal member of EA who leads organisations which are in turn corporate members, it was inevitable that Chalke's relationship with the Alliance, and with its Basis of Faith, would be questioned. It was also inevitable that having thus been drawn into the controversy, there would be pressure on EA to do something about it. Before examining EA's response and how that response led to the London symposium, it will be helpful to put the *Lost Message* issue more fully into context.

The Lost Message of Jesus was published in December 2003. Its chief aim was not to expound a detailed theology of the cross but rather to demonstrate "the core of Jesus' life-transforming, though often deeply misunderstood, message".[8] This core message was summarized in terms of God's kingdom or "inbreaking shalom" being available now to everyone through Jesus Christ.[9] However, it was Chalke and Mann's interpretation of the death of Christ which attracted the most attention.

Typically, evangelical crucicentrism has emphasised the "objective" nature of the atonement, whereby Christ's death is seen once and for all to have effected reconciliation between God and fallen, sinful human beings. Historically, this has been explained by various theories drawn from a wide range of biblical imagery, and evangelicals have characteristically acknowledged that orthodox understanding of it depends on a combination of such theories, rather than on any one in isolation. As the leading evangelical expositor of atonement, Leon Morris, put it, "Christ's atoning work is so complex and our minds are so small. We cannot take it all in. We need the positive contributions of all the theories, for each draws attention to some aspect of what Christ has done for us. And though in the end we cannot understand it all, we can thankfully accept 'so great a salvation'."[10] Thus, in accordance with Romans 5:15–21, evangelicals have recognised the theory of recapitulation, in which the life and death of the sinless Christ reverse Adam and Eve's disobedience and make human beings right with God. On the basis of texts like Matthew 20:28 and Mark 10:45, they have appreciated the dramatic theory, in which Christ's death achieves victory in a cosmic conflict between good and evil and secures humanity's release from bondage to sin. Citing John 10:18, evangelicals have also valued the commercial theory, in which Christ's death is seen as bringing infinite honour to God – an honour which is applied to human beings and thereby redeems the dishonour which attends their sinful state.[11]

Yet amidst these and other theories, penal substitution has widely been regarded as the "controlling model" within mainline evangelicalism – the *sine qua non* of evangelical soteriology. As construed from texts such as Isaiah 53:6–10, Romans 3:25, Hebrews 9:11–10:22 and 1 Peter 3:18, penal substitution presents Jesus' crucifixion as a vicarious sacrifice which appeased or "propitiated" God's wrath towards sin by paying the due "penalty" for that sin, which is suffering, death and condemnation. Whereas sinful humanity stood to incur this penalty, the sinless Christ incurred it for us on Calvary. Precisely because he is without sin, he was thus able to cancel or "expiate" the guilt which attends it, so bringing us forgiveness, imputing righteousness to us and restoring our relationship with God.[12]

The origins of penal substitution as a systematic model are much disputed, as the reader will see in various contributions to this volume. Sympathetic evangelical accounts characteristically trace its development through Clement of Rome in the first century, Cyril of Jerusalem in the fourth, Augustine in the fifth, John Calvin in the sixteenth, and John Owen in the seventeenth, ultimately ascribing its more detailed form to the nineteenth-century Princeton theologians Charles Hodge and Benjamin B. Warfield.[13] With this pedigree, penal substitution is often deemed by evangelicals to be the most fulfilling description of the role of the cross in the process of salvation.[14]

However, Steve Chalke and Alan Mann take a different view. In chapter 10 of *The Lost Message of Jesus*, they reject penal substitution on the grounds that it turns God from a loving Father into a vengeful tyrant, who "suddenly decides to vent his anger and wrath on his own Son". Then, either consciously or unconsciously echoing feminist theologian Rita Nakishima Brock, they provocatively cast this version of the atonement as a "form of cosmic child abuse".[15] They claim that as well as its being a "total contradiction of the statement 'God is love' ", it "makes a mockery of Jesus' own teaching to love your enemies and to refuse to repay evil with evil".[16] In a subsequent solo article, Chalke emphasises that this critique of penal substitution extends even beyond questions about "how the cross works" to "the very nature of

God, and as a consequence, the task of Christian mission and the attitude of the Church".[17]

Unsurprisingly, these charges have drawn a strong reaction. Reviewing *The Lost Message of Jesus* in June 2004, Mike Ovey and Andrew Sach accused Chalke and Mann of propounding "a wrong view of God", "a wrong view of man" and "a wrong view of the cross". Whereas the Bible often portrays God's "white-hot moral purity and indignation at sin", they wrote, *The Lost Message of Jesus* had "airbrushed" such divine attributes out of the picture. Similarly, they asked, "If God is not angry, and humans are not essentially guilty, then what job remains for the cross?"[18] Underlining these concerns, Garry Williams wrote that *The Lost Message of Jesus* offered no more than a "caricature" of penal substitution which would simply "not do".[19] Similar sentiments were expressed by Greg Haslam in a robust defence of penal substitution, which countered point by point the proposals made by Chalke and Mann.[20]

Despite these harsh appraisals, *The Lost Message of Jesus* attracted robust support from the Christian political think tank Ekklesia, from members of the Anabaptist Network and from correspondents to various Christian periodicals, not least the newspaper of Chalke's own denomination, the *Baptist Times*.[21] Furthermore, as early as June 2004, the Spring Harvest Leadership Team, of which Chalke is a prominent member, issued a statement stressing that he continued to uphold its own theological position.[22] Significantly, that position was and still is defined by the Evangelical Alliance Basis of Faith, as well as by the Lausanne Covenant (1974). Indeed, once Spring Harvest had issued this statement, it became impossible for EA to stay on the sidelines of the dispute.

As the Alliance sought to handle the growing debate on penal substitution responsibly, it needed to look beyond the few paragraphs that Chalke and Mann had devoted to the issue and facilitate a broadly based dialogue on the place and understanding of the atonement within evangelicalism. EA's theological commission was well aware that, while Chalke's profile had done much to bring evangelical doubts about penal substitution into the open, these doubts had been aired in various parts of the evangelical academy for some time. It knew Chalke and Mann were not the first evangelicals to critique the penal substitutionary theory, and they were unlikely to be the last. It noted that under the influence of William Law, certain nineteenth-century theologians like Thomas Erskine and George MacDonald had either significantly softened penal substitution or effectively abandoned it.[23] It realised that many in the so-called Liberal Evangelical movement of the 1920s had jettisoned penal substitution as "crude".[24] It also recognised that more recently a growing number of professing evangelical scholars had questioned penal substitution from various angles, among them Stephen Travis, Tom Smail, Nigel Wright, Clark Pinnock, Robert Brow, J. Denny Weaver, Christopher D. Marshall, Mark Baker and Joel Green.[25] Indeed, while acknowledging that *The Lost Message of Jesus* had done much to publicise this "dissenting" evangelical position, the commission stressed that it had not pioneered that dissent. Consequently, EA undertook to address the points Chalke and Mann had raised with reference to its own theological position, but to do so in the context of the wider academic evangelical debate. This strategy was then developed in three main stages.

First, on 7 October 2004, the Alliance convened a public dialogue on *The Lost Message of Jesus*, with a focus on the atonement.[26] Initially, it booked a room to hold 150 people for this event, but the interest aroused by the debate forced the venue to be switched to a larger space in the Emmanuel Centre, Westminster, which was filled by an audience of around seven hundred. Although Chalke was a keynote speaker, he was partnered by Stuart Murray Williams. On the other side, apologetics for penal substitution were offered by Simon Gathercole and Anna Robbins, with Mike Ovey appearing on the panel at Chalke's request in the question-and-answer session.

After hosting the October 2004 meeting and listening carefully to the arguments on both sides, the theological commission, board, and senior staff of the Alliance embarked on the second phase of its work on the atonement dispute. In early November 2004, it released a statement clarifying its stance on *The Lost Message of Jesus* and the interpretative parameters of its Basis of Faith with respect to the cross.[27] In this statement, EA acknowledged that certain self-identified evangelical scholars had questioned aspects of the penal substitutionary view, and it recognised the need to interact with their work. However, while welcoming careful and constructive reflection on the cross of Christ, it expressed concern that in Chalke's case there had been insufficient appreciation of the extent to which penal substitution had shaped, and continued to inform, evangelical understanding of the atonement. The statement went on to address the significance of this for the interpretation of its Basis of Faith. It noted that while the Basis did not use the explicit terms "penal", "penalty" or "punishment" in relation to what it called the "substitutionary sacrifice" of Christ, the executive council which approved the Basis in 1970 took it as entailing and implying penal substitution. It emphasised that its affirmations of universal human sin and guilt, divine wrath and condemnation, and the substitutionary, sacrificial and redemptive nature of Christ's death together comprised the key elements of penal substitution. The statement then urged that instead of dismissing penal substitution, Chalke should recognise its significant place in the range of atonement theories to which evangelicals have subscribed. It expressed concern that Chalke not only had pressed for his own anti-penal substitutionary view to be accepted within the Alliance but also had asserted that those who do hold it were doing serious damage to the church's witness and should abandon it for the sake of the gospel. This, said the statement, might compromise the spirit of the Alliance's so-called Practical Resolutions, which urge charity in evangelical disputes, not least where objections are being raised against well-established mainline evangelical doctrine.[28]

The statement accepted Chalke's point that evangelicals are often perceived as harsh, censorious and ungracious, and that this can hamper evangelism. But it denied his construction of a causal or necessary link between affirming penal substitution and *being* harsh, censorious and ungracious. In conclusion, it called on him to reconsider his approach to the issue. A month later, on December 10, 2004, Chalke and the EA general director, Joel Edwards, issued a joint statement pledging to "wrestle honestly together in applying the truth of Christ's substitutionary sacrifice, which is so central to our faith".[29] In keeping with this, they confirmed the third stage in the Alliance's strategy: the convening of the summer 2005 symposium on which this book is based.

Leaving aside the distinctives of his atonement theology, it can surely be agreed that the "honest wrestling" to which Chalke committed himself is a pledge which all in the debate should make. Even those who have reached what Dan Strange has called "cognitive rest" on penal substitution[30] need Leon Morris's reticence about any Christian's ability to exhaust the glory of the atonement with their human explanations. Yet of course, as we resolve to "know nothing except Christ and him crucified" (1 Cor. 2:2), we must at least *try* to articulate why Christ died and in what way. As the Alliance has sought to do this in the *Lost Message* controversy, one might wonder how it was so clear that the original drafters of the 1970 Basis meant to imply penal substitution, even though the text does not explicitly use the terms "penal" or "penalty". Herein lies an intriguing story – one whose twists and turns help to account for why EA arrived at the particular formulation of the atonement contained in the more recent version of its Basis of Faith, which was drafted between 2002 and 2005 and formally adopted in September 2005.

In helping to write EA's November 2004 statement on penal substitution, I consulted the Alliance archive and reviewed the executive council minutes to see if they shed any light on why the 1970 Basis was worded as it was.[31] Although the drafting process spanned three years from 1967 to 1970, and although other clauses went through several drafts, the relevant section on the cross – clause 4 – seems to have been settled early on and to have stayed the same almost to the end.[32] As we have seen, when the Alliance was formed in 1846, it adopted a doctrinal statement which affirmed Christ's "work of atonement for sinners of mankind". Clearly, the many disputes about the atonement which had developed between that point and the late 1960s prompted the EA executive council to tighten up its language on the cross. This it did with alacrity, as is seen by the introduction of terms like "substitutionary", "sacrifice", "sole", "all-sufficient", "redemption" and "guilt" in the revised Basis, all of which readily occupy the semantic field of penal substitution. Indeed, this vocabulary would appear to echo an even more explicit endorsement of the penal substitutionary view from an official Alliance report of the same period. *On the Other Side* was a special study on evangelism commissioned by the Alliance's executive council and was published in 1968. Here one finds a clear, unequivocal affirmation of penal substitution, which, given its parallel dating, can logically be read as an exposition of the language of the revised Basis:

> The judgement upon sin has been endured for man by Christ. God in Christ has taken the initiative in dealing with our sin and with the judgement upon it. By voluntarily giving himself to die upon the cross Christ suffered the worst that sin can do, including separation from His Father. God laid upon him all the consequence of human wrong-doing and wrong relationships, and He took upon Himself the penalty of our sin. This understanding of the Atonement, which is both clear and prominent in the New Testament, lies at the heart of the various biblical descriptions of Christ's death – e.g. sacrifice, redemption, justification, reconciliation.[33]

Given the clarity and directness of this statement, it seems unlikely that the final text of the revised Basis issued just two years later, in 1970, might imply any qualification of the classical penal substitutionary position. However, this deduction would be even more obvious were it not for the fact that an apparently inexplicable deletion was made from the revised Basis just prior to its adoption.

Right up to the eve of its incorporation into the Alliance's constitution, in the minutes of EA's executive council dated January 1970, the then-new EA Basis of Faith affirmed Christ's death as offering redemption from the "guilt, *penalty* and power of sin". This phrasing would have been familiar to many, as it had been lifted directly from the 1928 Basis of the InterVarsity Fellowship. Yet in the text eventually adopted into the constitution at EA's annual general meeting in July 1970, the word "penalty" had mysteriously disappeared, leaving the shorter formula "redemption from the guilt and power of sin". The mystery is especially deep given that the minutes from January 1970 record that everyone on the council accepted the draft with "penalty" in it, with the exception of Rev Ronald Taylor – a Methodist, now deceased. He, however, only wanted time to consult with Methodist Revival Fellowship about strengthening the clause on justification: he is not noted as having any objection to the word "penalty" in the clause on the cross.

Given that the minutes offer no explanation for this eleventh-hour omission of "penalty", I spoke to all those still alive who were on the executive council when the Basis was approved in July 1970. Only a minority are still living, but remarkably, none recalled any specific discussion on the cross at the time, and all were surprised when I pointed out the deletion of "penalty". Still, each took it as clearly implied in the text as they voted it through. Like everyone else consulted, David Pawson recalled no discussion of it at the council. Canon David Winter was a member of the drafting group appointed by the executive council to revise the Basis at that time. He recollected "one or two" on the executive council – himself included – who might have had "questions" about the traditional expression of penal substitution, but told me that this did not arise in discussions on the Basis itself. He added that the Alliance then was, if anything, more doctrinally conservative than it is now, and that the executive council as a whole would have taken the clause in question to affirm penal substitution, with or without the explicit term "penalty". Gordon Landreth was on EA's staff when revision of the Basis commenced in 1967, and took over as general secretary from Morgan Derham in 1968. He was *ex officio* on the drafting group but similarly could not recollect any specific discussion on the wording of the atonement clause. However, like David Winter, he did emphasise that the executive council at that time was a "fairly conservative group" and would certainly have seen penal substitution as entailed in the final wording, regardless of whether the word "penalty" was included. He did remember that certain executive council members were more influenced by the liberal trends of the time, but did not recall their pressing for any divergence from the traditional view of Christ's death as penal and propitiatory. Bishop Maurice Wood was present at the July 1970 AGM at which the Basis was adopted but could not recall any dispute about the wording of the atonement clause, nor any deliberate attempt to delete the term "penalty" from it. Even so, he insisted that the executive council would "unanimously" have taken the Basis to affirm penal substitution, since the elements of clauses 3 and 4 taken together (universal sin, human guilt, divine wrath, substitution, sacrifice, redemption) "clearly imply" it. The bishop also pointed out that John Stott was very much involved with the theological work of EA at the time and was and is a staunch proponent of penal substitution. David Abernethie was present when various drafts of the Basis were discussed but was absent from the July 1970 AGM which adopted the final version. He could not recall any direct discussion on the atonement. Like David Winter and Bishop Maurice Wood, he could not imagine why "penalty" fell out in the final stages, but told me that the relatively conservative council of the time would have "plainly assumed the Basis in its adopted form to affirm penal substitution". He added that an EA pamphlet produced and widely distributed in the 1980s under the title *Who Do Evangelicals Think They Are?* plainly uses the language of "penalty" in explaining what the EA Basis affirms about Christ's sacrificial death. Glyn Macaualy served on the executive council in the latter stages of the revision process and was present at the July 1970 AGM. However, he likewise did not recall any discussion on the atonement clause. He commented that some members of the executive council were certainly "more open than others" to influence from non-evangelical quarters, but did not think any of them would deliberately have sought to divert the EA from penal substitution.

All this presents a conundrum. Someone, for reasons lost in the mists of time, appears to have removed the key word "penalty" from the 1970 Basis of Faith. Possibly this happened by mistake, perhaps through a typing error. More likely, though, it was deliberate. We might speculate that the motive was a liberalising one, but we cannot be sure. Perhaps the anonymous deleter or deleters simply thought that "penalty" was already implicit and so removed it on the grounds that it was redundant. The point of this little exercise in redaction criticism is that it reveals a possible ambiguity on penal substitution within the *surface wording* of the 1970 Basis, even though all who were there and are still alive took the final, penalty-free version to imply penal substitution.

This curious manuscript quirk is worth considering not only in its historical context but also with respect to the updating of the 1970 text, which was well under way when the *Lost Message* dispute emerged, and which was completed shortly after the 2005 London symposium. There has been a degree of misapprehension and misinformation surrounding this process, so a factual account is in order.[34]

In January 2002, the Alliance theological commission formed a working group for the purpose of revising the 1970 Basis of Faith. At that point, a timetable for the project was produced which scheduled the adoption of a new Basis for February 2005 and legal incorporation of it into EA's constitution in September the same year. These deadlines were duly met; there was no modification of the schedule in reaction to the development of the atonement debate through 2004.

The Basis revision group met for the first time in March 2002. By the autumn of 2003, it had settled on the form of the words on the atonement which would be approved by the council in September 2005. Other clauses took longer to finalise: indeed, the paragraph on the last things was substantially reworded on the floor of the council in February 2005. Yet the atonement section was one of the earliest to be fixed. To recap: *The Lost Message of Jesus* was not published until December 2003 and did not begin stirring serious controversy until well into 2004. As such, it did not influence the wording of the atonement clause in the new text.

If the Alliance had introduced the language of "penalty" or "penal substitution" in the later stages of the revision process specifically to target Steve Chalke or any other individual, it could justifiably be accused of making one person more important than the whole organisation. To do this would abuse the Basis of Faith. Instead, the process of revision went much further back than the *Lost Message* controversy and reached its final stage according to EA's original intentions. Granted, if more radical members of the EA board or council had wished to alter the wording of the new Basis in a direction more explicitly favourable to a non-penal or anti-penal substitutionary view, they could have sought to do so during the revision process. However, no such alteration was proposed.

Despite all this, some have suggested that EA should have suspended or delayed the Basis revision process until well after the London symposium, to demonstrate its openness to new ideas on the atonement and to integrate those ideas into its statement of faith. Again, though, this mistakenly links two quite different processes. The production of the new Basis stood chronologically and motivationally distinct from the atonement controversy. EA's purpose when it began the revision in 2002 was not to change the substance of the 1970 version but rather to update and refine the style. Certainly, it aimed to add significant doctrinal content which the old text had overlooked – for example, on the virgin birth, mission and the general resurrection. Thus, the language of divine wrath and judgment is directly carried over from clause 3 of the 1970 text to clause 4 of the new Basis. However, since for whatever reason the 1970 Basis did not explicitly use the language of "penalty" and "penal" substitution, EA did not deem it appropriate to introduce it explicitly in the new version. Hence, it preferred the more straightforwardly biblical imagery of Christ's "paying the price" of our sin (cf. 1 Cor. 6:20; 7:23) and allowed this to carry the implication of penal substitutionary sacrifice which the EA council of 1970 had so clearly inferred from the earlier text.

This approach, in turn, raises a further question; namely, how much leeway might be allowed in the *interpretation* of the Basis, particularly with regard to those, like Chalke and the other doubters of penal substitution mentioned above, who wish to construe it in a non-penal substitutionary way? As one who affirms penal substitution, I find it difficult to endorse the statement in clause 4 of the new Basis which says that we are "corrupted by sin", and that this sin "incurs divine wrath",[35] without reckoning that part of the price paid by Christ was to suffer this same divine wrath on our behalf. Whether the Father suffers in some way with the Son or metes out his anger on Christ "from a distance" is a long-standing issue addressed elsewhere in this volume. However, I accept that the mercantile imagery of price-paying and "redemption" is not always or necessarily synonymous with the language of propitiation in Scripture.[36] I would also concede that this is a discoursal rather than a sentential inference on my part and may not be obvious from either of the two clauses taken in isolation.

Then again, even if the Alliance *had* chosen to describe Jesus as paying the "penalty" rather than the "price" of sin, would even this absolutely have clinched the matter? After all, one might say with Paul that the penalty or "wages" of sin endured by Jesus was death (Rom. 6:23) without dwelling on the propitiatory aspects of his passion. More subtly, Christopher Marshall and Nigel Wright alike affirm the penal nature of Christ's substitutionary atonement, but do so in ways which decouple the concept of penalty from that of propitiation, leaving the latter behind. Thus Marshall argues that "God suffers the penalty of sin not because God transfers our punishments onto him as substitute victim, but because Christ fully and freely identifies himself with the plight and destiny of sinful humanity under the reign of death, and pays the price for doing so."[37] Thus, too, Wright denies that Christ suffers "extrinsic" punishment at the hands of a wrathful Father but rather "bears that 'intrinsic' punishment whereby sin produces alienation from God, becoming vulnerable *to our self-inflicted judgement*".[38]

Faced with the sophistication of a Marshall or Wright, it becomes necessary to ask not only what the language of penal substitution might mean in and of itself but also what function it has come to perform within the pan-evangelical community – how it delineates evangelical orthodoxy, defines evangelical networks and drives evangelical discipleship. Such considerations take us beyond the sphere of semantic definition and into the sphere of speech act theory and linguistic pragmatics, where the use of language in particular contexts is taken to bear vitally on the construction of meaning.[39] Just as linguistic pragmaticians would ask what evangelicals *do* with the model of penal substitutionary atonement, so evangelicals need to ask the same question, even as they argue about what penal substitution itself refers to, and whether that reference is coincident with biblical reference to the death of Christ.

Addressing these broader questions of usage, context and social semiotics will prompt consideration of the extent to which penal substitution ought to define the limits of evangelical orthodoxy, whether it should function for evangelicals as a "centred" or a "bounded" set.[40] No doubt, faithful exposition of Christ's atoning death goes to the heart of true gospel ministry. Yet alongside all the key exegetical and theological work which appears in this book, these further ecclesiological and relational issues warrant close attention, lest the division which has plagued evangelical life and mission in the past be too heedlessly championed and that same gospel ministry be hampered.

Notes

1. David Bebbington, *Evangelicalism in Modern Britain: A History from the 1730s to the 1980s* (London: Unwin and Hyman, 1989), 17. Bebbington proposes that evangelicalism is characterised by biblicism, conversionism, activism and crucicentrism. It is often overlooked that this "quadrilateral" is an historian's description of what makes the evangelical movement distinctive

in relation to other strands of the Christian church, rather than a comprehensive prescription for evangelicalism as such. For alternative typologies of evangelicalism, see J. I. Packer, *The Evangelical Anglican Identity Problem: An Analysis* (Oxford: Latimer, 1978), 15–23; Robert Amess, *One in the Truth? The Cancer of Division in the Evangelical Church* (Eastbourne: Kingsway, 1988), 23–26; John Stott, *Evangelical Truth: A Personal Plea for Unity* (Leicester: IVP, 1999), 15–39.

2. Alister McGrath, *Evangelicalism and the Future of Christianity* (London: Hodder and Stoughton, 1995), 62.

3. Derek Tidball, *Who Are the Evangelicals? Tracing the Roots of Today's Movements* (London: Marshall Pickering, 1994), 98.

4. The full text of the LST's Doctrinal Basis can be viewed at *www.lst .ac.uk/whoweare/basis.php*.

5. For the new EA Basis and its predecessor, see *www.eauk.org/content manager/content/aboutthealliance/missionandbof.cfm*.

6. Steve Chalke and Alan Mann, *The Lost Message of Jesus* (Grand Rapids: Zondervan, 2003); Steve Chalke, "Cross Purposes," *Christianity*, September 2004, 44–48; Steve Chalke, interview on the atonement for BBC Radio 4 "Sunday," 3d October 2004; Steve Chalke, opening statement and response, "The Lost Message of Jesus: A Public Dialogue, 7/10/04," CD recording available from the Evangelical Alliance (London, 2004); Alan Mann, *Atonement for a Sinless Society: Engaging with an Emerging Culture* (Milton Keynes: Paternoster, 2005).

7. McGrath, *Evangelicalism*, 156–65.

8. Chalke and Mann, *Lost Message of Jesus*, 16.

9. Ibid., 113.

10. Leon Morris, "Atonement," in *NDT*, 56.

11. For evangelical summaries and assessments of the key atonement theories, see H. Wayne House, *Charts of Christian Theology and Doctrine* (Grand Rapids: Zondervan, 1992), 104–8; Millard J. Erickson, *Christian Theology*, 2nd ed. (Grand Rapids: Baker, 1998), 798–840; Wayne Grudem, *Systematic Theology: An Introduction to Biblical Doctrine* (Leicester: IVP; Grand Rapids: Zondervan, 1994), 568–607.

12. Tidball, *Evangelicals*, 98–115.

13. For a typical account along these lines, see Gordon R. Lewis and Bruce A. Demarest, *Integrative Theology* (Grand Rapids: Zondervan, 1996), 378–82.

14. James Denney, for instance, described assent to the defining component of penal substitution (propitiation) as the point "which ultimately divides interpreters of Christianity into evangelical and non-evangelical" (James Denney, *The Atonement and the Modern Mind* [London: Hodder and Stoughton, 1903], 82). Similarly, Millard Erickson devotes a whole chapter to it in his evangelical systematic theology, and titles that chapter "The Central Theme of the Atonement" (Erickson, *Christian Theology*, 798–840).

15. Chalke and Mann, *Lost Message of Jesus*, 182. Cf. Rita Nakishima Brock, "And a Little Child Will Lead Us: Christology and Child Abuse," in *Christianity, Patriarchy and Child Abuse: A Feminist Critique*, ed. Joanne Carlson Brown and Carole R. Bohn (New York: Pilgrim, 1989), 42–61.

16. Chalke and Mann, *Lost Message of Jesus*, 182–83.

17. Chalke, "Cross Purposes," 44.

18. Andrew Sach and Mike Ovey, "Have We Lost the Message of Jesus?" *Evangelicals Now*, June 2004, 27.

19. Garry Williams, "Cross Purpose: Replying to Steve Chalke on Penal Substitution," *Evangelicals Now*, October 2004, 26.

20. Greg Haslam, "The Lost Cross of Christ," *Christianity*, November 2004. Available online at *www.christianitymagazine.co.uk/engine .cfm?i=92&id=254&arch=1*.

21. For Ekklesia's comments on the atonement controversy prompted by *The Lost Message of Jesus*, see *www.ekklesia.co.uk/content/news_syndication/ article_040723pen.shtml*. See also *www.ekklesia.co.uk/content/news_syndica tion/article_04108ato.shtml*. For comment on the Anabaptist Network website, see *www.anabaptistnetwork.com/atonement*. For a review of the *Baptist Times* coverage, see *www.christiantoday.com/news/ministries/leading.newspaper .rebukes.evangelical.alliances.views.on.chalke/159.htm*.

22. The statement read as follows: "Questions have been raised following the publication of Steve Chalke's book *The Lost Message of Jesus*. It is of course the case that this book is not a treatise on sin and the atonement, but is rather, as its title states, a fresh exploration of the teachings of Jesus Christ in his earthly ministry. In response we wish to make the following points:

- As a member of the Leadership Team, Steve Chalke affirms the Spring Harvest theological position as outlined above
- He remains firmly committed to what David Bebbington calls the quadrilateral of priorities that mark the boundaries of evangelical faith; namely, crucicentrism, biblicism, conversionism and activism

- That the atonement lies at the heart of the Christian gospel
- Exploring the atonement is like gazing at a diamond with different facets
- Historically theological debate has focussed on different aspects of the atonement
- Steve's recent book should be read as a contribution to that ongoing discussion
- He, in common with all members of the Leadership Team, writes as an individual

Finally, we affirm the wonderful truth that 'Christ died for our sins according to the Scriptures, that he was buried, that he was raised on the third day according to the Scriptures.'"

23. For a thorough analysis of Erskine, MacDonald and others of this persuasion, see Don Horrocks, *Laws of the Spiritual Order: Innovation and Reconstruction in the Soteriology of Thomas Erskine of Linlathen* (Milton Keynes: Paternoster, 2004).

24. Bebbington, *Evangelicalism*, 200–202.

25. Stephen Travis, "Christ as Bearer of Divine Judgment in Paul's Thought," in *Atonement Today*, ed. John Goldingay (London: SPCK, 1995), 21–38; Tom Smail, "Can One Man Die for the People?" in Goldingay, *Atonement*, 73–92; Nigel Wright, *The Radical Evangelical: Seeking a Place to Stand* (London: SPCK, 1996), 58–72; Clark H. Pinnock and Robert C. Brow, *Unbounded Love: A Good News Theology for the Twenty-first Century* (Downers Grove, Ill.: IVP; Carlisle: Paternoster, 1994), 99–110; J. Denny Weaver, *The Nonviolent Atonement* (Grand Rapids / Cambridge, UK: Eerdmans, 2001); Christopher D. Marshall, *Beyond Retribution: A New Testament Vision for Justice, Crime and Punishment* (Grand Rapids; Cambridge, UK: Eerdmans / Auckland and Sydney: Lime Grove, 2001), 59–69; Joel B. Green and Mark D. Baker, *Recovering the Scandal of the Cross: Atonement in New Testament and Contemporary Contexts* (Downers Grove, Ill.: IVP, 2000), 23–32, 90–97, 173–75.

26. A recorded CD of this event is available from the Evangelical Alliance: "The Lost Message of Jesus: A Public Debate, 7/10/04." For details, see *www.eauk.org/contentmanager/Content/lmoj/questions.cfm*.

27. Online at *www.eauk.org/contentmanager/Content/press/statements/lostmessage.cfm*.

28. These Practical Resolutions were originally passed at the Alliance's inauguration in 1846. Having been updated, they now form part of a document

called the "Evangelical Relationships Commitment." Available online at *www. eauk.org/contentmanager/content/aboutthealliance/relationships.cfm*. The relevant clauses read as follows: "6. We call on each other, when speaking or writing of those issues of faith or practice that divide us, to acknowledge our own failings and the possibility that we ourselves may be mistaken, avoiding personal hostility and abuse, and speaking the truth in love and gentleness. 7. "We owe it to each other, in making public comment on the alleged statements of our fellow Christians, first to confer directly with them and to establish what was actually intended. Then to commend what we can, to weigh the proportional significance of what we perceive to be in error, and to put a charitable construction on what is doubtful, expressing all with courtesy, humility and graciousness."

29. Available online at *www.eauk.org/contentmanager/Content/press/2004/12/10.cfm*.

30. Daniel Strange, "Creation, Conquest and the Cross," Evangelical Library Lecture, 2005. Available online under the title "The Many-Splendoured Cross: Atonement, Controversy and Victory" at *www.elib.org.uk/lectures/el_2005_thecross.pdf*.

31. For the text of the 1970 Basis, see *www.eauk.org/contentmanager/content/aboutthealliance/missionandbof.cfm*.

32. "The substitutionary sacrifice of the incarnate Son of God as the sole all-sufficient ground of redemption from the guilt and power of sin, and from its eternal consequences."

33. *On the Other Side: Report of the Evangelical Alliance's Commission on Evangelism* (London: Scripture Union, 1968), 65.

34. Not least on the website of Ekklesia: *www.ekklesia.co.uk/content/news_syndication/article_050315alliance.shtml*.

35. "The dignity of all people, made male and female in God's image to love, be holy and care for creation, yet corrupted by sin, which incurs divine wrath and judgement."

36. Leon Morris, *The Atonement: Its Meaning and Significance* (Leicester: IVP, 1983), 169.

37. Marshall, *Beyond Retribution*, 62.

38. Wright, *The Radical Evangelical*, 69. My emphasis.

39. The seminal works on speech acts and speech act theory are J. L. Austin, *How to Do Things with Words*, 2nd ed. (Oxford: Oxford Univ. Press), 1962; and John Searle, *Speech Acts: An Essay in the Philosophy of Language* (Cambridge: Cambridge Univ. Press, 1969). Helpful textbooks on the broader

contextual linguistic discipline of pragmatics are Stephen C. Levinson, *Pragmatics* (Cambridge: Cambridge Univ. Press, 1983); Laurence R. Horn and Gregory Ward, eds., *The Handbook of Pragmatics* (Oxford: Blackwell, 2006).

40. For a helpful consideration of this "functional" problem for doctrine in pan-evangelical contexts, see Darrell L. Bock, *Purpose-Directed Theology: Getting Our Priorities Right in Evangelical Controversies* (Downers Grove, Ill.: IVP, 2002).

chapter two

the redemption
of the cross

steve chalke

"I don't judge you. I leave that to a wrathful, angry God to do."
– *Ned Flanders to his wayward neighbour, Homer Simpson*

The cross isn't a form of cosmic child abuse – a vengeful Father, punishing his Son for an offence he has not even committed. Understandably, both people inside and outside of the Church have found this twisted version of events morally dubious and a huge barrier to faith."[1]

When I penned this statement, as part of the text of *The Lost Message of Jesus*, I had no idea of the debate that it would ignite or the controversy it would stir. Some have claimed that this showed a naivety on my part, that I must have, or should have, anticipated the impact that my words would make. However, I was surprised because so many others had already written along similar lines and, in my opinion, had done so more extensively and eloquently than me. Indeed, according to David Hilborn, a critic of my position and at that time the Evangelical Alliance's head of theology, "We would underline that Steve Chalke is hardly the first Evangelical to critique the penal substitutionary theory of atonement. In recent times, a relatively small but growing number of professing Evangelical scholars, including James Dunn, Stephen Travis, Nigel Wright, Clark Pinnock, Robert Brow, Mark Baker and Joel Green, have questioned the biblical basis of penal substitution, and the importance accorded to it in Evangelicalism. *The Lost Message of Jesus* may have popularised this 'dissenting' movement, but it did not pioneer it."[2]

Though the sheer bluntness of my imagery shocked some, I contend that, in truth, it represents nothing more than a stark unmasking of what I understand to be the violent, pre-Christian thinking behind the popular theory of penal substitutionary atonement. Thus, whilst having great respect for many of those who hold what, I readily concede, is currently regarded as orthodoxy within modern evangelicalism, I will attempt to set out through this essay why I believe it to be biblically, culturally and pastorally deficient and even dangerous.

At this point, it would be helpful to talk definitions. Recently, N. T. Wright, in a paper titled "The Cross and the Caricatures,"[3] has contributed to what has become known as the *Lost Message of Jesus* debate. In it, he explains that, having read my book and talked with me, in his view, part of my understanding of the cross "amounts to a form of penal substitution", but one that "is quite different from other forms of penal substitution". In his terms, he is right. However, he goes on to comment that "it is his [Steven's] experience that the word 'penal' has put off so many people, with its image of a violent, angry and malevolent God, that he has decided not to use it." He is right again. I grieve over the depth of the damage that has been, and is being, done through the distortion, misrepresentation and misunderstanding of the purpose of the cross under the label of "penal" substitution. Indeed, N. T.'s comments are themselves made in the context of his severe, even damning criticism of *Pierced for Our Transgressions. Rediscovering the Glory of Penal Substitution*,[4] one of the latest books attacking my position. N. T. states, for instance, that "despite the ringing endorsements of famous men, it [*Pierced for Our Transgressions*] is deeply, profoundly, and disturbingly unbiblical." In my opinion, he is right once more.

It is for exactly this reason that I have only one point of difference with what N. T. Wright chooses to call penal substitution – the fact that he chooses to call it penal substitution at all. In my view, his understanding – with which I feel a deep resonance – is so far removed from what is so commonly taught under this label that, as he acknowledges, I believe it is better to abandon the use of the term altogether and restate the truth in fresh ways. Hence, for clarity, the penal substitution I reject, and with which I concern myself throughout this paper, is the penal substitution of the pulpit, the seminar room (one of the authors of *Pierced for Our Transgressions* is the principal of a theological college; the other two are theological students) and myriad other books of the same outlook – one or two of which I will refer to later in this paper. Meanwhile, I leave my friend N. T. to his attempt to redefine penal substitution as something, as he admits, very different to that which it currently is in the minds of both the church and society.

Biblical Issues

Douglas John Hall, in *The Cross in Our Context*, states, "One is surely bound to affirm that the actions of believers are usually the acting out of foundational beliefs, whether in conscious or unconscious ways. To state the matter the other way around: the foundational beliefs of a religious faith will find expression, one way or the other, in the deeds and deportment of its membership."[5]

What we believe is indissolubly linked to the way we behave. That hypocrisy is rampant is readily acknowledged – there is a huge aspirational gap between our desires and our delivery. But even recognition of this issue does not negate the core principle that our foundational beliefs filter into our responses, that our values have consequences for both our attitudes and actions. What we believe about the cross (and what God was doing there) will fundamentally shape our attitude toward, and involvement with, wider society. Inadequate doctrines of atonement lead to distorted understandings of God and humanity and result in an immature engagement in community and wider society.

But if erroneous theology leads to dysfunctional missiology, is there any connection between the public's almost universal perception of certain elements of the church as judgmental, guilt-inducing, censorious, finger-wagging, bigoted, and self-righteous and aspects of its theology of the cross? And if, as historian and scholar David Bebbington claims, one of the four pillars of evangelicalism (which together are known as the Bebbington Quadrilateral) is "crucicentrism", or cross-centredness,[6] why is it that our culture now views the death of Christ as no more than some kind of ancient myth or irrelevant religious event? Perhaps one factor is that our thinking about the cross has become distorted and thus our presentation of it is inadequate to engage the hearts and minds of our contemporaries both within and beyond the church.

Do we believe that Christ's death on the cross has any relevance or significance beyond the individual eternal destiny of his followers? What does the atonement mean for the wider affairs of our communities? What direction can our understanding of the atonement offer as we think about the global challenges faced by humanity at the beginning of the twenty-first century? Does the atonement speak to our government's foreign policy, the future of the Middle East, the war on terrorism, the challenge to the market economy of ethical trading, people trafficking and climate change? Does it address the hopes, ambitions and fears of our generation? Undoubtedly, a weakness of some modern theologies of atonement has been that they have simply failed to speak to, engage with, or challenge our culture in any significant way. I suggest that the penal substitutionary theory of atonement has failed us in exactly this way.

If we are to take the New Testament seriously, we must openly acknowledge that any robust theology of atonement is multicoloured rather than monochrome. No single theory can ever capture its breadth and profundity. The spectrum of complementary metaphors used by the writers of the New Testament, in their attempt to express the truth of the atonement, includes a clear substitutionary (though, I contest, not a "penal" substitutionary) element ("The Son of Man [came] ... to give his life as a ransom for many," Matt. 20:28), along with numerous others, among them identification ("I want to know Christ and ... the fellowship of sharing in his sufferings," Phil. 3:10), example ("If anyone would come after me, he must deny himself and take up his cross and follow me," Matt. 16:24) and representation ("For just as through the disobedience of the one man the many were made sinners, so also through the obedience of the one man the many will be made righteous," Rom. 5:19)

However, what has become known as penal substitution – the view of the cross which is common amongst evangelicals ("penal" referring to punishment, "substitution" to Christ's acting in our place) – does not fit comfortably amongst these. The shadow it casts does not match the picture of the cross painted by any of the New Testament metaphors. Although in some circles it has been held to be of huge importance, in my view it is simply not present in the biblical texts so often cited in its support.

Though often represented as a much older formulation, penal substitutionary theory, as it is understood and taught in many evangelical churches today, rests largely on the work of the nineteenth-century American theologian Charles Hodge, who, building on the work of John Calvin's legal mind, argued that a righteous God is angry with sinners and demands justice. God's wrath can be appeased only through bringing about the violent death of his Son. Joel Green and Mark Baker demonstrate in their book, *Rediscovering the Scandal of the Cross*, that, whereas supporters of penal substitutionary theory tend to quote the writings of various church fathers and early Christian writers to bolster their claims, their conclusion is more easily understood as an anachronistic "reading back" of modern views onto ancient texts, particularly into the work of Anselm of Canterbury (1033–1109).[7]

Supporters of penal substitution theory, following Hodge's lead, tend to hold it as a "God-given truth" – the only valid explanation of the atonement. Indeed, to question its legitimacy is viewed as tantamount to attacking the fundamentals of the faith itself. So it was that I recently had a conversation with one church leader who began by informing me that his view of the cross was "*the* biblical one". For him, not only does penal substitution theory sum up everything there is to say about the significance of Christ's death without remainder but also acceptance of it is a non-negotiable baseline of authentic Christian faith.

However, the supposed orthodoxy of penal substitution is greatly misleading. Although as a theory it is not as old as many people assume, it is actually built on pre-Christian thought. This is a point pressed by Professor George Eldon Ladd in *A Theology of the New Testament*: "In pagan Greek thought the gods often became angry with men, but their anger could be placated and the good will of the gods obtained by some kind of propitiatory sacrifice. Even in the Old Testament, the idea of atonement as the propitiating of an angry deity and transmuting his anger into benevolence is not to be found."[8] The emphasis on Yahweh's apparent appetite for continuous appeasement through blood sacrifice, present within some Pentateuchal texts, is to be understood in the light of later prophetic writings as a reflection of the worship practices of the pagan cults of the nations that surrounded the people of Israel. However, the story of Israel's salvation is the story of her journey away from these primal practices towards a new and more enlightened understanding by way of Yahweh's self-revelation.

At the heart of this important issue is the question about the meaning of the term "atonement" in the Old Testament. Indeed, Leon Morris, in his classic text, *The Apostolic Preaching of the Cross*, titles his section on atonement in the Old Testament "The Problem of Atonement".[9] However, having raised the question of the ambiguity of the term in its relationship to "blood" – the giving and taking of life – it is disappointing that he fails to pursue what he readily admits is a vital issue. Instead, though he recognises that "in other places atonement is connected with such ceremonies as the pouring of oil on the head of the cleansed leper (Lv 14:18,29), the offering of incense (Nu 16:46), the scapegoat (Lv 16:10), and there are others", he concludes that "these do not seem to forward our inquiry so we pass over them."[10]

Indeed, one of the challenging questions for those who hold a penal substitutionary view of the atonement is the fact that Jewish prophets of the eighth century BCE were clearly already moving beyond this concept. Thus, to defend the theory of penal substitution by arguing the meaning of this or that isolated biblical text ignores a deeper truth. The resonance of the scriptural witness, the overall flow of the narrative, and the unravelling story of salvation all speak with a different voice. So it is that, today, even the most orthodox Jewish teaching and practice has long since abandoned blood sacrifice. There is simply no Jewish scholar anywhere in the world who understands the sum content of the Old Testament text as an ongoing demand for propitiatory blood sacrifice.

The greatest theological problem with penal substitution is that it presents us with a God who is first and foremost concerned with retribution for sin that flows from his wrath against sinners. The only way for his anger to be placated is in receiving recompense from those who have wronged him, and although his great love motivates him to send his Son, his wrath remains the driving force behind the need for the cross.

If we follow Hodge's understanding of the atonement, it is Jesus' death alone that becomes our "good news". This approach reduces the whole gospel to a single sentence: "God is no longer angry with us because Jesus died in our place." Indeed, that is exactly why evangelistic presentations based on penal substitution often do not even bother to mention the resurrection: for them, it serves no direct purpose in the story of salvation.

Ironically, what Hodge most neglected was to let Jesus speak for himself. It is difficult to see how penal substitution fits with the words or attitude of Jesus. For instance, if the whole gospel centres on Jesus' death, what was the good news he told his followers to preach (Luke 9:6) before the crucifixion? And if God needed a sacrifice to placate his anger, how could Jesus forgive sins before his sacrifice had been made? In fact, why did Jesus preach at all? The rest of his ministry was ultimately unnecessary if it is only his death that makes things new. Surely we cannot embrace a theology in which Jesus' entire thirty-three-year incarnation could be reduced to a long weekend's activity.

It is interesting to note that in Jesus' own explanation of his Father's relationship with mankind, the story of the prodigal son, the father is not presented as angry or vengeful or as seeking justice and retribution; instead, he simply runs to greet his wayward child, showers him with gifts and welcomes him home (Luke 15:11–32). The father in the parable is wronged, but he chooses to forgive in order to restore a broken relationship – there is no theme of retribution. Instead, the story is one of outstanding grace, of scandalous love and mercy. How different it would read if penal substitution were the model of atonement offered.

In addition, we can note Jesus' teaching on anger (Matt. 5:22) and retaliation (Matt. 5:38–42). Is it not strange for Jesus (God incarnate) on the one hand to teach "do not return evil for evil" while still looking for retribution himself? Similarly, would it not be inconsistent for God to warn us not to be angry with each other and yet burn with wrath himself, or tell us to love our enemies when he obviously could not quite bring himself to do the same without demanding massive appeasement? If these things are true, what does it mean to "be perfect ... as your heavenly Father is perfect" (Matt. 5:48)? If it is true that Jesus is "the Word of God", then how can his message be inconsistent with his nature? If the cross has anything to do with penal substitution, then Jesus' teaching becomes a divine case of "do as I say, not as I do." I, for one, believe that God practices what he preaches. If the cross is a personal act of violence perpetrated by God towards humankind but borne by his Son, then it makes a mockery of Jesus' own teaching to love your enemies and to refuse to repay evil with evil.

So, what of God's anger? The most profound theological truth expressed in the whole canon of Scripture is that "God is love" (1 John 4:8). The Bible never defines God as anger, power or judgment; in fact, it never defines him as anything other than love. Love is not a quality that God possesses but rather is his divine essence itself – his essential being. And more than that, the Bible never makes assertions about God's anger, power or judgment independently of his love. God's anger is an aspect of his love, and to understand it any differently is to misunderstand it.

Every father will be wronged by his children; it is a simple fact. All of us who know the joy of raising children also know the pain of their rebelliousness – and yet no parent who loves their child ever seeks retribution for wrongs done to them. Parental anger, when it is motivated by genuine love, cannot be violent or destructive. Though in Scripture we read about God's various attributes, in truth, they are never more than repetitions and amplifications of the one statement that God loves. The reality of God's wrath is never in dispute. But only in light of our understanding of God as the perfect father can we begin to see that the objects of his burning anger are not his beloved children but the evils, attitudes and behaviours that ensnare and seek to destroy them.

Cultural Issues

Good Christian theology must be deeply and comprehensively informed by the Bible whilst at the same time be creatively alert and related to its specific cultural context.

A weakness of penal substitutionary theory is that it is culturally sluggish or even disconnected and, as such, fails to engage with or challenge our society and its macro values. For instance, the charge that "religion breeds violence" is one of the most common and popular complaints of all. However, Jesus' message was unambiguous. Reciprocal violence is a vicious circle – a downward spiral. Vengeance always leads to reprisal. Hatred and suspicion breed hatred and suspicion. Once installed within a community, they become self-perpetuating. Penal substitutionary theory betrays Jesus' attempt to root out the tendency of religion to lead to violence by inventing a theology of his death that is in direct opposition to his teaching. If the church could rediscover a deeper understanding of the cross, we could once again speak with prophetic power to a global society caught in the grip of the lie that violence can be redemptive. The church's inability to shake off the great distortion of God contained in the theory of penal substitution, with its inbuilt belief in retribution and the redemptive power of violence, has cost us dearly. As the world struggles to find a way out of the chaos resulting from the doctrine of "might is right" and "he who has the biggest guns wins," there is now an opportunity for the church to live out its commitment to the ethic of non-violence or "assertive meekness" demonstrated by Christ throughout his life and ultimately authenticated by his cross and resurrection. Jews, Muslims and Christians alike have to face up to the truth that their holy texts can be interpreted violently. Will our Christ-centred faith be part of the world's answer or part of its problem?

But a commitment to penal substitution also raises other ethical concerns. Indeed, it is open to the charge that it does little more than reflect the nineteenth- and twentieth-century culturally dominant values of individualism, autonomy and consumerism. Thus, the primary purpose for the cross becomes its instant "cash value" for the individual. By "praying the prayer", I am immediately moved from the wrong side of God's legal ledger to the right side. The great transaction is done. And what is more, not only am I no longer guilty but I can also cling to the belief that "once saved, always saved". My eternal destiny is guaranteed. Penal substitution offers instant forgiveness without challenging basic day-to-day moral behaviour.

It separates salvation from discipleship by disconnecting the way that Jesus lived his life from his saving work. Still further, because penal substitutionary theory tends to nurture a simplistic understanding of sin that is wholly individualistic and personal, it fails to address the corporate and systemic contexts of evil in our world. Thus, it is no surprise that those who subscribe to it tend not to be on the forefront of thinking about the major socio-political issues confronting us, such as racial reconciliation, wealth and poverty, and the environment.

Pastoral Issues

"I don't judge you. I leave that to a wrathful, angry God to do," thunders Bible- thumping, churchgoing Ned Flanders to his wayward neighbour, Homer Simpson. Of course, many Christians learn to live with the dichotomy caused by an uncritical acceptance of penal substitutionary theory. On the one hand, they believe in God's grace and goodness, but on the other, they believe that one of the central acts of their faith is bound up in his vengeance and wrath. The only way they cope with this tension is to dismiss it as "a divine paradox". However, for their friends and the rest of the world, it is simply a massive contradiction, the "elephant in the room".

Since my book was published, and in the serious theological debate that has followed it, some have sought to readdress their definition of penal substitution. I have witnessed various attempts to redraw, redefine, recast, remodel and rehabilitate the theory as "not really as violent and retributive a concept as *The Lost Message of Jesus* suggested". But the problem is simply this: this is not how the situation is perceived either within or beyond the church. So whilst I applaud these attempts to manufacture a kind of "penal substitution theory lite" – some of which will, no doubt, be represented in other contributions to this book – in my view, what we need is not a reworking but a renunciation. Why? Because even the most sophisticated and gracious attempts to nuance penal substitution have, in the end, failed to communicate anything other than a distorted view of God at a popular level.

Several months ago, a leading evangelical scholar gave me thirty minutes on why, in his view, I had misunderstood the issues and was living with a caricature of penal substitution which no one actually taught or believed. He then had to exit the room for a few minutes to take a phone call, leaving me alone in his study. At this point, his secretary, who had overheard some of our conversation, entered the room, thanked me for my book, told me that it had released her from the fear of an angry God that had been crushing her for years, urged me to keep speaking up, dried her tears and hurried away again. Two minutes later, the scholar returned to give me the benefit of a further fifteen minutes on why my views were out of step with anything being taught in the churches.

Though some are determined to hang on to a revised penal substitution theory, their presentation of it is not far from the popular version that has been and, to some extent, is still put forward. Pastorally, penal substitutionary theory, as represented in some of our songs (from which many Christians learn most of their theology), taught in some of our churches and written about in some of our paperback books, is, at the very least, open to huge popular misinterpretation and misrepresentation. To quote one writer, at the cross, "Man did his worst against Jesus. So did God."[11] Or in a review of *The Jesus Gospel* by Liam Goligher,[12] one of the flurry of books written to answer mine, Peter Lawrence wrote, "The problem with *The Jesus Gospel* as a book is that by the time I'd waded through the necessary blood in every chapter I came away with the view of a very gory God and not one I could easily fall in love with."[13] Perhaps those who reassure us that there is no cause for concern and that the popular presentation of penal substitution "is not as bad as all that" need to think again.

The Way Ahead

If penal substitution does not do justice to the story of our salvation through Christ, what other options are open to us? For me, the most empowering and motivating understanding of the atonement is that which, I believe, most closely resembles the thinking of the early church. As they struggled to make sense of Jesus' death and resurrection, the early church leaders (notably Irenaeus, Gregory of Nyssa and Origen) wrote about the cross in terms of a ransom.[14] Of course, Jesus said himself that he came "to give his life as a ransom for many" (Mark 10:45). But to whom was this ransom paid? The early church was adamant that it was not to God. As Origen put it, "To whom did he give his life as a ransom for many? Assuredly not to God — could it then be to the Evil One? For he was holding fast until the ransom should be given him, even the life of Jesus; being deceived with the idea that he could have dominion over it, and not seeing that he could not bear the torture in retaining it."[15]

From this commonly shared point of understanding, a diversity of thinking slowly developed which sought to be faithful to the various pictures of the impact of the cross used by the different New Testament writers. Only in

1930 did Gustav Aulen coin the term *Christus Victor* (Christ the Conqueror) as a kind of "umbrella" under which this spread of traditional understandings of the atonement could be gathered.[16] Within this, Christ's life, death *and* resurrection together are seen as his victory over all the forces of evil and sin, including the earthly and spiritual powers that oppress people. Indeed, it is Jesus' resurrection that gives the hope of the new heaven and the new earth, where sin is banished and all things are made right again. Jesus' emergence from the grave demonstrates that no political power, no unjust regime, no sinful structure can triumph, even in the infliction of death. It is Easter Sunday, not Good Friday, that shows the new kingdom in all its glory and God's love in all its fullness. On the cross, Jesus does not placate God's anger in taking the punishment for sin but rather absorbs its consequences and, as three days later he is raised, defeats death. It is the resurrection which finally puts the *Victor* in *Christus Victor*!

So it is that in and through Jesus' life, death and resurrection God confronts and dethrones the powers of evil. But in doing so, he will not use the tools of evil itself – those of coercion, unjust force, domination and violence. Instead, in weakness, he confounds Satan. He lures wielders of unjust power into exposing and discrediting themselves. Jesus, creatively and courageously, armed only with the non-violent power of truth and love, opposes and defeats sin and violence. Jesus contains evil, but evil cannot contain him. Jesus soaks up all that Satan can throw at him but will not submit. The second Adam is tempted in a garden but will not succumb. Straining with every last effort and breath, he hangs on to his Father. Satan is overcome. Sin, evil and death itself are defeated.

As the New Testament makes abundantly clear, the cross is cosmic in its impact, not just individual or personal. Through Christ's life, death and resurrection, God, because of his great love for us, has intervened to repair his broken relationship with a world out of harmony with his purpose. In the words of Gregory of Nyssa, "Thus, life being introduced to the house of death, and light shining in darkness, that which is diametrically opposed to light and life might vanish; for it is not in the nature of darkness to remain when light is present, or of death to exist when life is active."[17]

The cross is not a form of cosmic child abuse – a vengeful Father punishing his Son for an offence he did not commit. Rather than a symbol of vengeance or retribution, the cross of Christ is the greatest symbol of love and a demonstration of just how far God the Father and Jesus his Son are prepared to go to prove that love and to bring redemption to their creation.

Notes

1. Steve Chalke and Alan Mann, *The Lost Message of Jesus* (Grand Rapids: Zondervan, 2003), 182.

2. David Hilborn, "A Public Dialogue on Issues Raised by Steve Chalke's Book *The Lost Message of Jesus*," Evangelical Alliance press statement, October 2004.

3. All N. T. Wright quotes are from N. T. Wright, "The Cross and the Caricatures: A Response to Robert Jenson, Jeffrey John, and a New Volume Entitled *Pierced for Our Transgressions*," Fulcrum, Eastertide 2007, http://www.fulcrum-anglican.org.uk/news/2007/20070423wright.cfm?doc=205.

4. Steve Jeffery, Mike Ovey and Andrew Sach, *Pierced for Our Transgressions: Rediscovering the Glory of Penal Substitution* (Nottingham: IVP, 2007).

5. Douglas John Hall, *The Cross in Our Context* (Minneapolis: Fortress, 2003), 3.

6. David W. Bebbington, *Evangelicalism in Modern Britain: A History from the 1730s to the 1980s* (London: Unwin and Hyman, 1989), 3–17.

7. Joel B. Green and Mark D. Baker, *Recovering the Scandal of the Cross* (Downers Grove, Ill.: IVP, 2000).

8. George Eldon Ladd, *A Theology of the New Testament* (Grand Rapids: Eerdmans, 1974), 424.

9. Leon Morris, *The Apostolic Preaching of the Cross* (Leicester: IVP, 1965), 118.

10. Ibid., 121.

11. Roger Carswell, *Why Believe?* (Bromley: STL, 1990).

12. Liam Goligher, *The Jesus Gospel* (Carlisle: Authentic, 2006).

13. Peter Lawrence, "Review of *The Jesus Gospel*," *Christianity*, November 2006.

14. Green and Baker, *Recovering the Scandal*, 42.

15. Ibid., 122, citing Origen, *In Matthaeum* 16.8.

16. Ibid., 118.

17. Ibid., 123, citing Gregory of Nyssa, "The Great Catechism" 26.

biblical foundations

the theology of the atonement

i. howard marshall

A biblical understanding of atonement is concerned above all with the restoration of mutual, undistorted, unpolluted divine/human relationship,
not with the appeasing of a God angered by the misdeeds of his creatures."[1]
Alan Mann's statement represents the view of many theologians who reject the
concept of penal substitution as the principal means, or even as a subordinate
means, of understanding the significance of Christ's death.

One reason for this rejection is that such an understanding entails the
belief that God could not save sinners until he had first exercised violence
on his Son, and that the unacceptability of such violence indicates that penal
substitution cannot be the right way to understand the significance of the
cross.[2] Then it is argued that the concept is not well-founded in Scripture and
even represents a misinterpretation of scriptural teaching. This view is taken
by a number of conservative evangelical theologians[3] who agree that we are
saved from our sins solely by grace through faith on the grounds that God
sent his Son to die in our place and for our sins, but who want to understand
more fully what this means and what it does not mean. I shall argue that
the doctrine of penal substitution is well-founded in Scripture and that it is
defensible against the objections brought against it. I hope to argue in such a
way that, whatever may be the problems with the terminology, all of us may
recognise the validity and, indeed, the centrality of what is known by the
term "penal substitution" instead of repudiating the concept.[4]

In this paper, I am concerned with the biblical and theological foundations that underlie our preaching of the gospel and not with the evangelistic
edifice that we erect on these foundations. Therefore, even if we were to
conclude that we should not use terms like "penal suffering" or "appeasing

God" in our preaching, we still need to ask whether there is a place for them and what is meant by them in our technical theology.

A doctrine of the atonement has *inter alia* to deal with our situation as sinners in relationship to God, against whom we have sinned. Four views can be distinguished.

1. The principle of penal substitution does not figure in the New Testament at all.[5]
2. It is only one of the pictures, metaphors, or analogies used in the New Testament to express the significance of the death of Jesus Christ.[6] Some might argue that in this case it is of lesser importance or even dispensable.
3. It occurs to such an extent that it is not only indispensable but also the most important.[7]
4. It is the underlying principle present in all the others and the factor that makes them cohere.[8]

The Use of Metaphor

The New Testament uses various metaphors or analogies to explain the significance of what Christ did for human beings. I reiterate the point made by Henri Blocher that the metaphorical language used in the New Testament does convey truth and is to be taken seriously.[9] Against the suggestion that penal substitution is simply one metaphor among many and that we can dispense with it or place it on the margin, Trevor Hart comments that "the plurality of biblical imagery does not seem to be intended purely or even primarily as a selection box from which we may draw what we will according to our needs and the pre-understanding of our community ... the metaphors are not to be understood as exchangeable, as if one might simply be substituted for another without net gain or loss, but complementary, directing us to distinct elements in and consequences of the fullness of God's saving action in Christ and the Spirit."[10]

The Language of Judgment, Wrath and Punishment

If the cross is concerned "with the restoration of mutual, undistorted, unpolluted divine/human relationship, not with the appeasing of a God angered by the misdeeds of his creatures", why does this divine-human relationship need to be restored? Is it not because God is angered by the misdeeds of his creatures?

How else are relationships broken? Why was the death of Christ necessary to restore the relationship? I want to clarify the language of anger and appeasement in a way that will enable us all to say, "Well, maybe terms like 'penal' and 'anger' and 'appeasement' are open to misunderstanding, but properly understood they express the heart of the matter."[11]

The reality of final judgment as the active response of God to human sin is an absolutely central part of the predicament from which sinners need to be saved. In the last analysis, "the wages of sin is death." A complex network of terminology conveys this picture of judgment and condemnation.

Punishment. In the New Testament, the language of punishment does not figure all that prominently. In the parabolic teaching of Jesus, wicked servants will be punished when the master returns (Matt. 24:43–51; Luke 12:45–48). The noun is applied once to the eternal punishment of the wicked (Matt. 25:46). Those who disobey and reject the gospel will pay the penalty of eternal destruction (2 Thess. 1:9). A person who rejects the Son of God and the blood of the covenant deserves a greater punishment than somebody who rejected the law of Moses and was put to death (Heb. 10:29). The Lord keeps the unrighteous for punishment at the day of judgment (2 Peter 2:9).[12] That is the sum of references to divine punishment associated particularly with the day of judgment. However, to suggest that the comparative rareness of this term should keep us from putting the term "penal" in a central position in our doctrine would be premature.

Vengeance. Second, there is the concept of vengeance, sometimes rendered as "revenge". Persons who want to take vengeance for evils they have suffered are told to leave it to God, who will repay their opponents (Rom. 12:19, citing Deut. 32:35).[13] Human vengeance is liable to be sinful and therefore is prohibited, just as very firm limits are also set to the display of human anger. In 1 Thessalonians 4:6, God will take vengeance on those who wrong their brothers, taking the side of the wronged and acting against the wrongdoer. Sometimes he may do this through human agents.[14] In Luke 21:22, there are days of vengeance on Jerusalem, apparently as punishment for rejection of God. In 2 Thessalonians 1:8, God inflicts vengeance on those who do not know him and disobey the gospel (cf. Rev. 19:2).[15]

Wrath. The impression of sparsity that we gain from looking at punishment and vengeance is dispelled when we take note of the more frequent usage of the concepts of wrath and judgment. The noun *orgē* is common.[16] There is a future wrath (Matt. 3:7 par. Luke 3:7) or day of wrath; Jesus could feel anger at the hardness of the human heart (Mark 3:5; cf. the use of the verb in Mark

1:41 TNIV). God's wrath remains on those who reject the Son (John 3:36). There is a lengthy set of references to God's future but, to some extent, already revealed and active wrath in Paul, and it is this from which believers will be saved (Rom. 5:9).[17] It is anticipated in the reaction of magistrates (as agents of God) to wrongdoing (Rom. 13:4–5). It hangs over evildoers (Eph. 2:3; 5:6; Col. 3:6), and it comes upon unbelieving Israel, which hinders the evangelism of Gentiles (1 Thess. 2:16). Hebrews 3:11 and 4:3 cite Psalm 95:11 concerning God's attitude toward disobedient Israel. Revelation particularly emphasises the coming expression of the wrath of God and the Lamb (Rev. 6:16–17; 11:18; 14:10; 16:19; 19:15). Here the word "cup" is used, which is metaphorical for suffering and especially for suffering imposed by God (Mark 10:38–39; 14:36). The other term for wrath, *thumos*, is used by Paul for a human passion that is to be avoided (2 Cor. 12:20; Gal. 5:20; Eph. 4:31; Col. 3:8) and by John for the wrath of the devil (Rev. 12:12) and for the passion of the harlot (Rev. 14:8) and for various expressions of the wrath of God (Rev. 14:10, 19; 15:1, 7; 16:1, 19; 19:15). Here the reaction of God to the evil of the world is powerfully expressed.

Judgment. Far more common than these concepts of punishment and wrath is the use of the concept of judgment. It is no exaggeration to say that it is part of the framework of thought of the majority of New Testament books.[18] It is simply taken for granted and becomes thematic particularly in Matthew, John, Romans, Hebrews, James, 1 and 2 Peter, Jude and Revelation. God has appointed his Son to be judge, and we shall all appear before his judgment seat to be judged justly for what we have done. I do not need to give the evidence in detail.

Destruction and Death. Finally, the outcome of various sins is expressed in terms of destruction. Like judgment, this concept is extraordinarily pervasive in the New Testament. There is also the concept of death, both physical and ultimate. One manifestation of this is being sent to Gehenna by God himself (Matt. 10:28; Luke 12:5). The concept of torment is found occasionally, both in the imagery of some parables and in the description of the lake of fire, where it is used of the devil and his agents.

The New Testament Concept of Future Judgment

This compilation of the evidence leads to three significant conclusions:

1. There is a clear framework of thought in the New Testament which assumes a background of the future action of God against

evildoers, an action of judgment in which God displays his wrath against sin and carries out judgment involving the destruction or death of sinners.

2. There is no other kind of future scenario or description of the attitude and actions of God. This is not one type of metaphorical description among others. And there is no indication of a universalism in which all are saved and none are ultimately condemned.

3. This teaching becomes thematic on many occasions, and it lies at the centre of the evangelism of the early church in that salvation is deliverance from the consequences of sin and specifically from death and the wrath of God. Consequently, we cannot push it to one side as being less important than the other aspects of human sin and need.

There have been numerous attempts to argue that this wrath is not a feeling on the part of God, still less an arbitrary outburst of rage. Some would understand it simply in terms of the inevitable self-inflicted wounds of sin that God allows to happen. I can see no legitimate way of avoiding the fact that these terms refer to the attitude of God himself that results in action being taken against sinners.

1. The parallel language of judgment involves God, whether the Father or the Son, as the person who brings about this fate of sinners. If God is the agent in judgment, then equally he is the agent of wrath, particularly since it is so frequently referred to as his wrath.

2. This wrath is not arbitrary, uncontrolled rage. Critics tend to identify the feeling of wrath with an emotion that may be arbitrary, uncontrolled and intemperate. Whatever we may make of some of the more difficult material in the Old Testament, the New Testament does not ascribe such arbitrariness and selfish, uncontrolled anger to God. When Paul forbids the human activity of taking vengeance and says "leave it to God", it does not follow that divine vengeance is exercised in the same way as sinful, human vengeance.

3. If God feels other emotions, such as tender compassion, it is difficult to see why he should not feel revulsion against evil. If

he can bring his wrath to an end or turn from it (Exod. 32:12; 2 Chron. 12:12; Ps. 37:8; Hab. 3:2), then equally he can begin it (cf. Rom. 3:5; 9:22) or refuse to exercise it (1 Thess. 5:9). It is under his control.

4. Since wrath is called forth only when evil is present, to that extent it is not fundamental to God's character. But precisely the same thing could be said about grace and mercy, which are necessitated only when his creatures are in need caused by sin.

5. When Stephen Travis describes the nature of the wrath in Romans 1 as "God's allowing of people to experience the intrinsic consequences of their refusal to live in relationship with him" and contrasts this with "the retributive inflicting of punishment from outside",[19] this is a false antithesis in that it ignores the specific "God gave them up" language of Paul. To deny that God feels negatively about sin is a denial of the personal character of God, who reacts to the evil that ruins his creation and destroys his relationship with his creatures. It is to make the judgment something impersonal and mechanistic rather than the personal reaction of the living God. If we allow that God feels pain when he sees his creatures suffer, equally we must allow that he feels disappointment extending to wrath against those who cause the suffering. When Green and Baker say that human acts of wickedness "do not arouse the wrath of God but are themselves already the consequences of its active presence",[20] they fail to see that it was precisely the wrath of God that led to these consequences of sin.

Accordingly, the metaphor being used is that of the human response to persons who do wrong things. This attitude of strong disapproval may be expressed in a withdrawal of affection and an attitude of displeasure that makes the culprits feel uncomfortable and wish that they had not done the wrong action. One must carefully separate from this complex human attitude those elements which are themselves sinful, such as the overreaction in a fit of temper, the use of words like "revenge" and even "vengeance", which often include the assertion of one's superiority by a response that exceeds the original offence, and the use of superior power to crush the offender. A sinless divine expression of wrath, free from the elements that disfigure human wrath, is perfectly conceivable and proper.

To say that "wrath is not a divine property or essential attribute of God"[21] leads to a mistaken understanding of the cross. The God of the Bible and the God of the New Testament is fundamentally holy and loving. Both of these attributes are relational; they find expression in love towards his creation and yet also in judgment and wrath when that creation is spoilt by sin.

The Nature of Judgment

How are wrath and judgment expressed against the offender? In the human sphere, justice is the upholding of right against evil not simply by asserting the principle but by action against the offender, the latter being termed "judgment". The terms "punishment", "penalty" and "sentence" are commonly used to refer to this action or experience. These terms may cover a number of elements, not all of which are necessarily present on each occasion.[22] These include:

1. *Restraint and deterrence.* These refer to action to prevent similar evil deeds from happening, whether by some kind of restriction on the original offender or by warning examples to potential offenders. Detention in prison or some form of restraint may be necessary to stop the offender from re-offending or to warn others who may be tempted to similar crimes.

2. *Reformation.* The penalty imposed may be designed to educate and reform offenders so that they will see the wrongness of their actions and resolve to live differently. Ideally, we should like to see wrongdoers *repent* of the wrong they have done, but we have to be realistic and recognise that this happens less frequently. Perhaps the majority of people, including ourselves, keep the laws because we are afraid of being caught and penalised.

3. *Restitution.* Another vital element is restitution, either by giving back what has been taken or giving some kind of compensation where this is not possible (like money to a maimed person). Here justice is done to the victim of crime only when something can be done to undo the effects of the crime. This undoing is often imposed upon the guilty person (although it might also be done by the community).

4. But this raises the further question of whether there is more to justice than these three aspects, only the third of which is strictly concerned with *justice* as a principle. In some societies the *honour* of a person is affected and diminished by a crime, and it is held that the offender should make some kind of satisfaction to restore that honour. Such an idea lies behind the Anselmian type of understanding of the death of Christ.

More generally, it is thought that if a person causes somebody else to suffer, then they should be made to *suffer proportionately* to cancel the original evil deed. Till that happens, the guilty person remains guilty. Where the penalty consists in making restitution for the crime to the victim or to society more generally (e.g., by doing community service), there is not a problem. But in many cases, where restitution is not possible (or has not been developed), there may simply be the infliction of pain and loss upon the criminal, the payment of an arbitrary fine, or the imposition of a prison sentence.

Certainly the biblical principles are that whatever we sow we shall also reap (Gal. 6:7) and that we receive the due "reward" or "wage" of our sins (Rom. 1:27; 6:23; 2 Cor. 5:10; 11:15; 2 Peter 2:12–13; Rev. 18:6), which is painful and which is brought about ultimately by God.[23] In other words, something happens to sinners as a result of the sins for which they are responsible.

5. A major reason for the imposition of penalties is so that *society may express its disapproval of and rejection of evil and evildoers.* Society upholds justice and law by asserting that people must not disobey the laws as they please. We may put lawbreakers in prison for an arbitrary period of time, whereby we indicate to them and to the whole community that we are upholding justice (as we understand it) and will not tolerate lawbreakers in our society. There is a proper use of the principle of proportionality here.[24]

It almost goes without saying that the penalty is *painful*. It certainly is if it involves physical pain or being deprived of something that you enjoy, such as money or time. However, in some circumstances, it might be seen in a different light, as when the offender recognises the enormity of what has been done and is happy to make restitution for the offence, even though it involves personal cost.

I would therefore defend the proposition that in the divine-human context, the ultimate element in judgment is *exclusion from the community*, from the kingdom of God, of those who rebel against God and his requirements.[25] God says, "Depart from me" (Matt. 7:23; 25:41; Luke 13:27). This combines the two essential elements of upholding righteousness and excluding those who fail to do so.

But now the question arises whether this is rightly termed "retribution". Retribution refers to the reaction against the specific offender without specifying what is involved in the reaction.[26] Retribution is the action taken in order to uphold justice, restrain evildoers, undo the effects of the offence and, where the evildoer is irreformable, exclude that person from the community and its benefits.[27] And since the exclusion is exclusion from the blessings of the kingdom of God, it follows that this exclusion is experienced as painful by those who undergo it. I cannot see how deprivation of eternal life can be seen as anything other than a penalty or punishment upon the impenitent sinner.[28]

The Holiness and Righteousness of God

The New Testament uses this kind of language about God's judgment and wrath because he is holy (or righteous) and loving. Holiness and love are facets of the same character, but it is necessary to use both terms to bring out the irreducibility of the character of God to one or the other. The concept of divine fatherhood in the ancient world inevitably accommodated and required both of these ideas – the father is the upholder of justice within the family (1 Peter 1:17) and simultaneously the compassionate and loving carer for the family.

P. T. Forsyth has done the most to present a carefully wrought doctrine of atonement that takes God's holiness into account.[29] Forsyth seems to be overlooked by some critics of **penal substitution**[30] and some defenders as well,[31] but his work is significant in this discussion.

Forsyth laid extraordinary emphasis on the holiness and love of God, to the extent that he wrote frequently of holy love, and established that the holiness of God must figure centrally in any doctrine of the atonement. He states, "By the atonement, therefore, is meant that action of Christ's death which has a prime regard to God's holiness, has it for its first charge, and finds man's reconciliation impossible except as that holiness is divinely satisfied once for all on the cross. Such an atonement is the key to the incarnation."[32] It follows that the notion of judgment is inescapable: "The idea of God's holiness is inseparable from the idea of judgment as the mode by which grace goes into action."[33] God had to satisfy his holiness in dealing with the problem of sin, and he did so in the holy obedience and self-offering of his Son, through which reconciliation between God and the sinful world is achieved.

Alongside judgment, Forsyth upheld firmly the concept of the wrath of God as the reaction of holy love to sin: "The reconciliation has no meaning apart from guilt which must stir the anger of a holy God and produce separation from Him."[34] He insisted that "we do not only grieve God but we provoke His anger,"[35] and he strenuously rejected the idea that the law was "detached from God, and cut adrift to do its own mechanic work under His indifference".[36]

"Atonement means the covering of sin by something which God Himself had provided and therefore the covering of sin by God Himself."[37] What Christ did was "the perfect obedience of holy love which he offered amidst the conditions of sin, death and judgment".[38] "There is a penalty and curse for sin; and Christ consented to enter that region ... It is impossible for us to say that God was angry with Christ; but still Christ entered the wrath of God ... You can therefore say that although Christ was not punished by God, He bore God's penalty upon sin. To say that Christ was punished by God who was always well-pleased with Him is an outrageous thing. Calvin himself repudiates the idea."[39] Christ "turned the penalty He endured into sacrifice He offered. And the sacrifice He offered was the judgment He accepted."[40]

Ultimately, Forsyth sees his restatement of the doctrine as moving from an emphasis upon substitutionary expiation to what he calls "solidary reparation, consisting of due acknowledgement of God's holiness, and the honouring of that and not of His honour".[41] He suggests that "judgment is a much better word than either penalty or punishment", and interestingly, he would prefer to speak of representation rather than substitution, judging that "substitution does not take account of the moral results on the soul".[42] In my opinion, this does not mean that Forsyth rejected what is conveyed by the term "substitution" but that he thought "representative" was the more comprehensive and appropriate term to use, conveying what is meant by substitution and more.[43]

Here we have an exposition of the matter which takes holiness and wrath seriously, and that I find to be much more in tune with the teaching of the New Testament than the position of the anti-penal thinkers. The essential difference is that Forsyth and those like him hold firmly to the biblical teaching about the holiness and the wrath of God, which issue in his active judgment of sinners. They then embrace that understanding of the work of Christ which sees it as the active obedience and expression of holiness in which God himself bears the painful consequences of human sin, providing reconciliation with himself. God must be seen to be both just and the justifier, and this he did by himself bearing the judgment or penalty of sin.

Forsyth's view has seemed to some to be more like satisfaction than penal substitution.[44] But since what is satisfied is God's holiness rather than his honour, Forsyth does go in a somewhat different direction from Anselm. Forsyth in fact offers a classical statement of the evangelical doctrine. Similar things are said by theologians like Smail and Travis, and I think that it is fair to say that we are close to agreement on a positive statement of the work of Christ. But the difference is that I see this as an exposition of what is meant by penal substitution and appeasement of God rather than as a denial of these two categories of interpretation.

The vital point is that it is impossible to separate the personal and the judicial aspects in God as the sovereign ruler. God has to act in such a way that his justice is upheld (Romans 3), and this is achieved by the death of Christ, which enables him to pardon sinners while upholding justice. The judgment on sinners is exclusion from the family of God in that God dissociates himself from sinners. There can be no greater loss than that, and it is condign for sinners who have rejected the sovereign God's holiness and love. I cannot see any way of regarding this exclusion of sinners as anything other than the divinely imposed consequence or penalty for sin.

Thus, there is simply no basis for the common accusation that God's wrath is arbitrary or vindictive like a human outburst of temper. It is preferable to speak of wrath rather than anger or fury, since it is the latter terms that are most open to misunderstanding. However, we must not go to the opposite extreme and make the wrath impersonal, something that God does not feel.

It is inherent in this understanding that the death of Christ is not the event that persuades God, otherwise unwilling, to forgive. Rather, the death is purposed and initiated by God himself. The death is the death of God himself, since the Son is one with the Father, and we are correct to see God dying on the cross, as Charles Wesley clearly taught. The death is God's identifying with humanity in its need, and this is important in showing how God in Christ absorbs the suffering inflicted by evil and sinners on humanity. Some scholars complain that the idea of absorption is unbiblical.[45] I cannot see that the objection is justified, since we have to use terms that do not occur in the Bible in order to bring out its teaching.

The Underlying Principle?

The exposition of Forsyth has demonstrated that the penal substitution principle is clearly present in one New Testament understanding of the death of Christ. Is it principal and determinative? Space forbids a detailed demonstration of how the principle operates in the various other biblical ways of expressing the work of Christ.

1. Sacrifice. A fundamental way of understanding the death of Christ is in terms of sacrifice. The relevant patterns in the Old Testament are the sin and burnt offerings and the ritual of the day of atonement, which included the offering of a goat as a sin offering and the choice of another goat as a scapegoat over which were confessed all the sins of Israel. The scapegoat ritual pictured the "getting rid of" the sin rather than the sinners. The confession of the sin transferred the sin to the goat. When we read of Christ as the Lamb of God who bears the sins of the world, it is difficult to avoid the impression that the same kind of thing is happening.

A sacrifice can be understood in a broad sense as a penalty, although the specific language of penalty does not seem to be associated with it. This may be seen as an indication that the term "penal substitution" is too narrow to be applied strictly to every type of understanding of the death of Christ. It is better to think of a sacrifice as an offering made to God, but the fact remains that it is costly and involves the death of a victim that would otherwise have been spared.[46]

2. *Curse.* In Galatians 3:10–14, believers are bought back from the curse of the law by Christ's dying on the cross as one accursed. The curse of the law is its condemnation of sinners and statement of judgment over them. It is carried out on Christ and thereby sinners are delivered from it. Here the procedure of the Old Testament criminal law is used to explain the death of Jesus, and the element of penalty is conspicuous.

3. *Redemption and ransom.* A ransom is a payment that sets people free, often to deliver them from slavery and bondage. The price is a substitute for the person redeemed, and it is costly and painful. Here, the concept of substitution is present and the cost may be regarded as a penalty in the broad sense. This is manifestly the case where the redemption of people is effected by the precious blood of Christ. While the principle of penal substitution can be seen to be effective here, the rationale is not clearly worked out. The point of the metaphor is that people are in bondage to the power of sin and death, and the payment sets them free. The price is of infinite worth so that salvation is available for all people, even if not all accept it.

4. *Reconciliation.* Here the problem is the rebellion of the sinners against God and his consequent exclusion of them from fellowship. Romans 5 and 2 Corinthians 5 taken together make it plain that reconciliation takes place by the death of Christ, who is made sin on behalf of the sinners. The consequences of sin and specifically death are borne by Christ when he is made one with sinners, and in that sense the substitution is penal. Sinners are invited to receive the reconciliation that has been objectively achieved.

5. *Forgiveness.* In forgiveness, the offended person is prepared to overlook a fault and enter into a positive relationship with the offender. The offence is wiped away either without the imposition of a penalty or with mitigation of the penalty, provided the sinner is willing to accept the offer. Old Testament sacrifices could be understood as expressions of contrition. The sins in question were publicly confessed, and the sinner laid hands on the sacrifice to indicate that it was their sacrifice. In this way, the sacrifice could be said to take away sin.

In the New Testament, God, who provided the path of sacrifice in the Old Testament, now intervenes to provide a new offering, himself dying in the person of the Son, who has united himself with humanity to make the offering which will deal with sin. Christ or his name or his death are integral to the New Testament concept of forgiveness.[47] The sinner no longer needs to bring an offering to God, for Christ has already made that offering in the heavenly sanctuary. The conferral of forgiveness costs the sinner nothing, but it costs God everything.

It is clear that essentially the same basic principle is expressed in each of these different understandings of the death of Jesus. The principle of one person bearing the painful consequences of sin is the *modus operandi* of the different understandings of the cross. There are different nuances in these expressions of the nature of salvation. But the central action, common to them all, is God doing something in Christ that involves the death of Christ, who bears our sins and the painful consequence of them. Christ's sacrifice saves us from exclusion from the kingdom of God. The term "penal substitution" appropriately expresses this process.

The Objections Answered

Let us finally note some of the main objections brought against the doctrine.[48]

1. The alleged late origin of the doctrine. It is sometimes alleged that the doctrine of penal substitution virtually dates from the Reformation and was virtually absent or unformulated earlier. However, a distinction must be made between the existence of the doctrine and its prominence. The doctrine of penal substitution may not have been prominent before the Reformation, but this is quite different from saying that it was unknown. Thus, while Green and Baker can show how great stress is laid on the doctrine of recapitulation in Irenaeus, they also rightly point out that Irenaeus includes statements of propitiation.[49] If the doctrine was not central in patristic and medieval theology, that may be due to the general tendency to misunderstand the grace of God that T. F. Torrance rightly detected as occurring from an early stage.[50] That misunderstanding was not rectified until the Reformers brought the church back to the New Testament.

2. A God who needs to be appeased before he can forgive. It is easy for defenders of penal substitution to come under attack for allegedly presenting the matter as though it is only because of the cross that God is prepared to abandon his wrath and forgive sinners. Yet I am not aware that any responsible defenders of the doctrine take this point of view, and if there were, I would side with their critics.[51]

At the cross, it is God himself suffering with and on behalf of human beings. We may note the deep insight of Isaiah 63:9, which tells us that when Israel was afflicted by its enemies, "in all their distress he too was distressed, and the angel of his presence saved them". It could be argued that God only needs to uphold justice, with no duty to sinners beyond that. They have no claims on his mercy. Yet while James tells us that "judgment without mercy will be shown to anyone who has not been merciful", he then adds, "Mercy triumphs over judgment" (James 2:13). That principle must surely be true of God himself, and it reminds us that alongside justice lies the mercy of God, which goes beyond justice to deliver people who are under judgment.

The motive for Jesus' death is stated to be the loving purpose of God, and there is not the faintest hint in the New Testament that Jesus died to persuade God to forgive sinners. On the contrary, his death is part of the way in which God himself acts in his grace and mercy. Hence the death of Jesus is not a means of appeasing a Father who is unable or unwilling to forgive. It is what God himself does while we are yet sinners, and, because the reconciliation has already been made, sinners are urged to accept what God has done for them. It is true that the wrath of God is operative against sinners who have not accepted the gospel, but it is not true that God's wrath has to be appeased before he will be merciful.

3. Cosmic child abuse. The charge of cosmic child abuse is totally misplaced. It fails to recognise the points made above which emphasise that it was God who initiated the cross; it was God himself who suffered on the cross and bore the sin of the world. A parent who puts herself into the breach and dies to save her child from a burning house is considered praiseworthy. The God who suffers and dies in the person of Jesus for human sin belongs in the same category. It is true that the concept of God the Son suffering and dying is paradoxical and incomprehensible, and we have to recognise that fact, but that is what Scripture says.[52]

Conclusion

Salvation is possible through the death of Christ, who bears the consequence of sin, thus enabling us to avoid the painful penalty of life without God. In this way, the holy and loving God upholds righteousness through judging sinners and saving those who accept what he has done in his Son on their behalf. It is not a case of God punishing Christ but of God in Christ taking on himself the sin and its penalty. Indeed, at some point the challenge needs to be issued: where are these evangelicals who say that God punished Christ? Name them![53] Where are the evangelicals who will repudiate this statement, written by John Calvin: "We do not, however, insinuate that God was ever hostile to him or angry with him."[54] You will not find them among serious theologians, although I recognise that popular preachers may err in this respect. Further, it seems that much of this type of criticism comes from the more radical feminist type of theologian with an agenda that includes repudiation of essential features of biblical theology.

Nevertheless, this does not free us of the obligation to ask how we can present this doctrine in ways that do not lead to misrepresentation and misunderstanding. I regret that I have not even started to discuss this matter, but hopefully I have at least presented a case that helps to vindicate the traditional evangelical doctrine of the atonement, and I pray that it may help us towards an understanding of it that can command general assent and form the basis for our evangelism.[55]

Notes

1. Alan Mann, *Atonement for a "Sinless" Society: Engaging with an Emerging Culture* (Milton Keynes: Paternoster, 2005), 94. It is not clear whether this statement means that a biblical understanding of atonement is not concerned *at all* with the appeasing of God or that it is not concerned *primarily* ("above all") with the appeasing of God.

2. See the discussion in Joel B. Green and Mark D. Baker, *Recovering the Scandal of the Cross: Atonement in New Testament and Contemporary Contexts* (Carlisle: Paternoster, 2003), 30–31, 90–92.

3. Steve Chalke and Alan Mann, *The Lost Message of Jesus* (Grand Rapids: Zondervan, 2003); Green and Baker, *Recovering the Scandal*; John Goldingay, ed., *Atonement Today* (London: SPCK, 1995); Christopher D. Marshall, *Beyond Retribution: A New Testament Vision for Justice, Crime and Punishment* (Grand Rapids: Eerdmans, 2001); Tom Smail, *Once and for All: A Confession of the Cross* (London: DLT, 1998); Stephen H. Travis, "Christ as Bearer of Divine Judgment in Paul's Thought about the Atonement," in *Jesus of Nazareth, Lord and Christ: Essays on the Historical Jesus and New Testament Christology*, ed. Joel B. Green and Max Turner (Grand Rapids: Eerdmans, 1994), 332–45.

4. For a fuller treatment, see I. H. Marshall, *Aspects of the Atonement* (Milton Keynes: Paternoster, 2007).

5. Vincent Taylor (*The Atonement in New Testament Teaching*, 2nd ed. [London: Epworth, 1945], 197) commented that the New Testament teaching "comes so near, without actually crossing, the bounds of substitutionary doctrine".

6. So Colin E. Gunton, *The Actuality of Atonement: A Study of Metaphor, Rationality and the Christian Tradition* (Edinburgh: T & T Clark, 1988), but he does not regard it as dispensable.

7. So J. I. Packer, "What Did the Cross Achieve? The Logic of Penal Substitution," *TynBul* 25 (1974): 3–45.

8. David Peterson, ed., *Where Wrath and Mercy Meet: Proclaiming the Atonement Today* (Carlisle: Paternoster, 2001), 65; cf. John Stott, *The Cross of Christ* (Leicester: IVP, 1986), 159; J. I. Packer, "The Atonement in the Life of the Christian," in *The Glory of the Atonement*, ed. C. E. Hill and F. A. James (Downers Grove, Ill.: IVP, 2004), 416.

9. Henri Blocher, "Biblical Metaphors and the Doctrine of the Atonement," *JETS* 47, no. 4 (December 2004): 629–45. See also Blocher, "*Agnus Victor*: The Atonement as Victory and Vicarious Punishment," in *What Does It Mean to Be Saved? Broadening Evangelical Horizons on Salvation*, J. G. Stackhouse Jr. (Grand Rapids: Baker, 2002), 67–91. Also Blocher, "The Sacrifice of Jesus Christ: The Current Theological Situation," *EuroJTh* 8, no. 1 (1999): 23–36.

10. Trevor Hart, "Redemption and Fall," in *The Cambridge Companion to Christian Doctrine*, ed. Colin E. Gunton (Cambridge: Cambridge Univ. Press, 1997), 189–206, esp. 190. Hart himself appears to favour the "satisfaction" type of understanding and thinks that the development of theories

of penal substitution was not free from some misunderstanding of Scripture (201–2).

11. The term "appeasement" is perhaps too compromised to be usable, since it is very hard to use it of a God who takes the initiative in offering salvation to sinful human beings.

12. Or "while waiting for the day of judgment" (cf. NRSV).

13. The same Old Testament background is summoned in Heb. 10:30 to warn that God will judge those who reject his Son.

14. In Rom. 13:4, the magistrate is God's agent to carry out vengeance/punishment. Similarly, Paul expresses readiness to "punish" (lit. "avenge") every act of disobedience in the church at Corinth (2 Cor. 10:6).

15. In Rev. 6:10, the souls of martyrs ask God to judge and so avenge their blood. Here something is to be done to make up for their murder, presumably punishment of the wrongdoers. The prayer is answered according to the expression of praise in Rev. 19:2, which describes what God has done.

16. The verb "to be angry" (*orgizomai*) is not used directly of God, although it is used of characters representing God in two parables (Matt. 18:34; 22:7 par. Luke 14:21). This may be significant in avoiding the danger of thinking of God as exercising angry passions like human beings do.

17. Cf. 1 Thess. 1:10; 5:9; Rom. 2:5, 8; 3:5 (it is just); 4:15 (effect of God's law); 9:22 (seen in action against "the vessels of wrath").

18. The vocabulary is absent from Mark, Galatians, Ephesians, Philippians, Colossians, 1 Thessalonians, Titus, Philemon, 2 John and 3 John, but here, with the exception of the tiny books, other expressions convey the same essential reality.

19. Travis, "Christ as Bearer," 338.

20. Green and Baker (*Recovering the Scandal*, 55) make a contrast between God's striking out in vengeance against sinners and letting people suffer the consequences which are inherent in their own sins. But this does not take into account passages that speak of God's action subsequent to human sin (2 Thess. 1:6–9), or God expressing his wrath (Rom. 3:5), or God wishing to show his wrath (Rom. 9:22), or God's wrath coming upon disobedience (Eph. 5:6; Col. 3:6), or God swearing in his wrath (Heb. 3:11; 4:3), or God carrying out judgment. The term "vengeance" is not the best one for the holy response of God to sin, but the notion that God does not act in reaction to sin is false.

21. Green and Baker, *Recovering the Scandal*, 54.

22. See the discussion by Marshall, *Beyond Retribution*, for detail.

23. Cf. Blocher, "Sacrifice of Jesus Christ," 32.

24. Certainly if we took James 2:10 seriously, we would argue that any person who commits adultery is actually guilty of the much more serious and basic sin of disobedience to the law as divine command and therefore any individual sin is equally culpable, but on the human level we recognise that this is unjust and that proportionality is unavoidable.

25. Cf. Garry Williams, "The Cross and the Punishment of Sin," in Peterson, *Where Wrath and Mercy Meet*, 90–94. The concept of exclusion has a parallel in the Old Testament concept of exile as exclusion from the Promised Land of those who have broken the covenant, and some theologians want to understand "Christ's death on the cross as the divine punishment of exile" (Hans Boersma, *Violence, Hospitality and the Cross: Reappropriating the Atonement Tradition* [Grand Rapids: Baker Academic, 2004], 19, 174–77).

26. A dictionary definition (*The Concise Oxford Dictionary*) is "recompense usually for evil done, vengeance, requital".

27. My impression is that theologians use this term without defining and analysing it to any extent. Packer ("What Did the Cross Achieve?") uses it but does not discuss it.

28. On the impossibility of avoiding "violence" in this fallen universe, see especially Boersma, *Violence, Hospitality and the Cross*.

29. See L. McCurdy, *Attributes and Atonement: The Holy Love of God in the Theology of P. T. Forsyth* (Carlisle: Paternoster, 1999); P. T. Forsyth, *The Work of Christ* (London: Hodder and Stoughton, 1910; London: Independent Press, 1938); P. T. Forsyth, *The Cruciality of the Cross* (London: Independent Press,1909; Carlisle: Paternoster, 1997).

30. But not by Tom Smail, *Once and for All*, 45, 86–87, 98, 119, 186.

31. But not by Leon Morris!

32. Forsyth, *Cruciality of the Cross*, viii.

33. Ibid.

34. Forsyth, *Work of Christ*, 80.

35. Ibid., 241.

36. Ibid., 242.

37. Ibid., 55.

38. Ibid., 201.

39. Ibid., 147.

40. Ibid., 163.

41. Ibid., 164–65.

42. Ibid., 182.

43. If, however, "representative" means less than "substitute", then I have no doubt which term should be used. Cf. the discussion by Packer, "What Did the Cross Achieve?" 22–25.

44. T. H. Hughes, *The Atonement: Modern Theories of the Doctrine* (London: Allen and Unwin, 1949), 38–46.

45. Blocher, "Biblical Metaphors," 643.

46. Cf. Gordon J. Wenham, "The Theology of Old Testament Sacrifice," in *Sacrifice in the Bible*, ed. R. T. Beckwith and M. J. Selman (Carlisle: Paternoster, 1995), 75–87.

47. See Matt. 26:28; Luke 24:47; Acts 2:38; 5:31; 10:43; 13:38; Eph. 1:7; Col. 1:14; Heb. 9:22; 1 John 1:9; 2:12.

48. For a rebuttal of the objection that salvation by penal substitution does nothing to change the sinner, see my discussion of how the substitution of Christ identifies the believer with him in *New Testament Theology* (Downers Grove, Ill. / Leicester: IVP and Apollos, 2004), 223–26. For a fuller and deeper discussion, see James Denney, *The Death of Christ*, ed. R. V. G. Tasker (London: Tyndale, 1951; Carlisle: Paternoster, 1997).

49. Green and Baker, *Recovering the Scandal*, 121. See further Blocher, "Biblical Metaphors," 630–31, and Boersma, *Violence, Hospitality and the Cross*, 158–63, for other early writers.

50. T. F. Torrance, *The Doctrine of Grace in the Apostolic Fathers* (Edinburgh: Oliver and Boyd, 1948).

51. D. L. Edwards and John Stott, *Essentials: A Liberal-Evangelical Dialogue* (London: Hodder and Stoughton, 1988), 107–68.

52. Theologians of a so-called Arminian persuasion have difficulties with a common version of penal substitution which insists that it cannot be upheld apart from a belief in a doctrine of limited atonement, according to which Christ died only for the specific number of the "elect"; otherwise, it is argued, God would be demanding the penalty for sin twice from unbelievers, once from Christ and once from themselves if they do not accept salvation (Packer, "What Did the Cross Achieve?" 36–39). However, the logic of this position is faulty in that it assumes an inappropriate mathematical equivalence between the death of Christ and the penalty due to sinners, and its basis runs counter to the clear New Testament statements about the universal scope of Christ's death (John 3:16; 1 Tim. 2:6).

53. H. E. Guillebaud (*Why the Cross?* 2nd ed. [London: InterVarsity Fellowship, 1946], 145) explicitly repudiates the phrase "God punished Christ." Similarly, Stott, *Cross of Christ*, 150–51. There is a difference between saying that God in his Son, Jesus Christ, bore the penalty of human sin and saying that God punished him.

54. John Calvin, *Institutes of the Christian Religion* 2:16:11, trans. H. Beveridge (London: J. Clarke, 1953), 1.444.

55. For a fuller treatment of the issues discussed in this chapter, see I. H. Marshall, *Aspects of the Atonement: Cross and Resurrection in the Reconciling of God and Humanity* (Milton Keynes: Paternoster, 2007).

chapter four

atonement in
the old testament

christopher j. h. wright

Introduction

This essay is a broad reflection on how the Old Testament portrays what has gone wrong in human life and what it means for people and situations to be "put right". Atonement language is one part of this "putting right", but not the most prominent over all sections of the canonical traditions. Furthermore, this essay will cover a broad sweep of material in different parts of the Old Testament canon, and this necessarily means that it will lack exegetical or reflective depth. My hope, however, in offering this sketch is that it will motivate readers to explore specific themes or textual fields in greater depth for themselves.

The Problem

How does the Old Testament describe the human predicament? We need more than a simple word study on the various Hebrew terms for sin (though that is itself a significant and enlightening study). Broadly, the Old Testament portrays our predicament in terms of the following:

1. A relationship that has been broken: the relational aspect. The first account of trouble between God and humanity is described in relational terms. In the narratives of Genesis 2–3, it is the relationship between the man, the woman and God that is questioned and then spoiled. Throughout the rest of the Old Testament, relational metaphors for sin and its effects include adultery and other strong pictures of betrayal and ingratitude within a relationship that was meant to be built on love, trust, loyalty and commitment.

2. *The disturbance of* shalom: *the social aspect.* The narratives of Genesis 4–11 describe inter-human disorder at every level: envy, violence, murder, corruption, vengeance, arrogance. The rest of the Old Testament adds to this list all the other social sins of greed, injustice, socio-economic oppression, abuse of the poor, abuse of women and so on. In relation to these, one could add the ecological dimension, since our relationship with the earth is spoiled and the *shalom* that we should enjoy in our created environment is disturbed. The earth itself suffers because of human sin.

3. *Rebellion against authority: the covenantal aspect.* This aspect comes to prominence in relation to Israel. The first great apostasy of Israel after the exodus resulted in broken tablets of the law (Exodus 32–34). Sin among the redeemed people of God is portrayed, especially in the prophets, as disloyalty to the covenant Lord. This constitutes both apostasy and idolatry (cf. Jer. 2:13).

4. *Guilt that necessitates punishment: the legal aspect.* As early as Deuteronomy 32, the metaphor of the law court is used to portray the sin of Israel. Yahweh is the judge of Israel, the defendant. Forensic metaphors are used. This way of describing sin is also common in the prophets, using the language of offence, transgression, guilt and retributive justice.

5. *Uncleanness and pollution: the ritual aspect.* Here, sin is portrayed as dirt and defilement and includes "abomination" language. This more ritual way of viewing the effects of sin is not confined to the priestly materials of Leviticus, however. Ezekiel, who came from a priestly family, found many ways to communicate the disgusting, filthy nature of sin (e.g., Ezek. 4:12, 36:16–17). Using ritual metaphors, of course, did not mean he viewed sin as merely ritual. Ezekiel uses priestly language, but the evils he refers to are a comprehensive and devastating description of personal and social wickedness (cf. ch. 22).

6. *Shame and disgrace on oneself and/or on God: the emotional aspect.* The initial reaction to sin in the garden of Eden was the desire to hide and be covered. Sin produces shame in the presence of others and God. When sin advances, even the shame response is squashed, as Jeremiah observed when he spoke about people who could no longer blush (Jer. 6:15). Sin not only brings shame and disgrace on oneself; when it takes root and bears fruit among God's people, it results in shame and disgrace on God. Ezekiel called this the profaning of God's name among the nations (Ezek. 36:16ff.).

7. *An accumulating burden: the historical aspect.* The narratives of the Old Testament, from Genesis 4 onwards, show the accumulating effects of sin. Each generation builds on the sinful proclivities of the previous one. The sin of the

Canaanites, for example, is recognized in Genesis 15:16 as not yet having reached its full extent. Several generations later, it is cited as justifying the judgment of God by the agency of the Israelites (Deut. 9:4–6; Lev. 18:24–28). The book of Judges embodies this message, and the interpretation of the exile in the Deuteronomic history is a vivid portrayal of the accumulating historical weight of sin.

8. *Death: the final aspect.* The threat for disobedience in Eden was death, and indeed death invades human life soon after. But death also invades life long before we physically die, through the spoiling effects of disease, broken relationships, suffering, oppression and so on. The language of life and death, blessing and curse, destruction and blotting out is the constant accompaniment of the threats and the promises of the covenant relationship (cf. Deuteronomy passim, but especially ch. 30). Not surprisingly, Ezekiel, who graphically portrayed the death of exile, saw that the only solution lay in the resurrecting power of the Spirit of Yahweh.

Sin, then, in its broad Old Testament perspective, has a devastatingly wide range of effects. It breaks our relationship with God, one another and the earth; it disturbs our peace; it makes us rebels against God's authority; it makes us guilty in God's court; it makes us dirty in God's presence; it brings shame on ourselves and others; it blights us from the past and already poisons the future; it ultimately leads us to destruction and death.

The Patriarchs

How are things "put right" in Genesis? After the fall, the rest of Genesis shows a variety of ways in which God and human beings are involved in putting things right – whether in an immediate crisis or in longer-term hope and expectation. Some of these are as follows:

1. *By divine grace (Gen. 8:21).* The flood narrative begins and ends with God's grace. Noah "found grace in the eyes of the LORD" (Gen. 6:8). The story then proceeds through divine rescue, covenant promise and human *responsive* sacrifice. Initially, Noah does nothing but obey God's instructions. The saving work is entirely of God. The later act of sacrifice, however, is integrally connected to averting God's wrath (the "soothing aroma" that is characteristic of the effects of sacrifice in Leviticus) and the covenantal promise for the future that embraces all life on earth (8:20–22).

2. *By divine promise of blessing (Gen. 12:1–3).* In the context of the nations' rebellious arrogance in Genesis 10 and 11, the promise of God to *bless* all the nations through Abraham and his descendants is very good

news indeed. Putting things right for humanity will depend on God's will to bless, and in this text, God's blessing is anticipated to be individual, familial, national and global.

3. *By faith (Gen. 15:6)*. God's promise must be met by human faith, which is exactly Abraham's response. The text explicitly declares that God counts this as righteousness for him. This verse stands as a key principle in later biblical theology of justification by grace through faith.

4. *By doing righteousness and justice (Gen. 18:19)*. The ethical dimension of the required human response is here articulated through divine soliloquy about the purpose of God himself. God reminds himself that his long-term goal is to bring about what he had promised Abraham; namely, the blessing of all nations. To that end, he had chosen Abraham. And to that end, Abraham and his household after him were to be a community that would "keep the way of the LORD" by "doing righteousness and justice".

5. *By prayer (Gen. 18; 20:17)*. Abraham's remarkable intercession for Sodom and Gomorrah did not achieve the salvation of the cities. But God's rescue of Lot and his family is explicitly put down to God's remembering Abraham (Gen. 19:29). The reader is also taught to believe, with Abraham, that any putting right of things on earth depends on the twin foundational assumptions that Yahweh is "Judge of all the earth" and that he will always "do justice" (Gen. 18:25). Though counted righteous by God for his faith, Abraham was still a sinner, and several narratives feature his fallenness. But even as such, he proves the power of prayer in putting things right for a pagan king whom he had deceived (Gen. 20:17).

6. *By obedience (Gen. 22; 26:4–5)*. The culmination of the Abraham narratives comes in the profound story of the binding of Isaac. This test of obedience climaxes in the strongest and fullest affirmation by God of his promise to Abraham and his intention to bless the nations through him. It now takes the form of an oath on God's own self. And it explicitly links the promise to the proven obedience of Abraham, referring to this at the beginning and end of the promise (Gen. 22:15–18). The final phrase is unequivocal: "through your offspring all nations on earth will be blessed, because you have obeyed me." So as we put together the whole narrative of Abraham, it affirms the integral nature of grace and promise, faith and obedience. The concluding phrase cannot be construed as making God's promise or Abraham's salvation conditional on works. The point is rather that God sovereignly builds Abraham's obedience, as demonstrating the reality of his faith, into the outworking of his own gracious promise to bless humanity.

Apart from Genesis 8:21, although the patriarchs build altars, there is no clear picture of *sacrificial* atonement as a response to sin.

The Passover

In Israel's theology, the Passover was a blood rite initially connected with the exodus. Our theological interpretation of it must be closely connected to the exodus, which stands as the Old Testament model *par excellence* of Yahweh's acting in redemption to put things right. At least three key elements are involved in Passover ritual and theology.[1]

1. Protection from wrath and destruction. Though the vocabulary of atonement is not present, the sacrifice of a lamb is the central element. The blood ritual had an apotropaic force in protecting the Hebrew families from the wrath of the destroyer of the firstborn throughout the land. The effect of blood sacrifice in the averting of judgment is clear.

2. Liberation from oppression. Every celebration of the Passover focuses on the deliverance of the Hebrews out of slavery in Egypt. This happened according to God's promise and entirely by God's action. The whole focus is on the work of God in redemption. But because this was entirely an act of God, it required an appropriate human response, as was built into the whole covenantal nature of the relationship. One dimension of this follows immediately:

3. Consecration to Yahweh. Those whom God had redeemed from death were to regard themselves as now wholly consecrated to him. In the exodus, Yahweh was not so much liberating slaves from Pharaoh as reclaiming his own worshipers. The sacrifice of all firstborn animals and the redemption of firstborn sons was explicitly to remind the Israelites that every future generation belonged to Yahweh in perpetuity (Exod. 13:1–16). This is then carried forward into the demand that Israel should live in practical ethical holiness. So the Passover speaks not only of Yahweh's redemptive commitment to Israel, as demonstrated in history, but also of Israel's ethical commitment to Yahweh, to be demonstrated in life (cf. Exod. 19:6). The same dynamic is reflected in the combination of Passover and holiness imagery in 1 Peter 1–2, and in Paul's ethical use of the Passover tradition in 1 Corinthians 5:6–8.

The Great Apostasy

Exodus 32–34 records the great apostasy of the golden calf during Moses' absence on Mount Sinai. The situation was exceedingly serious, since God threatened immediate destruction of the whole people (Exod. 32:9–10). Moses recalls the event with horror, even forty years later, saying that God had been "angry enough to destroy *you*" (Deut. 9:18–19, in a context that anticipated God's destruction of the nations in Canaan). How could such an awful breach in the covenant relationship be put right? The narrative highlights several factors.

1. Intercessory prayer. The passionate prayer of Moses (Exod. 32:11–14, recalled in Deut. 9:25–29) appealed to three things:

- *God's covenant promise to Abraham.* God could not destroy Israel without breaking that promise and thereby acting inconsistently with his own character and being.
- *God's Sinai covenant with Israel.* This is seen in the reminder that Israel is "*your* people whom *you* brought up from Egypt".
- *God's name and reputation among the surrounding nations.* What would they think of a God who rescues his people only to destroy them a few months later?

The implication of this prayer is that putting things right depends entirely on God's character, promises and name. This dynamic is reflected in the prophets when God declares that his future saving acts will be "for my own sake" (e.g., Isa. 43:25; Ezek. 36:16–32).

2. Punishment. The people were spared from immediate destruction, but they did not go unpunished. This is seen in the slaughter of some by the Levites, the outbreak of plague, and the grinding of the golden idol to be drunk by the people (though the Deuteronomic recollection adds the detail that it was flushed away in a stream; very likely both elements were involved – one punitive, the other purgative).

3. Atonement. Interestingly, on this occasion, the vocabulary of atonement is used. Thus, in Exodus 32:30, Moses says to the people, "You have committed a great sin. But now I will go up to the LORD; perhaps I can make atonement [*kipper*] for your sin." While the predominant use of the *kipper* language comes in the context of the blood sacrifices in Leviticus, it is striking that Moses does *not* offer any sacrifice in seeking to avert God's threatened judgment, except for the remarkable self-offering that he proposes in 32:32. Rather he turns to prayer, and that indeed is atoningly effective. Perhaps there is some anticipation here of Psalm 51:16–17, that actually no sacrifice that Moses could offer could possibly have been adequate or appropriate.

The only hope lay in a "broken and contrite heart" and in the character and promises of God.

4. *The character of Yahweh.* In the context of God's withdrawal of the threat of judgment, restored commitment to go with the people, and a renewed covenant, Moses asks to know Yahweh even more closely. Yahweh's response takes the form of a revelation of his own name that becomes a key text throughout the rest of the Old Testament: "And he passed in front of Moses, proclaiming, 'The LORD, the LORD, the compassionate and gracious God, slow to anger, abounding in love and faithfulness, maintaining love to thousands, and forgiving wickedness, rebellion and sin. Yet he does not leave the guilty unpunished; he punishes the children and their children for the sin of the fathers to the third and fourth generation'" (Exod. 34:6–7). The paradox inherent in this self-description, that Yahweh is characterized by compassion, grace, love and faithfulness, and yet does not let sin go unpunished, is only finally resolved on the cross.

The Priests and the Levitical System

The language and concept of atonement abound in Leviticus, and we need to consider two main aspects of it: the connection with the sacrifices, and the Day of Atonement.

The Sacrifices

The Meaning of *Kipper*

There has been a prolonged debate over the best translation for the root *kpr* in its common piel form, *kipper*.[2] Apart from a much less likely meaning, derived from an Arabic cognate, "to cover over", there are two main candidates.

1. *To ransom.* In Exodus 30:11–16, money is taken as "atonement" or "ransom" for the lives of Israelites counted in the census. And in Numbers 35:29–34, no ransom is allowed in exchange for the life of a convicted murderer. This also seems to be the likely meaning in Leviticus 17:11, where the blood of an animal is said to be its *nephesh*, or "life", which "God has given to make atonement" – that is, as a ransom, or exchange, for the one who sacrifices it.

   The exact same Hebrew form is used in Exodus 30:16 and Leviticus 17:11 – "to *kipper* for your lives". That is, the money

(Exodus 30) or the animal blood (Leviticus 17) is an exchange, an equivalence, that provides a substitute for the life of the Israelite (in a census or as a sacrificing worshiper).

2. *To wipe clean* (with an Akkadian cognate). In Jeremiah 18:23, *kipper* is parallel to "blot out" (when Jeremiah prays that God will *not* do this with the sins of his persecutors). And this seems to be the commonest sense in Leviticus, where the word is frequently used in the rituals of purging or cleansing though the manipulation of the blood of sacrifice.

Perhaps either meaning is possible, depending on the context, though probably the second is commonest. Sacrificial blood is the instrument of cleansing, which thus effects what is necessary for sin to be forgiven and wrath averted.

"Soothing Aroma"

Gordon Wenham argues cogently that "soothing aroma" is a highly significant phrase which indicates that sacrifice effects a change in God's attitude towards the worshiper. That is to say, this metaphor expresses a propitiatory, as well as an expiatory, function. Yes, sacrifice expiates; it cleanses away the sins and offences for which it is offered. But it does so precisely in order to avert the wrath that those sins and offences would otherwise inevitably incur. Two text groups make this meaning clear.

1. *Genesis 8:21*: this is the first use of the phrase in the Hebrew Bible, and it refers to Noah's burnt offering. Wenham notes that the soothing aroma of that sacrifice did not, of course, prevent the flood, nor was it the instrument of saving Noah. However, it did precipitate *God's* benevolent and covenantal response that he would "never again destroy" the earth. There is a strong contrast with Genesis 6:5, where the same description of endemic human sin is found. The change between God's words and acts in 6:5 and in 8:21 is integrally connected to Noah's sacrifice as a "soothing aroma" and God's response to it.

2. *Leviticus 1:9; 2:2; 3:5; 4:31*: with reference to the burnt part of the respective sacrifices that are prescribed in these chapters. In all cases, the phrase "a soothing aroma" is closely linked to the declaration of *atonement* (i.e., the effect on the sin, offence, or

uncleanness: it has been wiped away) and to the declaration of *forgiveness* (i.e., the effect on the sinner-worshiper).

All this matches the theology of Leviticus 17:11. What happens in sacrifice is God-given ("I have given it to you"), but it is also God-affecting. Putting things right, then, includes both a God-orientated and a human-orientated dimension. Sacrifice both cleanses the worshiper and "soothes" the wrath of God. But inasmuch as it all comes from God in the first place, it retains its character as grace and cannot be construed as any kind of bargain, negotiation or *do ut des* relationship.

Maintaining or Restoring Social Order

Philip Jensen observes that sacrifice can function to initiate a fresh state of affairs that is desirable (e.g., the ordination of priests) or to correct a state of affairs that has degenerated (e.g., through pollution, sin, etc.). Also, it can function to restore and strengthen relationships – not only vertically with God but also horizontally within families and the community (e.g., the fellowship offerings).[3] So, in light of our observations about the human predicament, including the disturbance of *shalom*, we find in our Old Testament language of atonement and sacrifice in much more than individual terms. It had social and even cosmic significance. It was the means of preventing the slide into chaos and disorder, of sustaining the boundaries and regularities of an ordered world. Something of this deeper meaning also pervades what Paul has to say about the cosmic significance of the "blood of the cross" (e.g., Col. 1:20).

Life and Death

Sacrifice was not just about maintaining or restoring order; it was about resisting death and sustaining life. Wenham states, "Sin and uncleanness lead a person from the realm of life into the realm of death. Sacrifice stops this process, indeed reverses it. It gives life to those doomed to die."[4] God is the source of all life, so whatever was brought to him must be as perfect in its earthly life as possible, and all that was associated with death (corpses, discharges of the body, etc.) must be cleansed away. Sin and uncleanness were to be treated seriously, and the sacrifices inculcated this attitude.

Special Arrangements for the Poor

Finally, however, it is worth noting the significance of Leviticus 5:7 – 13, where further regulations are made, in relation to the sin offering, for those who could not afford the standard prescription of a lamb. They could bring two turtle doves instead. And if they could not afford even that, a few cups of flour would suffice. *And even this would still count as a sin offering!* Its atoning efficacy would be the same; the same words of atonement and forgiveness would be declared to the worshiper. Nothing could have made it clearer that the forgiveness of sin was entirely dependent on God and his grace – not on the size of the sacrifice, and not necessarily even on the presence of sacrificial blood, and least of all on the social or economic status of the worshiper. A poor Israelite who knew that he could come before God with nothing more than a few handfuls of flour, a contrite heart, and the spirit of true sacrificial confession, and then walk away with the words of forgiveness ringing in his ears was learning something very profound about the nature of Yahweh God and the meaning of divine grace.

The Day of Atonement

The Day of Atonement was an annual putting things right for the whole community in a highly symbolic way. The role of atoning blood in the four sacrifices was clearly to cleanse everything that was associated with God in the sanctuary, and at the same time to cleanse the people from the uncleanness of accumulated sins.

In Leviticus 16:11–22, we can see a double movement involving the two goats.

1. Spacially there is movement from the Holy of Holies in the sanctuary (where the blood of the sacrificed goat is taken) to the wilderness (where the live goat is driven off).
2. Spiritually there is movement from the holiest presence of God to its demonic opposite ("Azazel").

Space has a quality as well as a quantity in the priestly writings, and the two goats eventually encompass the extreme reaches of significant space in the priestly worldview. The blood of one goat reaches to the heart of holy space, whereas the other is driven out to where major impurities have their proper place (cf. Num. 5:1–3).[5] Atonement [sc. on the Day of Atonement], states Derek Tidball, "reaches right to the heart of God and propels sin to the furthest part of the earth. Cleansing comes from an act of God in his dwelling-place and leads to the removal of the problem as far away as it is possible to conceive."[6]

The effect of the complex ritual was not solely to atone for sin but was to restore harmony between God and Israel. The movement of the goats represents, or even effects, the reestablishment of the normative world order, thus allowing normal offerings to be resumed.[7]

All of the above speaks of a comprehensive response to sin and its effects. Putting things right in the Levitical system was far from narrowly individual or private. Rather, it was a system that tackled the effects of sin and uncleanness in every area of life, every dimension of space, and every relationship in the community. The overarching objective was to sustain or restore the normative pattern of healthy relationships, in personal, social and spiritual wholeness, cleanness and forgiveness.

The Prophets

Space precludes a detailed account of each prophet's characteristic "slant" on sin and its solution, but a few salient points may be mentioned.

1. Sharp perception of sin. Undoubtedly we owe to the great prophets of Israel a sharper, deeper and clearer perception of what sin is and does, a perception which complements the narrative portrayal in the historical books. The prophets expose both specific individual wickedness and general social ills. They put a spotlight on specific events and actions that breach covenant loyalty but also highlight endemic and structuralized injustice and oppression.

2. Rejection of corrupt sacrificial ritual. The prophets could not tolerate sacred rites in the context of social wrongs. There could be no putting things right with God by shallow cultic exuberance unless there were corresponding efforts to put things right horizontally within society. This is a fundamentally covenantal understanding of both relationships. The famous passages in which prophets vigorously reject the cultic activity of priests and worshipers should be seen not as hostility towards sacrifice and other rituals of Israel's worship in and of themselves but rather as a rejection of the worship of *these people*, in their persistent wickedness.[8] Moral obedience is thus prioritized over cultic observance – a point fully endorsed by Jesus himself.

3. The necessity of repentance. Jeremiah, perhaps more than any, called for the people to make a radical "turn" away from sin and back towards God. This is seen in his repeated use of the verb *sub* in its multiple forms. (See especially Jeremiah 3; 4; 7; etc.). Joel 2:12–17 provides a powerful litany on what true repentance means, while Ezekiel's appeals reach evangelistic levels in Ezekiel 18:30–32 and 33:10–11.

4. Covenant restoration. Putting things right for the prophets meant primarily the restoration of the broken covenant. For this, various metaphors were employed, such as a restored marriage (Hosea; Isaiah 50; 54) or restored relationship between parent and child (Jer. 31:9, 20). Ultimately, only a fully renewed covenant relationship would suffice, in which the original covenant realities would be fully guaranteed and experienced – wholehearted obedience, knowledge of God, assured relationship, and complete forgiveness (Jer. 31:33 – 34).

5. Dependence on grace. Ezekiel, who has the most severe portrayals of sin among all the prophets, also achieves the greatest insight into the miraculous grace of God. Any hope for Israel in exile flows only from God's will that they should live, not from any merit or potential of their own. His grace can purge the past, if they will acknowledge their guilt and turn from their wickedness (Ezek. 18:30 – 32; 33:10 – 11). His grace, meeting with practical repentance, can effect cleansing, regeneration, a new heart and spirit, and strength for obedience (Ezek. 36:24 – 28). But in the end, nothing short of resurrection, through the life-giving power of God's Spirit, will suffice (Ezekiel 37).

6. "For the sake of my name". Another emphasis of Ezekiel is that when God puts things right for Israel, it will have global effects. For not only Israel but all the nations will come to know the living God for who he truly is. "Then you [or they] will know that I am the LORD" is virtually Ezekiel's signature tune; the phrase occurs about eighty times in his book. It draws our attention to an essentially missional dimension in this whole matter. God's acts of grace and forgiveness have a revelatory purpose. God wills to be known to the nations not merely as the judge before whom they stand (or flee) but as the saviour to whom they can and must turn for salvation (cf. Isa. 45:22).

7. "By my righteous servant". In Isaiah 40 – 55, Yahweh alone is the God who puts things right, for "there is no God apart from me, a righteous God and a Saviour" (Isa. 45:21) and "in the LORD alone are righteousness and strength" (Isa. 45:24). Salvation and forgiveness come from the sheer grace of Yahweh and his choice to forgive and blot out transgressions (Isa. 43:25). But the anticipated vehicle or agent of this saving work of God will be the Servant of the LORD. His vicarious suffering and death will "bear" the iniquities of those who, having thought he was suffering under the judgment of God for his own sin, now realize that it was actually *our* sorrows, transgressions, iniquities and sins that were laid upon him. The language of sacrificial substitution and of vicarious sin-bearing runs through Isaiah 53 unmistakeably.

The Psalms

In the book of Psalms, we see Israel at worship. It is here that we will find how Israelites in the presence of God thought about sin and about how things could be put right. The following points stand out.[9]

1. There is a remarkable paradox that, on the one hand, we find a deeply penitential awareness of sin in several psalms, yet, on the other hand, an almost total absence of reference to atoning sacrifice. The sin offering is mentioned once, but even then only to reject it (Psalm 40)!

2. Sacrifices of various sorts are frequently mentioned, but broadly in contexts of thanksgiving, praise or joy in the communion of worship. The sacrifices normally referenced in Psalms are those that express what God has already done for the worshiper or in anticipation of what God is being asked to do – not in relation to confession of sin or guilt.

3. In fact, on several occasions sacrifice is decisively "relativized" or put in the context of other perspectives. Thus Psalms 40:6 and 51:16 state that obedience and contrition, not sacrifices, are what God desires. And Psalm 50:8–16 argues with intentional irony that while God is happy to receive the sacrifices of his people, the fact is that we cannot give him anything that does not already belong to him. God certainly needs no feeding at our hands, and we cannot influence him to overlook covenant wickedness by such means.

4. Accordingly, putting things right is once more seen as entirely a matter of God's character and grace. Psalmists frequently plead for forgiveness, cleansing, pardon, protection, renewal of life and so on. But this is done entirely on the basis of God's mercy, compassion, righteousness or promise. It is never the expected "product" or "benefit" of a sacrifice that has been made or promised. We may assume that the Israelites who wrote and sang these psalms were devout men and women who were in fact bringing their sacrifices to the sanctuary, in cultic as well as ethical obedience. But they never appeal to them as grounds for God's favour; rather they appeal only to the character and word of God himself. The book of Psalms does not deny Leviticus but, while

assuming it, points beyond it to the known mercy and grace of God, and indeed ultimately anticipates Hebrews in recognizing the inadequacy of all animal sacrifice in contrast to the only and all-sufficient adequacy of the self-sacrifice of Christ.

For Further Reading

Averbeck, Richard. "כפר." In *NIDOTTE*. Vol. 2., 689–710.

Beckwith, Roger T., and Martin J. Selman, eds. *Sacrifice in the Bible*. Carlisle: Paternoster; Grand Rapids: Baker, 1995.

Jensen, Philip. *Graded Holiness: A Key to the Priestly Conception of the World*. JSOTSup 106. Sheffield: Sheffield, 1992.

Tidball, Derek. *The Message of Leviticus*. Leicester: IVP, 2005.

Wenham, Gordon J. *The Book of Leviticus*. NICOT.

Notes

1. See further, T. D. Alexander, "The Passover Sacrifice," in *Sacrifice in the Bible*, ed. Roger T. Beckwith and Martin J. Selman (Carlisle: Paternoster; Grand Rapids: Baker, 1995), 1–24.

2. See the excellent discussion by Richard Averbeck in *NIDOTTE*, vol. 2, 689–710.

3. Philip P. Jensen, "The Levitical Sacrificial System," in Beckwith and Selman, *Sacrifice in the Bible*, 32.

4. Gordon J. Wenham, "The Theology of Old Testament Sacrifice," in Beckwith and Selman, *Sacrifice in the Bible*, 82.

5. Jensen, "Levitical Sacrificial System," 34.

6. Derek Tidball, *The Message of Leviticus* (Leicester: IVP, 2005), 196.

7. Jensen, "Levitical Sacrificial System," 34.

8. E.g., Amos 5:21–25; Hos. 6:6; Isa. 1:10–17; Mic. 6:6–8; Jer. 6:19–20; 7:21–23.

9. See further, Nigel Courtman, "Sacrifice in the Psalms," in Beckwith and Selman, *Sacrifice in the Bible*, 41–58.

chapter five

the atonement in the new testament

geoffrey grogan

The atonement is an important and heartwarming theme which should inspire both thought and worshipful devotion in the Christian. It is intimately related to the atonement teaching of the Old Testament. In this essay, we will consider the main New Testament books that give teaching on the atonement.

The Gospels and Christ's Teaching in Them

Many Christians studying New Testament atonement theology go straight to the Pauline Epistles. This is not necessarily the best place to start, for Paul's teaching is grounded not just on the Old Testament but on the teaching of Jesus. Many have attempted to drive a wedge between Paul's teaching and that of Jesus, representing Paul as the real author of atonement theology. So we will start with the Gospels. We will assume they give us an accurate account of the life and teaching of Jesus, and that the theological message of each is not imposed on but rather arises out of these facts.

Mark begins, "The gospel of Jesus Christ, the Son of God", which shows it is not just a record of facts but a message based on them. The early church came to apply this term to all four canonical gospels, for they all have this character. Each writer has his own way of stressing the importance of the cross, and each gives much space to the closing week of Jesus' life.

Early on, Mark records the baptism of Jesus, when the voice from heaven declares, "You are my Son, whom I love; with you I am well pleased" (Mark 1:11), often held to echo both Psalm 2:7 ("You are my Son") and Isaiah 42:1

("[my servant] in whom I delight"). So, unsurprisingly, the first half of the gospel focuses on Jesus as a person. He proclaims that God's kingdom is near and that his hearers should repent and believe the good news (Mark 1:15). The kingdom's power is shown in his miracles and in his grace when he forgives sins. Both the disciples and the readers are captured by the authority, the power, the wisdom and the caring love of God's Son. All this culminates when Peter confesses him as the Christ at Caesarea Philippi and in the transfiguration, which confirmed this confession.

In the gospel's second half, the emphasis moves to his destiny of suffering, reminding us that the servant passages in Isaiah culminate in the vicarious sufferings of God's servant in Isaiah 53. Because Jesus has been presented as so attractively godly, the reader identifies with the incomprehension of the disciples at talk of his death and then at that death itself.

Matthew has many of Mark's features, with some additional sayings about the cross, but his chief distinctive is his interest in the fulfilment of Scripture. The biggest concentration of fulfilment references after the early chapters is in the passion story, with two quotations from the Isaianic Servant Songs as particularly significant Scriptures among those quoted between these two groups (Matt. 8:17; 12:17–21).

Like Matthew and Mark, Luke records the baptism, temptation and sayings of Jesus on the way to Jerusalem. He alone tells the reader what Jesus, Moses and Elijah talked about on the transfiguration mount – "his departure [lit. "his exodus"], which he was about to bring to fulfillment at Jerusalem" (Luke 9:31). This suggests Jesus would effect typological fulfilment of the exodus from Egypt by delivering God's people from a greater bondage. Throughout Luke's gospel there is a strong sense of destiny for Jesus and his enemies, produced largely by the more than thirty references to Jerusalem, the particularly long length of Luke's account of the final journey to this city, and the reader's building anticipation as Jesus approaches the city.

The introduction to John's gospel, which is all of chapter 1, not just the prologue, contains many titles and descriptions of Jesus which point to his role. The striking utterance of John the Baptist, "Look, the Lamb of God, who takes away the sin of the world!" is underlined when its opening words are repeated a few verses later (John 1:29, 36). Its background is many-sided, reminding us of the binding of Isaac (Genesis 22), the lamb of the Passover (Exodus 12), the lambs of the perpetual sacrifice (Exod. 29:38–43), and the great final Servant Song (Isa. 52:13–53:12), particularly perhaps the first and last of these. Lambs were sacrificial animals, so we are not surprised by the emphasis on the blood of Christ in chapter 6. Eventually John underlines the unique finality of Christ's sacrifice by recording his great cry, "It is finished" (John 19:30).

What, then, did the cross mean for Jesus himself? Because the baptismal voice referred to the Isaianic servant, his death appears to have been in Jesus' mind throughout his ministry. Calvary was no afterthought but fulfilled the divine purpose. In the wilderness, he was tempted to abuse his powers as the Son of God to gain the universal crown without going the Servant's way of the cross, but he decisively rejected the satanic voice. Early in his ministry, he showed he knew that eventually he would be violently removed from his disciples (Mark 2:18–20). If they could expect persecution, as Mark 4:17 implies, how much more would this be true for him! After Peter's confession, his teaching became more explicit and emphatic.

He knew his death was essential (Mark 8:31; John 12:27), and in his mind it was something peculiarly dreadful, a deeply distressing baptism he must undergo (Luke 12:49–50), a bitter cup he must drink (Mark 10:38). Gethsemane reveals how terrible the contents of that cup were as Jesus anticipated them. In no sense, however, was this destiny forced upon him, because, although dreading it, he willingly accepted it as his Father's will. After the agony in the garden, he gave himself up to his enemies for his subsequent humiliation, scourging, impalement and death. He said of his life, "No one takes it from me, but I lay it down of my own accord. I have authority to lay it down and authority to take it up again. This command I received from my Father" (John 10:17–18). While he saw the participants in the crucifixion story to be fully responsible for their actions (John 19:11), there was, at the same time, a divine purpose in it (Mark 14:21).

Jesus said he was going to give his flesh for the life of the world (John 6:51) and that he would die for his sheep, his disciples (John 10:11–18; Luke 22:19–20). In fact, his life would be given up in their place, for "a ransom for many" (Mark 10:45) is literally "a ransom instead of many". This seems reminiscent of Isaiah 53, with its emphasis on sacrifice and penal substitution. What he bore in the place of sinners was the penalty for their sins. His blood established a covenant, a new relationship with God, as he affirmed at the Last Supper (Matt. 26:28), fulfilling God's great promise through Jeremiah (Jer. 31:31–34).

In his discourse on the bread of life in John 6, Jesus made it utterly clear, with vivid language that shocked many hearers, not only that he must die but also that he and his death would be valueless to others unless appropriated by them. Salvation from sin required his death, but individuals needed to exercise faith. Earlier he had said that when he was lifted up like the serpent in the wilderness, people must put their trust in him (John 3:14–16). Eating and drinking (John 6) and looking (implied in John 3:14–16 and made explicit by the Baptist in John 1:29) all present faith pictorially.

The cross is absent from the parables of Jesus except that of the vineyard tenants (Mark 12:1–12), where the emphasis, shortly before the crucifixion, is on the killing as a heinous act of rebellion against God. This absence should not surprise us. Most of the teaching about his death in the Gospels is given to the disciples, whereas the parables were delivered to a wider audience. Humanly speaking, with enemies present in the crowd, such a reference by Jesus could have become a self-fulfilling prophecy, and everything had to be in accordance with God's timetable, as we see from the many references to "the hour" or "his hour" in the Gospels, especially John's gospel (e.g., John 7:30; 13:1). Not only so, but any deeper teaching about the cross and its meaning would have been lost on the listeners. There were many other things the crowds needed to hear, and Jesus said them in the parables.

The Gospels record seven sayings of Jesus from his cross. Three quote the Old Testament, each from psalms in which the author faces enmity. This was, of course, the human cause of the cross so that it revealed human sin as well as divine grace. In quoting these Scriptures, Jesus identified himself with those who similarly endure suffering at the hands of others because of their faithfulness to God.

Two sayings require special mention. The awful Cry of Dereliction is recorded in two gospels (Matt. 27:46; Mark 15:34). Both writers leave it unexplained, driving the reader to seek clues to its meaning earlier in the gospel, perhaps in the Ransom and Last Supper sayings. Both writers and Luke mention the accompanying darkness, and Matthew in particular had recorded references by Jesus to outer darkness as the destiny of those God rejects (Matt. 8:12; 22:13; 25:30). Here, then, was the dreadful cost of the substitutionary ransoming.

John also records a profound saying from Jesus' lips, which in Greek is just one word, *tetelestai*, "It is finished" (John 19:30). What, then, was finished? His earthly life, his experience of suffering, his fulfilment of Scripture? Perhaps all of these, but most of all it was his work of atonement, a thought taken up also in the Epistle to the Hebrews and reflected too when the Synoptic Gospels record the rending of the temple curtain, the great veil that barred the entrance to the Holy of Holies. The old system of sacrifice had come to an end, so the symbolic barrier between God and sinful human beings was destroyed by God himself. The cross was not simply the evil deed of his enemies but something Jesus accomplished, a finished work of atonement.

The Preaching in the Acts of the Apostles

Sermons have an important place in Acts. The preachers are chiefly Peter and Paul, although there is also an address by Stephen. We will look later at the epistles of Peter and Paul but will consider their sermons now, as Luke presumably recorded them as typical of gospel preaching in the first period of the church's life.

The sermons make frequent references to the death and resurrection of Jesus. That assertions of the resurrection should be particularly frequent and emphatic is understandable when so many of them were delivered in Jerusalem, the very place where Jesus was crucified. The hearers needed to know that God had put them in the wrong by reversing what they and their compatriots had done in rejecting and killing Jesus. God had given Jesus a decisive vindication.

Is there, then, no doctrine of the atonement here? At first it seems not, but in fact there is. If Luke planned his gospel and Acts as two parts of one great story (note "began" in Acts 1:1), and we view them as an interpretative unit, we note that Jesus is the suffering and glorified Servant of God (Acts 3:13, 26; 4:27; cf. Luke 22:37; Isa. 53:12). The references to the cross as a tree in two sermons by Peter and one by Paul (Acts 5:30; 10:39; 13:29) would recall to any Jew (and also to Gentile proselytes and "God-fearers" through synagogue attendance) the words of Deuteronomy 21:23: "Anyone who is hung on a tree is under God's curse." The preachers would never have used the word "tree" unless for them it was loaded with significance.

What, then, was that significance? Did it mean that those who called for the crucifixion (the Jewish leaders) and those who actually impaled Jesus on the tree (the Romans) did so to show they regarded him as under God's curse (the Jews) or to put him to shame (the Romans)? If so, this word in the sermons would intensify the contrast between their treatment of Jesus and God's vindication of him.

This level of interpretation is by no means impossible, but it seems unlikely that this is all that these allusions mean. Both Peter and Paul mention the cross as a tree (1 Peter 2:24; Gal. 3:13–14), in each case interpreting it in terms of sin-bearing. This means they saw a divine purpose of atonement, indeed of penal substitution, in it. If what we have in Acts are sermon summaries, as their brevity suggests, the full versions may have included more theological explanation along these lines. Luke, a companion of Paul, was probably well aware of what meaning he attached to the tree.

Paul's theology of the cross, as we shall see, is associated with his teaching on justification. It is interesting therefore that in Paul's sermon at Pisidian Antioch, he asserts not only that "through Jesus the forgiveness of sins is proclaimed to you" but also that "through him everyone who believes is justified from everything you could not be justified from by the law of Moses" (Acts 13:38–39). Certainly the emphasis in the context is on the resurrection, but the verse which most reminds us of what Paul says here is Romans 4:25, where he links the cross and the resurrection most intimately – "He was delivered over to death for our sins and was raised to life for our justification."

The Teaching of Paul

Nobody has seriously doubted the centrality of the cross for Paul. He makes a number of references to the gospel he preached. First Corinthians 15:3–4 is particularly important, as he says, "For what I received I passed on to you *as of first importance*: that Christ died for our sins according to the Scriptures, that he was buried, that he was raised on the third day according to the Scriptures" (emphasis mine).

His doctrine of the atonement was many-sided.

Christ died "according to the Scriptures". At Thessalonica, Paul argued from the Scriptures that the Christ must suffer and rise from the dead, giving this as evidence of the messiahship of Jesus (Acts 17:2–3). In Ephesians 5:2 he says that Christ "loved us and gave himself up for us as a fragrant offering and sacrifice to God", and in 1 Corinthians 5:7–8 he wrote of Christ, as the Passover lamb, being sacrificed for us. This kind of language presupposes knowledge of the Old Testament background, well known not only to Hebrew Christians but to the Gentile proselytes and God-fearers.

Paul saw Christ's death to be propitiatory, substitutionary and justifying. In other words, he taught that because Christ took the punishment for our sins in our place, by God's initiating love and grace, we are given a right relationship with God. Faith, of course, is indispensable for securing this relationship in practical terms.

Whatever the main purpose of the Epistle to the Romans, it contains the nearest we have in Paul's writings to a systematic exposition of the gospel. Romans 3:25 occurs at a most important point in his argument. Here, avoiding any thought of humanly initiated appeasement, he writes that God set forth Christ as a *hilasterion* ("propitiation", ESV). Some translators and commentators view this word here as meaning "expiation" or "satisfaction for sin", which would not be altogether inappropriate. Leon Morris has argued persuasively, however, that this is too weak and that it should be rendered "propitiation", the turning aside of God's wrath.[1] He argues both from the word's Old Testament background through the Septuagint and also from its context here. Romans 1:18 – 3:20 is not simply about human sin but about the wrath and consequent judgment of God on that sin. Paul goes on to show that this propitiation is the basis of our justification by God.

Passages like Galatians 3:10 – 14 and 2 Corinthians 5:21 also teach the same truth and they do so in vivid, almost shocking language. That Christ became a curse for us or that God made him to be sin for us are expressions that remind us, both in their vividness and in their theology, of the great Cry of Dereliction. Vincent Taylor, who wrote three major studies of the atonement in the New Testament,[2] and who did not favour a theology of penal substitution, famously admitted that, although he felt it possible, it was not easy to interpret these verses in any other way than substitution.[3]

In 2 Corinthians 5:18 – 21, Paul also writes about our reconciliation with God through Christ. Sin has broken the relationship between God and ourselves, and God in his grace takes the initiative in reconciliation, to which we are to respond when it is made known to us through his ambassadors. We should note that even here, where the emphasis might seem to be on the subjective influence of God's offer of peace, Paul makes an important link with penal substitution in verse 21. Reconciliation is offered freely but at great cost to the one offering it. In Ephesians 2:11 – 18, he explores further implications of this, for as God has reconciled both Jew and Gentile to himself through Christ, he has also brought them together, destroying their hostility. The cross shows that God in Christ bears the cost not only of fellowship with him but also of fellowship with each other.

Paul also saw the cross as redemptive, and redemption has a rich Old Testament background. In Israel's God-given legal system, it meant the liberation of somebody who through poverty had sold himself and his services to another. It was secured by a near-kinsman by paying an appropriate price

(Lev. 25:47–53). Sometimes the word might seem a mere synonym of deliverance, as when God is said to have redeemed his people from Egypt or Babylon. The idea of a price paid is still present, however, as several passages refer to the expenditure of much power (e.g., Exod. 6:6; Deut. 7:8) or the giving of other nations as the people's ransom price (Isa. 43:3–4). If this seems far-fetched, we should remember that this is anthropomorphic language. In Paul's writings, redemption is a rich synonym for forgiveness (Col. 1:14). The price paid was Christ's blood (Eph. 1:7; Rom. 3:24–25) or his bearing of the curse the law pronounces against sinners (Gal. 3:13).

That Christ died for us and rose again has implications not only for our past in terms of forgiveness and justification but also for our future lifestyle. In Romans 5:12–21, Paul compares and contrasts Christ with Adam. These are the two representative men, for what they did deeply affected all those they represented – Adam by one trespass, and Christ by one act of righteousness (Rom. 5:18), his death for our sins (Rom. 5:6–11).

This passage is the theological basis of Romans 6, where Paul explores the significance of our union with Christ, believing that Christ represented us not in purely external fashion but as people united to him. Paul shows that representation implies participation. When Christ died, we died with him, and when he was raised, his emergence from the tomb to newness of life was ours too. This opens up both possibilities and responsibilities, for, in a decisive change of attitude, we should consider ourselves dead to sin and yield ourselves to him for his service. Because Christ's resurrection was followed by his ascension, Paul's consummate theological logic leads him to say that in him we too are exalted (Eph. 1:3), so that all heaven's resources become available to us for our life with him on earth.

Must we make a theological choice between penal substitution and participatory representation as Paul's atonement theology – or even as our own? No, for in Romans the first is the basis of the second. Neither do we have to choose between penal substitution and a *Christus Victor* theology, for in Colossians 2:13–14, the cancelling of our debt at the cross means also the defeat of the evil powers imprisoning us. No wonder Paul says that the message of the cross is the power of God and, because it was beyond human devising, the wisdom of God that cuts across all human wisdom (1 Cor. 1:18–31)! Who would ever have thought there could be such profound significance in a man hanging from a Roman gibbet?

All God's acts show something of his nature and character, and this is profoundly true of Christ's cross. Here, in the wonder of God's grace and because Christ died for our sins, he revealed his righteous character and made sinners right with him. No wonder Paul sees this as a great disclosure of the love of God in Christ (Eph. 5:2, 25). That he refers to this twice in one chapter clearly shows how much it meant to him. I have concentrated on passages in Paul's letters where reference to Christ's death is explicit, but the atoning work may often have been in his mind when he used phrases like "through Christ" or "through him". His sense of debt to Christ for dying for him was immense, and he gives this very personal expression in Galatians 2:20, where he writes of "the Son of God, who loved me and gave himself for me".

The Epistle to the Hebrews

We will make no assumptions about the author of Hebrews but will follow the majority view that the letter's recipients were a group of Jewish Christians belonging possibly to a church in Rome. Apparently discouraged by persecution, they were tempted to return to Judaism. The writer encourages them with the superiority of the revelation in Christ in so many ways, but he majors especially on Christ's high priesthood and the efficacy of his sacrifice for sins.

The author's main exposition of this theme begins at 4:14, but he anticipates this in 1:3 in saying that God's Son "provided purification for sins" and "sat down at the right hand of the Majesty in heaven". He also anticipates it in 2:17, where he says the Son became like his brothers in every way "in order that he might become a merciful and faithful high priest in service to God, and that he might make atonement [*hilaskesthai*] for the sins of the people". In this context, he writes too of Christ's tasting death for everyone and of the conquest of the devil through Christ's death (2:9, 14–15; cf. Col. 2:15).

The author believed the ultimate high priesthood required somebody fitted for it in character, experience and office. Christ was eminently fit because of his sympathy, his perfect endurance of temptation, his suffering (4:14–5:9; cf. 2:18) and because his priesthood, although not Aaronic, was "after the order of Melchizedek", an even higher order, as he shows by expounding Genesis 14 and Psalm 110 (7:1–28). He emphasises Christ's sinlessness and asserts that "he sacrificed for their sins once for all when he offered himself" (7:27), employing surely the most sublime reflective pronoun in all literature.

In 9:1–10:18, the author has chiefly in mind the comparisons and contrasts between Christ's work and that of the high priest on the Day of

Atonement. The old sacrifices gave ceremonial purity, making worship possible at the earthly tabernacle, but as animal sacrifices they could not satisfy the conscience (9:14; 10:2–4). By contrast, Christ's sacrifice, the obedient surrender of his life in death (10:5–10), was final (9:12, 26, 28; 10:10; cf. 7:27). He was the antitype also of the scapegoat, for he took away the sins of many (9:28). His sacrifice decisively did away with sin, and in virtue of it he entered not the earthly tabernacle but heaven itself (9:23–24). His sacrificial work complete, he sat down at the right hand of God (10:11–12; cf. 1:3; 12:2).

What did this imply for the earthly place of worship, the temple which had replaced the tabernacle? The old sacrificial system had now lost its validity. In fact, Jesus died even for the sins committed under the old covenant (9:15). So the writer says, in effect, "Don't go back, for there's no longer anything to go back to" (10:26; cf. 10:18). Moreover, such a return implied rejection of Christ's sacrifice, so it would be immensely serious and would receive severe judgment (10:26–31). Instead, as Christ suffered outside the city gate, we should be prepared for exclusion and disgrace too, while our sacrifices are no longer of animals but instead are praise to God and practical fellowship with others (13:11–16).

The First Epistle of Peter

While some have expressed doubts concerning the authorship of this circular letter, there are no real problems if we take seriously Peter's comment that he was helped in the task by Silas (5:12). Our understanding of its treatment of this theme is undoubtedly enriched if Peter is its author. For instance, in view of Peter's confession of Jesus as the Christ and his almost immediate rejection of his sufferings (Mark 8:27–32), it is most significant not only that he now frequently refers to those sufferings but also that, in doing so, he always calls Jesus "Christ" (1:11; 2:21; 3:18; 4:1, 13; 5:1). The union of messiahship and suffering, once so abhorrent, is now dear to his heart.

Peter is much aware of the Old Testament background to the cross, showing what he had gained from Jesus' teaching, particularly on the road to Jerusalem and after the resurrection. On the Jerusalem road, Jesus had predicted both his death and his resurrection, and Peter often links the two (1:11, 18–21; 3:18, 21–22; cf. 4:1). He had also observed the quality of his life, so that "the precious blood of Christ, a lamb without blemish or defect" (1:19) reflects not only Old Testament sacrificial teaching, which emphasised the quality of the offerings, but also the beautiful life Peter had been privileged to watch. He calls himself "a witness of Christ's sufferings" (5:1). Thus, observed fact and Old Testament teaching coalesced in his mind. What a powerful combination!

This union of Scripture and personal experience is found too in 2:21–25, where language quoting or reminiscent of Isaiah 53:4, 7, 9 and 11 is used. In 2:24, he quotes Isaiah 53:11, "He himself bore our sins in his body on the tree", which implies penal substitution. He then says, "So that we might die to sins and live for righteousness", which may well arise from a participationist theology like that in Romans 6. In fact, his main concern is to commend the example of Christ's attitude in his sufferings to those Peter was preparing to face, possibly suffering for doing good. We should not overlook this or play it down. Verse 24, however, shows that Peter is not implying that salvation is secured by following Christ's example rather than depending on his atoning work. Rather, we follow his example because of our concern to die to sins and live for righteousness as our grateful response to what Christ has done for us.

We note also that Peter refers to the sprinkling of Christ's blood (1:2). This could be a further Servant Song allusion (Isa. 52:15), or it could relate to the blood of the covenant (Exod. 24:6–8). Both this and the reference to the lamb may echo Peter's memories of Jesus' ministry (cf. John 1:29; Luke 22:20). He asserts too that this death was once for all and that it was the means of bringing us to God, perhaps alluding to the high priest's work on the Day of Atonement (cf. Heb. 9:28). At one point, he roots the atonement in eternity, for God's redemptive purpose was due to his choice of Christ as the Lamb before creation itself (1:18–20; cf. Acts 2:23).

The First Epistle of John

A distinctive feature of 1 John is the way John relates the atonement to God's character. First John 1:7 and 2:2 have as their background the great statement of 1:5: "This is the message we have heard from him and declare to you: God is light; in him there is no darkness at all." This reference to God's holy character is reflected in "the Holy One" in 2:20. The repeated statement "God is love" (4:8, 16) occurs in a passage where God's loving purpose in the coming of Christ is said to be an atoning one (4:9–12).

How then were God's holiness and love revealed simultaneously in one great divine act? This is expressed by *hilasmos*, which occurs in both contexts (2:2; 4:10). It is rendered "atoning sacrifice" in the NIV but is from the same word group as *hilasterion* in Romans 3:25 and, like it, means "propitiation". This is perhaps underlined when in 2:1 Jesus Christ is described as "one who speaks to the Father in our defense". This epistle might almost have been written to deal with modern misunderstandings of propitiation, for in 4:10 John says it was God in his love who sent his Son to be a *hilasmos*. This is not, therefore, the Son trying to change the mind of an unwilling Father, but it does mean we cannot avoid the thought of God's judgment by focusing on his love, for at the heart of that love's supreme manifestation it deals with the claims of his holiness.

The blood of Christ was important to John, for the phrase "water and blood" (5:6–8) probably refers to Christ's baptism, which inaugurated his ministry, and his death, which completed it, fulfilling its purpose. The words "he did not come by water only, but by water and blood" emphasise the significance of the blood, which was the means of cleansing from sin (1:7), a clear reference to sacrificial blood.

John gives a series of reasons for the Son of God's coming into the world. He came to take away our sins (3:5), to destroy the devil's work (3:8), and that we might live through him (4:9). These are summed up in the statement that he was sent to be the Saviour of the world (4:14), and, as we have already seen, this was through a lovingly provided propitiatory sacrifice.

The Apocalypse

We might not expect the Apocalypse, with its future orientation, to touch much on the finished work of Christ, but it does. John 1 contains many titles and descriptions of Jesus, and this is a feature also of Revelation 1–3. None is more important than the repeated "Lamb of God" (John 1:29, 36), and the Apocalypse uses "Lamb" of Christ twenty-six times. In the gospel, "lamb" is *amnos*, while here it is *arnion*, a diminutive. Greek diminutives had largely lost their distinctive force by then, but this could still possess enough diminutive nuance in people's minds to emphasise the contrast between the Lion and the Lamb at the latter's introduction in Revelation 5:5–6.

The Lamb features in several of the Apocalypse's paradoxes – for example in 6:16 and 7:17–but this introduction is particularly striking, for here the triumphant Lion is seen as a slain Lamb, the use of a perfect participle in the latter expression suggesting the abiding efficacy of his death. Although slain, he is standing, for his death was followed by his resurrection (cf. 1:18). His death is redemptive (5:9; cf. 1:5; 14:4), and because of it, the whole creation ascribes to him not only the power and strength of the lion but also so many distinctively divine qualities, making his worship appropriate (5:9–14). Because of it, too, he can open the scroll of destiny (5:1–9), and it is through his blood that the martyrs triumph over Satan (12:10–11).

In a book which features God's wrath and judgment and even "the wrath of the Lamb" (6:16), we should note that its first mention of the atonement sees it as expressing his love, and the Lamb's sacrifice is said to be "from the creation of the world" (13:8). His death, although a sinful act of human beings (11:8), was nevertheless God's eternal saving intention.

Summary

The crucifixion was both a heinous act of human sin perpetrated at Jerusalem and a most loving, gracious, holy and wise act of God conceived in eternity. Indispensable to the salvation of sinners, it was freely embraced by Jesus as God's will. It fulfilled the Old Testament; themes and language from passages like Exodus 12, Leviticus 16, the psalms of innocent suffering, and Isaiah 53 are used to interpret it. Sacrificial and sin-bearing language occurs frequently, and the cross is presented as a place of penal substitutionary atonement so final, so efficacious, that it did away with the Old Testament sacrificial system.

Through the cross, a new covenant was instituted involving forgiveness and a right status with God. Sinners are reconciled both to God and each other. Because Christ has dealt with sin, thus liberating sinners, the cross dealt Satan and his hosts a decisive blow. Christ's death was followed by his resurrection, which was God's vindication of him, and his representative death and resurrection open the way to godly living for Christians through their union with him. The atoning value of his death needs to be appropriated by faith in him. No wonder Christ is not only Lord of history and human destiny but the exalted focus of Christian worship!

Notes

1. Leon Morris, *The Atonement: Its Meaning and Significance* (Leicester: IVP, 1983), 163–70.
2. Vincent Taylor, *Jesus and His Sacrifice* (London: Macmillan, 1937); *The Atonement in New Testament Teaching* (London: Epworth, 1940); and *Forgiveness and Reconciliation*, 2nd ed. (London: Macmillan, 1946).
3. Taylor, *Atonement in New Testament Teaching*, 288–89. He also included Mark 10:45; Rom. 6:10–11; 2 Cor. 5:14; and 1 Tim. 2:5–6.

chapter six

why did christ die?

an exegesis of isaiah 52:13 - 53:12

sue groom

Introduction

The interpretation of Isaiah 53,[1] the fourth Servant Song, the song of the Suffering Servant, or rather the song of the Triumphant Servant, is hotly debated, particularly with respect to the identity of the servant. This is just one of the issues discussed by scholars over the centuries.

Other key issues include:

- Who are the speakers in the song? Who are the "he", "we", "I" and "they"?
- Was the servant an individual, or corporate Israel?
- How does this passage relate to the other Servant Songs and its own context?
- Did the servant die, or does the language use metaphors for extreme suffering?
- Is the language that of substitutionary or vicarious atonement?

Other questions often asked are:

- Was God the agent of the servant's suffering?
- Did the servant willingly embrace his suffering?

There are many problems with the Hebrew text of this passage: forty-six words do not occur elsewhere in Second Isaiah,[2] and it contains several *hapax legomena*. Some of our questions are not even addressed by the author.

Context

The historical context of this passage is usually taken to be the sixth century BCE. Israel is in exile; it is a time of profound searching. Hans-Jügen Hermisson helpfully summarizes Second Isaiah's message as follows: "A highway is built on which Yahweh leads his liberated people through the desert. This highway naturally leads from Babylon to Jerusalem. Such great signs and wonders are performed on this highway, as well as at its end, that the whole world is overcome and is being saved, streaming in and confessing the one and only God, the only saviour of Israel and the world."[3]

Exile itself was seen as a punishment for sins, so forgiveness of sins was another way of saying "end of exile". Lamentations 4:22 reads, "The punishment of your iniquity, O daughter Zion, is accomplished, he will keep you in exile no longer" (NRSV). The arm of the Lord, which will redeem Israel from exile and put evil to flight, is revealed, according to Isaiah 53, through the work of the servant of the Lord. N. T. Wright suggests that Second Isaiah as a whole was thematic for Jesus' ministry and kingdom announcement, which is to be understood as the historical and concrete acting out of the return of the Lord to Zion to defeat evil and to rescue his people from exile; that is, to forgive their sins at last.[4]

Overview of the Passage

There are two emphatic contrasts in Isaiah 53 – between the servant's exaltation and humiliation, and between what the people mistakenly thought about the servant and what was really the case. The change in perspective between then and now is not expressed by means of Hebrew tenses. The text does not determine whether various elements take place in the past, present or future; it only indicates the relational changes.

The passage begins and ends with divine speech (Isa. 52:13 – 15; 53:11b – 12). A series of correspondences between the prologue and epilogue show that they function as matching sections framing the body. The word for "my servant" appears only in these two sections (Isa. 52:13; 53:11), as does the word for "many" (Isa. 52:14 – 15; 53:11 – 12). They are written in the first person singular, from the perspective of "I".

The body of the passage (Isa. 53:1 – 9) speaks of the servant's humiliation and suffering as witnessed by the people. Verses 1 – 6 are written in the first person plural, from the perspective of "we". In verses 1 – 3, "we" considered the servant to be insignificant; in verses 4–6, "we" recognize that his sufferings were for us. There is no reason given for this change in perspective. In verses 4–5a, there is a strong contrast between what "we" believed was the source of the servant's suffering (God) and the actual source ("our sins"). The second half of verse 5 appears to be the heart of the whole poem. "The chastisement that made us whole was upon him and by his wounds he has healed us" (my trans.). It occupies the central place in the narrative section, and a number of words and motifs are repeated both before and after it. In verses 7–9, an onlooker describes how "he" suffers and dies, although "he" had done nothing wrong. In verses 10–11a, the same speaker recognizes that "his" sufferings were in accordance with the will of the Lord.

The idea that one who was despised and rejected should come to be exalted and victorious is a regular theme in earlier chapters of Second Isaiah (Isa. 41:14–15; 40:27–31). The belief that what happens in Israel affects the kings and many other nations is also found in Isaiah 49:1, 6 and 2:2–4.

The Identity of the Speakers

"I", the Lord, presents "him" for admiration as his servant and announces "his" supremacy (52:13). "I" also reports on the attitude of "them" to "him" (52:15). "They" mistakenly thought that "I" struck him (53:4), but "I" did lay suffering on "him" (53:6, 10), and "I" will give "him" a share of the spoils (53:12). The central figure of the passage is plainly "he". Most of the action is done to or by "him". "He" is the subject of twenty-one active verbs and eighteen passive verbs. "He" actually "does" very little. "He" is intensely present, although "he" is never named. "He" is silent.

"We" have heard the report (53:1) and once regarded "him" "stricken by God" (53:4). The attitude of "we" to "him" changes from one of hostility and scorn to appreciation. "Our" earlier view (vv. 2–3, 4b, 6b) was based on the logic of action-consequence: suffering is the result of sin. "Our" present view (vv. 4–6) is that the servant's suffering is the result of our actions. "We" could be the nations referred to in Isaiah 52:15. "We" could be the nation of Israel. "We" could be the collective voice of the prophets – a subset of the nation of Israel. If the servant is Israel, then "we" could be the nations looking on.

Brevard Childs states that the confessing "we" of the Old Testament is always Israel and not the nations.[5] The metaphor of "seeing" (52:15b; 53:1b) brackets that of "hearing" (52:15b; 53:1a), so the structure confirms continuity between "they" in Isaiah 12:15b and the confessing voice of "we" in

53:1–2. The identity of "we" and "they" virtually merges in the passage, as "he" is shown to have the same relationship to both. To begin, "he" is merely an object to "they", but by Isaiah 53:11–12, "they" are involved with "him".

Perhaps "we" could be whoever has been healed and is bewildered as well as grateful. As David Clines observes, "The poem is free to do its work by its very lack of specificity, its openness to a multiplicity of readings … refuses to let it be tied down to one spot on the globe, or frozen at one point in history: it opens up the possibility that the poem can become true in a variety of circumstances."[6]

The Identity of the Servant

The first suggestion regarding the identity of the servant[7] is that the servant is an individual with a divine commission to serve God's people. The fifteen historic individuals proposed basically fall into two categories: prophets and kings. Most are no longer advocated. Second Kings 17:23, in mentioning "his servants the prophets", portrays prophets as rejected figures who have spoken the truth from God. The experience of Jeremiah gave rise to the idea of the true prophet being a martyr figure.

Moses was a righteous individual who stood over against the people yet nevertheless suffered with them and on their account. He was assigned the role of the greatest and most efficacious intercessor who intervened with God on Israel's behalf. He rescued the nation from certain judgment and oblivion by putting his own life at risk in order that Israel might be saved. Nevertheless, he fell victim to the nation's sin in that he too failed to maintain holiness among the people. The death of Moses was an action which became necessary because of Israel's sins in the wilderness. R. E. Clements argues that the servant, like Moses, suffers both for and with the community he represents.[8]

Another suggestion, which stresses the political elements in the person and work of the servant, is that he is an anonymous contemporary of Second Isaiah. Second Isaiah himself has also been advocated, although both of these suggestions limit the horizon of the songs.

The appellation "my servant" appears eleven times in Isaiah prior to 52:13. All but one of those uses were explicitly applied to Israel or Jacob; that is, the people of God, who have been defeated and humiliated but have been chosen and will be redeemed by God (cf. Isa. 41:8–9; 42:19; 43:10; 44:1–2, 21; 45:4; 49:3, 6). A number of scholars have proposed that the servant is Israel appointed as God's agent in relation to other nations. In the fourth Servant Song, however, the personification of Israel is carried to the point where it is hard to escape the sense that he should be thought of as an individual who stood out as a representative and leader of the community.

H. H. Rowley argues that it is reasonable to ask whether there is not some development in the mission of the servant and whether what began as personification did not become a person. The first song has the closest connections with passages outside the songs: the author's thought is predominantly of a collective servant, Israel, destined to carry the light of true religion to the entire world in a mission of gentle persistence and unflagging zeal. In the second song, the prophet realizes that only a purified Israel can fulfil its mission; therefore, there is a mission to Israel as well as through Israel. The third song deals with the suffering and shame the servant will experience in execution of the mission. By this time, the prophet realizes that the mission will not be easy, but it is not clear whether he is speaking of a collective servant, or an individual representative and leader in whose person the mission of Israel can be both symbolized and supremely expressed. In the fourth song, the servant is unmistakably an individual, and the prophet perceives that suffering will be not merely incidental to the mission but its organ. He contemplates an individual who will supremely fulfil the mission of Israel through the organ of his own innocent suffering and who will pass through shame and death to exaltation and triumph.[9]

Did the Servant Die?

The servant is described as a person of stunted growth (Isa. 53:2), physically unattractive (53:2), and ostracized by people (53:3). The word used in verses 3–4 for "pain" (מַכְאֹב) is from the language of lamentation (cf. Ps. 38: 18; 69: 27; Job 33:19). As with here, in the Psalms it is always accompanied by being despised and rejected (נִבְזֶה וַחֲדַל; Ps. 22:7; 119:22; cf. Jer. 49:15). This is not necessarily a literal description but rather a stereotypical way of speaking about suffering generally. This leads to the argument that the servant did not actually die. But from the narrator's point of view, the servant's death is a thing of the past: "he poured out his life unto death" (Isa. 53:12); "he was cut off from the land of the living" (53:8). Hence, the majority of commentators believe that he died. H. M. Orlinsky is one of those who remain unconvinced: he considers verses 7–9 to be hyperbole.[10]

Isaiah 53 contains the essential elements to classify as an individual psalm of thanksgiving: a narrative of the sufferer's experiences and an act of recognition of God's intervention to rescue him. However, there is one great difference: the standard speaker is the former sufferer, who comes to offer thanks to God. Here it is a group of onlookers who speaks.

Does Isaiah 53 Use the Language of Atonement?

The verb יָזֶּה ("sprinkle") which occurs in Isaiah 52:15 is the language of the sacrificial cult. Elsewhere (e.g., Lev. 14:7; Num. 8:7) it takes an object which is a liquid and an indirect object prefixed by the preposition עַל. In Isaiah 52:15, that would imply that the servant is sprinkling the nations upon something else. Some suggest the nations are sprinkling the servant for fear of contamination. It does not easily make sense in the current context, hence a second root, נזה, is often suggested, from an Arabic word meaning "to leap, to spring up", which gives the translation "to startle" in the NRSV. This is confirmed by the LXX rendering θαυμάσονται, "will wonder".

The word אָשָׁם, which occurs in Isaiah 53:10, is a sacrificial term usually translated "guilt offering" (cf. Lev. 5:1–19), but it can mean an "obligation arising from guilt" or a means of "wiping out guilt" (Num. 5:8; 1 Sam. 6:3–8) or just "guilt" (Jer. 51:5; Ps. 68:22). In contrast to the context here, the guilt offering was the one sacrifice for which the individual had to realize their own guilt and make their own offering.

The phrase סבל עון used in Isaiah 53:11 refers to the consequences of sin in Lamentations 5:7: "Our fathers sinned and are no more; and we must bear their guilt" (JPS). The more common phrase נשא עון does not occur in Isaiah 53. However, the situation in Ezekiel 4:4–6 appears to be similar to that of Isaiah 53:11–12. As part of a sign of prophecy, Ezekiel was to "bear [נשא] the guilt [עון] of the house of Israel". But his symbolic portrayal of a year of Israel's punishment indicates only how long the exiles will suffer, and there is no stress on Ezekiel's righteousness or his suffering innocently as an atonement for the sins of others.

In the priestly tradition, Moses linked "bearing the guilt of others" to "making atonement" when he reminded Aaron that the Lord "gave it to you for bearing the guilt [לָשֵׂאת אֶת־עֲוֹן] of the assembly in order to make atonement for them [עֲלֵיהֶם לְכַפֵּר] before the Lord" (Lev. 10:17). However, the priest was never construed as innocent or suffering for others in his task. He too had to make atonement for his own guilt and was himself in danger of punishment if he did not live according to the commandments of the Lord.

The scapegoat has often been cited in connection with Isaiah 53. The ceremony surrounding the scapegoat was a unique part of the annual Day of Atonement (Lev. 16:1–25). After Aaron, the high priest, had made atonement for himself, he made atonement for Israel by laying his hands on the head of the scapegoat and confessing all the guilt (עָוֹן) of Israel and their transgressions (פֶּשַׁע), indeed all their sins (חַטָּא), and then sending the goat off into the wilderness (Lev. 16:21). Leviticus 16:22 explains that "the goat will bear [נָשָׂא] on itself [עָלָיו] all their guilt [עָוֹן] into a solitary land." Like the servant, the scapegoat was a living creature and bore a guilt not its own. It was also sent out into the wilderness, a place of suffering. However, the servant suffers without the people's knowing it at the time, let alone placing their hands upon him. He does not "get rid" of their sin; he endures it, and he bears it. The idea of God's accepting a human sacrifice for sin is entirely foreign to the Old Testament tradition.

Moses offered to be blotted out of the book of life to atone for the sins of Israel after the incident with the golden calf (Exod. 32:30–35). The Lord's answer was clear: the one who sinned will die, not you. Even the transfer of guilt between father and son is not possible, according to Ezekiel 18:20.

Isaiah 53 appears to use the language of "bearing guilt" in a unique way.[11] It should be noted that the one who has borne (נָשָׂא) the sins of others (Isa. 53:12) will be the one who is lifted up (נָשָׂא) by the Lord (Isa. 52:13).

The fourth Servant Song is a cleverly crafted piece of poetry with much repetition. The verb פָּגַע is used in verse 6 with the preposition בְּ-, giving "the Lord laid on him the iniquity of us all." It also appears in verse 12 with the preposition לְ-, giving "and for the transgressors he [the servant] intercedes." Hermann Spieckermann argues that by using this one verb differently both of the Lord and of the servant, an agreement of wills is made evident.[12] He sees the main idea behind vicarious suffering to be the close community of will between the Lord and his servant, with the intention of wiping out the guilt for many.

Paul Hanson reads Isaiah 53:11–12 as follows: "What is being described is not a scapegoat loaded with the iniquity of the people and then slaughtered capriciously as a substitute. Rather we encounter one who, having identified his human will with divine redemptive purpose, enters into solidarity with a people at their nadir point, in their guilt-ridden disease, and acts in partnership with God to break the bondage that is destroying them. The result is that they are shocked to their senses, accept the divine gift of healing, and thus are restored to the righteousness that enables them to carry on their vocation as God's people."[13]

The human limitations of the servant mean that the text of Isaiah 53 could never mean the same thing when applied to him as it means when it is applied to Christ. As Daniel Bailey points out, what is wrong with servant theology is that it is not incarnational Christology. What sinners need is to die and rise with Christ; they cannot die and rise with the servant, not as a historical figure and not in the terms in which the text describes the relationship between the one and the many.[14]

According to *Inkludierende Stellvertretung*, because of Christ's pre-existence and divine status, he can enter our human place in a way that does not displace but incorporates us. Christ did not die in place of humanity; he died while he was in the place of humanity. Christ has not simply come alongside the sinner in order to take away something – namely, guilt and sin – he has rather become identical with the sinner in order, through the surrender of his life, to lead sinners into union with God, opening up to them fellowship with God for the first time. "Inclusive place taking" is not human but divine place taking. Isaiah 53 read in this way becomes a new text. François Kabasele Lumbala, writing from an African perspective, reminds us that "it is not adequate to apply the characteristics of the servant to Jesus in order to grasp the entire meaning of the text."[15]

Isaiah 53 in the New Testament

Out of the twelve verses of the song of the Suffering Servant, ten of them are quoted or alluded to in the New Testament. Luke has Jesus quoting Isaiah 53:12 and applying it to himself: "For I tell you, this scripture must be fulfilled in me, 'And he was counted among the lawless'; and indeed what is written about me is being fulfilled" (Luke 22:37 NRSV). Mark's Jesus is thought to be alluding to Isaiah 53:2–3 and Psalm 22:6–7 when he says, "How then is it written about the Son of Man, that he is to go through many sufferings and be treated with contempt?" (Mark 9:12 NRSV). πολλὰ παθη is the contemporary Greek equivalent of יֵחָל and so is thought to evoke Isaiah 53. There are also allusions to Isaiah 53 in Mark 9:31, 10:33 and 10:45, which says, "For the

Son of Man came ... to give his life a ransom for many" (NRSV). Nowhere else in the life and faith of Israel do we find reference to a saviour figure who gives his life in a way that benefits "the many". "The many" also feature in the words of institution at the Last Supper (Mark 14:24). Matthew comments on Jesus' miracles of healing by quoting from the LXX of Isaiah 53:4: "This was to fulfill what had been spoken through the prophet Isaiah, 'He took our infirmities and bore our diseases'" (Matt. 8:17 NRSV).

In Acts 8 we encounter the Ethopian eunuch reading from the scroll of Isaiah. Acts 8:32–33 quotes the text of Isaiah 53:7–8 from the LXX, which is a free rendering of the difficult Hebrew text. The quotation breaks off at precisely the point where the passage begins to speak of interpretation. It is quoted without reference to the meaning of Jesus' death. If the atonement is so important, why is it missed? Mikeal Parsons suggests that the eunuch was most probably excluded from the cultic community on account of his physical defect and Ethiopian origin. He was therefore attracted to the figure in Isaiah 53, and to include references to the servant's vicarious suffering would have served as an obstacle to his identification with the social location of the sufferer.[16]

Paul, in his letter to the Romans, sees the Jews' rejection of Jesus as a fulfilment of Isaiah 52:15. Basing his words on the LXX, he writes, "But not all have obeyed the good news; for Isaiah says, 'Lord, who has believed our message?'" (Rom. 10:16 NRSV). He also uses this same verse (again quoting the LXX) in Romans 15:21 to promote preaching to the Gentiles. Paul's primary use of Isaiah 53 in Romans is not christological but missiological. However, in Romans 4:25, 2 Corinthians 5:21 and 1 Corinthians 15:3, he appears to proclaim Christ's death on the cross as the fulfilment of the song.

First Peter 2:22–25 (with clear allusions to a wider passage using words from the LXX text of Isa. 53:4–6, 9, 12) provides moral exhortation for slaves to be submissive to their masters and to put up with undeserved punishment. This is because Christ himself suffered for them, leaving them an example to follow. The author then progresses to the idea that Christ's suffering has atoning value. This is an example of Isaiah 53 used in a way Christians expect. It is used creatively, not as a proof text. The servant suffers as result of the sin of others. His sufferings in turn lead to their restoration and forgiveness. However, Morna Hooker asserts that there is no need to interpret this in terms of "substitution". She writes, "What we have in Isaiah 53 is much better described as representative suffering rather than vicarious suffering: as inclusive place-taking rather than exclusive place-taking."[17]

Translation and Exegesis
Isaiah 52:13

הִנֵּה יַשְׂכִּיל עַבְדִּי יָרוּם וְנִשָּׂא וְגָבַהּ מְאֹד

> Behold, my servant shall prosper,
> he shall be exalted and carried and lifted up high.

The verb שׂכל, usually translated "to be wise", can also mean "to prosper" (cf. Deut. 29:8; 1 Kings 2:3). The Targum adds the words "my messiah" after "my servant". The language of being high and lifted up (יָרוּם וְנִשָּׂא) is used four times in Isaiah and nowhere else in the Old Testament. It refers to God (cf. Isa. 6:1; 33:10; 57:15).

Isaiah 52:14

כַּאֲשֶׁר שָׁמְמוּ עָלֶיךָ רַבִּים
כֵּן־מִשְׁחַת מֵאִישׁ מַרְאֵהוּ וְתֹאֲרוֹ מִבְּנֵי אָדָם

> Just as many were appalled at him,
> so disfigured was his appearance from that of a man,
> his form from that of humanity.

The verb שׁמם, "to be desolate" or "to be appalled", is used of the devastation of places in Isaiah 49:8, 19 and of a bereaved wife in 54:1. The pronominal suffix עָלֶיךָ, "to you", is usually amended to read as "to him", giving "many were appalled at him." Where MT has מִשְׁחַת, "disfigured" (a *hapax legomenon*), 1QIsa has an additional *yod*, giving "I have anointed."

Isaiah 52:15

כֵּן יַזֶּה גּוֹיִם רַבִּים עָלָיו יִקְפְּצוּ מְלָכִים פִּיהֶם
כִּי אֲשֶׁר לֹא־סֻפַּר לָהֶם רָאוּ וַאֲשֶׁר לֹא־שָׁמְעוּ הִתְבּוֹנָנוּ

> So he shall startle many nations,
> because of him kings shall keep their mouths shut,
> for what has not been told them they shall see
> and what they have not heard they shall consider.

The verb יַזֶּה, "sprinkle", elsewhere (e.g., Lev. 14:7; Num. 8:7) takes an object which is a liquid and an indirect object prefixed by the preposition על. Here it would imply that the servant is sprinkling the nations upon something else. Some suggest the nations are sprinkling the servant for fear of contamination. Young argues for "he will (at some time in the future) besprinkle, i.e. purify many people from their sins."[18] A second root, נזה, is often suggested from an Arabic word meaning "to leap, to spring up", hence "to startle" (NRSV). The LXX has θαυμάσονται, "will wonder".

Isaiah 53:1

מִי הֶאֱמִין לִשְׁמֻעָתֵנוּ וּזְרוֹעַ יְהוָה עַל־מִי נִגְלָתָה

> Who would have believed our report?
> And the arm of the Lord, to whom has it been revealed?

וּזְרוֹעַ יְהוָה, "the arm of the Lord", emphatically positioned here, occurs also in Isaiah 51:9 in an impassioned cry for God to act in his mighty saving power as in former times (cf. 40:10–11; 48:14; 51:5; 52:10). Isaiah 59:1–2 declares, "No, the Lord's arm is not too short to save, or his ear too dull to hear; but your iniquities have been a barrier between you and your God, your sins have made him turn his face away and refuse to hear you" (JPS). 1QIsa has אֶל־מִי, "to whom", rather than עַל־מִי, "upon whom".

Isaiah 53:2

וַיַּעַל כַּיּוֹנֵק לְפָנָיו וְכַשֹּׁרֶשׁ מֵאֶרֶץ צִיָּה
לֹא־תֹאַר לוֹ וְלֹא הָדָר וְנִרְאֵהוּ וְלֹא־מַרְאֶה וְנֶחְמְדֵהוּ

> He grew up like a tender plant before him and like a root from the
> dry earth
> > there was no form to him nor majesty, that we should look at him
> > and no appearance that we should desire him.

יוֹנֵק (the only occurrence of this form) literally means "a suckling". The noun is used of both children and plants. The parallelism here suggests plant imagery. The LXX renders this phrase "we brought a report as a child." לְפָנָיו, "before him", most probably refers back to "the Lord". Both Rachel and Joseph are described as being of יְפַת־תֹּאַר וִיפַת מַרְאֶה, "beautiful form and beautiful appearance" (Gen. 29:17; 39:6). Esther is described as having יְפַת־תֹּאַר וְטוֹבַת מַרְאֶה, "beautiful form and good appearance" (Est. 2:7).

Isaiah 53:3

נִבְזֶה וַחֲדַל אִישִׁים אִישׁ מַכְאֹבוֹת וִידוּעַ חֹלִי
וּכְמַסְתֵּר פָּנִים מִמֶּנּוּ נִבְזֶה וְלֹא חֲשַׁבְנֻהוּ

Despised and deserted by men, he was a man of pains and knowing sickness.

As one who hid his face from us, he was despised and we took no
account of him.

The verb חדל literally means "to cease, to be lacking". It is used in a similar
context in Job 19:14, which is rendered "my relatives and my close friends have
failed me" in the NRSV and "my relatives have gone; my friends have forgotten me" in the JPS. אִישִׁים is not the usual plural form; it may be used here
for assonance with the singular form. The word used here and in verse 4 for
"pain", מַכְאֹב, is the language of lamentation (cf. Ps. 38:18; 69: 27; Job 33:19).
As here, in the Psalms it is always accompanied by being despised and rejected,
וַחֲדַל נִבְזֶה (Ps. 22:7; 119:22; cf. Jer. 49:15). The noun מסתר, "hiding", occurs
only here. 1QIsa has מסתיר, probably a hiphil participle, "one who causes faces
to hide". The LXX renders "his face is turned away", the Syriac "we turned our
faces from him", and the Targum "when the presence of the Shekinah was with-
drawn from us". Moses hid his face because he was afraid to look at God (Exod.
3:6); the Lord hid his face from his rebellious people (Deut. 31:17–18; cf. Isa.
8:17; 54:8; 64:7). In the language of lamentation, the psalmists beg God not
to hide his face from them (Ps. 13:1; 27:9; 44:24; 69:17; 88:14; 102:2; 143:7;
cf. Job 13:24), yet the Lord did not hide his face from the poor (Ps. 22:24) and
his servant did not hide his face from insult and spitting (Isa. 50:6).

Isaiah 53:4

אָכֵן חֳלָיֵנוּ הוּא נָשָׂא וּמַכְאֹבֵינוּ סְבָלָם
וַאֲנַחְנוּ חֲשַׁבְנֻהוּ נָגוּעַ מֻכֵּה אֱלֹהִים וּמְעֻנֶּה

Surely, it was our sicknesses he carried and our pains he bore.
But we accounted him stricken, smitten and afflicted by God.

In this verse there is a noticeable contrast between "him" and "us" produced by the emphatic use of the pronoun הוא and first person plural suffix -ֵינוּ. The LXX removes any suggestion of divine intent here: "And we
considered him to be in distress and under a stroke of misfortune and under
oppression." The language of carrying and bearing, נשׂא and סבל, also occurs

in verses 11–12 (see detailed notes there). The verb נָגַע, "to touch" or "to strike" (also in v. 8), is used many times in the prohibitions of Leviticus 11. The noun indicates a mark or plague (cf. Leviticus 13–14) and is sometimes associated with leprosy (e.g., 2 Kings 15:5).

Isaiah 53:5

וְהוּא מְחֹלָל מִפְּשָׁעֵנוּ מְדֻכָּא מֵעֲוֹנֹתֵינוּ
מוּסַר שְׁלוֹמֵנוּ עָלָיו וּבַחֲבֻרָתוֹ נִרְפָּא־לָנוּ

> But he was pierced because of our transgressions,
> he was crushed because of our iniquities.
> The chastisement that made us whole was upon him
> and by his wounds he has healed us.

Once again emphatic pronouns are used to indicate the contrast between "him" and "us". The form מְחֹלָל, "pierced", occurs only here. The same verb is used of the Lord piercing the dragon in Isaiah 51:9 (cf. Job 26:13; Ezek. 32:26) and in the psalmist's lament, "I am poor and needy and my heart is pierced within me" (Ps. 109:22). The verb דכא (also in v. 10) indicates more than mere bruising; it suggests breaking into pieces: "the Lord crushed Rahab" (Ps. 89:10; cf. Isa. 3:15). The noun formed from this root means "dust", as in "you return man to dust" (Ps. 90:3; cf. Job 4:19). However, it is also used in the language of lament (Ps. 143:3). The preposition מִן usually means "from" but is taken as "on account of" here. מוּסַר is not a legal term but rather suggests discipline or correction as in the chastisement of a child by a parent. The noun חבורה occurs only in Isaiah 1:6, describing the back of the rebel, and in the language of lament: "my wounds stink and fester because of my folly" (Ps. 38:5).

Isaiah 53:6

כֻּלָּנוּ כַּצֹּאן תָּעִינוּ אִישׁ לְדַרְכּוֹ פָּנִינוּ
וַיהוָה הִפְגִּיעַ בּוֹ אֵת עֲוֹן כֻּלָּנוּ

> All of us like sheep have erred, each turning to his own way,
> and the Lord laid on him the iniquity of us all.

כֻּלָּנוּ, "all of us", emphatically begins and ends the poignant confession. "We" are like a flock of sheep going astray; this contrasts with the servant being like a single silent sheep or ewe in the next verse. The hiphil of the verb פָּגַע (also in v. 12) means "to cause to light upon". With the preposition -בְּ it can mean "to intervene" or "to intercede" (Isa. 59:16; Jer. 15:11; 36:25). The subject "the Lord" is emphasized. All of us went astray, and the Lord caused the servant to suffer the consequences of all of our wanderings.

Isaiah 53:7

נִגַּשׂ וְהוּא נַעֲנֶה וְלֹא יִפְתַּח־פִּיו
כַּשֶׂה לַטֶּבַח יוּבָל וּכְרָחֵל לִפְנֵי גֹזְזֶיהָ נֶאֱלָמָה
וְלֹא יִפְתַּח פִּיו

He was oppressed and he was afflicted, but he did not open his mouth.
Like a sheep brought to slaughter and like a ewe, dumb before her shearers,
he did not open his mouth.

The verb עָנָה, "to be afflicted" (also in v. 4), is often found in psalms of lamentation (e.g., Ps. 116:10; 119:67, 71, 107). The noun שֶׂה is used regularly in the cultic laws, whereas רָחֵל is not. In any case, the comparison with sheep here concerns patient acceptance, not ritual sacrifice. The language of Jeremiah 11:19 is reminiscent of the first line here, but the emphasis there is on a lack of awareness, whereas here it is on the silence of the sheep. The prophets and psalmists are not usually silent in the face of suffering (however, cf. Ps. 38:14; 39:2). However, the servant's behaviour here is consistent with Isaiah 42:1–4 and 50:4–9. Some delete the last clause as dittography, but the repetition fits the style of poetry here. The Targum reads, "He will deliver the mighty ones of the peoples as a lamb to the slaughter."[19]

Isaiah 53:8

מֵעֹצֶר וּמִמִּשְׁפָּט לֻקָּח וְאֶת־דּוֹרוֹ מִי יְשׂוֹחֵחַ
כִּי נִגְזַר מֵאֶרֶץ חַיִּים מִפֶּשַׁע עַמִּי נֶגַע לָמוֹ

From oppression and from judgment he was taken away.
And as for his generation, who will recount
that he was cut off from the land of the living,
struck down because of the transgression of his [lit. "my"] people?

Or:

> By oppressive judgment he was taken away.
> Who has considered his generation?
> For he was cut off from the land of the living,
> because of the transgression of my people he was struck down.

The first part of this verse is notoriously difficult because of the various possible interpretations of the preposition מִן. Does it mean the servant was delivered from these things? Does it mean he was taken away because of these things? Does it mean he was taken away having been deprived of these things? The NRSV has, "By a perversion of justice he was taken away." The JPS, reading a hendydias, has, "By oppressive judgment he was taken away." The LXX reads ἐν τῇ ταπεινώσει ἡ κρίσις αὐτοῦ ἤρθη, "In his humiliation his judgment was taken away." Some read the Hebrew as indicating that he was taken away without having a fair trial. The noun עֹצֶר is rendered "oppression" in its only other occurrence (Ps. 107:39); the verb indicates "to shut up, imprison". The only other occurrences of מִשְׁפָּט with the preposition מִן are Psalm 119:102, 120, where the context is departing from, or being in awe of, the Lord's judgments. מִשְׁפָּט can indicate "the place of judgment" or "justice".[20] לֻקָּח, "he was taken away", can mean to death: it is used in Genesis 5:24 and 2 Kings 2:3 for Enoch and Elijah respectively. In Proverbs 24:11, the text includes the words "to death". If we take דּוֹר to mean "generation" or "line", then the idea could be that the servant dies childless in a culture in which this meant to have lived an utterly futile life. Its exact meaning here is uncertain. It is also debatable whether אֵת is the direct object indicator or whether it means something like "as for". Both the JPS with "Who could describe his abode?" and the NRSV with "Who could have imagined his future?" take it as the direct object indicator. The verb שִׂיחַ occurs in the Psalms with the preposition -בְּ, where it is usually rendered "meditate on, recount" (Ps. 119:15, 23, 27, 48, 78, 148). Only in Psalm 143:5 does it take the same form (polel imperfect) as here. It is used with a direct object in Proverbs 6:22 to indicate the reproving function of wisdom. Another difficulty is מִפֶּשַׁע עַמִּי, "the transgression of my people". The LXX has ἀπὸ τῶν ἀνομιῶν, indicating "the rebellious". נֶגַע לָמוֹ literally means "stricken to him". The LXX reads "led to death", ἤχθη εἰς θάνατον.

Isaiah 53:9

וַיִּתֵּן אֶת־רְשָׁעִים קִבְרוֹ וְאֶת־עָשִׁיר בְּמֹתָיו
עַל לֹא־חָמָס עָשָׂה וְלֹא מִרְמָה בְּפִיו

His grave was appointed with the wicked, with the rich in his
death,
although he had done no violence and no deceit was in his
mouth.

עָשִׁיר, "a rich person", is often emended to "evildoers" (עֹשֵׂי רַע) to fit
with רְשָׁעִים, "the wicked", but the LXX has the plural "the rich" and the Targum has "those that are rich in possessions they have obtained by violence"
(cf. Mic. 6:12; Jer. 9:22). בְּמֹתָיו literally means "in his deaths"; the LXX,
Vulgate and Targum read the singular. 1QIsa reads בומתו, meaning "high
place", as in a burial mound.

Isaiah 53:10

וַיהוָה חָפֵץ דִּכְּאוֹ הֶחֱלִי אִם־תָּשִׂים אָשָׁם נַפְשׁוֹ
יִרְאֶה זֶרַע יַאֲרִיךְ יָמִים וְחֵפֶץ יְהוָה בְּיָדוֹ יִצְלָח

Yet, it was the will of the Lord to crush him with sickness.
When his life shall make an offering for sin,
he shall see his offspring, he shall prolong his days,
and the will of the Lord, by his hand, will prosper.

חָפֵץ literally means "to delight" but also indicates purpose: God willed
this. דַּכְּאוֹ is a Piel infinitive construct with a third masculine singular suffix
"to crush him" (cf. v. 5) and הֶחֱלִי is a hiphil perfect third masculine singular
form meaning "his sickness" (cf. vv. 3–4). נַפְשׁוֹ, "his life", is the subject of
the second phrase: the servant offers his own life. אָשָׁם is a sacrificial term
usually translated "guilt offering" (cf. Lev. 5:1–19), but it can mean an "obligation arising from guilt" or a means of "wiping out guilt" (Num. 5:8; 1 Sam.
6:3–8) or just "guilt" (Jer. 51:5; Ps. 68:22). The guilt offering was the one
sacrifice for which the individual had to realize their own guilt and make their
own offering. The LXX avoids identifying the servant's suffering with the
Lord's will and has the Lord vindicating the righteous one by cutting short his
agony and saving him from death at the hands of wicked people. It requires
a sin offering from members of the congregation. The Targum reads, "And it

was a pleasure before the Lord to refine and purify the remnant of his people, to cleanse their soul from sin. They will gaze upon the kingdom of the messiah; they will increase sons and daughters; they will prolong days, and the servants of the law of the Lord will prosper in his pleasure."[21] Long life was a sign of God's favour and blessing, a notable contrast to verse 8.

Isaiah 53:11

מֵעֲמַל נַפְשׁוֹ יִרְאֶה יִשְׂבָּע בְּדַעְתּוֹ
יַצְדִּיק צַדִּיק עַבְדִּי לָרַבִּים וַעֲוֹנֹתָם הוּא יִסְבֹּל

> After the toil of his life he shall see,
> he shall be satisfied with his knowledge.
> The righteous one, my servant, showed himself righteous for the
> many
> and he bore their guilt.

The LXX and 1QIsa add the object "light" to the end of the first phrase (as does NRSV; cf. Isa. 60:19–20). Instead of the common root ידע, some have proposed another root, ידע II, meaning "to be submissive, humiliated". Some translate "by his knowledge shall my righteous servant justify many". The hiphil imperfect third masculine singular form יַצְדִּיק indicates "to show himself righteous". The first person singular form occurs in Exodus 23:7 and Job 27:5, where it means "I will declare righteous." The LXX has "to vindicate the righteous one who serves the many well", making the Lord's vindication of the servant the dominant theme, rather than the servant's justification of the many. Many scholars omit צַדִּיק, "the righteous one", on the grounds of dittography.

Isaiah 53:12

לָכֵן אֲחַלֶּק־לוֹ בָרַבִּים וְאֶת־עֲצוּמִים יְחַלֵּק שָׁלָל
תַּחַת אֲשֶׁר הֶעֱרָה לַמָּוֶת נַפְשׁוֹ וְאֶת־פֹּשְׁעִים נִמְנָה
וְהוּא חֵטְא־רַבִּים נָשָׂא וְלַפֹּשְׁעִים יַפְגִּיעַ

> Therefore I will give him a share of the many
> and with the mighty he will share the spoil,
> because he poured out his life to death
> and let himself be counted with the transgressors.
> Yet he has carried the sins of the many
> and for the transgressors he intercedes.

The verb חלק means "to divide, apportion". Here it occurs in the piel imperfect with two prepositions in the first clause. The same construction is found in Joshua 13:7, where the Lord tells Joshua to "divide this land into portions for the tribes"; and with the qal perfect tense in Job 39:17, where the Lord "gave her no share of understanding". עֲצוּמִים literally means "the mighty", although in Proverbs 7:26, again in parallel to בָרְבִּים, it can be rendered "the countless". שָׁלָל is usually interpreted as material possessions and worldly power, but it can be a metaphor indicating that the servant will be integrated again into the community from which he had been separated by illness and suffering (cf. Jer. 39:18; 45:5). The hiphil verb הֶעֱרָה, "to be naked, empty", is active and causative here; the LXX uses a weaker passive voice here: "his soul was given up to death." The hiphil of the verb פָּגַע means "to cause to light upon, to cause to reach". The only other occurrence of this verb with the preposition -לְ is in Genesis 23:8, where NRSV translates "entreat for me" and JPS "intercede for me".

Notes

1. Conventional shorthand for Isaiah 52:13 – 53:12

2. J. Muilenberg, "The Book of Isaiah: Chapters 40 – 66, *The Interpreter's Bible*, vol. 5 (Nashville: Abingdon, 1982), 614.

3. Hans-Jügen Hermisson, "The Fourth Servant Song in the Context of Second Isaiah," in *The Suffering Servant: Isaiah 53 in Jewish and Christian Sources*, ed. Bernd Janowski and Peter Stuhlmacher (Grand Rapids: Eerdmans, 2004), 18.

4. N. T. Wright, "The Servant and Jesus: The Relevance of the Colloquy for the Current Quest for Jesus," in *Jesus and the Suffering Servant: Isaiah 53 and Christian Origins*, ed. William H. Bellinger Jr. and William R. Farmer (Harrisburg, Penn.: Trinity Press International, 1998), 294.

5. Brevard S. Childs, *Isaiah*, Old Testament Library (Louisville: Westminster John Knox, 2001), 413.

6. David J. A. Clines, *I, He, We, They: A Literary Approach to Isaiah 53*, JSOTSup 1 (Sheffield: Sheffield Academic, 1976), 62.

7. The most detailed historical study is Christopher R. North, *The Suffering Servant in Deutero-Isaiah: An Historical and Critical Study* (London: Oxford Univ. Press, 1948).

8. R. E. Clements, "Isaiah 53 and the Restoration of Israel," in Bellinger and Farmer, *Jesus and the Suffering Servant*, 54.

9. H. H. Rowley, *The Servant of the Lord and Other Essays on the Old Testament* (London: Lutterworth, 1954), 54.

10. H. M. Orlinsky, "The So-Called 'Servant of the Lord' and 'Suffering Servant' in Second Isaiah," in *Studies on the Second Part of the Book of Isaiah*, Supplements to Vetus Testamentum 14 (Leiden: Brill, 1967), 1–133.

11. Cf. J. Alan Groves, "Atonement in Isaiah 53: For He Bore the Sins of Many," in *The Glory of the Atonement: Biblical, Historical and Practical Perspectives*, ed. Charles E. Hill and Frank A. James III (Downers Grove, Ill.: IVP; Leicester: Apollos, 2004), 61–89.

12. Hermann Spieckermann, "The Conception and Prehistory of the Idea of Vicarious Suffering in the Old Testament," in Janowski and Stuhlmacher, *Suffering Servant*, 6.

13. Paul D. Hanson, "The World of the Servant of the Lord in Isaiah 40–55," in Bellinger and Farmer, *Jesus and the Suffering Servant*, 18.

14. Daniel P. Bailey, "Concepts of *Stellvertretung* in the Interpretation of Isaiah 53," in Bellinger and Farmer, *Jesus and the Suffering Servant*, 240.

15. François Kabasele Lumbala, "Isaiah 52:13–53:12: An African Perspective," in John R. Levison and Priscilla Pope-Levison, *Return to Babel: Global Perspectives on the Bible* (Louisville: Westminster John Knox, 1999), 104.

16. Mikeal C. Parsons, "Isaiah 53 in Acts 8: A Reply to Professor Morna Hooker," in Bellinger and Farmer, *Jesus and the Suffering Servant*, 115.

17. Morna D. Hooker, "Did the Use of Isaiah 53 to Interpret His Mission Begin with Jesus?" in Bellinger and Farmer, *Jesus and the Suffering Servant*, 98.

18. Cf. Muilenberg, "Book of Isaiah," 618.

19. Bruce D. Chilton, *The Glory of Israel: The Theology and Provenience of the Isaiah Targum*, JSOTSup 23 (Sheffield: JSOT, 1982), 92.

20. Cf. David J. A. Clines, ed., *The Dictionary of Classical Hebrew*, vol. 5 (Sheffield: Sheffield Academic, 1993–2001), 556–57.

21. Chilton, *Glory of Israel*, 91.

chapter seven

penal substitutionary atonement in paul

an exegetical study of romans 3:25 – 26

rohintan k. mody

Introduction

The book of Romans is central to the theology of the New Testament and indeed the entire Bible. As well, it is universally agreed that Romans 3:21 – 26 is central and important to the Pauline gospel.[1] Thus, C. H. Dodd calls this passage a return to Paul's original thesis in 1:17 and "a key passage in Paul's teaching".[2] John Ziesler argues that the passage is "a major turning point in the letter, where we move from problem to answer".[3] Thus, whatever understanding of the atonement is present here is central to Paul's gospel.

In this essay, we will argue that penal substitutionary atonement is present in Romans 3:21 – 26 and, therefore, is at the heart of Paul's gospel. We will first focus on God's love as the foundation for the atonement. Then, we will put forward a definition of penal substitutionary atonement so that the precise issue under debate is clear. We will focus upon verses 25b – 26, since if penal substitution is present here, it will throw light upon the rest of the passage. We will counter the arguments that penal substitutionary atonement is not present in verses 25b – 26 and present a case that it is. Then we shall briefly turn to consider whether redemption in verse 24 implies "cost" and whether propitiation or expiation is present in verse 25a. Lastly, we shall briefly review other passages in Paul where penal substitutionary atonement is present.

The Foundation: The Love of God

The foundation for any discussion about the atonement must be the love of the triune God. Out of love for us sinners, God puts his beloved Son forward as our penal substitute (1 John 4:8–10). Paul exclaims in wonder that the Son gave himself up to death out of love for him, a sinner and persecutor of Christ (Gal. 2:20). The cross shows God's love (Rom. 5:8), a love revealed by the Holy Spirit (Rom. 5:5). The love of God is central to penal substitution.[4] Out of love, the triune God provides Christ as our substitute, bearing our punishment, so that evil is defeated, and we are justified, forgiven, washed and re-created.

A Definition of Penal Substitutionary Atonement

The doctrine of penal substitutionary atonement has two distinct aspects, which shall be considered in turn.[5]

Penalty or Punishment

The penalty or punishment aspect of penal substitutionary atonement tends to include three elements. First, the penalty is a response to a particular offence or set of offences (transgression or a set of transgressions against a law/ standard or laws/standards). Second, a legitimate authority administrates the penalty. Third, the penalty means the imposition of a state of affairs on an offender that the person would prefer not to experience.[6] In formulations of penal substitutionary atonement, the punishment is specifically retribution (i.e., a punishment that is deserved or merited for the offence). This retributory aspect is separate from a punishment designed simply to influence a change in behaviour or as a deterrent. God administers the penalty in his judicial capacity because of humanity's transgression of his laws or standards. Specifically, the penalty for sinners means experiencing the wrath of God and, consequently, death.[7]

Substitution

Substitution can be defined as follows: person X excludes person Y and takes his place in an act Z. This is different from representation or inclusion, in which person X includes person Y in an act Z. Thus, in terms of penal substitutionary atonement, it means that Christ, by his death on the cross, excluded sinners from the punishment due for their sinful transgressions.[8] This means the *transference of the whole penalty for sin* from the sinner to Christ.

It is important to note here that penal substitutionary atonement does *not* negate a representative or inclusive view of the cross. Without our inclusion with Christ, there is an unjust substitution – one man who has nothing to do with others is punished for what they did. Yet, Christ also dies as a substitute. How then can Christ be both our representative and our substitute? With Christ's death, the senses of inclusion and substitution are different. Legally, he is one with us by taking on our humanity and suffering and dying in the flesh. Mystically, he is one with us in our spiritual union with him.[9] But in terms of experiencing the punishment, we are excluded. There is a difference between our unity as one mystical body in Christ and our distinction as two conscious agents – one, Christ, who experiences the punishment, and the others, us, who do not.[10]

Therefore, it is no objection to penal substitutionary atonement to say that Paul and the New Testament more widely conceive of the atonement in representative and inclusive terms as Christ's triumph over evil and as re-creation. But the question is whether Paul and the rest of the New Testament conceive of the atonement in substitutionary terms with regard to the penalty due for sin, *as well as* in representative and inclusive categories and as the defeat of evil and as re-creation.[11]

Thus, penal substitutionary atonement can be defined as follows: *Jesus Christ by his death on the cross exclusively bears the wrath of God and the retribution for sinful transgressions against God's law in the place of sinners.*[12]

The Just Justifier: Penal Substitution in Romans 3:25b–26

This paper will concentrate on the second half of verse 25 and its continuation in verse 26, because that section clearly talks about penal substitution.[13] Here we will first focus upon the NIV translation, which takes a very particular stance on this question involving penal substitution; second, we will explain the opposing view, which excludes penal substitution; third, we will explain why this opposing view is wrong and why the NIV is basically right in saying that penal substitution is in view here.

The Penal View: The NIV Translation

The NIV translates Romans 3:25–26 in the following way:

> ^{25}God presented him [Jesus] as a sacrifice of atonement,
> through faith in his blood. He did this to demonstrate his
> justice, because in his forbearance he had left the sins com-
> mitted beforehand unpunished – ^{26}he did it to demonstrate
> his justice at the present time, so as to be just and the one
> who justifies those who have faith in Jesus.

According to the NIV, the theology of penal substitution is clearly present. The sins of the old covenant have been left unpunished – they were
not ultimately dealt with by the sacrificial system. This leads to an implied
question: Is God unjust because he just lets sins go, forgives without punishment? The answer is no, because now God has demonstrated his justice
by punishing those sins (and, of course, ours too) in Jesus' death upon the
cross. As a result, then, God is both just (as one who punishes sins) and the
justifier (who acquits us and therefore saves us).

The Non-penal View: John Ziesler

In modern scholarship, however, a number of interpreters have moved
away from this position, and one of the clearest accounts of the alternative
position comes in John Ziesler's Romans commentary.[14] His understanding
of Romans 3:25a – 26 can be summarized as follows:

> ^{25}He did this (i.e. God presented Jesus as a sacrifice) to
> demonstrate *his righteousness, which is observed in his forgiving*
> *former sins* in his forbearance; ^{26}he did it to demonstrate at
> the present time that *he himself is righteous in that he justifies*
> *him* who has faith in Jesus.[15]

This view departs from the traditional view of penal substitution in four
key areas:

1. God's righteousness in the passage is purely his saving righteousness. The
idea lying behind the NIV's translation is that God's righteousness is basically
double edged: it consists both in the fact that God punishes sin and in the
fact that it results in our salvation. Ziesler, however, maintains that the basic
meaning of the phrase "the righteousness of God" in Paul is purely salvific.
Hence, he does not see in these verses any reference to a retribution expressed
in God's punishment of sin.

2. God's righteousness consists in the passing over of sins; his righteousness
and the passing over of sins are not in tension with one another. In the NIV's

version, there is a problem generated by God's having not punished sins in the past – a problem solved by God's punishment of those sins now in Jesus and his death. Ziesler, on the other hand, does not see a tension between righteousness and "passing over" at all. This leads to Ziesler's third point.

3. God's passing over sins is God's forgiveness, not his ignoring them. Here the debate is over the Greek word *paresis*, which is difficult to translate, because it comes up only once in the New Testament. The NIV takes this as referring to God's passing over sins in the sense of leaving them unpunished. Since Ziesler sees the overwhelming emphasis in the passage as being on God's salvation, he takes the word in an even more positive way, as referring to forgiveness.

4. God's being both "righteous and the justifier" are essentially the same thing. This is Ziesler's fourth point. Going back to the idea in the NIV translation, we see that the revelation of God's righteousness in Jesus Christ does two things: (1) it answers the potential problem that God was unjust in leaving former sins unpunished, and (2) it brings about salvation in making people right with God. But in Ziesler's interpretation, it is only the second part that comes into play. It is not that God is both just and the justifier, as if these are two different things.[16] Ziesler translates the word for "just" as "righteous".[17] Then he argues that the verse is saying it is because God is righteous that he is the justifier. Hence, "he did it to demonstrate at the present time that he himself is righteous *in that* he justifies him who has faith in Jesus."

Summary of the Different Views

	NIV	Ziesler
God's righteousness...	was *in question because of* his passing over sins.	is *expressed by* passing over (=forgiving sins).
	expresses *both* his punishment of sins *and* his salvation of sinners.	expresses only salvation.

Defence of the Penal Substitution View

There are problems with Ziesler's view, and on these particular points, the NIV does better.

Objections Answered and Penal Substitutionary Atonement Justified

God's Righteousness: Only Saving?

First, there is a problem with seeing, as Ziesler does, God's righteousness as only referring to his salvation, and the passage as a whole as not focusing upon issues connected with God's wrath.[18] Ziesler's view is surprising because from Romans 1:18–3:20, God's wrath and human sin are the dominant themes. Indeed, Ziesler himself sees 3:25–26 as the answer to the problem raised by 1:18–3:20.[19] There, God's wrath and judgment against human sin are the problem. Thus, God's righteousness here must deal with his own wrath in order for 3:25–26 to be the answer to the problem of 1:18–3:20.[20]

The fact that God's righteousness and his condemnation are not contradictory terms can be seen in part of the context of the passage we have been focusing on. In Romans 2:5, Paul states, "You are storing up judgment for yourself for the day of God's wrath [orges], when his *righteous judgment* [dikaiokrisias] will be revealed." Further, in Romans 3:5, the righteousness of God is contrasted with Jewish unrighteousness and must refer to God's attributive justice seen when he inflicts his punishing wrath:

> But if our unrighteousness [adikia] brings out God's righteousness [dikaiosunen] more clearly, what shall we say? That God is unjust [adikos] in bringing his wrath [orgen] on us? (I am using a human argument.)

This point is reinforced in 2 Thessalonians 1:6–9, where the language is *not* about punishment being the impersonal consequence of sin but rather is about a personal and active involvement by God. There is an expression of God's righteousness/justice in that he rescues the afflicted and punishes the afflicters:

> [6]God is just [dikaion]: He will pay back [antapodounai] trouble to those who trouble you [7]and give relief to you who are troubled, and to us as well. This will happen when the Lord Jesus is revealed from heaven in blazing fire with his powerful angels. [8]He will punish [ekdikesin] those who do not know God and do not obey the gospel of our Lord Jesus. [9]They will be punished [diken] with everlasting destruction and shut out from the presence of the Lord and from the majesty of his power.

Paresis = Forgiveness?

Linguistically, there are also problems with the notion that *paresis* means "forgiveness".[21] First, although the noun is not used elsewhere in the New Testament, the verbs from which it comes – *pariemi* and its cognate *parerchomai* – are used. Therefore, these cognates, since they are used in the New Testament, are relevant to the discussion.[22] In Luke 11:42, it does not mean "forgive" but rather means "to leave alone", referring to a matter that is not acted on.[23]

> Woe to you Pharisees, because you tithe your mint, dill, and all manner of garden herbs, but *pass by* [*parerchesthe*] justice and the love of God. You should have practised these as well, without *ignoring/neglecting* [*pareinai*] the former.

Second, Douglas Moo argues that *paresis* does not mean "forgiveness" when applied to *legal charges or sins* but means "postponement of punishment".[24] This is significant because the problem being dealt with here is sins: "All have sinned and fall short of the glory of God" (Rom. 3:23). These sins matter because they infringe on God's law, a law that is not above God but involves the satisfaction of God's own justice.[25]

Third, Moo also observes that if *paresis* means "forgiveness", this also means that the preposition *dia* is given an instrumental sense of "through", which is an unlikely use of *dia*.[26] It is more likely that *dia* here means "because".

Fourth, if *paresis* means "forgiveness", it makes the revelation of God as "just" (*dikaion*) redundant, given that God is already the "justifier" (*dikaiounta*).[27] We must remember that the entire passage of Romans 1:18–3:20, with its description of wrath and judgment, is relevant, and the problem of God's wrath and judgment finds its resolution here.[28] As a result, the NIV is right when it refers to God's *not punishing* the sins committed beforehand.

God's Patience

There is another link with Romans 2, and therein we have a truly decisive argument in favour of the penal substitution interpretation. It is important to note that the time or the state in which God passed over sins was "in his forbearance" – the Greek word is *anoche*, used in the New Testament only here and in Romans 2:4. In Romans 2:4, *anoche* is used to refer to the period in which God, out of his kindness, does not punish sins but gives people an opportunity to repent:

> Or do you despise the riches of his kindness and forbearance [*anoche*] and patience [*makrothumias*], not knowing that the kindness of God is to lead you to repentance?

With this parallel in mind, when Paul talks about God's "forbearance", the meaning is clearly a period of patience in which he leaves sin unpunished. It is important to note that "forbearance" (*anoche*) does not mean a patient delay in wiping out sin later, given that verse 3 talks about God's judgment and verse 5 talks about the day of wrath when God's judgment is revealed. Rather, in verse 4 *anoche* means a delay of God's judgment.[29] In Romans 9:22, we see similar language with a similar noun, "patience" (*makrothumia*), to that of Romans 2. Here, God's patience is clearly a delay in wrath and judgment:

> What if God, choosing to show his wrath [*orgen*] and make his power known, bore with great patience [*makrothumia*] the objects of his wrath [*orges*] – prepared for destruction?

In 2 Peter 3:9, there is also this idea in the context of the day of judgment and the destruction of the ungodly and the elements (vv. 7–10):

> The Lord is not slow in keeping his promise, as some understand slowness. He is patient [*makrothumei*] with you, not wanting anyone to perish, but everyone to come to repentance.[30]

Hence, we can return to Romans 3:25, which states that it was in God's *forbearance* that he passed over sins. In other words, this is about a period when, as a kind of interim measure, God holds back. This does not mean there was no punishment of sins in the Old Testament period. It means that God did not exact the full and immediate punishment for sin at that time.[31] Thus, it is after the Old Testament period that God acts decisively to punish sin fully in the death of Christ. There is probably an echo here of the Old Testament idea that God is slow in his anger (cf. Exod. 34:6), *but now* (Rom. 3:21), in the cross, God has at last executed judgment against sin. So it is no surprise that we have this sequence of thought in Romans 3:25–26:

- God passed over sins *previously committed* in the time of his forbearance (v. 25),
- but now *in the present time*, he demonstrates his righteousness (v. 26).

That is why this forbearance cannot be God's forgiveness of sins: it is a time when he patiently endures sins, knowing that he will decisively deal with them in Christ's death.

The Tension between God's Justice and His Justification

As a result, it is unlikely that God's righteousness is *expressed in* his passing over sins; rather, this is something which God's righteousness will remedy. The demonstration of God's righteousness shows that he is "both just and the justifier"; importantly, there are two elements here, not just one.[32] He *is* just *in himself* (*einai auton dikaion*) and has shown his justice in that in Christ's death, he punishes the previously unpunished sin. And he is the justifier in that in Jesus' atoning work, he frees his people from the penalty of sin.

Present here is not only the idea of punishment but also the idea of substitution. It is Christ who is punished exclusively in our place, so that we do not bear the punishment of our sins. It is precisely because of this punishment that, since we are included in Christ, God justifies us. This is surely good news, and indeed the heart of the Pauline gospel.

Redemption as Involving Cost

In Romans 3:24, Paul states that justification comes through God's free grace through the redemption found in Christ:

> and are justified freely by his grace [*dorean te autou chariti*] through the redemption [*apolutroseos*] that came by Christ Jesus.

The word "redemption" (*apolutrosis*) has been usually thought to bear the connotations of "ransom", given that it is a compound of *lutrosis*, which means "ransom".[33] In the second and first centuries BC, "redemption" often referred to the "ransoming" of prisoners of war, slaves and criminals (see Mark 10:45).[34]

Ziesler argues that the concept of ransom has no place here; there is no suggestion of any price being paid to the devil or anyone else.[35] For Ziesler the image of redemption reminds us that the focus of the passage is on justification/acceptance and the removal of guilt.[36]

In the old Greek Old Testament, *apolutrosis* is used of the redemption of Israel from Egyptian slavery.[37] In Exodus 13:1–16, the firstborn of Israel, man and beast, are consecrated to God. Yet these firstborn are to be redeemed through the payment of a lamb, a lamb that is both representative of the firstborn and also a substitute for the firstborn. Here payment secures redemption, and the redemption involved with the firstborn is closely linked with retelling the narrative of the redemption from Egyptian slavery.[38]

Further, one possible aspect to the background of "redemption" may also lie in the legal language of Exodus 21:30 and 30:12.[39] In Exodus 21:30, if an Israelite irresponsibly causes death, then he himself should be put to death. However, if the family of the deceased consent, then, "he shall give for the redemption of his life [*lutra tes psuches*] whatever is imposed of him." Similarly, in Exodus 30:12, at Moses' census, in order to avoid the plague, "each shall give a ransom for his life [*lutra tes psuches*] to the Lord."

Returning to Romans 3:24, given that we receive redemption as a free gift of grace, we pay nothing. The idea is that Christ redeems humanity under the sentence of death at the cost of his own life as both representative and substitute (see Mark 10:45).[40] It is important to stress that this is not the payment of a price to the devil but rather a cost incurred as a penalty under God's law. Indeed Ziesler himself says that the redemption here is "costly, for it involved the death of Christ on the cross".[41]

The Debate on Expiation and Propitiation in Romans 3:25a

Much of the debate on penal substitutionary atonement has focused upon what is often thought of as the most important word in the whole discussion – the Greek word *hilasterion* in Romans 3:25a.[42] Indeed, Daniel Bailey has written a monograph on this one word.[43]

This was a subject about which there was fierce debate decades ago between C. H. Dodd and the senior evangelical scholar Leon Morris. The debate was about whether *hilasterion* referred to expiation (the cleansing or wiping way of sins) or propitiation (the appeasement or satisfaction of God's wrath). Dodd's view was that Paul means only expiation here – that Jesus dealt with our sins by taking them away and that he did not have to deal with God's wrath.[44] Morris's view was, by contrast, that Paul actually says Jesus was appeasing God's wrath, and by doing so expiated sin.[45]

It is important to note here that Morris's view is far from the pagan view of propitiation; namely, that humanity satisfies the wrath of the gods by the unwilling sacrifice of an innocent victim. Ziesler (no proponent of propitiation) correctly states that on the propitiation view, it is God himself who provides the means of propitiation, and there is no suggestion that God is placated by anything men or women do or offer.[46] Further, the propitiation stems from God's *love* (see 1 John 4:10).

The contrast between the two views can be seen really clearly when we compare two translations of Romans 3:25a:

> For God designed him [Jesus] to be the means of expiating sin.
> — *NEB*

> [Jesus] ... whom God put forward as a propitiation.
> — *ESV*

Many may think that this is the key to the debate over whether Paul emphasises penal substitution.[47] However, we have already shown that penal substitution is clearly present in 3:25b–26 and is implied in the idea of redemption; therefore the debate over propitiation versus expiation should not be seen as the only key as to whether penal substitution is present in Paul.

Yet it seems likely that the historical reference of *hilasterion* is, in common with its normal meaning in the old Greek translation of the Old Testament, actually the *place of atonement*, the mercy seat, especially in reference to the Day of Atonement ritual in Leviticus 16:2, 13–15, where the high priest sprinkles the blood of the sin offering.

However, this raises the conceptual question of whether Paul sees *hilasterion* in Romans 3:25 merely in expiatory terms or gives it in his mind a propitiatory element as well. We shall argue that a propitiatory element is present here for four reasons. First, *hilasterion* does clearly mean "propitiation" in non-biblical Greek, and it is unlikely that the biblical authors would use it in such a way that the word lost all nuances of propitiation.[48]

Second, cognates of *hilasterion* are used to mean "propitiate" or "propitiation" in biblical Greek. So, for example, in Numbers 25:4 LXX, the Lord commands the execution of the judges so that God's fierce anger (*orge thumou*) may be turned away from Israel, but this command is not carried out. Then Phinehas kills Zimri and Cozbi, and in verse 11, the Lord commends

Phinehas for causing his wrath to cease so that Israel was not consumed. In verse 13, the Lord grants Phinehas a perpetual priesthood because he made atonement (*exilasato*) for Israel. This act of atonement is both human and substitutionary (Zimri and Cozbi die); it propitiates God's anger, for the plague stops; and it leads to God's declaration of righteousness for Phinehas. The language of wrath, judgment, death that turns away anger, and atonement suggests that cognates of *hilasterion* are used to mean propitiation in biblical Greek.[49]

Third, returning to Romans, the language of God's wrath and judgment in Romans 1:18–3:20, and our conclusions regarding penal substitution in verses 25b–26 and redemption in verse 24, suggest that *hilasterion* does imply that Paul could think in terms of propitiation. Further, Paul states that this *hilasterion* is "by his blood" in verse 25a. "Blood" here signifies Christ's death, and blood is used in conjunction with salvation from God's wrath in Romans 5:9. This also points towards propitiation, since God's wrath had not commenced its full punitive operation until the cross of Christ. For Paul, sin is not only a wound to be cleansed but also an offence against a God who needs to be propitiated.

Fourth, given the above three points, the question becomes whether Paul would have read Leviticus 16 as implying that the mercy seat, *hilasterion*, has a conceptual sense of propitiation. Leviticus 16:2, 13 warns that Aaron should come before the mercy seat only on the Day of Atonement and should do so with the proper incense. God is present in the cloud over the mercy seat, and the smoke stops the person from seeing the holy presence of God and so dying ("No one shall see God and live"). To bring improper incense means death, since in Leviticus 10, Nadab and Abihu are killed by a fire from God for bringing an unlawful incense offering. The infringement of God's holiness brings death, and God demands that he will be treated as holy (v. 3). In verse 6, Moses warns Eleazar and Ithamar to perform their duties properly, otherwise God's wrath would come upon Israel. Leviticus 16:1 then links chapter 10 to the provisions regarding the Day of Atonement by reminding readers about the death of Aaron's sons.[50] The implications of this are that God is present in his awesome holiness; to approach the mercy seat without the necessary provision is to risk disaster.

Gordon Wenham argues that the high priest, in order to protect himself against the wrath of God, has to prepare a censor of fine incense, and the smoke from the incense covers the mercy seat. Wenham notes that sometimes incense can avert the wrath of God, and this idea may underline the use of incense over the mercy seat here.[51] Thus, in Numbers 16, Korah and his men are portrayed as illegitimate priests, and their unlawful incense offering provokes God to destroy Korah and his men. Then God starts to destroy Israel through a plague, but the lawful incense offering of Aaron, the legitimate priest, satisfies God's wrath and makes atonement.[52] This implies that the point of the incense offering is not only to legitimate the true priest but also that only the true priest can offer incense that appeases God's wrath. So in Leviticus 16, under the cover of the lawful incense offering which protects the high priest from death, the high priest can sprinkle the mercy seat with the blood of the sacrificed bull as a purification offering.[53]

Given these four arguments, the concept of propitiation does seem to be present in Romans 3:25a. As Tom Wright says, "Paul's context here demands that the word [*hilasterion*] not only retains its sacrificial overtones (the place and means of atonement), but that it carry with it the note of propitiation of divine wrath – with, of course, the corollary that sins are expiated."[54]

Elsewhere in Paul: A Very Brief Summary

It is also clear that penal substitution is found in a number of places elsewhere in Paul.

In Romans 4:25, Paul alludes to Isaiah 53:5, 12:

> He was handed over for our trespasses [*paredothe dia ta paraptomata*]
> and was raised for our justification.

The language of "handing over" clearly points to Christ's death for sins, and thus all that has been said above regarding Christ's death applies.[55] The allusion to Isaiah 53 evokes the context of the Suffering Servant.[56] At the very least *Paul* reads Isaiah 53 in penal substitutionary terms.[57] The allusion to Isaiah 53 also reflects the Jesus tradition of the Son of Man being "handed over" to the hands of men.[58]

The clearest of all – perhaps even clearer than Romans 3 – is Romans 8:3:

> God sent his Son in the likeness of sinful man to be a sin offering, and
> so *he condemned sin in the flesh* [*katekrinen ten hamartian en tei sarki*].

Here, importantly, Paul connects the incarnation to the atonement, since God sends his Son into the world. In his humanity, Christ represents us.

But God also condemns sin in the flesh, where the reference can be only to the flesh of Jesus as the place sin is punished. The sin that properly belongs to the flesh of humanity is condemned in Christ, who came in the likeness of sinful flesh.[59] Also important is Galatians 3:13:

> Christ redeemed us from the curse of the law by becoming a curse for us, as it is written, "Cursed is everyone who is hung on a tree."

Paul here does not say that God cursed Christ, but the law is *God's* law. So Christ bears the curse of the law, which in the Old Testament is God's punishment for breaking the law, and thus Christ bore this legal curse *in our place*.[60]

Most important of all are the formulae very common in the New Testament to the effect that "Christ died for us" or "Christ died for our sins."[61] First Corinthians 15:3 is a good example:

> For what I received I passed on to you as of first importance: that *Christ died for our sins* [*huper ton harmation hemon*] according to the Scriptures.

This common formula taps into an important assumption in Paul's understanding of the Old Testament. From the Old Testament ("according to the Scriptures"), Paul understands that God's punishment for sin is death.[62] The Scriptures here are focused on Isaiah 53 because of the close verbal links and parallels between "Christ died for sins" and Isaiah 53:4–8, 11–12.[63]

As a result of God's punishment for sins, it could easily be that "we died for our sins", but in the revolutionary salvation that God brings about, Jesus is the Suffering Servant who bears the sin of many and the punishment that we deserve.[64] It important to note that Paul is restating the heart of the gospel (1 Cor. 15:1); this is of "first importance" (v. 3); this formula of Christ's dying for sins is common to all the apostles (vv. 3, 11); and this is what the Corinthians believe and by which they will be saved, providing they continue to hold to it (v. 2).

Conclusion

The exegesis offered above, primarily of Romans 3:25b–26 but also of other texts, makes it difficult to resist the cumulative Pauline evidence for penal substitution.[65] Penal substitution is not merely one motif among many others from which we may choose; it is at the heart of the Pauline gospel in Romans 3. Indeed, the entire narrative movement from Romans 1:18 to 4:25 is, in Andrew Lincoln's phrase, "from wrath to justification".[66] This is a justification that is dependent on penal substitution, the solution that deals with the problem of wrath.[67]

Some of the distaste that people can feel with penal substitution is an aspect of their general distaste for salvation as a legal judgment. It is, of course, more than that, but it is not an unfortunate or worrisome thing that the legal aspects are integral to it. God's passing over sins beforehand meant that there was always a possibility that his judgment on us was only a matter of time. But now the revelation of God's righteousness in Jesus Christ means that he is both just in having punished sin and the justifier of those who have faith in Jesus.

The implications of penal substitution for our lives are spelled out in Romans 3:27–31: no boasting; justification by faith, not the works of the law; a God for all peoples; and an upholding of the law.[68] A further implication is assurance: "There is now no condemnation for those who are in Christ Jesus" (Rom. 8:1).

Ultimately, just as the foundation is divine love, the goal is the glory of God. God, out of amazing love, gave Christ as our penal substitute. This means that penal substitution must result in and end with our being lost in wonder, adoration and praise (Psalm 150). Penal substitution results in the glory of God. This is the heart of the Pauline gospel. A rejection of penal substitution is a rejection of the heart of the Pauline gospel. *Soli Deo Gloria.*

Notes

This paper is based upon a draft lecture on Rom. 3:25–26 which was prepared by Dr Simon Gathercole for the EA-LST symposium in July 2005. In the event, he was unable to deliver it personally because of the terrorist events in London of 7/7. I am indebted to Dr Gathercole for graciously allowing the incorporation of his lecture into this paper, and his kindness in allowing it to appear solely under my name. I thank Dr Gathercole profusely. I also thank Dr Garry Williams and Abraham Kuruvila for reading and commenting upon a draft of this article. Any remaining faults are, of course, my sole responsibility.

1. The passage is the "centre and heart of the whole of Romans 1:16b–15:13", according to C. E. B. Cranfield (*The Epistle to the Romans*, ICC, vol. 1 [Edinburgh: T & T Clark, 1990], 199), while the great German scholar Ernst Käsemann calls it "the central concept of Pauline theology" (Käsemann, *Commentary on Romans*, ET [Grand Rapids: Eerdmans, 1980], 320).

2. C. H. Dodd, *The Epistle of Paul to the Romans*, MNTC (London: Collins, 1959), 73, 83.

3. John A. Ziesler, *Paul's Letter to the Romans* (London: SCM, 1989), 106–7.

4. Note here D. A. Carson, *The Difficult Doctrine of the Love of God* (Wheaton, Ill.: Crossway, 2000), that in Scripture, the love of God is spoken of in different senses. Love does not exclude wrath.

5. See the classic studies by J. I. Packer, "What Did the Cross Achieve? The Logic of Penal Substitution," in *Celebrating the Saving Work of God* (Carlisle: Paternoster, 1998), 85–124; John R. Stott, *The Cross of Christ* (Leicester: IVP, 1986); David Peterson, ed., *Where Wrath and Mercy Meet* (Carlisle: Paternoster, 2001); and Charles E. Hill and Frank A. James III, eds., *The Glory of the Atonement: Biblical, Historical and Practical Perspectives*, Festschrift for Roger Nicole (Downers Grove, Ill.: IVP; Leicester: Apollos, 2004). See also Steven Jeffery, Michael Ovey and Andrew Sach, *Pierced for Our Transgressions: Rediscovering the Glory of Penal Substitution* (Nottingham: IVP, 2007).

6. See Oliver O'Donovan and R. J. Song, "Punishment," in *NDT*, 547–49.

7. Death here is spiritual death and, ultimately, hell. This death is not sprung on humanity by the whims of a capricious God. Man was warned (Gen. 2:17; Exodus 20).

8. Note the review of notions of substitution or exclusive place-taking (*exclusierende Stellvertretung*) in German scholarship in Daniel P. Bailey, "Concepts of *Stellvertretung* in the Interpretation of Isaiah 53," in *Jesus and the Suffering Servant: Isaiah 53 and Christian Origins*, ed. William H. Bellinger Jr. and William R. Farmer (Harrisburg, Penn.: Trinity Press International, 1998), 251–59.

9. Here Christ is not the unwilling victim of a cosmic miscarriage of justice, but is, with the Father, the judge of humanity (cf. Acts 17:31), and the Son who delights to do his Father's will (John 5:30). God in Christ is the lawgiver, the judge, the offended party, and the bearer of punishment. Thus, penal substitutionary atonement is not "cosmic child abuse".

10. We are indebted for this point to Dr Garry Williams. Note here also that in terms of legal punishment, Christ is also one with the Father; thus Christ is *not* bearing the punishment as a foreign third party.

11. In other words, penal substitutionary atonement does not mean that there is no sense that Christ includes us upon the cross. Penal substitutionary atonement does not exclude other aspects of the atonement.

12. This definition leaves open the question whether the sinners for whom Christ is the substitute are all human beings (universal atonement) or believers alone (limited atonement).

13. For a more detailed discussion, see Simon J. Gathercole, "Justified by Faith, Justified by His Blood: The Evidence of Romans 3:21–4:25," in *Justification and Variegated Nomism*, ed. D. A. Carson, P. T. O'Brien, M. A. Seifrid, vol. 2, *The Paradoxes of Paul*, WUNT (Tübingen: Mohr; Grand Rapids: Baker, 2004), 147–84, esp. 168–83 on penal substitution, and 177–81 on Rom. 3:25–26.

14. Ziesler, *Paul's Letter*, esp. 115–16. Ziesler's position is followed, for example, by Stephen H. Travis, "Christ as Bearer of Divine Judgment in Paul's Thought about the Atonement," in *Jesus of Nazareth, Lord and Christ: Essays on the Historical Jesus and New Testament Christology*, ed. Joel B. Green and Max Turner (Grand Rapids: Eerdmans; Carlisle: Paternoster, 1994), 332–45.

15. This translation is based on the NIV and the NRSV (which is the translation used throughout the commentary) but modified on the basis of Ziesler's translations of some of the individual components in his comment.

16. Ziesler, *Paul's Letter*, 115–16.

17. Semantically, it is possible, since in Greek *dikaios* can mean either "just" or "righteous". The question is what Paul means here.

18. Ziesler (*Paul's Letter*, 116) says that humans are objects of wrath but nevertheless believes that *paresis* means forgiving sins as part of God's strategy. Ziesler's comments seem to imply that God's wrath is dealt with merely by his forgiveness rather than by the satisfaction of justice as well.

19. Ibid., 106–7.

20. For a discussion of the Pauline concept of righteousness, see Mark A. Seifrid, "Paul's Use of Righteousness Language against Its Hellenistic Background," in Carson, O'Brien, Seifrid, *Justification and Variegated Nomism*, 105–46

21. For the meaning of *paresis*, see BDAG, 776; LSJ, 1337.

22. For *pariemi*, see BDAG, 777; LSJ, 1340. For *parerchomai*, see BDAG, 775–76; LSJ, 1337.

23. This sense is confirmed by the LXX usage of "leave alone" in Exod. 14:12; Num. 13:20; Jdt. 12:12; 4 Macc. 5:29; cf. Prov. 15:10. See also Jdt. 5:21: "But if they are not a guilty nation, then let my lord pass them by [*pareltheto*]; for their Lord and God will defend them, and we shall become the laughingstock of the whole world."

24. Douglas Moo, *The Epistle to the Romans*, NICNT (Grand Rapids: Eerdmans, 1996), 238n95.

25. Thomas R. Schreiner, *Romans*, BECNT (Grand Rapids: Baker, 1998), 192.

26. Moo, *Epistle to the Romans*, 238–39.

27. John Piper (*The Justification of God: An Exegetical and Theological Study of Romans 9:1–23*, 2nd ed. [Grand Rapids: Baker, 1993], 144) points out that to take *paresis* as forgiveness "does not necessarily weaken the case for penal substitution here, since it could merely be the forgiveness shown in the OT period and this creates the same problem for justice as God's leniency of punishment, i.e. the issue would be: if God forgives the OT saints, on what just basis does he do so? Thus, for *paresis* as forgiveness" to be a decisive objection against penal substitution, proponents would have to show that the "forgiveness" refers to the present forgiveness of Christ.

28. Gathercole, "Justified by Faith," 180.

29. Ibid., 181.

30. See also 1 Tim. 1:16; 1 Peter 3:20.

31. Schreiner, *Romans*, 197.

32. Cranfield (*Epistle to the Romans*, 213) argues that it is no objection against penal substitution that *edeisis* could be translated "a showing forth" or "an expression" rather than "proof" because the point here is not just God's being seen to be righteous but God's *being* righteous.

33. Moo, *Epistle to the Romans*, 229.

34. See the evidence in Leon Morris, *The Apostolic Preaching of the Cross* (London: Tyndale, 1955), 22–26.

35. Exod. 15:13 is used by Socinians as a standard text to prove that redemption involves no price, since neither Pharaoh nor anyone else is paid. Our thanks go to Dr Garry Williams for drawing our notice to this point.

36. Ziesler, *Paul's Letter*, 111.

37. LXX Exod. 6:6; 15:13, 16; Deut. 7:8; 9:26; 13:5; 15:15; 21:8; 24:18.

38. The words used in verses 13 and 15 are *allasso, lutroo, lutromai*.

39. See Simon J. Gathercole, "The Cross and Substitutionary Atonement," *Scottish Bulletin of Evangelical Theology* 21, no. 2 (2003): 152 – 65.

40. Schreiner, *Romans*, 190. A lamb cannot truly represent us, given that it is dumb animal, but Christ in his humanity can be a true representative.

41. Ziesler, *Paul's Letter*, 111. See especially I. H. Marshall, "The Development of the Concept of Redemption in the New Testament," in *Reconciliation and Hope: New Testament Essays on Atonement and Eschatology*, ed. F. S. Leon Morris and R. Banks (Grand Rapids: Eerdmans, 1974), 153 – 69, who suggests that while "price" is not always specified, "cost" is invariably present.

42. Cognate terms, *hilaskomai* is present in Heb. 2:17, and *hilasmos* in 1 John 2:2 and 4:10, but these terms are a matter of debate as well.

43. Daniel P. Bailey, "Jesus as the Mercy Seat: The Semantics and Theology of Paul's Use of *Hilasterion* in Romans 3:25" (PhD diss., University of Cambridge, 1999).

44. C. H. Dodd, *The Bible and the Greeks* (London: Hodder, 1935); Dodd, *Epistle of Paul*, 78 – 79.

45. Leon Morris, *The Cross in the New Testament*, Mount Radford Reprints 19 (Exeter: Paternoster, 1976); Morris, *Apostolic Preaching*, 125 – 87.

46. Ziesler, *Paul's Letter*, 112.

47. It should be noted here that propitiation does not necessarily mean penal substitution; see Gathercole, "Justified by Faith," 178.

48. Linguistically, it is important to note that there is plenty of evidence from pagan Greek sources to indicate that *hilasterion* and cognates did have a propitiatory sense. For examples, see Morris, *Apostolic Preaching*, 126 – 29, 155; LSJ, 827 – 28.

49. See also Ps. 105:29 – 31 LXX (106). Paul clearly knows Ps. 105 LXX (106), since he alludes to verse 20 in Rom. 1:23, and he is also aware of Numbers 25, since he alludes to it in 1 Cor. 10:8. See also Exod. 32:14; Num. 16:46; Lam. 3:42; 2 Kings 24:4; Ps. 78:38; and Morris, *Apostolic Preaching*, 136 – 56.

50. Note here in 16:1 that the LXX adds that the reason the sons of Aaron died is that they brought "strange fire" (*pur allotrion*) before God.

51. Gordon J. Wenham, *The Book of Leviticus*, NICOT (Grand Rapids: Eerdmans, 1979), 231.

52. Gordon J. Wenham (*Numbers*, TOTC [Leicester: IVP, 1981], 139) says of Num. 16:46ff. that Korah's illegitimate incense provokes God's wrath,

but the incense of Aaron assuages it. The same view of the propitiatory effect of the incense offering is present in Wis. 18:21, cf. Sir. 45:16.

53. We are not denying the expiatory effect of the blood of the bull in Leviticus 16; we are merely pointing out that propitiation is also present.

54. N. T. Wright, "Letter to the Romans: Introduction, Commentary and Reflection," in *NIB*, vol. 10 (Nashville: Abingdon, 2002), 393–770, 476.

55. The preposition *dia* is here used in the sense of "because".

56. For a discussion of Isaiah 53, see John H. Oswalt, *The Book of Isaiah, Chapters 40–55*, NICOT (Grand Rapids: Eerdmans, 1998), 373–410, and Jeffery, Ovey, Sach, *Pierced*, 52–61. Brevard S. Childs (*Isaiah*, Old Testament Library [Louisville: Westminster John Knox, 2001], 415] dismisses R. N. Whybray's conclusion (*Thanksgiving for a Liberated Prophet: An Interpretation of Isaiah 53*, JSOTSup 4 [Sheffield: JSOT, 1978]) that there is no substitution in Isaiah 53 as "bland and even superficial".

57. Peter Stuhlmacher, *Revisiting Paul's Doctrine of Justification: A Challenge to the New Perspective*, with an essay by Donald A. Hagner (Downers Grove, Ill.: IVP, 2001), 131.

58. See Peter G. Bolt, *The Cross from a Distance: Atonement in Mark's Gospel*, NSBT 18 (Downers Grove, Ill.: IVP; Leicester: Apollos, 2004), 52–58.

59. See here also 2 Cor. 5:19–21, where Jesus is "made" sin; also Eph. 2:14.

60. N. T. Wright (*The Climax of the Covenant: Christ and the Law in Pauline Theology* [London and New York: Continuum, 1991], 153n54) correctly here rejects as spurious an antithesis between "participation" and "substitution".

61. See Matt. 26:28; Mark 14:24; Luke 22:19–20; Rom. 5:6, 8; 8:32; 1 Cor. 11:24; 15:3; 2 Cor. 5:14–15; Gal. 1:4; 3:13; Eph. 5:2; 1 Thess. 5:10; 1 Tim. 2:6; Titus 2:14; Heb. 2:17; 9:28; 10:12; 1 Peter 2:24; 3:18; 1 John 2:2; 4:10; cf. Col. 2:14.

62. See, for instance, Gen. 2:17; 3:19; Lev. 22:9; Num. 18:22; 2 Sam. 12:13; 1 Kings 16:18–19; Ps. 49:14; 78:50; Prov. 11:9; 14:12; Isa. 53:12; Ezek. 3:20; 18:4, 20.

63. See Otfried Hofius, "The Fourth Servant Song in the New Testament Letters," in *The Suffering Servant: Isaiah 53 in Jewish and Christian Sources*, ed. Bernard Janowski and Peter Stuhlmacher, trans. D. P. Bailey

(Grand Rapids: Eerdmans, 2004), 163–88, 177, and Gathercole, "The Cross."

64. Here we take "for" (*huper*) as having a substitutionary sense "in our place" (in addition to that of "for our sakes"). See Daniel B. Wallace, *Greek Grammar beyond the Basics: An Exegetical Syntax of the New Testament* (Grand Rapids: Zondervan, 1996), 383–89.

65. The problem opponents of penal substitution have is that it is almost impossible to deny, given that Jesus died on the cross, not us, and that God was angry at our sin and yet Jesus' death deals with the problem of our sin. Therefore, Jesus must be, in some sense, our penal substitute.

66. Andrew T. Lincoln, "From Wrath to Justification," in *Pauline Theology*, ed. Donald Hay and E. Elizabeth Johnson, vol. 3, *Romans* (Minneapolis: Fortress, 1995), 130–59.

67. This is not to say it is merely a "mechanism". Rather, Paul presents penal substitution as the solution to the principal problem: God's wrath and judgment. Anger and love are not here opposites. We reiterate that penal substitution is above all a demonstration of God's amazing grace and love. Paradoxically, those who deny penal substitution out of a concern for God's love end up denying the full measure of God's love and grace; what could be more loving than the triune God, out of love, satisfying his own wrath and taking the punishment we deserve so that we may be free?

68. For the theme of boasting, see Simon J. Gathercole, *Where Is Boasting? Early Jewish Soteriology and Paul's Response in Romans 1–5* (Grand Rapids: Eerdmans, 2002).

chapter eight

the atonement
in hebrews
steve motyer

Introduction

The debate about penal substitution as a model for the atonement must take full account of Hebrews, which is certainly one of the central atonement texts in the New Testament. As we look at Hebrews, it is vital that we hear it in its own terms, carefully listening for its distinctive message. Hermeneutically, we need to attend to the author's message for his readers, and it is highly unlikely that he expected them to read his letter through the spectacles of an atonement theology provided by Paul, Matthew or John. Theologically, we need to bear in mind that the very diversity of Scripture is part of its God-givenness for us. A wholehearted belief in scriptural authority will, in this instance, "let Hebrews be Hebrews"[1] and speak to us in its authentic tones.

We need to be ready, therefore, to hear something about atonement which no other part of the New Testament says. At the outset I share my conviction – for which this essay will provide ample evidence – that penal substitution does not provide a useful summary of Hebrews' teaching about the atonement, and that Hebrews does indeed say different things about what Jesus did for us on the cross – things that are truly glorious and worship-raising but are not penal substitution.[2]

A vital introductory point to make is that Hebrews' argument depends on a contrast between the old covenant and the new. The author is engaged in a careful balancing act. He wants to say that the same God who spoke through the prophets has now spoken through his Son (1:1–2), so that both covenants are from God. But at the same time, the new covenant is "better" than the old (a favourite word in Hebrews), and this "betterness" produces some sharp contrasts between them. Because of Christ, Hebrews is looking at the Old Testament with new eyes, taking a dramatic sideways look at Moses, the exodus, and the whole life and religion of Israel.

So when it comes to Hebrews' theology of atonement, we cannot assume the author is simply importing Old Testament atonement theology unchanged. He is working with Old Testament ideas and images drawn from the sacrificial cult, but our vital task is to hear the fresh thing he is doing with them because of the fresh revelation in Jesus.[3]

Hebrews 8 – 10

I begin with this central section of the letter because this is where we find sacrificial language most clearly, and this where people most readily find penal substitution. However, a sacrificial understanding of the death of Jesus does not, in itself, imply penal substitution. Sacrifice is a grander idea and does not in itself require a narrative of God's judicial wrath needing to be satisfied. We start our exploration of Hebrews' atonement theology by looking at the long quotation from Jeremiah 31 in Hebrews 8:8 – 12, which introduces and dominates the whole section.

Jeremiah's "New Covenant" Prophecy

This is the longest sustained quotation from the Old Testament in the New, here introducing the whole following section. In the author's use of this quotation, the emphasis falls not on continuity but on contrast: God announces a "new covenant" through his prophet because there is something wrong with the old one (8:7), and thus, by announcing the new, God makes the old *really* old – in fact, past its sell-by date (8:13).

The problem with the old covenant was that it was broken. The new one will be "not like the covenant which I made with their fathers on the day I took them by the hand to lead them out of the land of Egypt – because they did not abide by that covenant with me, and I turned away from them, says the Lord" (8:9).[4] According to this text, a new covenant is needed because though he "turns away", God does not abandon his people. The new covenant is based on a whole new relationship with God (8:10 – 11) because of a whole new forgiveness of sins (v. 12).

There is a hidden factor in this reference to the forgiveness of sins, which helps to explain the need for a new covenant. Israel's sin of apostasy (8:9) amounts to a so-called high-handed sin, for which no atonement is possible under the old covenant. Numbers 15:30–31 explains it very clearly: the sacrificial cult provides for "unintentional" sins – either sins which are committed in ignorance, or sins which do not amount to conscious and deliberate rebellion against the relationship with God which the covenant creates. But by definition, if someone rejects the covenant relationship, then the covenant's provision for atonement cannot apply! Israel is in this state, according to Jeremiah, and God promises a new covenant under which that terrible rebellion will be forgiven and a new relationship with him will be created. This relationship will be marked by much greater intimacy, with God's law written on people's hearts and everyone knowing the Lord without the need for teachers (8:10–11). This reference to the lack of teachers is also relevant to the overall theme because the priests were the teachers under the old covenant.

Then the Argument Develops

In chapters 9 and 10, the author develops this contrast between the two covenants in order to highlight the new thing that God has done in Christ, in particular the new atonement made through him. He highlights five ways in which atonement under the new covenant differs from atonement under the old:

1. *Place.* An earthly sanctuary is replaced by a heavenly one, and Jesus, our High Priest, enters the heavenly Most Holy Place on our behalf (9:11–12). See also 9:24.

2. *Focus.* Old covenant atonement focused on "regulations for the body" (9:10) so that people could participate physically in an earthly cult. But new covenant atonement focuses on "cleansing the conscience" (9:14), the part of the human person left untouched by ritual washings (9:9). See also 10:1–2.

3. *Scope.* Old covenant atonement dealt with "sins of ignorance" (9:7) – sins which were less than a full and conscious rejection of the covenant relationship. But new covenant atonement, through the blood of Jesus, brings cleansing even of such "dead works" (9:14): these are "works that lead to death", deliberate high-handed rebellion against God.[5] So Jesus allows us to understand that, even though it was not supposed to happen under the old covenant, God still forgave and accepted high-handed rebels like King David, who seduced his servant's wife and had him murdered when she got pregnant. There is no basis for this forgiveness within the Old Testament. The author of Hebrews

goes on in 9:15 to explain that because of the death of Jesus, "transgressions" of the old covenant can be forgiven.

4. *Means.* Jesus offers "his own blood" (9:12), "himself" (9:14, 25), "his body" (10:10). There is a huge contrast between this and "the blood of goats and bulls" (9:13; 10:4) which featured centre-stage in the old covenant rituals, especially on the Day of Atonement. The self-offering of Jesus is what makes new covenant atonement crucially different from sacrifices in the Old Testament, as we will see.

5. *Timing.* For the author of Hebrews, the repetition of the old covenant sacrifices underlines their ineffectiveness (10:1–2, 11). Day after day (7:27) and year after year (10:1), the cult offered the same sacrifices. But the sacrifice of Jesus takes place "once for all" (9:26, 28). This "once for all" event takes place "at the end of the ages" (9:26), which means, in Hebrews, that time is collapsed around the atonement achieved by Jesus. Like the high priest on the Day of Atonement, he has now entered the Most Holy Place, the heavenly sanctuary. We are now waiting outside for him to reappear, like the crowd of Israelites gathered outside the central sanctuary on the Day of Atonement, ready to cheer the moment when the high priest emerged unscathed from the divine presence (9:28).

But That Leaves Us with a Vital Question

So in all these crucial respects, the sacrifice of Christ is different from those of the old covenant. This means we cannot use the Old Testament to explain what God was doing in Christ. He has done something new. So we need carefully to consult Hebrews again, asking a double-sided question: (1) what exactly is achieved by the death of Christ, and (2) how?

The what is easier to answer than the how, but of course the how takes us into our interest in the mechanism of atonement, and of penal substitution in particular. The next two sections of this essay look at these two questions, devoting more space to the how question.

What Is New Covenant Atonement Designed to Achieve?

Hebrews 9:14 is a key trinitarian statement expressing in a nutshell what God has done for us in Christ. In 9:14, the purpose of the atonement is "to purify our conscience from dead works". As we saw above, "dead works" in all likelihood means "every kind of sin that leads to death, including the most vile, deliberate rejections of God's will – the things for which there was no atonement under the old covenant". And as we will see, death is the keynote here. The work of atonement in Hebrews focuses upon our deliverance from death, because that is our fundamental existential problem. The accent falls not so much on our guilt as on our mortality: not on our sinful lives before a holy judge but on our hopeless death in impurity and alienation.

But "works that lead to death" are covered by the cleansing achieved by Christ. No sin is beyond the scope of his high-priestly work. Cleansing or purifying is close in Hebrews to the notions of perfecting and sanctifying: these three words are frequently connected (see 2:10–11; 10:1–2, 14) and between them occur no fewer than forty-eight times in Hebrews.

Here in 9:14, our purification is linked to the blamelessness of Christ, who offers himself "through the eternal Spirit" to God. His blamelessness is to be connected with his sinlessness, which features in Hebrews 4:15. This blamelessness or sinlessness is not a static quality or piece of equipment with which Christ is kitted out, like the blemish-free sacrifices demanded under the old covenant. Jesus' blamelessness, on which our purification rests, is a hard-won quality in Hebrews for which he fights and gains through much testing. As we will see in our "how" section, this is vital to our understanding of atonement. And in 9:14, it is the Holy Spirit who is the agent of the self-offering of Jesus in his blamelessness.

The author picks this up in 10:14–18, where he links back to his Jeremiah quotation, drawing the threads of this long central section together. Here we discover that our cleansing is mediated to us through the sacrifice of Christ, and we discover that, for us too, the Holy Spirit is the agent. The translation of this passage is disputed because translators have failed to be sufficiently guided by an awareness that letters like Hebrews were written in order to be heard, not to be seen in print. Here is a paraphrase that reflects the thought of this powerful passage:

> By one sacrifice he has perfected for all time those who are being sanctified. And [so that we may know this is true of us too] the Holy Spirit testifies to us: for after saying, "This is the covenant I will make with them after those days," the Lord then says, "I will put my laws in their hearts, and write them on their understanding, and I will remember their sins and their rebellions no more."

This construction, followed by the Jerusalem Bible, is how the passage would naturally be heard. The effect of this is to identify the testimony of the Holy Spirit as the Jeremiah 31 experience of transformation of heart and forgiveness of sins. Just as the Holy Spirit enabled Jesus to live out his relationship with God through much testing and to offer himself sinlessly for us, so the Spirit brings us into new covenant intimacy with God, having been forgiven and now living in deep knowledge of him.

Hebrews 10:14–18 then leads into 10:19–25, the paragraph which summarises the central section of the letter and therefore plays a vital role in Hebrews' atonement theology. The what of atonement focuses finally on enabling us to "approach" (10:22) and "enter the sanctuary". In this paragraph, the author applies priestly language to all of us, because we are to follow where Jesus, our "great priest", has gone before.

This is the point where Hebrews departs most radically from the religious structure of the Old Testament. It was never a goal of Old Testament religion for the whole of Israel to qualify for entry into the Most Holy Place. In fact, as 9:1–10 points out, the tabernacle/temple was structured deliberately to keep people out – or rather, to keep God in, defended by a series of concentric barriers from direct contact with sinful human beings. But by his incarnation in his Son, God has magnificently swept all these barriers aside. The new covenant truly is new. We now "have boldness to enter the sanctuary by the blood of Jesus" (10:19) because his entry there heralds ours. We stand in trembling awe on the very threshold of the Most Holy Place, approaching it like the other priests who stood outside while the chief priest entered, hovering on the doorstep of heaven where our Saviour has already entered. Worship, in Hebrews, is electric with the nearness of God.

How Are the New Covenant Blessings Achieved by Christ's Death?

That brings us from the what to the how. How does Jesus' sacrifice win this entry for us? Is penal substitution the mechanism in Hebrews? Rather than focus the discussion directly around that question, I want to consider carefully what we actually find in Hebrews and then come back to that question briefly at the end.

The picture in 10:19–22 is graphic: Jesus' flesh – that which he offered on the cross – is the veil through which we dare to pass into the very sanctuary of God. But how does his sacrificed flesh secure this access for us? We will look first at the answer to this given in the immediate context (10:5–18), and then we will move back to the opening presentation of the work of atonement in Hebrews 2–5, which lies behind this central section of the letter.

Jesus offers a sacrifice of himself different in kind from the sacrifices of the old covenant. This contrast is explored through the dramatic quotation of Psalm 40:7–9 LXX in 10:5–7. This psalm expresses one of those strange contradictions in the Old Testament which the author of Hebrews loves to exploit in order to relate Jesus to what went before. Even though the sacrificial cult was ordained by God, here is a text that denies it: the sacrifices are not God's will, and instead God's will is going to be done by another who "comes" to do it and for whom God has "prepared a body". The author's comment is pointed: "he abolishes the first in order to establish the second" (10:9) – the old sacrificial system applies no more because it has been superseded by a different kind of sacrifice, a "single sacrifice for sins" (10:12), "the offering of the body of Jesus Christ once for all" (10:10). This offering is the will of God by which we have truly been sanctified from sin, sanctified in conscience (9:14). The offering of Jesus' body achieves something deeply "spiritual" – a cleansing and purification that fully restores us to eternal relationship with God.

But how does the sacrifice of the incarnate body of Jesus Christ actually work for us, to effect our cleansing and to institute a whole new covenant relationship between God and us? For the essence of Hebrews' answer to this, we have to go back to chapters 2–5, and in particular to chapter 2. There we are given the fundamental perspective from which to view the sacrifice of Jesus. In this section, we find that four basic points are made about his death and about atonement. These points follow from each other logically, as they trace the movement of the argument in Hebrews 2:

1. *His death first and foremost qualifies the Son of God to be the Greatest Human Being.* This is the message of the quotation of Psalm 8 in Hebrews 2:6–8, a quotation which heads the entire argument and theology of the letter. The dramatic message is that this Son of God, the agent of all creation on behalf of his Father (1:1–4), has become "for a little while lower than the angels". Here is another sideways look at an Old Testament text in light of Jesus. Psalm 8:5–6 underlines the enormous dignity of humankind: in God's eyes, we are barely less than the angels, commissioned by God to rule the world, with "all things put under their feet"! But the author is acutely aware that this vision does not match human reality, for "we do not yet see everything in subjection to him" (2:8b). In particular, it is the universal rule of death which defeats and frustrates the vision

of humanity expressed so powerfully in Psalm 8. How can we "have dominion" over all things when death has dominion over us? (See especially Heb. 2:15.)

The author's response is clear: "But we see Jesus, who for a little while was made lower than the angels, now crowned with glory and honour because of the suffering of death, so that by the grace of God he might taste death for everyone" (2:9). Jesus rescues the veracity of Psalm 8 by becoming the Human Being (the "Son of Man") in whom universal dominion is a reality.

While he could be this by virtue of his incarnation, at the end of 2:9 the author subtly introduces the idea that it is not just his incarnation but particularly his death which qualifies Jesus to rule in the Psalm 8 way. Why is this? Why is his death necessary to the package? This leads into the second point, which picks up the connection between 2:9 and 2:10.

2. His incarnation means sharing our suffering, with death as its supreme expression. Hebrews 2:10 is one of the most profound statements in the whole letter – maybe in the whole New Testament. It begins with "for" (omitted in TNIV and NRSV) because it sets out to explain the reference to Jesus' "death for everyone" at the end of 2:9. Verse 10 says that his death was "fitting", because if he was successfully going to bring many "sons" to glory (i,e,, make Psalm 8 true for others too), then he himself would have to be "made perfect through sufferings". Verse 10 introduces for the first time the journey metaphor, which is crucial for Hebrews' theology of atonement. Jesus is our "Pioneer", who "leads" sons to glory. But we who follow go only where he has already gone before us. And he goes before us through a process of "perfecting through suffering", by the will of God.[6]

This is a challenging idea in two respects: In what way does Jesus need to be "made perfect"? And why "through sufferings"? The first question is particularly pressing because of 4:15: how does "being made perfect" sit alongside his sinlessness? We will explore this further under the fourth point, but for now we need to stick closely to the journey metaphor as the author unfolds Jesus' role as our Pioneer and High Priest. Notice how the picture of the exodus underlies the author's expansion of 2:10 in 2:14–15. We need to be freed from slavery, not from political bondage but rather from something far more serious, from the "fear" of death (here "fear" means "power, domination, control" – actually "sphere" rather than "fear"). That is what Jesus does, but not by some mighty decree of banishment or destruction whereby death and the devil are powerfully dismissed from planet earth. Rather, he nullifies the power of death by sharing in it.

And that leads us to the second puzzle: why "through sufferings"? Hebrews 2:10 is picked up and expanded in 5:7–10, which focuses upon the experience underlying Jesus' perfecting. In these verses, the author undoubtedly has Jesus' Gethsemane experience in mind (Mark 14:32–42). Jesus, too, "fears" what is about to happen to him. But his fear turns into a sacrifice of "prayers and supplications, with loud cries and tears", offered up in faith to the God "who is able to save him from death". In Hebrews, Jesus' suffering in Gethsemane is as much a sacrifice as his subsequent death. God hears his cry and saves him, not from death, but rather after it. So, though he is God's Son, he has to go through death holding on in faith to his Father's power and intention to deliver him, "learning" an obedience which could be learned no other way. He learns to obey and trust God through death, and thus "having been made perfect, he became the source of eternal salvation for all who obey him" (5:9). If we will obey him – that is, follow him on the same journey of faith through which he "learned obedience" – then we too will be saved eternally.

3. Atonement thus arises fundamentally out of the incarnation, rather than just out of Jesus' death and resurrection. In Hebrews, atonement proceeds from relationship. "Since, therefore, the children share flesh and blood, he himself likewise shared the same things, so that through death he might destroy the one who has the power of death" (2:14). The "blood" that Jesus sheds in his death (9:12) is the blood that he takes in his birth. Because of this emphasis on sharing our blood, family terms are vital in 2:10–18: he *had* to become like his "brothers" in every respect (2:17), and he is not ashamed to call us "brothers" (2:11), although we could equally well be called "sons" (2:10) or "children" (2:13–14). The crucial family term is that we are "seed of Abraham" (2:16), because it was Abraham who heard the covenant promise of salvation and held on to it by faith (6:13–15). As one of us, Jesus' key testimony is, "I will trust in him" (2:13a, quoting Isa. 8:17), so that his faith is the same as our faith (or the other way round!). It is the faith that sustained him through his entire experience of flesh and blood, carrying him right through Gethsemane and the cross to his Father's presence "behind the veil". (See Heb. 6:19–20; 12:1–3.)

4. The fundamental action in atonement is, therefore, that he goes before us. The title High Priest is first applied to Jesus in 2:17, as the climax of the agenda-setting presentation of the work of atonement in 2:5–18. For Hebrews, it is supremely the action of the high priest on the Day of Atonement which makes this title applicable to Jesus. As one of us (5:1), he precedes us through death and into the Most Holy Place, so that, joined to him in obedience and faith, we may tread in his footsteps and enter also.

Jesus is perfected first (2:10; 5:9; 7:28), then we are perfected after him (10:14; 11:40; 12:23). This perfecting, because it applies both to the Saviour and to the saved (cf. 2:11), is quite delicate to define. It cannot be straight moral perfecting, which applies to the saved but not to the already sinless Saviour. Nor can it be the perfection of appointment to high-priestly office or more broadly the perfection of vocational fitness (two of the scholarly theories), because these apply to the Saviour and not to the saved. It is also more than the perfection of passing the test, because in this case we might expect "approved" or "certified" rather than "perfected". It is rather, I think, the perfection of the end of the Story. It attaches to the person as well as to the achievement: Jesus, the Son of God, has become something that he was not – he has become the High Priest and the Saviour, and, therefore, "after he had provided purification for sins, he sat down at the right hand of the Majesty in heaven" (1:3), his sonship translated into heirdom (1:2).

Perfection is thus part of the journey metaphor in Hebrews. It is reaching the *telos*, something already achieved by our forerunner (6:20; 7:28) and fundamentally true of us even now, so complete is his work (10:14), but something finally true of us only when we join the Party on Mount Zion (12:22–23).

So the law of atonement in Hebrews strongly emphasises the metaphor of the journey. Atonement (at-one-ment) takes place under the leadership of Jesus Christ, who goes before us through suffering and death and opens the way for us to follow because he unites heaven and earth in his own person: the Son of God who is crowned with glory and honour because he tasted death for us. He "comes" for us (10:7), to do the will of God by perfecting us along with himself! He is "the beginner and perfecter of faith" (12:2). The faith that marks the saved is the faith of Jesus, who clings to his Father in the face of death and passes the test because his confidence in God is unshaken. This is the faith of Abraham and his seed (11:8–19). His death is the door to the Most Holy Place for us, because it is the door for him before us, and we are his "brothers".

Finally, Thinking More Widely

This is not penal substitution but something even more compelling and vigorous. We are not dealing here with a static satisfaction of a principle of justice in God or a negative dealing with wrath on our behalf. We do not find any notion of bearing punishment in our place. These ideas are completely foreign to Hebrews. Whether we find them elsewhere in the New Testament is beyond the scope of this essay. What we do find in Hebrews is a powerful, worship-evoking presentation of a God who "brings" his firstborn into the world (1:6), so that he may lead a redeemed people in a mighty new exodus out of the power of death into God's rest, away from Mount Sinai and up to Mount Zion (12:18–24). He does this by embracing our suffering and death along with our flesh and blood, thus becoming the High Priest who leads his people, as one of them, into the Most Holy Place. Within the traditional models of atonement, Hebrews fits most closely with a representative view, although that pale metaphor hardly does justice to the depth and power of Hebrews' picture of a High Priest who attains perfection and brings his people with him.

It would be possible to argue that I have carefully avoided the theme of God's judgment, which is prominent in Hebrews, and that taking it into account would change the picture considerably.[7] Is it not true that Hebrews presents the judgment of God with great force (see 3:7–19; 6:8; 10:26–31; 12:25–29), including some terrifying texts: "It is a dreadful thing to fall into the hands of the living God ... for our 'God is a consuming fire'" (10:31; 12:29)? Hebrews 9:27 could be read as the starting point of its atonement theology: "It is destined for us to die once, and after that the judgment." Do not these texts present the fundamental reason for the atonement in the first place – we need to be rescued from the judgment of God?

This argument relies on importing a perspective from elsewhere – most usually, from the Old Testament. A penal substitutionary interpretation of Hebrews argues that in the Old Testament, the judgment of God is the fundamental presupposition of atonement and must be in Hebrews also, since the letter views the atoning work of Christ through Old Testament spectacles. In response, I offer the following reflections.

As stated above, it is misleading to assume that Hebrews simply imports Old Testament ideas unaltered by the new word spoken in Jesus. Even if the judgment of God is the presupposition of Old Testament atonement theology, it is not so in Hebrews. Here, God's judgment is seen not as his response to our sin but as his response to our rejection of his Son. Judgment is posterior, not anterior, to the work of salvation. This is true even in Hebrews 9:27.[8]

Why is this? One could argue that it is a consequence of the issue addressed in Hebrews: the author is concerned that his readers are intending to abandon their faith, so inevitably God's judgment is presented in this way, as part of his strategy to warn them of the consequences. If they reject the Son, they will fall under the dreadful judgment of God. But if the author were presenting the work of atonement in a cooler, more detached way, would he not start with the judgment or wrath of God as the fundamental issue with which atonement deals? In fact, does he not hint that this is the case in 1:9? In the foundational texts with which he begins the letter, he quotes Psalm 45:7, applying it to Jesus: "You love righteousness and hate wickedness." Does not this imply that he comes to deal with our wickedness?

Yes, it does. The author has already said that Jesus comes to "make purification for sins" (1:3). But nowhere does he hint that the problem with sin is essentially that God does not like it, so that we are helplessly under God's condemnation. The essence of the problem lies elsewhere. The essence of our human problem, for the author of Hebrews, is that we inhabit a world that cannot sustain a permanent relationship with God, our Creator. He begins and ends the letter by writing powerfully about the impermanence and fragility of the world, compared, on the one hand, with the awesome power and life of the Son of God (1:10–12) and, on the other, with the "unshakeability" of the kingdom of God (12:26–28).

Just as the world is destined to die (1:11), so are we (2:15). But God has determined to redeem us from it, so that we do not die but "receive a kingdom that cannot be shaken" (12:28). And that is where "the purification of sins" comes in, because it is sin that violates our relationship with God and so implicates us in the impermanence and death of the world. The problem, for our author, is essentially cosmic.

And that is why the solution, for him, is essentially incarnational. We have a Saviour who shares our flesh and dies our death, and then "by the power of his indestructible life" (7:16) enters the heavenly sanctuary ahead of us. He binds the fallen cosmos together, uniting earth and heaven by his blood, so that we too may have "confidence to enter". The final vision of Mount Zion in 12:22–24 is the author's evocative picture of where we're headed: the sounds of the party drift down the slopes as we climb towards the lights and just begin to make out the faces of those who have gone before, whose laughter now rings out as they gather around "Jesus, the mediator of a new covenant" (12:24).

One of the many creative features of Robert Gordon's recent commentary on Hebrews is the way in which he notices the prominence of the theme of death in chapter 11. The characters in the heroes gallery all, in different ways, faced and overcame death – just as, at the end of the roll call of faith, Jesus, our Pioneer, has done (12:1–2).[9] In Hebrews, the atonement focuses on death as that which violates our humanity by destroying our capacity for intimate relationship with our Creator. But because of Jesus, "We are not marked by shrinking back into destruction, but by faith so that we gain our lives" (10:39).

It is fitting that, in his closing blessing, the author picks up the gospel metaphor of the Good Shepherd, who leads, provides for, and dies for his sheep before rising to a glorious new life (13:20–21): "May the God of peace, who brought up from the dead, by the blood of the eternal covenant, that Great Shepherd of the sheep, Jesus our Lord, equip you with every good thing so that you may do his will, working in you what is pleasing in his sight, through Jesus Christ, to whom be glory for ever and ever. Amen."

Notes

1. I allude to the title of James D. G. Dunn's influential essay "Let John Be John" in P. Stuhlmacher, ed., *Das Evangelium und die Evangelien: Vorträge vom Tübinger Symposium 1982* (Tübingen: Mohr, 1983), 309–39. Dunn too was arguing that John should be heard carefully in his own right, distinct from the voice of later doctrinal disputes and formulations.

2. I do not concern myself in this paper with the definition of "penal substitution". There are, of course, several versions of it.

3. I have not laden this paper with scholarly references and discussions, for clarity's sake. But those in the know will recognise the scholarly discussions buzzing in the wings. There are just a few references to wider literature in relation to some of the more important points that follow.

4. The translations of texts from Hebrews in this paper are my own.

5. This interpretation of "dead works", both in 9:14 and in 6:1, is proposed by Robert Gordon both in his commentary *Hebrews* (Sheffield: Sheffield Academic, 2000) and in "Better Promises: Two Passages in Hebrews against the Background of the Old Testament Cultus," in *Templum Amicitiae: Essays on the Second Temple Presented to Ernst Bammel*, ed. W. Horbury, JSNT-Sup 48 (Sheffield: Sheffield Academic, 1991), 434–49.

6. The standard (and excellent) treatment of the vital theme of perfection in Hebrews is that of David Peterson, *Hebrews and Perfection: An Examination of the Concept of Perfection in the Epistle to the Hebrews* (Cambridge: Cambridge Univ. Press, 1982). The view I defend here is a little closer, however, to that of Oscar Cullmann than to Peterson's: Oscar Cullmann, *Christology of the New Testament* (London: SCM, 1963), 92–101.

7. This was indeed the response of some hearers when I gave this paper at the EA-LST atonement consultation in July 2005.

8. "It's appointed for human beings to die once, and then face judgment" – this sounds at first like the fundamental problem facing humanity. We have to face the Judge! But "judgment" does not mean "condemnation" here: it means "scrutiny, division, verdict", with the implication that the verdict may be either further death, or life. Here, the author is thinking especially of the "verdict unto life" that awaits us, because he is pointing out the parallel between what happens to us (death, followed by verdict) and what happens to Christ (death, followed by the glorious second coming as Saviour – like the high priest reappearing out of the sanctuary at the end of the Day of Atonement ritual). There's no doubt that, for the author of Hebrews, the criterion of God's verdict is whether people have embraced his Son.

9. Gordon, *Hebrews*, 17, 129.

theological contributions

must we imagine the atonement in penal substitutionary terms?

questions, caveats and a plea

joel b. green

I believe in God the Father Almighty, Maker of heaven and earth.
And in Jesus Christ his only Son our Lord; who was conceived by
the Holy Spirit, born of the Virgin Mary, suffered under Pontius Pilate,
was crucified, dead, and buried; the third day he rose again from the
dead; he ascended into heaven, and sits at the right hand of God the
Father Almighty; from thence he shall come to judge the quick and
the dead.

I believe in the Holy Spirit; the holy catholic church; the communion of saints; the forgiveness of sins; the resurrection of the body; and
life everlasting. Amen.

I begin with a recitation of the Apostles' Creed for three reasons. First,
incorporating the statement *crucifixus est sub Pontio Pilato* into its rule of
faith, the early church testified to its conviction that the crucifixion of Jesus
Christ under Pontius Pilate was an unassailable historical event.[1] Second, by
this statement, early Christians underscored what is indisputable in the New
Testament: Jesus' demise at the hands of Roman justice, represented theologically in the phrase "Christ crucified", is central to comprehending the eternal
purpose of God as known in Israel's Scriptures. The plot line of God's purpose
passes through and cannot bypass the execution of Jesus on a Roman cross.
Emphatically put: no cross, no Christianity. Third, given the importance of

the crucifixion of Jesus to our faith, it must not escape our attention that, on the question of *how* Jesus' death is salvific, the creed is silent.

The creed is uncommitted regarding the nature of the atonement. From this, I want to draw out what I take to be a self-evident corollary: namely, that one can inhabit the land of Christian orthodoxy, classically defined, without embracing a particular theory of the atonement, be it the now-regnant penal substitutionary model or some other. Of course, in making this claim, I also recognize that the Apostles' Creed does not stand alone, neither in defining the faith of the church nor in its lacuna with regard to defining doctrinal orthodoxy concerning the soteriological significance of Jesus' death. On the particular nature of the atonement, the great ecumenical councils were similarly silent. Moreover, the "rule of truth" or "rule of faith", as this was articulated variously in the ante-Nicene period, leaves undeveloped, or at least underdeveloped, how best we might construe the soteriological ramifications of the cross of Christ. As any history of atonement theology will demonstrate, the post-apostolic church did not speak with one voice when it sought to articulate *how* Jesus' death was salvific.[2] In short, I am working from the assumption that the faith of the church and Christian identity are not in the dock as we engage these important questions about the nature of Christ's atonement. This allows a certain freedom of inquiry and urges hospitality toward persons and faith communities holding views other than one's own.

As my contribution to this conversation, I want to pursue two agendas. First, in response to the task given me by the editors of this book, I want to raise some questions regarding one view of the atonement – specifically, the model of penal substitutionary atonement. I hope to demonstrate through a range of considerations why I find this way of articulating a theology of the atonement wanting. Some may find it puzzling that I do not seek to make my case on narrowly exegetical grounds. They will ask, What of Galatians 3? What of Romans 8? What of 2 Corinthians 5? And so on. I am not blind to the importance of a close reading of the text for theological hermeneutics. I am cognizant of the fact, though, that an essay of this kind would allow for exegetical inquiry into only a small sampling of texts, so that, even were I able via exegetical navigation to convince my readers on the texts I might have chosen, questions would remain: what about those texts with which I did not engage? Additionally, when it comes to the status we allow the penal substitutionary theory of the atonement, I doubt that more exegesis will provide us with any knock-down arguments, whether pro or con. As Howard Marshall has helpfully observed, the apostle Paul in particular and New Testament thought more generally "is more concerned with the nature of salvation than the precise way in which it has been achieved"[3] – which I take to mean that Marshall would agree that the struggle here will not be resolved on exegetical grounds alone. Instead, my sense is that larger issues are operating, some at a taken-for-granted level, and that putting some of these on the table and naming them is one way that I can press the conversation forward. Along the way, I want, second, to draw attention to a constellation of concerns that I regard as important in our contemporary thinking about the atonement. Given the more narrow focus of this project on the theory of penal substitutionary atonement, I will not be drawing these issues together into a constructive proposal, but I hope it will be nonetheless clear that I regard Jesus' death as rich with soteriological significance.[4]

Penal Substitutionary Atonement: Some Questions and Caveats

For most Christians in North America and the United Kingdom, to speak of the atonement is almost invariably to speak of penal substitutionary atonement. Gone are the days when discussions about atonement might signal the term's derivation from the combination "at + one + ment" in Middle English, and so refer generally to reconciliation.[5] Gone are the days when "atonement" might refer more broadly to the doctrinal affirmation of "the benefits of Christ's death for us". The model of penal substitutionary atonement is so pervasive that many Christians may wonder whether the saving significance of Jesus' death can be understood in any other way. Indeed, so pervasive is this model that, for many, to call it into question is tantamount to undermining the whole of Christian soteriology. Nevertheless, important issues must be raised.

The Context of Jesus' Death on a Roman Cross

"To state the matter somewhat provocatively, one could call the Gospels passion narratives with extended introductions."[6] In what must be one of the most-quoted footnotes in the history of scholarly writing, Martin Kähler penned these words more than a century ago (1896), thus setting the stage for twentieth-century study of the passion narratives of the Gospels. Read in its context, Kähler's comment was designed to draw attention away from the Gospels as biographies of Jesus concerned to trace the development of Jesus' self-consciousness, observing instead that the Gospels were emphatic not about Jesus' inner life but regarding his activity. Irrespective of Kähler's own agenda, his claim participated in the move to segregate the New Testament accounts of Jesus' death from those of his life. Thus it was that, from the turn of the twentieth century into the 1960s, the accounts of Jesus' suffering and death were isolated from study of the Gospels more generally.[7]

Irrespective of the particular objectives of its proponents, the effect of the ascendency of penal substitutionary atonement as the regnant model for explaining the saving death of Jesus has been the same: to divorce Jesus' life from the passion event, as though the only significant thing about Jesus was his death. Jesus was born in order to die. Why did God become human? In order to bear on the cross the punishment for our sin.[8] But this proposal neglects what we know historically, fails to account for the nature of the witness of the New Testament itself, diminishes the significance of the incarnation, and (as I will suggest later) unacceptably truncates the portrait of faithful human life as the imitation of Christ.

This is not to deny the centrality of Jesus' death as the actualization of God's purpose. That Jesus' passion carries this significance is clear from the explicit predictions of Jesus' suffering and death (e.g., Mark 8:31; 9:31; 10:33–34), as well as from the numerous sayings, both indirect and in a variety of forms (parables, pronouncement stories, narrative episodes, aphorisms, etc.), through which Jesus anticipates and charges with meaning his violent end.[9] Materials drawn from the Psalms of the Suffering Righteous are everywhere to be found on the terrain of the gospel passion narratives, and this further embeds Jesus' suffering and death in God's plan.[10]

How does Jesus' death reveal as well as serve the purpose of God? The Gospels and Acts show how Jesus' death and resurrection place the spotlight on particular emphases in Israel's Scriptures. In our reading of the Old Testament, we might fail to notice such motifs as the inevitable rejection and death of God's spokespersons (for example, Neh. 9:26; Jer. 2:30; 26:20–23; cf. Mark 6:4). We might bypass the persistent view that, rather than rescue people *from* suffering, God saves people *through* suffering – a pattern found in the stories of Joseph and Daniel, for example, and in the Psalms of the Suffering Righteous.[11] In our reading of Israel's Scriptures, we might be tempted to overlook such texts in favor of others, such as those that promise destruction of our enemies and our own rise to power. Doing so, we would find ourselves keeping company with Jesus' disciples, who, in their obtuseness, held on to such Old Testament threads; but this kept them from understanding Jesus and his mission (e.g., Luke 9:43–46; 18:31–34). They needed to reread their Scriptures in ways that took seriously how the cross casts its shadow backward over the whole of Israel's story. But if the cross serves as a hermeneutical key for comprehending the purpose of God, it is also true that Jesus' death on a Roman cross makes no sense apart from the pattern of his life.

In a recent monograph, Stephen J. Patterson has conveniently summarized three ways in which the significance of Jesus' death is and must be worked out in relation to the character of his life.[12] First, because Jesus died as a victim, and particularly as a victim of imperial brutality, the cross points to Jesus' life as a life of resistance to earthly empire. Second, because Jesus died the death of a martyr, the cross points to Jesus' life as one of courageous commitment to the kingdom of God – a commitment that attracted hostility in life as in death. Third, Jesus died a sacrificial death, pointing both to the character of Jesus' life as acceptable before God ("without defect or blemish", 1 Peter 1:19) and faithful toward God, rather than in fidelity to the Roman Empire and imperial worship.

From the perspective of the Gospels, then, the cross of Christ cannot be understood apart from the wider context of this narrative. The Gospels are unanimous in their testimony that Jesus anticipated his death; in the charged environment of Roman Palestine, how could he not have done so? To admit this is to open the door to the probability that he reflected on its significance and did so in a way that intimately related it to his mission to redeem the people of God. By this I mean that Jesus was no masochist looking for an opportunity to suffer and die, but saw that his absolute commitment to the purpose of God might lead, in the context of "this adulterous and wicked generation" (Mark 8:38), to his death. This, as he discerned and embraced in prayer on the night of his arrest, was the cup given him by God (Mark 14:32–42; Luke 22:39–46).

His mission, as this is known to us in the Gospels, is directed toward revitalizing Israel as the people of God. Pursuing this aim compelled him to proclaim the intervention of God's rule and to embody the ethics of this kingdom, and this brought him into conflict with the conveyers of Roman and Jewish ideologies and practices. From this perspective, we may regard nothing of significance in Jesus' practices as irrelevant to his execution; everything – his interpretation of Israel's Scriptures, his practices of prayer and worship, his astounding choice of table companions, his crossing of the boundaries of clean and unclean, his engagement with children, his miracles of healing and exorcism – leads to the cross. Calling twelve disciples as representative of restored Israel, weaving the hopes of new exodus and the eschatological era into his ministries of word and deed, speaking of the fulfillment of God's promises to Israel, his prophetic action at the temple in anticipation of a temple not made by human hands – in all of these ways and more, Jesus countered the present world order and maintained that God was at work in his person and mission. This led him to a form of execution emblematic of a way of life that rejected the value of public opinion in favor of status before God and inspired interpretations of his death that accorded privilege to the redemptive power of righteous suffering. The way was opened for Jesus' followers to ascribe positive value to his shameful death and thus learn to associate in meaningful ways what otherwise would have been only a clash of contradictory images: Jesus' heinous suffering and his messianic status.

Over against the model of penal substitutionary atonement, then, God's saving act is not his response to Jesus' willing death, as though, in a forensic exchange, our punishment by death was suspended by Jesus' execution. God sent his Son to save, but this is worked out in a variety of purpose statements: to fulfill the law (Matt. 5:17), to call sinners to repentance (Matt. 9:13), to bring a sword (Matt. 10:34), to give his life as a ransom for many (Mark 10:45), to proclaim the good news of the kingdom of God in the other cities (Luke 4:43), to seek and to save the lost (Luke 19:10), and so on. Even the Ransom Saying is exegeted by the parallel description of Jesus' mission: "The Son of Man came not to be served, but to serve" (Mark 10:45). God's saving act is the incarnation, which encompasses the whole of his life, including – but not limited to – his death on a Roman cross.

To admit all of this, however, is to pull the rug out from under any interpretation of Jesus' death that separates Jesus' life from his death. Indeed, apart from this larger narrative, we have little on which to base any claim regarding the soteriological significance of Jesus' execution. Someone might say, as Rudolf Bultmann said, that, for his part, Paul seemed quite capable of interpreting Jesus' death (and resurrection) without any concern for the manner of Jesus' life, that Jesus' earthly life, apart from the "that" of his earthly life, was irrelevant to Paul: "Jesus' manner of life, his ministry, his personality, his character play no role at all; neither does Jesus' message."[13] But this way of construing Paul's interests has been countered repeatedly by reference both to evidence of the Jesus tradition in Paul's letters and to the theological significance for Paul of Jesus' life.[14]

In short, it is not clear to me how the model of penal substitutionary atonement can help but strip Jesus' death from its historical context in the Roman world and from its narrative context in the Gospels. Theologically, the model of penal substitutionary atonement eclipses the historical particularity of Jesus' crucifixion, resulting in a serious deficit of interest in the incarnation and in Jesus' human life and mission.

A Misshapen View of God

In his critical engagement with the book I co-authored with Mark Baker, *Recovering the Scandal of the Cross*, Kevin Vanhoozer voices a complaint to which Dr Baker and I have become accustomed – namely, that our characterizing the god of penal substitutionary atonement as "emotion-laden ... ever on the verge of striking out" is nothing but a caricature. As Vanhoozer observes, God's wrath is interpreted in a variety of ways by those who hold to penal substitutionary atonement.[15] Although we are happy to grant this point, Dr Baker and I remain unrepentant insofar as our concern was not so much with the carefully nuanced discussions of penal substitutionary atonement that occupy theologians as with the way the atonement is conceived and articulated at the popular level by Sunday school teachers, Christian camp counselors, preachers, evangelists, in sermons, in praise songs, around campfires, and in small group Bible studies. It is against this backdrop that we wrote,

> We must face the reality that, even when it is articulated by its most careful and sophisticated adherents, penal substitutionary atonement remains susceptible to misunderstanding and even bizarre caricature. Accordingly, the drama of the death of Jesus becomes a manifestation of God's anger – with God as the distant Father who punishes his own son in order to appease his own indignation. One of us has received a report from a friend leading a Sunday school class in which a boy observed, "Jesus I like, but the Father seems pretty mean!" "Why is God always so angry?" another friend asked.[16]

Two issues surface in these comments, both troubling: a misshapen image of God as angry with us and a denial that the work of God the Father and of Christ the Son are one (that is, a severance within the Godhead).

I have already drawn attention to the usual defense of the model of penal substitutionary atonement put forward by its champions in the face of these concerns. As John Stott writes in response to the critical remarks of Sir Alister Hardy, "He caricatured the Christian understanding of the cross in order the more readily to condemn it."[17] While granting this point, it should not escape us that it is precisely this sort of caricature that is held by many Christians, persons who either have never heard a more nuanced accounting of penal substitutionary atonement, on whom such subtlety is lost, or who simply reject any such attempts at refining this atonement theory. Should the proponents of penal substitutionary atonement assume responsibility for the way in which their theory is heard? How many readers must respond wrongly to an utterance before the nature of the utterance itself demands scrutiny? Should not an articulation of a doctrine, such as this particular model of the atonement, be assessed at least in part with respect to how it has been received and is now represented more generally within the church?

In large part, the pivotal issue here has to do with God's wrath. With reference to Romans 3:25, for example, J. I. Packer has recently urged that "it is the sacrificial death ('blood') of Jesus Christ, God's incarnate Son, that quenches divine anger against sinners, just because Christ's death was a vicarious enduring of the penalty that was our due."[18] With regard to Romans 3:21–26, Derek Tidball writes similarly, first, that "the wrath of God against sin" expresses God's "personal anger at evil leading to his punishment of those who commit it" and, second, that we cannot but conclude that the cross of Christ turns away God's wrath. Even though Romans 3:21–26 does not develop the need for justification through the redemption that is in Jesus Christ in terms of the need to assuage God's wrath, the problem of divine wrath, Tidball writes, is "clearly assumed", developed as it was earlier in Paul's letter, in Romans 1–2.[19]

Let me raise three questions here. First, by what logic can it be assumed that anger is quenched by acting upon it in just this way? That is, if we were to grant the first two stages of Packer's soteriological scheme – the penalty due us on account of our status as sinners is death, and this penalty was an expression of divine wrath – on what basis does it follow that Jesus' dying quenches the anger directed at us by God? Does the transfer of guilt satisfy the demands of justice? Given the anthropathy at work in attributing anger to Yahweh, can we so easily escape the reality that redirecting anger at an innocent party does not necessarily return the guilty party to good graces? If this logic is explanatory of the divine economy, how are we to understand those biblical accounts in which forgiveness is extended apart from the satisfaction of wrath (e.g., Luke 7:36–50)?

Second, if God's anger can sometimes be understood in Old Testament texts in relation to retributive punishment, then is it not of consequence that the antidote to God's wrath is not therein developed in those same texts in sacrificial terms? Indeed, although the animal sacrifice may represent those for whom the sacrifice is offered, we find no exposition of the ritual act as satisfaction or penalty.[20] John Goldingay observes, "The problem of sin in Leviticus is not that sin involves infidelity or disloyalty which makes God angry but that sin pollutes, stains, and spoils, and thus makes people repulsive.... Sacrifice does not directly relate to anger."[21] As Bruce Baloian summarizes, "What is striking is that the OT portrays the turning of his wrath as coming to an end not as a result of repentance, but because of Yahweh's mercy."[22] Similarly, on the basis of some New Testament texts, someone might want to insist that God's wrath is addressed by means of the cross of Christ, but this is hardly the same thing as insisting that this was the consequence of God's redirecting his wrath onto his Son, Jesus of Nazareth. Indeed, the inference that God's wrath might be turned away from sinful humanity only by God's finding in Jesus a substitute object for his wrath is both logically unnecessary and exegetically suspect.

The third concern has to do with the presumption made by some with regard to the implicit need to assuage God's wrath in Romans 3. Let me respond to this presumption while also saying more about the presumed relation of wrath, sacrifice and atonement in the Old Testament.

In the Old Testament, the concept of atonement is the resolution of estrangement between two parties whose relationship has been interrupted or broken by sin or by some other infraction and is generally tied to the rites of sacrifice and mediation. In divine-human relations, God is the source of atonement, even in those texts where God provides the means for achieving atonement.

Since early in the twentieth century, debate has revolved around whether the work of atonement might best be characterized as expiation (God's freeing and cleansing people from the onus and blemish of sin) or as propitiation (sacrifice as a means of averting God's wrath). Against the claim that Israel had no notion of propitiation (e.g., Dodd), some have emphasized the need in atonement to assuage God's wrath in the face of human sin (e.g., Morris).

As Richard Averbeck has demonstrated, the linguistic evidence related to the use of the verb "to atone" (כפר) in the Old Testament prioritizes a definition of atonement as "to wipe away" or "to cleanse", though not exclusively so.[23] In any case, against the backdrop of Paul's world, it is crucial that we not confuse the wrath of Yahweh with the retributive and capricious dispositions of the Greek and Roman gods, to whom sacrifices were offered in order both to placate the deities and to solicit their favor. In spite of popular views of "the Old Testament God", divine wrath in the Old Testament is not well represented by views of this kind. In fact, Old Testament scholars today continue to debate precisely how to work out the meaning of "anger" when applied to God.[24] Indeed, according to his own self-description, the God of Israel is "slow to anger and abounding in steadfast love" (e.g., Exod. 34:6; Num. 14:18). In the Old Testament, anger appears as God's response to sinful acts rather than as a description of God's general disposition toward humanity.[25]

Among the sacrifices and sacrificial offerings developed in the Old Testament, the most important for our purposes is the purification offering (חַטָּאת; e.g., Lev. 4:1–6:7; 6:24–7:10; see Leviticus 16), the focus of which is on cleansing the effect of sin, cultic impurity. This way of explaining the atoning work of sacrifice has been argued persuasively by Jacob Milgrom, though his view is susceptible to a reduction of the purification offering to a concern only with contamination of the temple. Clearly, however, this rite cannot be segregated from forgiveness of sins (e.g., Lev. 4:20, 26, 31; 16:16). Milgrom himself interprets atonement as redemption through the substitution of an animal for a human being (Leviticus 16), as well as purification of the sanctuary and, by extension, of the community of God's people (e.g., Lev. 15:31; 16:19).[26] Thus, in the rite of sacrifice, the laying of hands on the beast's head signals the importance of identification or representation – with sinners identifying themselves with the beast and the beast now representing sinners in their sin. And so the shedding of blood – with blood understood as the substance of life, sacred to God – signifies the offering of the lives of those for whom the sacrifice is made.

In short, if we were to insist that Paul's logic depends on an Old Testament notion of atoning sacrifice, it would not be clear either why this would be related to assuaging God's wrath nor in what way best to articulate the instrumentality of that atonement.

However, even this line of inquiry begs the question, What of the wrath of God in Romans 1? As Paul develops the concept in this context, wrath is the active presence of God's judgment toward "all ungodliness and wickedness" (1:18).[27] The wrath of God here is neither vindictive indignation nor the anger of divine retribution, but the divine response to human unfaithfulness. In Romans 1, wrath is not an anticipated future threat but is already present, for God is now handing people over to experience the consequences of the sin they choose (1:18, 24, 26, 28; cf. Wis. 11:15–16; 12:23). That this is so is underscored by our recognition that, in his representation of the human situation in Romans 1:18–32, Paul works with the portrait provided already in Wisdom of Solomon 13:1–15:6.[28] This is not to say that wrath for Paul is merely imminent nor that Paul's view is confined to God's wrath in the present, as Romans 2:5–10 demonstrates.[29] Nor am I identifying wrath with an impersonal set of rules of the game of the universe, as though by doing so one might segregate God from wrath. Instead, in my narrow focus here on Romans 1, I am recognizing that wrath is being worked out as divine action in the present world. From the human side, in Romans 1, ungodliness and unrighteousness are identified with a general disposition to refuse to honor God as God and to render him thanks. Sin – that is, the proclivity to act as though things created, including ourselves, were the Creator and such expressions of sin as lust, gossip, envy, deceit, same-sex relations, rebelliousness toward parents, and the rest are themselves already expressions of the wrath of God. They evidence the moral integrity of a God who takes sin seriously.

It is God's moral character that Paul is defending here, and he does so by showing the progression from (1) the human refusal to honor God, with its consequent denial of the human vocation to live in relation to God, to (2) God's giving humanity over to its own desires – giving humanity, as it were, the life it sought apart from God – and to (3) human acts of wickedness. In this economy, wicked acts do not stir up the wrath of God but are themselves already the consequences of the active presence of God's wrath. That is, sinful activity is the result of God's letting us go our own way, and this letting us go our own way constitutes God's wrath. To crib the language of Wisdom, God "torments" those who live unrighteously by allowing them their own atrocities (Wis. 12:23). In Paul's own words, the wrath of God is revealed in God's giving humanity over to their lusts, over to their degrading passions, and over to their debasement of mind (Rom. 1:18, 24, 26, 28). Our sinful acts do not invite God's wrath but prove that God's wrath is already active. What is needed, then, is not a transformation of God's disposition toward the unrighteous and the ungodly but rather a transformation on the human side of the equation.

In short, penal substitutionary atonement is implicated in a view of God that either is itself theologically problematic or at the very least lends itself easily to grim distortion. What is more, its focus on deflecting divine wrath from sinful humanity onto Jesus is logically deficient and exegetically problematic.

At Home, Especially, in the Modern West

How might one explain the ascendency of the theory of penal substitutionary atonement as a description of the saving work of Christ? My own sense is that, whatever its etiology, the popularity of this model has less to do with exegesis and historical theology, more to do with its incubation in an environment structured around individualism and mechanism.

By mechanism, I refer to the inheritance bequeathed us by René Descartes, the polymath who, during his intellectually formative years, was impressed by the hydraulic machines animating the figures of Neptune, Diana and other mythical personages in the royal gardens of St Germain, by mechanical dolls in the windows of upscale shops, and by the intricate mechanics by which tower clocks kept the time of day. "It seemed perfectly natural for one witnessing the incredible mechanization of the physical world to think that natural bodies may also possess clocklike mechanisms to propel them into motion."[30] His work *Le Monde* (1633) developed his mechanistic analysis of both inanimate and living bodies, including the human person. One of his chief interests was how the human soul, itself an unextended, immaterial substance, could activate the physical machinery of the material body. As is well known, his solution was to locate the "seat of the soul" in the pineal gland, the movement of which was capable of stimulating a system of hydraulics causing muscle movement. To the influence of Descartes we could add others, including Isaac Newton, whose mechanics emphasized cause-effect relations in a way having direct bearing on our theological concerns. In the universe propelled into being by such explanations, is it any wonder that the theological enterprise has little room for mystery and beauty? Our social world is a mechanistic one where technique reigns, so it is no surprise that we are unsatisfied with views of the atonement that do not clarify "how" in objective, cause-effect relations.

By individualism, I refer to the penetrating analysis of contemporary human identity in the West by Charles Taylor. In *Sources of the Self*, Taylor demonstrated that personal identity has come to be based on presumed affirmations of the human subject as autonomous, disengaged, self-sufficient and self-engaged.[31] In the garden of cultural individualism, what theology is cultivated? Let me mention only a few corollaries: (1) sin is understood naturally in autobiographical terms and little space is allowed for the recognition of systemic evil; (2) justice is understood similarly, in autobiographical terms, and little space is allowed for the recognition of corporate justice; (3) humans not only possess free will but also are self-autonomous. Who is to blame? Who cast the first stone? Such questions seem natural to us: results for me come from my decisions; they are nothing more than what I deserve, my reward or punishment as appropriate. In such a world, a penal justice system only makes sense, and it is no surprise that we have now before us a widespread assumption that the death of Jesus is best understood in penal categories and soteriology in forensic terms focused on the status of the individual before God.

What sort of soteriology would follow from an anthropology not so cozy with the modern era, such as the anthropology we find in Scripture? As Robert Di Vito has argued, the construction of personal identity that pervades modernity is at odds with biblical anthropology at almost every turn.[32] Speaking particularly of the Old Testament, but in terms that in broad outline would be at home similarly in the New, Di Vito emphasizes, among other things, (1) the construction of the self as deeply embedded in social relationships, so that notions of self-responsibility, autonomy and personal freedom are eclipsed by that of a moral community, (2) the assumption that a person *is* one's behavior, and (3) an emphasis on external authority, specifically on the moral competence of Yahweh alone. Within this accounting of human identity, an atonement theology focused so narrowly on the individual as moral agent would appear to be an alien intrusion.

Happily, concerns of this nature, and others besides, have been taken seriously by Kevin Vanhoozer, whose constructive proposal for explicating God's gift of Jesus' death "for us" goes a long way toward addressing the captivity of thinking about the atonement to modern categories and sensibilities. For him, the cross of Christ exceeds our attempts to explain it, and the version of the model of penal substitutionary atonement he sketches locates this theory in the pantheon of atonement theologies (without insisting that it is either the base on which the others are built or the one that rules the rest), is sensitive to inter-trinitarian relations, and is oriented toward corporate images of covenantal blessing.[33] The jury is out, though, on whether other proponents of the model of penal substitutionary atonement will enter the territory Vanhoozer has so ably opened for exploration. Hence, it is not clear to me that the proponents of penal substitutionary atonement are sufficiently critical of the cultural influences of the modern era that, at the very least, contribute to the reductionism of the saving work of Christ along mechanistic and individualistic lines. Such considerations cause me to wonder whether proponents of penal substitutionary atonement are not far more concerned with identifying the "how" of our salvation than either the Bible or the tradition has been, and it is unclear how this model is capable of addressing the corporate dimension of salvation so important to biblical faith.

Penal Substitution and Anemic Salvation

The prevailing model of the atonement, focused as it is on the individual, on a forensic judgment, and on the moment of justification, is an obstacle to a thoroughgoing soteriology oriented toward holiness of life. That is, an exaggerated focus on an objective atonement and on salvation as transaction undermines any emphasis on salvation as transformation, and it obscures the social and cosmological dimensions of salvation. If the purpose of God will be actualized in the restoration of all things, then how is this purpose served by a theory of penal substitutionary atonement? How does the model of penal substitutionary atonement carry within itself the theological resolution of racism? What becomes the soteriological motivation for engaging in the care of God's creation? Against the backdrop of texts like Colossians 1:15–20 and Ephesians 2, these are not peripheral questions.

As the New Testament has it, what happened on the cross had universal significance: for Jew and Gentile, for slave and free, for male and female. The work of Christ on the cross has as its object even the cosmos, giving rise to images of new creation (2 Cor. 5:17) and all-encompassing reconciliation (Col. 1:15–20). The atonement is not narrowly focused on the individual's relationship with God but involves persons in their relationships with the world and with others, both neighbor and enemy. The cross is about salvation as a call to reflect in day-to-day life the quality of life exhibited in Jesus' death on behalf of others.[34]

Again, if salvation is focused, as it is under the model of penal substitutionary atonement, on a transaction by which persons are declared not guilty on account of the substitutionary work of Christ to satisfy God's wrath, what generates or funds the ongoing dynamic of salvation? Is the work of salvation as transformation unrelated to the atoning work of Christ? Where does the model of penal substitutionary atonement make room for the portrait of discipleship as following Jesus on the way of the cross? Are we not told in the model of penal substitutionary atonement that the cross of Christ and the discipleship of cross-bearing are disjoined in their significance? How can this be, given their manifest inseparability in Scripture?

In short, the model of penal substitutionary atonement provides, at best, no basis for a thoroughgoing soteriology and, at worst, stands in its way.

Conclusion

Other questions and concerns might be raised,[35] but with these our four questions – or, rather, these four constellations of questions – I have sought to draw attention to the range of issues that I regard as particularly troubling to the theory of penal substitutionary atonement. These have to do with questions of logic, history and the incarnation, formulations of the doctrine of God, exegesis, the history of effects, the nature of the Christian life (including soteriology, social and environmental ethics, and interrelated concerns with the way of the cross and the doctrine of sanctification), cultural assumptions and more. In other words, as some theologians have begun to insist, the atonement cannot be articulated in a way that isolates the saving significance of Jesus' suffering and death from the whole of Jesus' ministry, from the Christian life, or from the rest of the theological enterprise.[36] These questions, I must quickly add, are not fatal to our belief in the atonement, even if they do suggest why some of us find the model of penal substitutionary atonement lacking.

That the champions of the model of penal substitutionary atonement will claim to have resolved, or to be able now to resolve, these varied questions, I have no doubt. Indeed, I imagine that these champions will find incredulous the reality that I and others remain unconvinced by attempts thus far to satisfy such questions as these, just as I and others are incredulous that these questions have not already toppled the hegemony of the theory of penal substitutionary atonement within evangelical Christianity. And so I end as I began: with a plea that we remind ourselves, often, that debates regarding the appropriateness of penal substitutionary atonement as an exposition of the saving message of the cross of Christ comprise an intramural conversation, and not one that can serve to distinguish Christian believer from non-believer or even evangelical from non-evangelical.

Notes

1. A. E. Harvey, *Jesus and the Constraints of History* (Philadelphia: Fortress, 1982), 11.

2. For example, Gustaf Aulén, *Christus Victor: An Historical Study of the Three Main Types of the Idea of the Atonement* (1931; London: SPCK, 1975); Herman-Emiel Mertens, *Not the Cross, but the Crucified: An Essay in Soteriology*, LTPM 11 (Louvain: Peeters; Grand Rapids: Eerdmans, 1992), 63–84.

3. I. Howard Marshall, "The Development of the Concept of Redemption in the New Testament," in *Jesus the Saviour: Studies in New Testament Theology* (Downers Grove, Ill.: IVP, 1990), 239–57 (250).

4. For two brief examples of constructive accounts of the atoning significance of Jesus' death (atonement as sacrifice and as illumination), see Joel B. Green, "A Kaleidoscopic View," in *The Nature of the Atonement: Four Views*, ed. James K. Beilby and Paul R. Eddy (Downers Grove, Ill.: IVP, 2006), 157–85.

5. See, however, Joseph A. Fitzmyer, "Reconciliation in Pauline Theology," in *No Famine in the Land: Studies in Honor of John L. McKenzie*, ed. James W. Flanagan and Anita Weisbrod Robinson (Missoula, Mont.: Scholars Press, 1975), 155–77.

6. Martin Kähler, *The So-Called Historical Jesus and the Historic Biblical Christ* (ET; Philadelphia: Fortress, 1964), 80n11.

7. The introduction of redaction criticism and, then, various forms of literary criticism worked to reintegrate passion accounts into their respective Gospels; see, for example, Frank J. Matera, *Passion Narratives and Gospel Theologies: Interpreting the Synoptics through Their Passion Stories*, Theological Inquiries (New York and Mahwah, N.J.: Paulist, 1986).

8. The allusion to Anselm's treatise *Cur Deus Homo* is deliberate, though this is not to say that Anselm ought to be read as a proponent of penal substitutionary atonement as this is articulated today. See, for example, Joel B. Green and Mark D. Baker, *Recovering the Scandal of the Cross* (Downers Grove, Ill.: IVP, 2000), 126–36; Darby Kathleen Ray, *Deceiving the Devil: Atonement, Abuse and Ransom* (Cleveland: Pilgrim, 1998), 8–13.

9. For example, Mark 2:20; 9:12–13; 10:38, 45; 12:1–12. See Joel B. Green, *The Death of Jesus: Tradition and Interpretation in the Passion Narrative*, WUNT 2:33 (Tübingen: Mohr, 1988), 148–54; Scot McKnight, "Jesus and His Death: Some Recent Scholarship," *CurBS* 9 (2001): 185–228 (201–3).

10. See, for example, Joel Marcus, "The Old Testament and the Death of Jesus: The Role of Scripture in the Gospel Passion Narratives," in *The*

Death of Jesus in Early Christianity, ed. John T. Carroll and Joel B. Green (Peabody, Mass.: Hendrickson, 1995), 204–33 (206–9).

11. This was ably documented in George W. E. Nickelsburg Jr., *Resurrection, Immortality and Eternal Life in Intertestamental Judaism*, HTS 26 (Cambridge, Mass.: Harvard Univ. Press, 1972).

12. Stephen J. Patterson, *Beyond the Passion: Rethinking the Death and Life of Jesus* (Minneapolis: Fortress, 2004). Patterson's skepticism regarding the historical veracity of key aspects of the gospel narratives and his discounting the potential of some atonement theologies to account for these central motifs of the narrative of Jesus' life are insignificant to his basic observations regarding the interpretation of Jesus' death "as an inevitable part of his life, and end fitting of the kind of life Jesus lived" (123).

13. Rudolf Bultmann, *Theology of the New Testament*, 2 vols. (New York: Charles Scribner, 1951–55), 2:293–94.

14. See, for example, G. N. Stanton, *Jesus of Nazareth in New Testament Teaching*, SNTSMS 27 (Cambridge: Cambridge Univ. Press, 1974).

15. Kevin J. Vanhoozer, "The Atonement in Postmodernity: Guilt, Goats and Gifts," in *The Glory of the Atonement: Biblical, Historical and Practical Perspectives; Essays in Honor of Roger Nicole*, ed. Charles E. Hill and Frank A. James III (Downers Grove, Ill.: IVP, 2004), 367–404 (376), with reference to Green and Baker, *Recovering the Scandal*, 53.

16. Green and Baker, *Recovering the Scandal*, 30.

17. John Stott, *The Cross of Christ* (Leicester: IVP, 1986), 112.

18. J. I. Packer, "Anger," in *New Dictionary of Biblical Theology*, ed. T. Desmond Alexander and Brian S. Rosner (Downers Grove, Ill.: IVP, 2000), 381–83 (382).

19. Derek Tidball, *The Message of the Cross: Wisdom Unsearchable, Love Indestructible* (Leicester: IVP, 2001), 184–99.

20. See, for example, James D. G. Dunn, "Paul's Understanding of the Death of Jesus as Sacrifice," in *Sacrifice and Redemption: Durham Essays on Theology*, ed. S. W. Sykes (Cambridge: Cambridge Univ. Press, 1991), 35–56; more broadly, Robert J. Daly, *The Origins of the Christian Doctrine of Sacrifice* (Philadelphia: Fortress, 1978), 11–35. Gordon Wenham imagines, however, that the "pleasing odor" from the sacrifice quiets "divine uneasiness" ("The Theology of Old Testament Sacrifice," in *Sacrifice in the Bible*, ed. R. T. Beckwith and M. J. Selman [Grand Rapids: Baker; Carlisle: Paternoster, 1995], 75–87 [80]). Even if this reading of נוח is sustained, however, this

idea would relate only to the burnt offerings, as opposed to the "purification" (or sin) offerings or "restitution" (or guilt) offerings that provide better analogs for the New Testament presentation of the sacrifice of Christ.

21. John Goldingay, "Your Iniquities Have Made a Separation between You and God," in *Atonement Today: A Symposium at St John's College, Nottingham*, ed. John Goldingay (London: SPCK, 1995), 39–53 (51); see further, Goldingay, "Old Testament Sacrifice and the Death of Christ," in *Atonement Today*, 3–20.

22. Bruce Baloian, "Anger," in *NIDOTTE*, 4:377–85 (384).

23. C. H. Dodd, "ἱλάσκομαι, Its Cognates, Derivatives and Synonyms in the Septuagint," *JTS* 32 (1931), 352–60; Leon Morris, *The Apostolic Preaching of the Cross*, 3rd ed. (Leicester: IVP, 1965); Richard E. Averbeck, "כפר," in *NIDOTTE*, 2:689–710.

24. See Jan Bergman and Elsie Johnson, "אָנַף," in *TDOT*, 1:348–60; Gary A. Heron, "Wrath of God (OT)," in *ABD*, 6:989–96.

25. See John Goldingay, *Old Testament Theology*, vol. 1, *Israel's Gospel* (Downers Grove, Ill.: IVP, 2003), 140.

26. Jacob Milgrom, *Leviticus*, 3 vols., AB (New York: Doubleday, 1991–2001); Milgrom, *Studies in Cultic Theology and Terminology*, SJLA 36 (Leiden: Brill, 1983). See further, B. Lang, "כפר," in *TDOT*, 7:288–303; Gary A. Anderson, "Sacrifice and Sacrificial Offerings (OT)," in *ABD*, 5:870–86.

27. See Stephen H. Travis, "Christ as Bearer of Divine Judgment in Paul's Thought about the Atonement," in *Jesus of Nazareth, Lord and Christ: Essays on the Historical Jesus and New Testament Christology*, ed. Joel B. Green and Max Turner (Grand Rapids: Eerdmans; Carlisle: Paternoster, 1994), 332–45.

28. On Paul's engagement with this Jewish text, see Francis Watson, *Paul and the Hermeneutics of Faith* (London: T & T Clark, 2004), 405–8.

29. In what sense, then, can Paul speak of the "wrath to come" (cf. 1 Thess. 1:9–10)? This is the climactic, end-time scene of judgment when those who prefer to worship idols rather than the living God receive from God the fruits of their misplaced hopes and commitments.

30. Stanley Finger, *Minds behind the Brains: A History of the Pioneers and Their Discoveries* (Oxford: Oxford Univ. Press, 2000), 74.

31. Charles Taylor, *Sources of the Self: The Making of Modern Identity* (Cambridge, Mass.: Harvard Univ. Press, 1989).

32. Robert A. Di Vito, "Old Testament Anthropology and the Construction of Personal Identity," *CBQ* 61 (1999): 217–38; see also Klaus Berger, *Identity and Experience in the New Testament* (Minneapolis: Fortress, 2003).

33. Vanhoozer, "Atonement in Modernity."

34. Cf. Michael J. Gorman, *Cruciformity: Paul's Narrative Spirituality of the Cross* (Grand Rapids: Eerdmans, 2001).

35. For examples of catalogs old and new, see Frances Young, *Sacrifice and the Death of Christ* (London: SCM, 1975), 85–100; Patricia A. Williams, *Doing without Adam and Eve: Sociobiology and Original Sin*, Theology and the Sciences (Minneapolis: Fortress, 2001), 180–98.

36. See, for example, Kathryn Tanner, "Incarnation, Cross and Sacrifice: A Feminist-Inspired Reappraisal," *Anglican Theological Review* 86 (2004); Leanne van Dyk, "The Three Offices of Christ: The *Munus Triplex* as Expansive Resources in Atonement," *Catalyst* 25, no. 2 (1999): 6–8; Robert Sherman, *King, Priest and Prophet: A Trinitarian Theology of Atonement* (London: T & T Clark, 2004).

chapter ten

penal substitution

a response to recent criticisms

garry williams

Contemporary Criticisms of Penal Substitutionary Atonement

Steve Chalke has said that he has felt "in the dock" during the debate concerning penal substitution provoked by his book *The Lost Message of Jesus*. This is understandable, but we need to remember that the controversy has actually arisen because the doctrine of penal substitutionary atonement has been put in the dock. The initiating accusation here is an accusation against the doctrine of penal substitution and, therefore, against those who hold to it. They – we – are the ones in the dock. There is a move here to exclude and lay to rest a view of the atonement. This is ironic, since opponents of penal substitution often call for what Chalke has described as a "multicoloured rather than monochrome" view of the cross, but it is they who reduce the historical diversity by rejecting one major model.[1]

The criticisms of penal substitutionary atonement which have arisen even just within this recent debate are legion, and in works on the subject, they often come like machine gun fire. I focus here on four main charges, reducible to the three categories of God, the individual and doctrinal isolationism. The first charge is that penal substitution entails a mistaken doctrine of God, principally in that it ascribes retributive justice to him. The second, also a charge relating to the doctrine of God, is that penal substitution conflicts with the doctrine of the Trinity by severing the Father from the Son. The third is that penal substitution grows out of modern Western individualism with its conception of "autobiographical justice".[2] The fourth is that penal substitution is guilty of doctrinal isolationism, an inability to look beyond itself. This charge consists of a cluster of three subcriticisms with a common core. The claim is that penal substitution cannot embrace three vital aspects of the Christian faith. It has no place for the life of Jesus; it cannot account for the cosmic scope of the work of Christ on the cross; and it undermines the need for moral renewal in the life of the believer subsequent to conversion. In its stronger form, this last subcriticism develops into the charge that penal substitution not only cannot support sanctification but also mandates wrong, abusive behaviour.

In this essay, I wish to begin to address these four criticisms, examining whether they make sense in themselves, whether they apply to the doctrine of penal substitutionary atonement as it has been understood in the history of the church, and whether they take due measure of the biblical data regarding God's justice and his action in the atoning work of the Lord Jesus Christ.[3]

God: Divine Retribution
Faustus Socinus, Steve Chalke and Jesus' Example

A key argument used by opponents of penal substitution is that retributive punishment is ruled out by Jesus' own teaching on how we should relate to one another. A form of this argument was used as far back as Faustus Socinus in 1578, but it has been used more recently by Steve Chalke.[4] The argument states that there must be a fundamental continuity between the way God acts and the way he commands us to act. Chalke judges that this kind of continuity is disrupted by penal substitutionary atonement because it depicts a God who himself exacts punishment, yet at the same time commands his people not to do so. This, he fears, turns God into a hypocrite: "If the cross has anything to do with penal substitution, then Jesus' teaching becomes a divine case of 'do as I say, not as I do.' I, for one, believe that God practices what he preaches!"[5] In short, Jesus tells us to turn the other cheek, so how could God punish in a way that exacts satisfaction for sin? If God denies us retribution, he must eschew it himself.

For many, the background here is found in the work of Walter Wink.[6] He argues that the pattern of violence on earth reflects the pattern of violence which is believed to occur in heaven. He cites the Babylonian *Enuma Elish* myth as an ancient instance of the view that violence is "the central dynamic of existence" which "possesses ontological priority over good".[7] In this ancient "myth of redemptive violence", it is the spiral of heavenly violence which triggers the creation itself and then continues through history: "Heavenly events are mirrored by earthly events, and what happens above happens below."[8] As in heaven, so on earth. Applying this model to penal substitutionary atonement suggests that divine retribution must be mirrored by human retribution, and therefore that the doctrine either fails to reckon with the mirroring of heaven on earth when it resists this conclusion, or else it contradicts the teaching of Jesus.

In reply to this Socinian argument, there is a clear counter case which implies a quite different construal of the relationship between divine and human justice. The apostle Paul distinguishes sharply the different ways that justice should operate between human beings on the one hand, and between God and creation on the other. At the end of Romans 12, he follows Jesus in teaching that we must not take revenge. This would be the perfect opportunity to point out that we must not because God does not, but in a striking move, Paul does the opposite. He explains that individuals must not take revenge precisely because God *is* going to do so: "Beloved, never avenge yourselves, but leave it to the wrath of God; for it is written, 'Vengeance is mine, I will repay, says the Lord'" (12:19, quoting Deut. 32:35). From here, Paul moves to argue in 13:1–7 that God has given a limited remit to the governing authorities to implement this final justice in the present time by the power of the sword. Thus, Paul denies vengeance in the sphere of relationships between individual people and at the same time ascribes it to God, who shares it in limited part with the ruling authorities. Where Chalke infers that God would never do what he tells us not to do, Paul argues exactly the opposite. God tells us not to do what he does precisely because he does it. God says, "Do as I say, not as I do," and justly so, since he is God and we are not.

Stephen Travis and Retribution

The Definition of Retribution

It is argued, most notably by Stephen Travis in *Christ and the Judgment of God*, that retribution has little place in the biblical doctrine of punishment as a whole. This argument has been influential, and Joel Green draws on Travis's work. Travis writes that "the judgment of God is to be seen not primarily in terms of retribution, whereby people are 'paid back' according to their deeds, but in terms of relationship or non-relationship to Christ."[9] Everything in

Travis's work rests on the definition of the nature of retribution itself. This should not surprise us, since it is obvious that whether we find retribution in Scripture depends on how we first define it. At the start of his book, Travis defines retribution as having five key characteristics. His list is drawn from W. H. Moberly's work *The Ethics of Punishment*, in which it is given as an expansion of Hugo Grotius's definition in *De Iure Belli ac Pacis*. Punishment, Grotius states, is "the infliction of an ill suffered for an ill done". Travis summarizes Moberly thus:

1. What is inflicted is an *ill* – something unpleasant.
2. It is a *sequel* to some act which has gone before and is disapproved by authority.
3. There is some *correspondence* between the punishment and the deed which has evoked it.
4. The punishment is *inflicted from outside*, by someone's voluntary act.
5. The punishment is inflicted on the *criminal*, in virtue of his offence.[10]

The emphasis on act or deed here is vital to Travis's project. He explains: "We may pose the question whether there is any real place for retribution (in the sense defined above) in the context of personal relationships. People are rewarded or punished not because of their character, but because of some specific overt act which they have done. Retribution thus operates on a less than fully personal level, and it deals with externals."[11]

Retribution Flowing out of a Deed

First, I wish to take exception to point 4, the claim that the punishment being inflicted from the outside is integral to retribution. It is clear that a punishment can in a strong sense flow out of a deed and still be retributive. In a human system of justice, we cannot redesign the natural order so that our acts have internal consequences. But with God the Creator, it is quite possible for a punishment to be intrinsic, to follow from an act, and yet still to be retributive in character. Such an intrinsic result might still have all of the other characteristics of punishment: it might be an ill, following an act, corresponding to it, being imposed on the criminal. The kind of process described in the Proverbs in which someone digs a hole and falls into it can, when the process is created and sustained by God, still be understood as retributive.

There is something very strange going on here in Travis's use of his sources. The difficulty is that Moberly himself agrees with my reading at this point and explicitly qualifies his fourth point in a way that distances his position from that taken later by Travis. When Moberly states the fourth element, he expresses it like this: "(4) The punishment is *inflicted*. It is imposed by somebody's voluntary act." So far Travis is reading him accurately. But then Moberly continues, "Disagreeable consequences which follow wrongdoing by natural causation, as disease or poverty sometimes follow, are not 'punishment' unless they are supposed to be deliberately brought about by some superhuman personal agency."[12] In other words, Moberly, in his very definition, states that point 4, externality, would not be required to find retribution in the actions of a superhuman being like God. According to Moberly, if a punishment is internal rather than external, then it may, if it comes from God, still be retributive.

As we realize this, a crack shatters out through much of the exegesis in *Christ and the Judgment of God*, because the use of externality to deny retribution is pervasive. Take this comment for example: "The Jesus of the synoptic gospels sometimes uses retributive words, and some of these judgment-sayings are expressed in talionic *form*. But the *content* of such sayings generally undermines a strictly retributive interpretation."[13] How so? Because, to take the example of the treasure-in-heaven passage, "Jesus pictures people's destinies as the end-result of their desires rather than as a recompense imposed from outside."[14] According to Moberly's definition, this kind of connection between act and consequence, if established by God, may still be understood as a retributive process.[15] The interposition of a mediating natural means between God and the sinner which brings about the punishment does not remove the retributive role of God; it simply shifts the moment of its imposition. Instead of being imposed at the moment of punishment, it is set up at creation. Or rather, because God sustains the creation, it is still imposed by God as it happens. In him we live and move and have our being, and that includes the penal processes of creation.

We should also note in passing that Travis's claim that divine punishment always flows out of the act by itself will not account for a great deal of the biblical evidence, most notably events such as the plagues on Egypt and the last judgment.[16] The plagues involved natural phenomena, but in terms of their occasion and intensity did not just happen according to the normal operation of biological processes. The era of the exodus was not just a good time for frogs, gnats, flies and locusts, let alone for the death of firstborn children. Even more clearly, on the last day, Jesus Christ will intervene in history as judge. He will stop the progress of world history, raise the dead and pronounce judgment on them. Left to itself, this would not happen to the world. Much punishment in Scripture is irrefragably extrinsic.

Retribution as Responsive to Character as Well as Acts

Second, Travis is wrong when he claims that on a retributive understanding of punishment "people are rewarded or punished not because of their character, but because of some specific overt act which they have done." The biblical accounts of retribution make clear that this is a false antithesis, since according to Scripture, punishment is imposed both for acts and the character behind them, the acts serving as evidence of the character. For example, in Matthew 25:31–46, we find that on the day of judgment Jesus will reward those who have shown kindness to others. He will judge them on the basis of their acts as public evidence, but these acts will be taken as an indication of the individual's disposition toward Christ himself. The acts reveal the disposition, so that the deed of giving a drink serves as evidence of a caring attitude to Jesus himself. Here we are dealing with the theological link between the tree and its fruit (cf. Matt. 7:16–20). To hold that God is interested in the disposition behind the deed does not mean that he cannot therefore punish retributively. There is nothing to prevent God's retributively punishing a person for his disposition as well as his acts, using the acts as evidence for the disposition.

Retribution as Relational Punishment

Third, it is clear in Scripture that when God punishes retributively, he punishes relationally. Many critics of penal substitution view retributive punishment as non-relational and impersonal. For example, consider the contrast drawn by Travis: "the judgment of God is to be seen not primarily in terms of retribution ... but in terms of relationship or non-relationship to Christ." According to Travis, retribution and relationship are alternatives; retribution cannot be relational. There is, however, no reason why non-relationship to Christ should not actually be a retributive punishment. Travis posits an antithesis where none need be found.

Retribution entails two elements, as Grotius made clear in the work upon which Moberly draws. First, it entails "an ill suffered *for* an ill done" – that is, an ill which is responsive to an ill. Second, it involves "an *ill suffered* for an ill done" – that is, the infliction of some kind of proportioned pain. So long as the non-relationship with Christ is the deserved result of character or conduct, and so long as it involves some kind of pain (which separation from Christ most surely does), then it is retributive *and* relational. The category of exclusion from a loving relationship with Christ *is* a relational category. The sinner stands in a relationship of hostile confrontation with Christ. For these reasons, we have no grounds for holding that retribution is incompatible with the justice that God exemplifies or demands in Scripture.

God: The Doctrine of the Trinity

Joel Green and Mark Baker argue that "any atonement theology that assumes, against Paul, that in the cross God did something 'to' Jesus is ... an affront to the Christian doctrine of the triune God."[17] Following Stephen Sykes, they explain that the problem is with the idea of Jesus as the object of the Father's action: "The New Testament portrays Golgotha along two story lines – one with God as subject, the other with Jesus as subject. It will not do, therefore, to characterize the atonement as God's punishment falling on Christ (i.e., God as subject, Christ as object) or as Christ's appeasement or persuasion of God (Christ as subject, God as object)."[18] Or again, specifically on Paul: "Paul does not treat God as the subject and Jesus as the object of the cross."[19] If penal substitution depicted the cross as simply "God as subject, Christ as object," as Green and Baker characterize it, then it would indeed be problematic. But it does not, and no thoughtful proponent of penal substitution has ever portrayed it in this fashion. Witness John Stott, for example: "We must never make Christ the object of God's punishment or God the object of Christ's persuasion, for both God and Christ were subjects not objects, taking the initiative together to save sinners."[20]

The reason that no conscientious advocate of penal substitution thinks of the Son simply as the object of the Father's action is that the doctrine has been formed within a conscious, mature doctrine of the Trinity. Penal substitution relies on a careful grounding in Augustine's principle that since the Father, the Son and the Holy Spirit are inseparable, so they work inseparably.[21] The principle is plainly stated and applied to the work of Christ by Reformed theologians. John Owen, for example, in *The Death of Death in the Death of Christ*, states it as follows: "The agent [i.e., the subject] in, and chief author of, this great work of our redemption is the whole blessed Trinity; for all the works which outwardly are of the Deity are undivided and belong equally to each person, their distinct manner of subsistence and order being observed."[22] The Reformed conception of the covenant of redemption between the persons of the Trinity in eternity shows how Christ is in every action of God *ad extra* the subject. The persons of the Trinity covenant with each other in eternity to act together in all of their purposes.[23]

Scripture also plainly depicts Christ as the subject in going to the cross. Jesus insisted, "I lay down my life, that I may take it again. No one takes it from me, but I lay it down of my own accord" (John 10:17–18), and Paul wrote that Jesus "gave himself for me" (Gal. 2:20). So in agreement with Green and Baker, we must reject the ludicrous railroad illustration where the father switches the points to rescue his passengers and in so doing kills his wandering son.[24] The son has no idea what is going on and should not have been standing around on a railway track in the first place. Taken with its full implications, this illustration is a travesty of penal substitution. Even if such implications are excluded and the illustration is intended solely to demonstrate the Father's generosity in giving his Son instead of others, the picture is still misleading. But it is not enough for critics of penal substitution to engage with such caricatures of the doctrine; they have a responsibility to distinguish more carefully the crude from the sophisticated and to deal with it at its best.

Thus, the Lord Jesus Christ was the subject of the atonement. But can he also be the object of the Father's act? Clearly, as Stott explains, he cannot be the object in an unqualified sense, because such an object does not will what happens to him. But might he not be the *willing* object? Might he not be the subject purposing what happens to him as the object? It should be obvious that we cannot on the basis of trinitarian theology say that the Son can *never* be the willing object of the Father's activity. Witness the description of the multiple activities where the Father is the subject and the Son the object in Scripture: "the Father loves the Son" (John 3:35); the Father "sent the Son into the world" (John 3:17); the Father "has granted the Son also to have life in himself" (John 5:26); the Father set forth the Son as a ἱλαστήριον (Rom. 3:25). No one can deny that the Father acts on the Son, provided we are clear that the Son also wills the action.

More likely then, the problem is thought to be specifically with the Father's activity causing the Son to suffer. The difficulty here is that there is plain biblical testimony to the Father's acting on the Son at the cross, in the suffering of the cross, and specifically in the penal suffering of the cross. Isaiah 53 speaks of the suffering of the "servant of the Lord", which is understood in the New Testament as a description of the suffering of Christ (e.g., 1 Peter 2:21–24). Verse 6 says that "the LORD has laid on him the iniquity of us all," and verse 10 that "it was the will of the LORD to crush him with pain." In Mark 14:27 and Matthew 26:31, Jesus quotes Zechariah 13:7: "You will all become deserters; for it is written, 'I will strike the shepherd, and the sheep will be scattered.' But after I am raised up, I will go before you to Galilee." Interestingly, the Hebrew and the LXX have a second-person imperative here, addressed to Yahweh's sword: "Awake, O sword … Strike." But in the Gospels, this is changed to the first-person future, πατάξω, thus actually emphasising the personal involvement of Yahweh rather than the more impersonal image of the sword: "I will strike."[25] Joel Marcus notes this in a book edited by Green himself. He explains that in the Gospels, "divine responsibility for the attack on the shepherd is made explicit" in what he describes as a "forthright acknowledgement of the divine role in the wounding of the shepherd".[26] Here, then, are two statements that the Father purposes the suffering of the cross, indeed that he wills the crushing and striking of the Son, who also wills the same acts.

It is of further significance that in the context of Isaiah 52–53, the suffering in question is specifically penal. This emerges at the end of chapter 53 with the use of two expressions: "and he shall bear their iniquities" (הוּא יִסְבֹּל וַעֲוֺנֹתָם, v. 11) and "yet he bore the sin of many" (וְהוּא חֵטְא־רַבִּים נָשָׂא, v. 12). The verb-noun combinations in these phrases (and the reversed pairings of סָבַל with חֵטְא, and נָשָׂא with עָוֹן are used widely in the Old Testament to describe bearing sin, guilt and punishment (e.g., *inter alia* Gen. 4:13; Lev. 5:17; Num. 5:31; 14:34; Lam. 5:7). Here, in Isaiah 53, it is evident from the connection with sin and the suffering of the Servant that they have a penal connotation. Thus we find in verses 6 and 10 statements that the Lord willed the suffering of the Servant in a context where that suffering is defined as being penal, and indeed atoning (v. 5). Likewise, in the New Testament, we read that the Father "condemned sin in the flesh" (Rom. 8:3) of his Son. There is, therefore, biblical testimony to the action of the Father toward the Son, specifically in laying iniquity on him and condemning it in him. To state what ought to be obvious: he punished the sin that had been transferred to Christ, not Christ regarded in and of himself, with whom in this very act he was well pleased.

We must also note that the reverse is the case with the persons of the Trinity. Just as the Son cannot be the object in an unqualified sense, but he can be the subject and the *willing* object, so the Father cannot be the object in an unqualified sense, but he can be the subject and the willing object. This emerges most clearly in the intercessory work of the Son and the Spirit. The Son intercedes with the Father for us (Rom. 8:34). So too the Holy Spirit intercedes for us (Rom. 8:26). The Father is the willing subject and object of the intercessory work of the Son and the Spirit. Furthermore, if we deny that the persons of the Trinity can be at once the willing subject and object of one another's actions, then we must deny not only penal substitution but also the love of each person for the others and the sending of the Son, who comes willingly. Ultimately, the logical implication of the denial that one person of the Trinity can act on another is the denial of the distinction between them – namely, modalism.

The Individual

Joel Green and Mark Baker assert that penal substitution coheres "fully with the emphasis on autonomous individualism characteristic of so much of the modern middle class in the West",[27] This is a very strange line of criticism of penal substitution, since penal substitution itself relies on a denial of individualism. No proponent of penal substitution has ever conceived of it as the transfer of punishment between two wholly unrelated persons. Indeed, the more individualistic penal substitution becomes, the less tenable it is, since it holds precisely that the guilty individual is not punished for his or her sins as an individual. Rather, corporate categories are powerfully at work in the historic doctrine of penal substitution.

The corporate-covenantal context of penal substitution is clearest in the seventeenth century, the period when it reached its zenith in response to the Socinian critique. John Owen emphasises the corporate Christ as the ground for substitutionary punishment:

> He [God] might punish the elect either in their own persons, or in their surety standing in their room and stead; and when he is punished, they also are punished: for in this point of view the federal head and those represented by him are not considered as distinct, but as one; for although they are not one in respect of personal unity, they are, however, one, – that is, one body in mystical union, yea, *one mystical Christ*; – namely, the surety is the head, those represented by him the members; and when the head is punished, the members also are punished.[28]

This account of penal substitution is far from being individualistic. Rather, it is mystical, stressing the spiritual bond between the believer and Christ.

It is also notable that there are patristic examples of the consciously reflective use of union with Christ. For example, Eusebius of Caesarea introduces the theme of union with Christ to explain the justice of penal substitution:

> And how can He make our sins His own, and be said to bear our iniquities, except by our being regarded as His body, according to the apostle, who says: "Now ye are the body of Christ, and severally members?" And by the rule that "if one member suffer all the members suffer with it," so when the many members suffer and sin, He too by the laws of sympathy (since the Word of God was pleased to take the form of a slave and to be knit into the common tabernacle of us all) takes into Himself the labours of the suffering members, and makes our sicknesses His, and suffers all our woes and labours by the laws of love. And the Lamb of God not only did this, but was chastised on our behalf (περὶ ὑμῶν κολασθείς), and suffered a penalty (τιμωρίαν ὑποσχών) He did not owe, but which we owed because of the multitude of our sins; and so He became the cause of the forgiveness of our sins, because He received death for us, and transferred to Himself the scourging, the insults, and the dishonour, which were due to us, and drew down on Himself the apportioned curse, being made a curse for us. And what is that but the price of our souls? And so the oracle says in our person: "By his stripes we were healed," and "The Lord delivered him for our sins," with the result that uniting Himself to us and us to Himself, and appropriating our sufferings, He can say, "I said, Lord, have mercy on me, heal my soul, for I have sinned against thee."[29]

Hence we find even in the early church a thoroughly theological account of the unique justice of penal substitutionary atonement that repudiates the individualism with which proponents of the doctrine are erroneously charged. It is certainly not the case that penal substitution is, as Chalke says, "not even as old as the pews in many of our church buildings".[30]

There is an irony here. It is in fact the critics of penal substitution who have embraced individualism, not its proponents. Here is the view, for example, of the Church of England's 1995 Doctrine Commission report *The Mystery of Salvation*: "in the moral sphere each person must be responsible for their own obligations. Moral responsibility is ultimately incommunicable."[31] Penal substitution is denied in this report because the authors endorse this species of individualism. If, as Green and Baker argue, we are heading into a postmodern culture which holds to "a communal accounting of human nature", then contrary to their expectation, penal substitution has a bright future and will preach well.[32]

Doctrinal Isolationism
Penal Substitution and the Life of Jesus

The first criticism here is that penal substitution cannot make sense of the life of Jesus. If Jesus needed to die this death, why did he need to live this life? It may be true that the link between penal substitutionary atonement and the life and ministry of Jesus has not always been made sufficiently clear, but it certainly can be made, and needs to be made. One important example will suffice to illustrate how the connection can be established. Recent New Testament scholarship, for instance the work of N. T. Wright, has emphasised how Jesus is depicted in the Gospels as the one in whom the destiny of Israel is fulfilled. Jesus, the representative Messiah of Israel, is the New Israel. As such, like Israel, he is tempted in the wilderness. Yet unlike Israel, he stands firm in the face of temptation. In significant senses, Israel in the first century remains in exile. Jesus is the one who, as the representative of Israel, is exiled on the cross and in his resurrection returns from exile. He thus renews Israel and opens the way for the blessing to come to the nations. As Wright has shown, this theme explains much of the teaching and many of the symbolic actions of Jesus.[33] Here, then, is a dominant aspect of the life of Jesus. Yet here too we have, rooted in the life of Jesus, the pattern of penal substitutionary atonement. Jesus is Israel, and he is exiled. Exile is the punishment for Israel's disobedience, and Jesus takes it on himself as the New Israel. Having borne the penalty for sin, he then rises to life and brings forgiveness. From this historical basis, penal substitution explains how the curse borne by Jesus was not just the curse of the Jews but the curse of all those under bondage. And so the doctrine of the atonement is very clearly tied to the life of Jesus as the New Israel.

Penal Substitution, Cosmic Renewal and the Resurrection

Second, it is asserted that penal substitution cannot make sense of the cosmic scope of the work of Christ on the cross. Green and Baker write, "A gospel that allows me to think of my relationship with God apart from the larger human family and the whole cosmos created by God – can it be said that this gospel is any gospel at all?"[34] Related to this, we find the charge that penal substitution cannot cohere with an emphasis on the resurrection: "because of the singular focus on penal satisfaction, Jesus' resurrection is not really necessary according to this model."[35] Let it be said that we must affirm the importance of an individual's personal relationship with God: every individual's greatest need is reconciliation with God. But clearly the merely personal is inadequate. Penal substitution actually explains very well the cosmic effect of the cross and in so doing demonstrates the centrality of the resurrection.

The narrative of Genesis 2–3 shows that the fall disordered the whole creation, with the serpent seeking to rule Eve, Eve seeking to rule Adam, and Adam seeking to rule God. The whole resulting complex of woe was the death threatened in Genesis 2:17. The serpent said that man would not die, but he was wrong. Though he did not die bodily at once, he died spiritually. To put the entire creation right, to reverse the effects of sin, to reorder all of the different relationships, something had to be done with that curse of spiritual death. Penal substitution teaches that on the cross, the Lord Jesus Christ exhausted the disordering curse in our place. It is for this reason that there can be resurrection and new creation, because the obstacle to it has been removed. Penal substitution is therefore the prerequisite for a strong doctrine of the resurrection as the beginning of the new creation, not a detractor from it. If the penalty has not been borne by Christ, then the creation is still under the curse, still disrupted, and incapable of being renewed.

Penal Substitution and the Moral Renewal of the Believer

Third, it is alleged that penal substitution provides no basis for moral renewal in the life of the believer subsequent to conversion. Here we need to remember the link in Paul's theology between the definitive death of the believer in Christ and the ongoing death to sin of the believer day by day. This is particularly clear in Romans 6, where Paul argues that since we have been baptised into the death of Christ (v. 3) and have died with him (v. 5), we must consider ourselves dead to sin (v. 11). This idea of being united to Christ in his death is integral to penal substitution. Union with Christ explains the justice of the transfer of sin to Christ: we are "one body in mystical union, yea, *one mystical Christ*", as Owen put it. If we have died with him as he died, as he bore our penalty for us, so we must reckon ourselves dead to sin. The foundational doctrine of union with Christ forges an indissoluble link between penal substitution and personal sanctification.

Penal Substitution and Abuse

Finally, what about the dark side of this criticism, the accusation that penal substitution is tantamount to child abuse, a charge leveled by some feminist theologians and taken up by Steve Chalke?[36] The claim appears to be that the infliction of pain on a child by a parent is unjust and that penal substitution mandates such infliction. There is an immediate problem here with the criticism; namely that when the Lord Jesus Christ died, he was a child in the sense that he was a son, but not in the sense that he was a minor. As an adult, Jesus had a mature will and could choose whether to cooperate with his Father. So we are in fact looking at a father and an adult son who will together for the father to inflict suffering on the son, as we have seen in our trinitarian exposition.

But there is a major problem here for the critics of penal substitution. While they have taken up and used the feminist critique of the cross as a critique of penal substitution, that criticism originated as a critique not of penal substitution but of the Christian doctrine of redemption generally. It attacks the general idea that the Father willed the *suffering* of the Son, not the specific idea that he willed the penal substitutionary suffering of the Son. Here is the criticism, as found in the work of Joanne Carlson Brown and Rebecca Parker: "The central image of Christ on the cross as the savior of the world communicates the message that suffering is redemptive.... The message is complicated further by the theology that says Christ suffered in obedience to his Father's will. Divine child abuse is paraded as salvific and the child who suffers 'without even raising a voice' is lauded as the hope of the world."[37] Furthermore, it is evident that Brown and Parker attack not just the idea that Jesus was a passive sufferer but even the idea that he was the active subject of the cross, an idea Green and Baker endorse. Brown and Parker argue that if Jesus was active in accepting his suffering, then we have a model of the victim of suffering being responsible for it, and that such a model would mandate blaming victims. They make this move when they criticise Jürgen Moltman's statement that Jesus suffered actively: "Jesus is responsible for his death on the cross, just as a woman who walks alone at night on a deserted street is to blame when she is raped."[38]

For many feminists, their criticism results in the rejection of Christianity because the religion undeniably involves the idea that God purposed the sufferings of Christ. Others try to rescue a reinvented theology, but the effort is futile. In the end, if purposed redemptive suffering is regarded as unacceptable, Christianity has to go. The reason is that the child abuse problem, as understood by these feminist theologians, remains with any model of the atonement that maintains divine sovereignty, even in a limited form. Unless we remove the suffering of the Son from the realm of events over which God rules, then God wills it. A similar point is made by Hans Boersma: "Only by radically limiting Christ's redemptive role to his life (so that his life becomes an example to us) or by absolutely dissociating God from any role in the cross (turning the crucifixion into a solely human act) can we somehow avoid dealing with the difficulty of divine violence."[39] Hence there is a trajectory from unease with penal substitution to a denial of the sovereign rule of God over the cross and, thence, we may presume, the world. In the more frank writers, this trajectory emerges clearly. J. Denny Weaver, for example, in arguing for a non-violent view of the atonement which he terms "narrative Christus Victor," sees that to succeed, he must remove the cross from the plan and purpose of God. He explains that Jesus was not sent with the intention that he should die, that his death was not the will of God, and that it was neither required nor desired by God: "In narrative Christus Victor, Jesus' mission is certainly not about tricking the devil. Neither did the Father send him for the specific purpose of dying, nor was his mission about death.... And since Jesus' mission was to make the reign of God visible, his death was not the will of God as it would be if it is a debt payment owed to God. In narrative Christus Victor, the death of Jesus is clearly the responsibility of the forces of evil, and it is not needed by or aimed at God."[40] Yet in terms of the metaphysics of the divine relationship with creation, even this view is unsustainable. So long as God sustains the world in which the Son suffers, then in a strong sense, he wills the suffering of the Son. If he does not stop history as the first blow is about to be struck, then he wills that the Son suffers. There is something that prevents him intervening to rescue his beloved Son, some purpose he intends to achieve through the suffering, and therefore a strong sense in which even such a diminished god as Weaver's wills the suffering. If someone else had wrested from God his work in sustaining the world, if we lived and moved and had our being elsewhere, then perhaps we could say that God did not will the suffering of the Son. But if purposed redemptive suffering is problematic, then on any view where God maintains some kind of control of his creation, even in a limited fashion at arm's length, the feminist criticism finds its target. And that target is not just penal substitution.

We therefore need to ask about the criticism itself. Is it valid? It is evidently not so with regard to penal substitutionary atonement. According to penal substitution, the cross has the character not simply of suffering but of necessary penal suffering for a good end. It is in this sense violent, but not reducible to the single category of violence. The cross was violent, but there was more to it than merely an act of violence. We can understand this if we consider scenarios in which a father and his adult son together purpose that the son should suffer. Imagine, for example, the father who directs teams of Médecins Sans Frontières, sending his son into an area where he and the son know that the son may suffer greatly. The father wills to send the son, and the son wills to go. There is no injustice here, because the purpose is good and both parties are willing. The same applies in the case of penal substitution.

In fact, the feminist criticism really only applies when we deny penal substitution, because it is then that we are in danger of denying the necessity of the suffering of the Son. According to penal substitution, the necessity of punishment arises from God's own nature and his divine ‌‌‌‌‌. He is bound only by who he is, by faithfulness to himself.[41] On the other hand, if we opt for some kind of voluntarist account wherein the suffering of the Son is not a necessity arising from divine justice, then we are left with the feminists' question at its most acute point. If God can freely remit sins, we must ask, why did the Father send the Son purposing his death, as Acts 2:23 says? The more deeply we understand the Trinity, the love of the Father for the Son, the more we will ask why a loving Father would lay the burden of suffering on his eternally beloved Son. Penal substitution preserves a necessity, which alone explains why this needed to happen as part of God's saving plan. Remove the necessity, deny penal substitution, and then the suffering of the Son is unjustifiable. The feminists' criticism attains its full force, because the Father wills the suffering of the Son for no necessary reason.

Christus Victor, for example, taken by itself without penal substitution, does not explain why Christ needed to suffer like this. Deny penal substitution and *Christus Victor* is hamstrung. Hence it is that in Colossians 2:13–15, the victory over the rulers and authorities is accomplished by forensic means, by the cancellation of the legal bond (χειρόγραφον; 2:14). Victory is exegeted by Paul in legal terms. Penal substitution is central because of its explanatory power with regard to the justice of the other models of the atonement. Note that such a claim affirms rather than denies the existence of other models, but it also affirms the centrality of penal substitutionary atonement to them. Without penal substitution, the feminists who reject Christianity are right that the Father has no sufficient reason to inflict suffering on the Son. A cross without penal substitution therefore would indeed mandate the unjustified infliction of suffering on children, because it would have no basis in justice.

Conclusion

It is no exaggeration to say that proponents of penal substitution are currently charged with advocating a biblically unfounded, systematically misleading and pastorally lethal doctrine. If the attack is simply on a caricature of the doctrine, all is well and good. Then the way forward is simple: the critics need to say that they do believe in penal substitution itself and just not in warped forms of it. But if the accusation is indeed an accusation against penal substitution itself, as it surely is, then I fear that we cannot simply carry on as we are. I am mindful both of the injunctions of the Lord Jesus Christ to seek peace, and of the ways in which he and his apostles make clear that there are issues over which division is necessary. Does not the present debate over penal substitutionary atonement fall into this category of issues that require separation? I find it impossible to agree with those who maintain that the debate is just an intramural one which can be conducted within the evangelical family. It is hard to maintain this when it has been acknowledged by all parties that we are arguing about who God is, about the creedal doctrine of the Trinity, about the consequences of sin, about how we are saved, and about views which are held to encourage the abuse of women and children. So long as these issues *are* the issues, and I believe that they have been rightly identified, then I cannot see how those who disagree can remain allied without placing unity above truths which are undeniably central to the Christian faith.

Notes

1. Steve Chalke, "Cross Purposes," *Christianity*, September 2004, 44–48 (44).

2. Joel B. Green and Mark D. Baker, *Recovering the Scandal of the Cross: Atonement in New Testament and Contemporary Contexts* (Downers Grove, Ill.: IVP, 2000), 29.

3. I am very grateful to Steve Jeffery and Tom Watts for their meticulous technical contributions to the process of revising this piece for publication.

4. Faustus Socinus, *De Iesu Christo Servatore* 3.2, in *Opera Omnia*, vols. 1–2 of Bibliotheca Fratrum Polonorum Quos Unitarios Vocant, 8 vols (Irenopoli: post-1656), 2:115–246. "As we saw elsewhere, Paul likewise instructs us to be imitators of God: just as he forgave our sins through Christ, so we should forgive each other. But if God so forgave our sins through Christ that he yet demanded the punishments of them from Christ himself, what prevents us, on the basis of Paul's command, as imitators of God, from seeking satisfaction for ourselves for the offences of our neighbour not from the man himself, but from anyone else, as we were just saying?" (my trans.).

5. Chalke, "Cross Purposes," 47.

6. For example, in the recent debates, Stuart Murray Williams has cited Wink in a number of his oral critiques of penal substitutionary atonement.

7. Walter Wink, *Engaging the Powers: Discernment and Resistance in a World of Domination* (Minneapolis: Fortress, 1992), 14.

8. Ibid., 13, 15.

9. Stephen H. Travis, preface to *Christ and the Judgment of God: Divine Retribution in the New Testament* (Basingstoke: Marshall Pickering, 1986).

10. Ibid., 3 (italics original), summarizing W. H. Moberly, *The Ethics of Punishment* (London: Faber and Faber, 1968), 35–36.

11. Ibid., 5.

12. Moberly, *Ethics of Punishment*, 35–36.

13. Travis, *Christ and the Judgment of God*, 134 (italics original).

14. Ibid., 134.

15. At the Evangelical Alliance symposium, Graham MacFarlane and Stuart Murray Williams also adopted this naturalist view of punishment where it is reduced to being the organic consequence of an action. They too fall prey to the same criticism: if God created the process, then God is involved, and it is his process.

16. I. Howard Marshall also made this point at the Evangelical Alliance symposium.

17. Green and Baker, *Recovering the Scandal*, 57.

18. Ibid., 113; cf. S. W. Sykes, "Outline of a Theology of Sacrifice," in *Sacrifice and Redemption: Durham Essays in Theology*, ed. S. W. Sykes (Cambridge: Cambridge Univ. Press, 1991), 282–98 (294–95), cited in Green and Baker, *Recovering the Scandal*, 96.

19. Green and Baker, *Recovering the Scandal*, 96.

20. John R. W. Stott, *The Cross of Christ*, 2nd ed. (Leicester: IVP, 1989), 151. Given Stott's position as a whole, I understand this statement to exclude only the notion that Christ was the object without being the subject, not the notion that he was in any sense the object.

21. Augustine, *De Trinitate* 1.4.7.

22. John Owen, *The Death of Death in the Death of Christ* 1.3, in *The Works of John Owen*, ed. William H. Goold, 23 vols. (Edinburgh: Banner of Truth Trust, 1967), 10:163.

23. Hence, Owen speaks of "an authoritative imposition of the office of Mediator, which Christ closed withal by his voluntary susception of it, willingly undergoing the office" (ibid., 164).

24. Green and Baker, *Recovering the Scandal*, 141.

25. The Hebrew reads הַךְ (hifil imperative masculine singular of נָכָה), the LXX πατάξατε (second person plural aorist imperative active of πατάσσω), and the New Testament πατάξω (first person singular future indicative active of πατάσσω).

26. Joel Marcus, "The Old Testament and the Death of Jesus: The Role of Scripture in the Gospel Passion Narratives," in *The Death of Jesus in Early Christianity*, ed. John T. Carroll and Joel B. Green (Peabody, Mass.: Hendrickson, 1995), 205–33 (225–26).

27. Green and Baker, *Recovering the Scandal*, 213.

28. John Owen, *A Dissertation on Divine Justice* 2.5, in *Works of John Owen*, 10:598 (italics original).

29. Eusebius of Caesarea, *Demonstratio Evangelica* 10.1, in *The Proof of the Gospel*, ed. and trans. W. J. Ferrar, 2 vols (Eugene, Ore.: Wipf and Stock, 2001), 2:195–96. Likewise, Cyril of Alexandria: "The Only-begotten was made man, bore a body by nature at enmity with death, and became flesh, so that, enduring the death which was hanging over us as the result of our sin, he might abolish sin; and further, that he might put an end to the accusations of Satan, inasmuch as we have paid in Christ himself the penalties for the charges of sin against: 'For he bore our sins, and was wounded because of us,' according to the voice of the prophet. Or are we not healed by his wounds?" (*De adoratione et cultu in spiritu et veritate* 3.100–102 [PG 68:293, 296; my trans.].

30. Chalke, "Cross Purposes," 45.

31. Church of England, *The Mystery of Salvation* (1995; London: Church House, 1997), 212.

32. Green and Baker, *Recovering the Scandal*, 29, cf. 32.

33. These themes recur many times in Wright's work, but a good starting point for exploration is chapter 12 of *Jesus and the Victory of God* (London: SPCK, 1996). Wright is, of course, repeatedly negative about the idea that we find in the Gospels "an abstract and timeless system of theology" (603), but this is just the point: his work shows that by beginning with the history of Jesus and his vocation, it is possible to lay out a biblical theology which grounds a penal substitutionary understanding of the cross.

34. Green and Baker, *Recovering the Scandal*, 213–14.

35. Ibid., 148.

36. Chalke, "Cross Purposes," 47; Steve Chalke and Alan Mann, *The Lost Message of Jesus* (Grand Rapids: Zondervan, 2003), 182.

37. Joanne Carlson Brown and Rebecca Parker, "For God So Loved the World?" in *Christianity, Patriarchy, and Abuse: A Feminist Critique*, ed. Joannne Carlson Brown and Carole R. Bohn (New York: Pilgrim, 1989), 1–30 (2).

38. Ibid., 18.

39. Hans Boersma, *Violence, Hospitality, and the Cross* (Grand Rapids: Baker Academic, 2004), 41, cf. 117.

40. J. Denny Weaver, *The Nonviolent Atonement* (Grand Rapids.: Eerdmans, 2001), 132.

41. *Contra* Green and Baker: "Within a penal substitution model, God's ability to love and relate to humans is circumscribed by something outside of God—that is, an abstract concept of justice instructs God as to how God must behave" (*Recovering the Scandal*, 147).

chapter eleven

atonement, creation and trinity

graham mcfarlane

Introduction

This essay is an attempt at giving a wider evangelical response to the question as to why God created what has become a seemingly dysfunctional creation. To do this will require conversation within three significant theological arenas: a Judaeo-Christian doctrine of creation, some New Testament perspectives concerning the person and work of Jesus Christ, and a trinitarian understanding of divine identity and being.

Creation

We start with creation – the stage within which the drama of redemption and divine disclosure unfolds, a drama, it must be said, that consists of two inextricably bound acts.

Creation as Faithful and Good

The purpose of the doctrine of creation, according to the Judaeo-Christian faith, is to articulate an understanding of reality as perceived from within the context of a dynamic, personal and existential relationship with the living God. As such, it is a specifically theological understanding of reality – a way of describing creaturely existence, whether personal or impersonal, in relation to its Creator, the God of Abram, Isaac and Israel, the God and Father of our Lord Jesus Christ.

From this specifically theological perspective, we may rightly talk of creation as a "matrix of creaturely associations",[1] as a realm of interrelated and interdependent relations or associations, in which each aspect of the created order stands in deep association with the whole. All that exists does so within a network of relational associations that, when fulfilled, promise abundance and security (the consequences of the Lord God's blessing and proper husbandry), that are personally expressed through being in proper association with oneself, with those around, and with the Lord God.

This allows us to talk about an ontology of faith – in which creation exists as a matrix of faithful relational associations within and without creation. This constitutes the created order not only as faithful, since all that exists comes into being from one who invests faith in it, but also as undeniably good, since the one who calls it into existence and exercises faith in it happens to be the Creator, God. Only as a result of this prior faithful benevolence can we then say that what is created is good and that it is called into faithful relation with its Creator and all other aspects of the created order. In so doing, creation accords proper worth, offering the right glory back to its Creator. Herein, we touch base with the primary impetus for God's creative acts and the reason why God bothered to create in the first place.

A Tempting Aside

At this point, however, it is worth noting one possible theological temptation to be avoided – namely, creating familiar discourses concerning Creator and creation as though they share similar attributes. Rather, the Judaeo-Christian doctrines of creation make clear from the outset that there is a clear distinction between the being of God and that of creation. Consequently, two methodological distinctions are to be maintained before proper talk concerning the relationship between creation and Creator can occur. The first concerns the *ontic* – what we describe as reality, whether divine or creaturely. The second concerns the *epistemic* or hermeneutical – what we understand of that reality.

The tensions between these two fields of inquiry constitute subsequent doctrine and belief. Such activity is tensive in the sense that our *interpretations* concerning what we think reality to be do not necessarily correspond to *reality in and of itself*, nor do they carry univocal or permanent meaning: there is clear development within Scripture. This point is particularly apropos in our considerations concerning the relations between created and uncreated realities.

Consequently, whatever we want to say about the various creaturely associations that make up creation, we start with clear methodological distinctions, since they determine what can and cannot be said about the relation between the two and, therefore, what can be said about the way in which the brokenness between them is resolved. The biblical testimony concerning these boundaries is couched in the language of holiness: holiness not as a purely moral parameter but much more as one that describes the ontological difference between the Creator and all that is created.

In whatever way, then, we describe creation's relationship with Creator, it cannot be one that suggests a natural correspondence or a family likeness. Whether pre- or postlapsarian, a doctrine of creation that corresponds best to both divine reality and our canonical understanding of that reality is one in which this relationship between creation and Creator is maintained. The reason for this is simple: that which is created is not the Creator. There are no organic, essential, immediate, direct associations between the two.

Hence, it is our doctrine of creation that provides the backdrop against which our thinking of the cross and the Trinity must be developed. This fundamental article of faith narrates both divine and human identities and provides the conceptual grammar for our beliefs. As such, it determines just what can and cannot be said about the nature of the problem and how it should be resolved. With this in mind, we may now address our second consideration concerning creation.

Creation as Fallen and Unfaithful

Left on its own, the distinction between creation and its Creator results in forms of ontological dualism. However, a dialectic emerges within the same creation stories that suggests, at the same time, a union of Creator and creature is possible in the form of a very specific relationship. Adam, as male and female, is positioned at the apex of creaturely associations. Thus, Genesis 1:26–27: "'Let us make man in our image, after our likeness; and let them have dominion over the fish of the sea, and over the birds of the air, and over the cattle, and over all the earth, and over every creeping thing that creeps upon the earth.' So God created man in his own image, in the image of God he created him; male and female he created them" (RSV). Two interrelated theological premises are established here. On the one hand, God's otherness poses certain epistemological concerns about how we ever come into relationship with such a being and how we may be assured of knowing God personally. On the other hand, the canon expresses the collective memory of the people of God, that God overcomes the gulf by means of a series of mediatory functionaries.

Both criteria are of fundamental importance to any subsequent under-standing of the cross. Our humanity is established within a matrix of relations and associations: *we are* to the degree *we relate* – as ego and other, as self and neighbour, as creature and Creator. This is why God created; this is humanity living as it was intended. As John Zizioulas pus it, "It is communion which makes beings 'be': nothing exists without it, not even God."[2] In doing so, humans mediate – reflect – the divine within creation.

However much the *imago Dei* is a product of creation and as such is conditioned like the rest of creation by its material and biological constitu-tion, there is a higher, more fundamental determination operating – namely, one that is immaterial and non-biological. *Human* being is determined not in terms of its biological existence alone but much more so by a relational identity. Our true identity is discovered and established only to the degree that the matrix of relations established at creation informs each.

- Creation, then, is a set of creaturely-material relational associations
- These associations are, in turn, constituted by what we may describe as "mutual relational expectations" that constitute each particular relation. Thus, being a son or daughter is constituted by the relational expectations specific to that relation, which, in turn, differ from those that constitute being a mother or father, employee or employer. Thus, our identities are not biologically derived (this constitutes *what* I am): rather, they are relationally derived (constituting *who* I am) and have meaning only in terms of the mutually agreed expectations to which each relationship holds.
- It is only to the degree that we live within and fulfil these expec-tations that we have life in all its potential and abundance.

When applied to our relationship with God, these relational expecta-tions are expressed primarily in terms of blessing and dominion – of "do this and live" as counterpoint to the Tempter's "you surely shall not die" – not a biological death in any automatic sense but certainly a relational death. The acts of unbelief and distrust bring about a relational morphing wherein the relationship which constitutes the first couple as good and life-sustaining becomes distorted and death-bearing. As a result, what was initially created good becomes an altogether different personal reality. Thus, at the very core of the Genesis narrative is the call to live a life of faithful relational associations with self, fellow humans and God – a call to trust the divine word over all others and to live, therefore, in fidelity and trust.

So, What Has Gone Wrong?

Interestingly, the Genesis account is very specific in diagnosing the problem: the human creature acts in such a way as to be "like one of us, knowing good and evil".[3] Herein lies the human fault line. Sure, the act of disobedience enacted by the first Adam and perpetuated by all subsequent human beings has significant rational consequences. It manifests itself in how we think and then in how we act.

However, this cannot be the primary meaning of Genesis 3:22, since we have already established that human identity is fundamentally a relational issue. As such, the human fault line has to do with who we are and is to be understood in terms of our relational dysfunctioning. That is, sin is to be understood first as the manifestation of disordered relating and relationships: human beings are no longer content to find their meaning within the symphony of creation, as its fullest and highest expression. The human predicament has now to do with who we are – of seeking to be like the Creator. Through being enlightened as to the knowledge of good and evil, human beings – who already possess the relational ability to image God within creation – now actualise their own ability for self-determination. It is they who decide what is good and what is ill. As a result, rather than living in faithful and trusting relationship with Creator and creation, the human creatures determine what is good and what is evil in relation solely to themselves, rather than in relation to their Creator. What results is nothing less than a relational catastrophe.

Consequently, what was intended for mutual benefit, where each part of creation contributed to the goodness of the whole and generated a power for the good, has become enslaved to a counterpower. Paul describes this power, in terms we would use today, as a cosmic terrorist that has taken creation captive and that works as a counterforce to that which was originally intended.[4] As a result, a two-dimensional dislocation arises within creation.

First, at the personal level, chaos erupts at the very apex of creation, resulting in human beings experiencing three-dimensional alienation:

- alienation in relation to one's self, since our own self-relationship is dependent upon a more primary relationship with God.
- alienation in relation to the other, since to be an embodied self requires the presence of an embodied other.

- alienation in relation to the Creator, since all ongoing acts of self-determination are directed against the very one on whom our self-actualisation develops.

Second, at the impersonal level, this alienation works itself out three-dimensionally:

- materially, in relation to biological networks which take millennia to unravel, with catastrophic ecological consequences.
- culturally, where we as human beings actualise our self-determination socially, where the *imago Dei* becomes the *imago mundi* and creates in its own image worldviews that take centuries and millennia to burn out.
- personally, the most immediate stage in which the human pathology reveals itself in the death of relationships over days, weeks, years and ultimately in the eventual death of the image-bearer.

The evidence, then, is that these creation stories are as relevant today as they were a few millennia ago.

First, they reinforce at a theological level not only that creation is the arena within which the subsequent arena of re-creation is set but also that creation itself now requires redemption. The network of creaturely relationships itself is in need of re-creation – due to the human creature's acts of self-determination, a distorted (at best) and diabolical (at worst) set of relations exist that can work themselves out only in counterpoint to the Creator's original intentions for creation.

Second, what now dominates is a distinctive relational and, therefore, personal power at work within creation working itself out in relation to self, neighbour and God. Without intervention, it will work itself out more widely in a three-dimensional pathology. Sin, a relational dysfunction, when left to its own devices, brings about the destruction of every creaturely relational association, whether at the level of interpersonal relationships or at the wider level of biospheric extinction.

Third, it is proper to locate the drama of redemption within the stage of creation. We do so because our understanding of creation provides the blueprint for redemption and therefore informs what can and cannot be said about the means by which the pathology may be redressed and redeemed.

Christological Associations

Thus far, I have articulated the boundaries to be respected if we are to understand the nature of atonement. The Creator seeks to establish a network of relations capacious enough, via the human image-bearer, to bring glory to the Creator by offering up an embodied reflection of the unity inherent within creation. There is a desire for inter- and intrarelationship, between creation with creation, and creation with Creator. It is established in fidelity, in trust, in conformity to the Creator's original intentions. Within this network of relations, there is blessing, life and power at work that reflect the very being of God.

This sets the scene for any subsequent understanding of the solution. Yet if there is no unmediated contact between Creator and creation, and the image is distorted beyond apparent repair, how then are we able to talk meaningfully of a solution that involves the death of the Son of God on a cross?

I want to suggest that Scripture offers us a threefold answer.

1. Get Wisdom

The first response centres on a Judaeo-Christian cosmogony and cosmology – on how creation comes into being and is understood to exist. In its earliest form, we are told that creation comes into existence by the divine act of speech and is mediated in the synthesis of breath and word. In its later, fuller sense in Proverbs 8:22–36, this agency is more specific: it is through Wisdom that everything comes into being, until eventually Wisdom is installed as a royal ruler over the created order.

Wisdom, neither God nor separate from God, but rather the personification of God's intentions for his creation, is a heuristic means of talking about the Creator-creation relationship that safeguards the identity of both. On the one hand, creation corresponds to all that the Creator intended as good and pleasing. It can do so because it comes into being and is resourced by God's own Wisdom. On the other hand, Wisdom is not Yahweh but a means of safeguarding the Creator as he reaches out of his holiness and initiates creation. The point to note here is this: whatever creation is within this theological matrix, it comes into being in a mediated, not direct, manner and does so through the medium of Wisdom.

Wisdom, then, assumes a creative identity that serves the people of God well in times of distress and national disaster. Psalm 137:1, 4 express the exiles' despair as they experience firsthand a disrupted creation: "By the rivers of Babylon, where we sat down and wept when we thought of Zion ... how could we sing the Lord's song on foreign soil?" The temple is destroyed, the people displaced and the Lord God thoroughly displeased. In this cultural and cultic displacement, profound psycho-theological tremors are felt. How can the nation exercise trust in their God? How do they know that God's promises have not been overturned? How do they know, contrary to their neighbours, that chaos and chance are not ultimate? In essence, what grounds have they for any hope of rescue, redemption and reconciliation with the God of their forebears?

The answer is located in Wisdom theology. Only the one who creates has the power to re-create. If all that exists comes into being through Wisdom, who personified all that is good and who ordered not only creation but the Creator's relation to creation, then it follows that the same *modus operandi* applies for redemption and the re-creation of all that exists. To be saved, then, is to correspond one's life to the benchmark – to Wisdom. Get wisdom, and live!

2. Find Christ

When the New Testament writers consider the person and work of Jesus the Christ, they undergo what might be called a Jewish, post-foundationalist, post-traditional paradigmatic change. They are forced to reconsider their perception of how the network of creaturely associations works in the light of Jesus' death and resurrection. God has clearly endorsed the ministry and person of Jesus by raising him from death. In turn, he has exalted Jesus to a name as high as his own and, in so doing, predicated to him attributes previously thought proper only to the Lord God. It is to Jesus, not Yahweh, that every knee shall bow: it is Jesus, not the Father, whom the Spirit makes present; it is Jesus, not God, who is the first and last. Clearly, the first Jewish Christians are more than comfortable in worshiping Jesus, according to him a relational association that is not creaturely but proper only to the Creator.

All this is more than vivid Semitic theological imagination at work. What it signifies is that a new set of associations has entered the stage of creation. What was hitherto attributed abstractly to Wisdom is earthed in the history of one man's fidelity to God, neighbour and self. Whereas Wisdom's credentials to save were located in a prior act of creation, Jesus' salvific status (he is the one God endorses through resurrection even in the most accursed of deaths) affirms his right to be recognised as the one in whom all things come into being and without whom nothing would exist.[5] Paul, too, articulates this association of relations in Colossians 1:15–20, arguing similarly that Christ holds a status in relation to creation that is subsequently reflected in the act of re-creation within the church. This relational trajectory runs through Ephesians 1:9–10, 20–23, where allusions of Jesus Christ's cosmic and creational identity are made, and is fulfilled in Revelation (1:8, 17) when the relational association of being the first and the last explicitly unites Jesus with the Lord God.

What this sample of texts reveals is that in his association to the created order, Jesus Christ embodies the very power that brought creation into being. It is Jesus who now performs the mediating role of Wisdom. In him, the Creator-creation association is reestablished by virtue of his relational fidelity to his God and Father and to his neighbour. It is right and proper, then, to stress the centrality of Jesus, the wisdom of God, as the one who is able to bring about our redemption because he was involved, in some mysterious but not puzzling way, in the genesis of creation itself.

3. See God

Jesus is not accomplishing something on behalf of creation alone. It is God who was in Christ reconciling the world to himself and doing so through the empowering agency of the Spirit. Yet even in the act of re-creation, it is a Godhead veiled in flesh, an incarnate deity, whom we meet. The Son of God comes to us as one whose relational association to God the Father is mediated through the humanity of Jesus of Nazareth. That he alone lives in relational harmony with the Father is evidenced in his being filled with the Spirit, who alone generates life in all its fullness. Only in Jesus is the association of relations restored and the point of contact between Creator and creation re-established in the image-bearer. As such, we are now able to turn to consider the meaning of the cross from within this matrix of relational associations.

The Cross

What, then, does the cross mean within this relational matrix? Certainly, it cannot be reduced to a univocal answer: the cross addresses a multilayered network of relational associations it seeks to resolve. In addition, as Alister McGrath reminds us, "The cross has always maintained a resistance against reductive interpretation. We cannot distil the meaning of the cross into a simple proposition on the basis of which we can deduce further propositions.

As Luther pointed out: 'the wisdom of the cross is hidden in a deep mystery.' At the end, the cross, itself mysterious, points to an even greater mystery which lies behind it – the living God."[6]

When understood from the perspective of creation and the Father's participation in the act of redemption through the mediating presence of the Son empowered by the Father's Spirit, there are some helpful pointers. Let me highlight two important considerations in light of the act of unbelief and distrust on the part of the first couple and perpetuated by all subsequent humans – except Jesus, of course.

1. The "What" of Atonement

The cross signifies that our human actions carry with them real consequences, that within creation there is an inbuilt penalty clause for relational unfaithfulness, and that this lies at the very heart of the created order. Without exception, actions within creation have consequences for good and for ill. There is a reckoning we must address, whether in relation to the ground we are called to till and over which we exercise dominion, or in relation to our private associations with ourselves as psychosomatic beings, or with those around us, or with our Creator-Redeemer God. It is this:

- in relation to creation as the arena of labour and produce, there is the curse (rather than blessing) of disorder and mistrust.
- in relation to interpersonal relations between ego and other, self and neighbour, whether male to female, or female to male, there is dysfunction and disharmony.
- in relation to human procreation, what was good becomes painful and disordered, thus laying foundations for subsequent generational discord.
- in relation to God, a relation of openness becomes disordered wherein sin distorts the creature's perception of God and becomes blinded to the Creator's goodwill.

This is *what* the cross signifies: the breakdown of creaturely associations carries with it significant consequences, ultimately leading to the death of the persons involved as well as the destruction of their habitat. The consequences are what follow from the creature's desire for self-determination. They are unavoidable and are part of the woof and warp of the created order. In this sense, John McLeod Campbell is correct in saying that on the cross, the Son offers up a perfect amen to the Father's judgment on humanity's sin.[7] A Judaeo-Christian doctrine of creation insists that there is a cost to our acts of self-determination, and that this cost is to be located within the fabric of creation and to be understood as the penalty for its own acts of self-determination.

2. The "How" of Atonement

Here we are confronted with the very nature of God. Once again, the Genesis narrative offers us a window: as a result of the relational breakdown, the Creator extends grace towards those who have been unfaithful. The act of exclusion from the original soil is a gift to the unfaithful image-bearers. It is performed to limit the scope of their actions' consequences – lest they eat of the tree of life itself and live an eternal life of self-determination with all its catastrophic consequences (Gen. 3:23). Whilst the creatures have broken the network of relational associations that links them with God, it would appear that it is not a two-way break. Rather, we see the character of the Creator, whose initial instinct is to save the fallen image-bearers and preserve them from the ultimate consequences of their actions.

Here we discover the foundation for later interpretations of the cross as the place where the Lord of creation both covers our sins and stems the consequences of our relational dysfunction, and discover that it is an act of God's initiative, not ours. This is a gift that is given when not merited, and as such, one that is received only through trust on the part of both parties. It is a demonstration of the nature and character of divine love: one that does not demand justice alone before forgiveness is acquired and the relationship restored but makes provision to arrest the destructive consequences of the faithless creatures' actions. Herein we are confronted with the manner by which divine love covers sin. Divine grace precedes divine retribution. Such is the nature of the network of associations now operative within creation.

For instance, in Israel's escaping the tyranny of Egypt (Exodus 12), this divine gifting operates in terms of interchange and identification: interchange in that the sacrificed lamb stands in place of the firstborn, and identification in that the household identifies with the symbol of life. In so doing, the lamb secures their escape. What underscores the act of putting the lamb's blood on the lintels of one's home is an expression of trust, of relational fidelity, of faithful dependence upon the God who has revealed himself to Moses. What we have here is the outworking of the original ontology of faith, of creaturely dependence upon God and upon one's neighbour (in this case, the word of Moses and, therefore, dependence upon Moses himself).

Alternatively, the Levitical rite of the Day of Atonement, in Leviticus 16, describes the removal of sins that cannot be washed away or bought off (since they are to do with one's being). Again, a collective identification and interchange lie at the heart of the ritual. We see the manipulation of a distorted association of relationships with the aim of resolving what has gone wrong. First, there is recognition of the consequences of sins that cannot be washed away or paid for by the goat's death (Lev. 16:18–19). Note that the blood of bull and goat serves to "cleanse" the Holy of Holies as well as the high priest, so that the people are represented before a holy God. The existential impact of the scapegoat cannot be minimised; Yahweh graciously provides the scapegoat in order to arrest the potentially catastrophic dynamic of sin that comes about as a result of the sins of their hearts, of self-actualisation, the deliberately rebellious responses of each personality whether in relation to self, neighbour or God. As in the garden, so in the desert; God makes provision for his people by dealing with the sins that cannot be atoned for. Hence, the scapegoat is not killed but led out to the desert as a symbolic reminder of the fact that the sins are removed in an inversion of the distorted relational associations that got the nation to this place initially. Once again, it is God who provides the covering for sin, and does so in order to achieve the intended goal for creation in the first place: relationship. It is an underscoring of the fact that atonement has to do not only with personal forgiveness but also with the reordering of creation itself.

In this enactment, I want to suggest that divine justice is still being met.

Divine Justice

First, there is creational justice, a rule of creation to which we must adhere. The biblical witness suggests that this can occur only sacramentally. This is seen in the sacrifices of Abel or of the cultus, in the demonic release into a herd of pigs, in the personal expressions of forgiveness each of us is required to demonstrate prior to divine forgiveness, and ultimately in the death and resurrection of Jesus Christ or in the familiar elements of bread and wine. Herein lies the twofold rationale for substitution. First, the life of one is given for the other as evidence of the fact that a space-time-historical relational break has occurred that must be addressed before it can be resolved. Second, the severity of the consequence reflects the degree of relational dysfunctioning: it reveals the true state of the sinner's being, and only the removal of the sinner will remove the root of sin. As such, there is a personal, not merely practical, transferral taking place in the act of substitution: it is primarily about one's being, not one's doing. Only when this relational association is restored can resurrection occur and the prospective dimension of atonement be actualised in restored relationship.

Second, there is a divine and personal justice: we sin against persons, not an impersonal creation. The Law given to Moses represents an intrinsic part of what this kind of love looks like – we do not lie, because God is true; we do not kill, because God is life; we do not covet, because God provides all our needs – and this Law is fulfilled in loving God with all our heart, mind, soul and strength. Here we confront the substitutional nature of God's justice. Yes, there is what we may describe as "raw justice", where we are simply given over to the ultimate consequence of our actions – death – and justice is done. In this sentence, God's law is upheld and the sinner proven guilty. However, within this relational understanding of creation and Creator, the gracious act on the Father's part in giving up his Son to mediate his love and become a substitute in human form enables us to avoid reifying two theological control mechanisms. The first concerns the necessity for purely penal interpretations of the death of Christ that source the penal dimension and its consequences in the character of God. Such a controlling mechanism inevitably results in the premise that God does not necessarily need to love but he does need to judge.[8] This introduces the second control mechanism: that atonement is primarily a desire for justice. Rather, for the restoration of a relationship and, therefore, atonement to occur, divine love reshapes divine justice and does so by going beyond the boundaries established by normal law. However, atonement is the means by which personal relations are restored, and as such, the imperative driving such reconciliation is a relational one, whatever its juridical outworkings may be.

God the Father achieves this by meeting us not abstractly within creation as his wisdom but personally in his Son, who became one of us, who ultimately acts as the guarantee for our reconciliation. We are empowered to believe that this is a possibility within the present created order because:

- we hold to a robust biblical doctrine of divine agency, which understands creation to be the work of a wise and dependable Creator in which human beings are the point of contact between the purely immanent (creation) and the purely transcendent (God).

- the means by which the association of relations between God and creation privileges divine love over human understandings of justice is rooted firmly in the fact that God does not give us up to the consequences of our actions, thereby fulfilling the law. The mystery that is expressed on the cross demonstrates the extent to which the Father seeks us out in order that the torn fabric of our relational associations may be restored to its rightful glory. It is because of this priority of love that I believe any doctrine of atonement worth the term "biblical" must move in two dimensions:

1. It must maintain a sacramental notion of a sacrificial substitute in which the power and the pathology of sin is destroyed: only incarnation makes this possible.

2. It must turn on the notion of resurrection, since the imperative of atonement is driven by the desire for relationship. Herein we are confronted by the tri-personal dimension of atonement: in the humanity of the obedient Son empowered by the Spirit, the Father's disposition towards creation and unfaithful humanity in particular is actualised. The barrier to relationship and the power holding us and the rest of creation in captivity is destroyed through the self-giving of the Son to the full consequences of our dysfunctional ways of relating and the Father's response to this. As a result, the consequences of the Son's faith in the Father are demonstrated in the power displayed in raising him from the dead to a position of power and authority in which the rest of the faithful live and have their hope.

Conclusion

Let me end with two points concerning the meaning of the cross in dialogue with a doctrine of creation and divine trinitarian identity.

First, I have sought to present a framework within which we might see the death of Christ from a slightly different vantage point. This involves a relational understanding of creation. As such, there has to be a wider, what we may describe as cosmic, dimension to the act of atonement in which we see the tri-personal acts of God at work. I do so on the grounds (a) that such an approach corresponds better to the biblical testimony, and (b) that in order for theological reflection to have any practical meaning within the church, it must first diagnose the problem. To do so necessitates being able to identify not only what is malfunctioning but also what is healthy. In biblical terms, this is our doctrine of creation.

Second, we are able better to understand the human pathology that requires an act of incarnation, death and resurrection. The act of human self-determination has unleashed catastrophic consequences within the creaturely order: it is the personal nature of sin, a problem too big for the human creature to resolve due both to the cosmic character it assumes as well as its personal outworkings in our individual and corporate selves. And since it involves our very selves, it follows that the pathology is removed to the degree we are removed. In this enactment of atonement, justice will be served, but at the cost of any relationship. We require, rather, the actions of another who deals with both the object and subject of offence and yet safeguards our personal integrity: a handling of us in relation to the other and the other in relation to us. Only in this manner – of sacramental mediation – are we translated from the consequences of our own dismal relations and associations into the kingdom of God.

Finally, a proper understanding of atonement that is both biblical and contemporary understands not only the what and why of atonement but can also articulate the how of our salvation. I have argued that the primary manner is that of self-giving sacrifice as the expression of the Creator's intention for relationship. It is this witness that expresses both understanding and articulation of the dynamics of atonement, for through it, we are empowered to see, beyond our own perceptions, the Father's desire for relationship given sacramental expression in and through the faithfulness of Jesus Christ, his incarnate Son, and endorsed in power and new life through the energising agency of the Spirit.

Notes

This paper was first delivered at an Evangelical Alliance – London School of Theology symposium on atonement and has been written up as a paper to be read publicly. Hence, there is little, if any, footnoting. I have, however, footnoted any specific references made to other scholars' work.

1. Michael Welker, *Creation and Reality* (Minneapolis: Fortress, 1999), 13.
2. John D. Zizioulas, *Being as Communion* (London: St Vladimir's Seminary Press, 1985), 17.
3. Gen. 3:22.

4. See B. R. Gaventa, "The Cosmic Power of Sin in Paul's Letter to the Romans: Toward a Widescreen Edition," *Interpretation* 58, no. 3 (2004): 235.

5. John 1:1–3; Heb. 1:2–4.

6. Alister E. McGrath, *The Enigma of the Cross* (London: Hodder and Stoughton, 1987), 88.

7. John McLeod Campbell, *The Nature of the Atonement* (Edinburgh: Handsel, 1996), 118.

8. Jonathan Edwards, *The Works of Jonathan Edwards*, vol. 18, *The "Miscellanies" 501–832*, ed. Ava Chamberlain (New Haven: Yale Univ. Press, 2000), 439. Edwards argues that God's majesty should be vindicated by "either equivalent punishment, or an equivalent sorrow and repentance".

chapter twelve

the logic of penal substitution revisited

oliver d. crisp

When I survey the wondrous Cross,
On which the Prince of Glory died,
My richest gain I count but loss,
And pour contempt on all my pride.

– Isaac Watts

It is notorious amongst theologians that there is no single theory of the atonement upon which all Christians agree. Nevertheless, evangelicals have, for the most part, traditionally maintained that only the doctrine of penal substitution is an adequate account of the atonement, and that only this particular theory of atonement can assure believers that they are, indeed, saved. For instance, evangelical New Testament scholar Simon Gathercole, in a recent essay endorsing penal substitution, says, "In the case of substitution, however, it seems that the combination of the Bible's clarity on the issue ... and the fact that it is an essential requirement for assurance means that it is not a legitimate area of disagreement amongst Christians."[1]

Similar sentiments can be found elsewhere.[2] Yet despite this defence of the doctrine, there are serious problems with the internal logic of penal substitution. These problems are often alluded to in the literature on the subject and known amongst historians and theologians working in this area. However, I want to suggest that, contrary to contemporary defenders of penal substitution like Gathercole, these problems have not been adequately resolved. More work is needed on them to demonstrate that penal substitution is a viable theory of the atonement.

In this chapter, I shall begin by setting forth the assumptions that lie behind the traditional penal substitutionary theory of the atonement. Then I shall consider the doctrine proper and address myself to what seem to be five systemic problems for the logic of penal substitution. I do not claim these are the only problems facing the doctrine, but I do think they are five of the most serious.[3] I will argue that, although some of these problems can be overcome by a careful explanation of penal substitution, several interrelated issues are problematic for the doctrine as it has been traditionally understood. It may be that there is another way of understanding the doctrine that avoids these problems. At the end of the essay, I shall hint at how such a rehabilitation of penal substitution might proceed.

Assumptions

J. I. Packer, in his influential essay on the logic of penal substitution, summarises the doctrine in these words: "The notion which the phrase 'penal substitution' expresses is that Jesus Christ our Lord, moved by a love that was determined to do everything necessary to save us, endured and exhausted the destructive divine judgement for which we were otherwise inescapably destined, and so won us forgiveness, adoption and glory. To affirm penal substitution is to say believers are in debt to Christ specifically for this, and that this is the mainspring of all their joy, peace and praise both now and for eternity."[4] Following in the spirit of Packer's description, there seem to be several assumptions required. These are:

(A1) Divine justice is retributive and inexorable.
(A2) Sin requires an infinite punishment.
(A3) Satisfaction for sin must be made either in the punishment of the sinner or in the person of a vicar.

Each of these needs some explanation before we may proceed to unpack the doctrine proper. We shall consider each of them in turn.

Regarding Divine Retributive Punishment

I take it that the central notion behind a retributive theory of punishment is the idea of proportionality between punishment and crime, expressed in the principle "the punishment must fit the crime." But as I have argued elsewhere, there are two versions to the retributive theory of punishment involved in a penal substitution theory.[5] The stronger of the two states that divine justice does not permit forgiveness. The weaker version of the doctrine claims merely that divine justice does not require forgiveness. If divine justice does not permit forgiveness, then sin must be dealt with; it cannot be simply passed over or forgiven without a proportional punishment being meted out. There might be a number of reasons offered as to why this is the case. For instance, following Kant, we might say that there is a categorical obligation to apply a certain penalty for a certain crime, and that not to impose such a penalty would be objectively morally wrong. Applied to divine justice, this would mean that God has a categorical obligation to apply certain penalties in order to remain a moral being. He has to punish sin according to the idea of proportionality just outlined. It is not the case, on this view, that God could choose some other, alternative means of punishment, or forgive the sin without any punishment being suffered by the sinner or some penal substitute.

However, it seems to me that this poses considerable problems for a right understanding of the divine nature. Even if one were to ground this moral obligation in the divine nature itself, rather than in some deontological moral standard external to God (thereby ameliorating some of the more obvious problems that would result from the application of the Euthyphro Dilemma to this issue), this still means that God has certain moral obligations that he has to discharge. This is a problem if one thinks that God has no moral obligations, strictly speaking.

Alternatively, one might say that God has to punish sin because there is something about divine justice that is inexorable. That is, divine justice must be satisfied. If this is the case, then God cannot pass over or forgive sin without punishment or else he would cease to be a moral being in that he would be acting contrary to his essentially just nature. Obviously, this raises the question of whether divine justice is, in fact, inexorable. On the strong view of divine justice, this would seem to be the case. Such a strong view of divine justice involves the following assumptions:

1. A person should not be treated any worse than they deserve.
2. A person should not be treated any better than they deserve.
3. One person should be treated in the same way as another for comparable crimes. Punishment should be fair.[6]

Fairness on its own need not mean justice is inexorable. A particular police force might decide that they will have a one-day amnesty for illegal firearms, allowing people to hand in their weapons without fear of punishment on that particular day. This seems fair because no one is treated differently from another on that particular day. But this would mean that these people are being treated better than they deserve. In this case, justice has given way to clemency for the limited period of the amnesty. Human societies might allow this, but divine justice cannot without violating tenet 2 in our tenets of justice. Similarly, if God decided that all people possessing illegal firearms were to be hauled over hot coals for a thousand years, this might appear to be fair in that all receive the same punishment. But it would violate the condition that persons are not treated any worse than they deserve, for no one deserves to be hauled over hot coals for a thousand years merely because they have been caught possessing an illegal firearm.

These intuitions about divine justice dovetail with what we have said about retributive punishment. Retribution means the punishment must fit the crime. It must be fair and proportional, and therefore not too severe or too lenient. If this applies to divine justice as the strong view of divine justice claims, there does seem, *prima facie*, to be something inexorable about that justice. God, it would seem, has to punish sin rather than pass over or forgive it without punishment.

It seems that most theologians who have advocated penal substitutionary theories of atonement have subscribed to the strong view of divine justice according to a retribution model of punishment. To take just one example, the Dutch-American Reformed theologian Louis Berkhof states, "When man fell away from God, he as such owed God reparation. But he could atone for his sin only by suffering eternally the penalty affixed to transgression. This is what God might have required in strict justice, and would have required, if He had not been actuated by love and compassion for the sinner. As a matter of fact, however, God appointed a vicar in Jesus Christ to take man's place, and this vicar atoned for sin and obtained an eternal redemption for man."[7]

Of course, one could adopt the weaker view of divine justice on a retributive model, the view that divine justice does not require forgiveness. On this view, God is not required to forgive the sinner without punishment, but he could do so. But then some justification would have to be offered for (a) why God does forgive some without punishment and not others (if one is a particularist and does not believe all human beings will be saved), and (b) how it is that forgiving some but not others is consistent with the three tenets of justice outlined above. For it does not seem fair to treat some sinners one way, visiting divine justice upon them in punishment, and some sinners another way, granting them the benefits of divine grace.

Recently, Richard Swinburne has defended the notion that divine justice does not require punishment.[8] Swinburne claims that atonement involves four constituents: repentance, apology, reparation and penance. A guilty person should demonstrate repentance for a sin committed and apologise, seeking to make reparation where possible. Finally, the guilty person should seek to demonstrate their penitence by a supererogatory act, which shows the offended party that they are truly sorry.

Swinburne applies this to the divine-human relationship in the following way. Human beings have acquired guilt through sin against God. This guilt is problematic because human beings are obliged to render to God a moral life. God may deal with this in one of two ways. He could forgive the sin, with no further satisfaction required, if the sinner is truly repentant and apologises. In this way, divine justice does not require punishment for satisfaction. However, God could require reparation and penance for the sin committed. Clearly, it is difficult for human beings to offer reparation for a sin committed against God, so God may provide a means by which reparation and penance for the guilt of sin can be made, via the work of Christ. When the sinner sincerely repents of his sin and apologises to God for what he has done, pleading the work of Christ as a satisfaction for reparation and penance that the sinner himself cannot offer, God will forgive that sin in virtue of Christ's vicarious work.

Swinburne is right that atonement normally comprises repentance, apology, reparation and penance with respect to human relationships.[9] But defenders of a traditional version of penal substitution maintain that this cannot apply *mutatis mutandis* to divine-human relationships for three reasons. First, the inexorableness of divine justice means that it is not possible for God to permit forgiveness without punishment because this would be contrary to the divine nature. Second, it is not possible for human beings to offer adequate reparation and penance for their sinful condition. Third, it is not the case that God could have used any means by which to ensure vicarious reparation and penance. As Steven Porter points out, this makes the cross an arbitrary choice for the satisfaction of sin.[10] And the cross is anything but an arbitrary choice by God.

Regarding Infinite Punishment

This brings us to the second assumption lying behind penal substitution: the claim that only an infinite punishment provides the correct "fit" for the crime.[11] In brief, the central idea is that the dignity of God is infinite, which means that the seriousness of an offence committed against God is infinite, or infinitely surpasses that of other offences. Assuming a retributive punishment thesis taken with the strong view of divine justice, we could outline the following argument for an infinite punishment thesis:

1. God is worthy of infinite regard.
2. The gravity of an offence against a being is principally determined by that being's worth or dignity.
3. There is an infinite demerit in all sin against God, such that all sin is infinitely heinous.

This argument assumes that in the case of divine-human relationships, the status of the person offended (God) is of crucial importance in determining the severity of the punishment to be meted out.[12] Sin against a being of infinite honour and worth has consequences for the sinner that are themselves infinite. This sort of argument undercuts the Swinburnian thesis about divine justice. For if this sort of argument is cogent, then sin is so serious that it is not possible for God merely to forgive sinners without adequate reparation and penance being made,[13] To borrow the language of scholastic theology, the satisfaction of divine justice is absolutely necessary. It is not merely hypothetically necessary. It is in the nature of God to punish sin inexorably because of the heinousness of sin (hence, absolutely necessary). It is not the case that God decrees that sin will be punished in this way, although he could have decreed some alternative to this (hence, hypothetically necessary).[14] In what follows, I shall assume that it is coherent to claim that God metes out infinite punishment for all sin on the basis of this sort of argument.[15]

Regarding the Satisfaction of Punishment

The third assumption has to do with the satisfaction of punishment. According to those who defend penal substitutionary theories of atonement, divine retributive justice, taken on a strong view of divine justice according to an infinite punishment thesis, ensures that punishment for sin is meted out in order that divine justice is satisfied. This punishment can be meted out in the person of the sinner, in hell, or in the person of Christ, who is able to offer a sacrifice for sin of infinite worth and able to atone for the sin of those he has come to save (the elect). Satisfaction depends upon the notion that the punishment offered is able to satisfy the offended honour of the divine agent. Since this has to be an infinite, retributive punishment in order to fit the crime, this means that either divine honour is satisfied by the infinite punishment of the sinner in hell, or by Christ's taking on the penal consequences of the sin for the sinner and dying to satisfy divine justice.

Penal Substitution and Its Problems

With these assumptions in place, we come to the substance of the doctrine of penal substitution. To begin with, it is important to see that punishment and atonement are not the same things. Thus, Swinburne states, "Punishment is something imposed by the wronged party (in this case, God); atonement is offered voluntarily."[16] But this can be accounted for in a version of penal substitution:

1. All sinners are guilty and stand under divine judgment (from [A1] and [A2]).
2. God would be just if he punished all human sinners in hell infinitely (from [A3]).
3. However, God could satisfy his perfect justice by punishing a substitute in the place of the sinner (from [A3]).
4. God will not punish the sin of all human beings in the person of a substitute, since it is in the nature of God to display his divine justice and his divine mercy, thereby vindicating his nature before his created order.
5. Therefore, the sin of some sinners will be punished in the person of Christ, their substitute for sin (the elect). The sin of other sinners will be punished in hell (the reprobate).

According to penal substitutionary accounts of the atonement, Christ's work on the cross is the voluntary taking up of the penal consequences of the sin of human beings as a substitute for that sin. So Christ voluntarily takes on the sin of elect human sinners in order to satisfy the requirements of divine justice. But this is not an offering made apart from the penal consequences of the actions of sinful humanity. It is an offering made in substitution for those penal consequences. Christ takes on the penal consequences of sin for elect human beings by being punished in their place. This, according to L. W. Grensted, involves a "legal fiction".[17]

But some theologians have claimed, in addition to this, that Christ takes on the sin of fallen human beings who are elect, and the guilt for that sin. But this is deeply problematic. Some may think that Christ cannot become a penal substitute for us because this would mean taking upon himself a debt that cannot be transferred from us to Christ (or from one person to another at all). If Christ takes on only the penal consequences of my sin, perhaps this problem can be ameliorated. But this still means that he takes on the punishment for my crime even if he does not take on the crime itself, or the guilt for that crime. And it is unclear how anyone can take on the penal consequences of another person's crime.

The logic of penal substitution raises many problems besides that pertaining to the claim that Christ somehow acts as a vicar for elect sinful human beings. The first of these has to do with whether the doctrine of penal substitution reduces the love of God to something arbitrary. This, allegedly, is because the doctrine means God chooses to love only an elect, less than the total number of humanity, on no other basis than that he wills to do so. Hence, penal substitution appears to smack of divine megrim in that God simply decides whom he will save and whom he will damn.

The second problem is that the doctrine means God cannot forgive sin without a reparation being made that is sufficiently valuable to offset the sin committed. Built into this theory of atonement is the idea that God is "wroth" with sin and must deal with it according to his inexorable retributive justice in the person of the sinner or a vicar. But this seems to limit God from being able to simply forgive sin. Furthermore, it has been thought to make God a moral monster, extracting punishment from sinners born with original sin who cannot save themselves.

The last two problems are interrelated and pertain to the question of the transfer of sin and guilt from the sinner to Christ and, in turn, the transfer of Christ's righteousness from Christ to the sinner. On the question of the transfer of sin, the following distinction needs to be observed. There are some debts that can be transferred from one person to another and some debts that cannot. According to Francis Turretin, debts in the first instance are called pecuniary debts.[18] So if Smith owes a financial debt to Jones, his debt can be paid by Wayne, since the financial penalty must be met, nothing more. However, in the case of penal debts, the same conditions cannot apply. A penal debt involves more than the debt itself; it involves the person who has committed the crime that has generated the debt. So if Smith has killed Jones, Wayne cannot take his place and act as his substitute in the way he could with respect to Smith's financial debt to Jones. Smith's sin means Smith has to serve the punishment for his crime. This is a problem for penal substitution if acting as a penal substitute entails the transfer of sin from the sinner to Christ, not just the transfer of the penal consequences of that sin from the sinner to Christ.

Similarly, if guilt is non-transferable, and the transfer of guilt is a constituent of penal substitution, this would constitute a second fatal flaw in the theory. Consider the case of Smith once more. In the first instance, Wayne can step in and pay the money owed, thereby settling the debt. But in so doing, he cannot take upon himself the guilt of Smith. Smith alone is guilty of incurring that debt, even if Smith is not the one who pays the debt. Smith's guilt in this instance is not transferable to Wayne. This problem is even more pronounced in the case of Smith murdering Jones. Here Smith is guilty of the crime, and nothing Wayne can do will render Smith innocent of that crime. Even if Smith, Jones and Wayne were living in a society in which penal substitutes could take the place of convicted criminals and serve their punishment, that does not mean the person taking the punishment of another also takes on the guilt for that punishment. It seems that the guilt accruing to a crime like murder is irremovable and non-transferable.

Responding to the Problems

Let us respond to each of these problems in turn.

Does *Penal* Substitution Make Sense?

First, can Christ be a penal substitute at all? As Berkhof puts it, "All those who advocate a subjective theory of the atonement raise a formidable objection to the idea of vicarious atonement. They consider it unthinkable that a just God should transfer His wrath against moral offenders to a perfectly innocent party, and should treat the innocent judicially as if he were guilty. There is undoubtedly a real difficulty here, especially in view of the fact that this seems to be contrary to all human analogy."[19]

Traditionally, defenders of penal substitution have sought to avoid this problem by appealing to a concept of legal "relaxation". God can "relax" the punitive requirement of divine justice so that a substitute can take on the penal consequences of the sin of another. This could take one of two forms. First, God could relax the punitive requirement of divine justice by allowing that a substitute could, in certain circumstances, take on the penal consequences of another's crime where the substitute is not required to pay an equivalent penalty. That is, God can decide that, in the case of the substitute, he is willing to admit a punishment of inferior value to that required by strict justice. In scholastic theology, this is called "acceptation".[20] (A variation on this form of legal relaxation would be that Christ's work is a satisfaction not because of its intrinsic worth but because God deigns to graciously accept it as a satisfaction for the crime committed, though he need not do so.)[21] Alternatively, God could relax the punitive requirement that justice be meted out only to the guilty party and allow a substitute to take the penal consequences of the crime instead of the guilty party. In this second form, the doctrine of legal relaxation applies only to the question of who serves the punishment, not whether the punishment is served to the full. On this second view, the punishment must be served to the full; there is no relaxation of the requirements of divine justice. The relaxation pertains to whether the perpetrator of the crime is punished or a penal substitute is punished instead.[22]

Let us apply this second form of legal relaxation to penal substitution. God may decide that he is willing for Christ to take the place of the sinner and suffer the penal consequences of the crime of that sinner, as if he were that sinner. Here also there are two ways in which this could be construed. First, one might think that this arrangement cannot mean that the sinfulness of those human beings Christ came to save is actually transferred to Christ. Nor can it mean that the actual righteousness of Christ is really transferred to the sinner in place of their sinfulness. This, according to Berkhof, is "utterly impossible".[23] The reason being, as we have already noted, that it is not metaphysically possible for the sin and guilt of one person to transfer to another person. According to Berkhof, all that can be transferred from one agent to another is the guilt of sin as liability to punishment. The sinner remains the guilty party, and their liability to guilt does not transfer.[24] The sinner remains the one who has sinned, and the actual property of having committed this sin does not transfer. But that aspect of the guilt for the sin committed which renders the sinner liable for punishment is transferable, and Christ can suffer as a substitute for this liability to punishment. So on this first view, all that is transferred from the sinner to Christ is the culpability for sin, not the sin itself, nor the fact that this particular person is guilty of having committed this particular sin. (In other words, not original sin as such or the whole of original guilt but merely the culpability aspect of original guilt is transferred to Christ.)[25]

On the second view, we could apply the legal relaxation of penal substitution in the following way. God does transfer the sinner's guilt and sin to Christ, and he does transfer the righteousness of Christ to the sinner. So legally and metaphysically speaking, the sinner is righteous. Further, legally and metaphysically speaking, Christ is the sinner and guilty for that sin, and therefore punishable for it. However, I cannot make any sense of this view as it stands. It seems to me that the person who has committed a particular crime is guilty of having committed it, and that liability to guilt cannot simply be transferred from one individual to another. Nor, it seems to me, can the sin itself, if it is a penal rather than pecuniary debt, be transferred from one person to another. If one suggests that, though this is true in the case of creaturely legal transactions, the case with the transaction between the Father and the Son in the atonement is an exception, the problem remains. So without some further argument to make sense of this view, it seems to me that it is mired in considerable conceptual problems that make it untenable.[26]

Assuming the second legal relaxation of penal substitution cannot work, we are left with the first way. This seems to be the way most defenders of penal substitution think of the transference of punishment from the sinner to Christ in the atonement. Take, for example, Calvin's exposition of this: "To take away our condemnation, it was not enough for him to suffer any kind of death: to make satisfaction for our redemption a form of death had to be chosen in which he might free us both by transferring our condemnation to himself and by taking our guilt upon himself." Moreover, "Thus we shall behold the person of a sinner and evildoer represented in Christ, yet from his shining innocence it will at the same time be obvious that he was burdened with another's sin rather than his own.... This is our acquittal: the guilt that held us liable for punishment has been transferred to the head of the Son of God."[27]

Note that Calvin emphasises the fact that Christ takes up the guilt of sinful human beings by transferring the condemnation of sinful human beings to himself. It is not his own sin with which he is burdened. He has transferred to himself the guilt that belongs to sinful human beings. This "legal fiction" involves nothing more than this transfer of the penal consequences of guilt. So it seems from this passage that Calvin's view is compatible with Berkhof's notion of liability to punishment. It is this liability that Christ took upon himself in the atonement, according to this version of penal substitution.

So the answer to how Christ can be a penal substitute involves a concept of legal relaxation that applies to Christ's atonement. Christ is able to take on the punishment for sin because God decides that Christ's work satisfies the requirements for sin. And God is willing to accept Christ's work as a substitute for the sin of those human beings whom Christ came to save. Defenders of penal substitution admit that there is no real precedent for this in human affairs. But they typically appeal to the unique circumstances involved in Christ's atonement: the fact that it is God who decides whether to allow satisfaction to be made for sin, that God the Father covenants with God the Son to bring this satisfaction about, that no sinful human being could make this satisfaction, and that only the Son could achieve this satisfaction in the person of Christ. In taking on this role, the Son acts as both voluntary substitute, taking on the penal consequences of the sins of others, and as the one who is able to offer satisfaction for this sin. Both punishment for the sin of human beings and satisfaction of divine justice is rendered in the one atoning act of Christ.

All this presumes that (a) divine retributive justice is inexorable and must be satisfied, and (b) the legal relaxation of punishment in the case of the atonement is consistent with this divine justice. Only if God is not able to accept the satisfaction of a substitute in the stead of sinners is God unable to allow Christ's atonement to count as a penal substitution for sin. Yet even if this point is granted, this still does not show that God is just in accepting the substitution of an innocent party (Christ) instead of the punishment of the sinner. It still does not show how a penal substitute is a just substitute. So it does not seem to me that the traditional argument in defence of the justice of penal substitution is sufficient for the purpose of making sense of this aspect of the doctrine.

Does Penal Substitution Make the Atonement Arbitrary?

We come to the second problem for penal substitution: whether it makes the atonement arbitrary. Let us assume, for the sake of the present argument, that it is arbitrary. Why should this be a problem for the defender of penal substitution? Presumably because penal substitution means God chooses to save a particular number of humanity less than the total number of humanity via this sort of atonement. But if this is the problem, it is not a problem with the theory of penal substitution as such but with a particular construal of this theory along the lines of the doctrine of particular redemption. Penal substitution does not entail particular redemption. What is more, other theories of atonement could be understood along particular-redemptionistic lines. So this sort of argument is not about penal substitution at all but about particular redemption, which is a separate, although related, issue.

To make this clear, consider the fact that penal substitution could be combined with a version of universalism. It could be that God arbitrarily decides to save all humanity through the penal substitutionary work of Christ. Assume that God does decree this in such a way that Christ's saving work is effectively applied to all humanity. It follows that no one (at least, no human) is damned; all humans are saved. Assume also that God arbitrarily decides to save all humanity rather than merely some of humanity, via penal substitution. I presume that far fewer contemporary theologians would have a problem with this application of penal substitution than they would with a particular-redemptionistic application of penal substitution, despite the fact that both versions of the doctrine involve an arbitrariness problem. So it is not penal substitution as a theory of atonement that is in question here but the way in which this theory is applied: as a means to a particular redemption less than the total number of humanity, or as a means to the particular redemption of all of humanity in a version of universalism, or some other view. In this respect, penal substitution is in the same metaphysical boat as all other theories of atonement that claim there is no optimum number of people that are saved.

Some theologians will respond by saying that there is an optimal number of humans that God saves. Universalists might claim this. But also, some who take a particular-redemptionistic view might claim this. One could argue that God saves a particular number of human beings less than the total number of humanity because this is the right number to display God's mercy and grace in salvation, and his justice and wrath in damnation. For, it might be thought, it is in the nature of God to display both these attributes in his works optimally, and God has ordained that this optimal state of affairs obtains.

I do not intend to argue for this claim. I am simply pointing out that some theologians might be attracted to this sort of justification for believing that a particular-redemptionistic argument could be conjoined with a doctrine of penal substitution without conceding at the outset that this entails that the number of humans saved via the atonement is arbitrary. In a similar fashion, the universalist would claim that only the salvation of all humanity represents the optimal number of human beings saved, because it is the objectively morally best outcome. Moreover, if God is essentially benevolent, he will ensure that all humanity is saved because the salvation of all humanity is the objectively morally best outcome.

So the defender of penal substitution has a decision to make. On the one hand, he could embrace the notion of particular redemption and state that Christ dies for some elect, not the whole of humanity. This leaves two possible options: concede that the exact number of the elect is arbitrary as far as we can tell, or present an argument that the number of the elect is not arbitrary. On the other hand, the defender of penal substitution could embrace the notion of universal redemption and state that Christ dies for the whole of humanity and that God ensures that all humanity are saved by this work. This also leads to two possible options: either concede that this divine decision to save all humanity is an arbitrary one, or present an argument that it is not an arbitrary decision to save all humanity, but that this is an objectively morally better state of affairs than the salvation of some number less than the totality of humanity.

These two ways of thinking about the relationship between penal substitution and the arbitrariness problem are not exhaustive of all logically possible options. One could take the view that penal substitution makes the salvation of all humanity possible, but not actual. But then, it seems, God does not decree the number of the elect. Nor does he decide that some particular number of humanity is the right number of saved humanity and brings about just this world as a result of that decision. Or if he does, he does not determine that there shall be just this number of humans saved and that this is the best number. On this view, the problem of arbitrariness does not apply in the same way.

So penal substitution, understood in terms of particular redemption, does not necessarily entail an arbitrariness problem. God may have a reason for saving just the number he does, on this view. But what if he does not? What if one concedes that the number of humanity saved via the atonement is arbitrary? This question, as I hinted earlier, is broader than the doctrine of penal substitution. Other theories of atonement are also liable to this sort of criticism. This is, of course, merely *ad hominem*. If the defender of penal substitution embraces the claim that God ordains to save a particular number of humanity via the atonement without sufficient justification for this decision, then an arbitrariness problem does follow. But the theologian need not embrace this conclusion simply because they think penal substitution is right.

Why Cannot God Simply Forgive Sin without Punishment?

The force of this line of criticism has already been considerably reduced by the exposition of the assumptions behind penal substitution. If divine justice is both retributive and inexorable such that God cannot permit forgiveness without punishment or satisfaction, then God cannot simply forgive sin without satisfaction being made. Of course, the critic could claim that this conception of divine justice is a travesty. But then some argument has to be offered as to why it is a travesty, and why some alternative conception of divine justice is preferable. Even if we concede that divine benevolence does require that God loves all humanity equally and savingly, this does not entail that God cannot or will not require satisfaction for sin, only that God will not let any human being be lost. It is perfectly consistent with this view of divine benevolence for God to save all humanity through the penal substitution of Christ.

In any case, it seems to me that divine benevolence need not mean God has to love all humanity equally *and* savingly. Divine benevolence is consistent with God's loving all his creatures but saving only some of them. Salvation is dependent not merely on divine benevolence but also on divine grace. God may love the sinner but hate the sin and punish it in hell, just as the parent may love the child who is sentenced to life imprisonment for murder. So a distinction needs to be made between divine benevolence and grace in this respect: even if divine benevolence is an essential attribute of God, it does not follow that God has to save all humanity, because grace is not inexorable in the same way that justice is. From this it seems to me that the traditional view of divine retributive punishment as inexorable is not a travesty but is coherent. So this argument against penal substitution fails.[28]

Can Sin and Guilt Be Transferred to Christ?

It should be clear from the foregoing that defenders of penal substitution have not usually been guilty of claiming that there really is a transference of properties from the sinner to Christ, or from Christ to the sinner, in sin, guilt and Christ's righteousness, respectively. Rather, in the classical doctrine of penal substitution, God takes Christ's satisfaction of the penalty due for sin as a penal substitute for the sin of humanity on the basis of a legal relaxation whereby Christ is able to take upon himself the liability to punishment for the guilt of sin. Nothing is transferred from the sinner to Christ beyond this "legal fiction". But Christ is punished as if he were the guilty party, though he is not, strictly speaking. The punishment served is therefore not numerically the same as that owed by the sinner (it cannot be, because the sinner does not serve it; Christ does). Nevertheless, an infinite punishment is served upon Christ; hence, it is a punishment that is qualitatively the same as that which would have been served upon the sinner had Christ not acted as substitute.[29] So on this view, the punishment due for the guilt of sin may be transferred in an action of legal relaxation on the part of God. This, it is claimed by defenders of penal substitution, is still just because it fits with the forensic nature of the atonement, outlined thus far. But can the liability for penal debts be transferred from one individual to another? If a murderer were able to have the culpability for his crime transferred to another, surely, we would think, this would make a mockery of justice. But this is just what is involved in penal substitution. The murderer remains the one who has committed the crime. He remains the one guilty of committing the crime. But the penal consequences of the crime are transferred to a vicar who serves the punishment in his stead. Despite the valiant attempts of theologians past and present to make sense of this claim, I cannot.

Conclusions

Not all of the problems we canvassed seem insurmountable for the doctrine of penal substitution. The claim that God could just forgive human beings without punishment seems wide of the mark. The claim that penal substitution makes God's action in election seem arbitrary does not necessarily obtain, and even if it does, it may not be a fatal problem. But the central problem with penal substitution remains: it is not possible for the sin and guilt of one individual to be transferred to another individual. Even if penal substitution means only that the penal consequences of sin are transferred from the sinner to Christ, there is still the transference of the penal consequences of sin to contend with, and it seems monumentally unjust to punish an innocent party in the place of a guilty one for a penal debt. Perhaps God can relax his justice to the extent that he can accept a vicarious satisfaction of the infinite debt owed by human beings instead of punishing them. If God can do this, it is a legal arrangement that has no obvious parallel in human penal transactions and still appears to be unjust, even if it is not arbitrary. And this problem alone poses serious difficulties for the traditional arguments for penal substitution.

However, matters are not as bleak as this might suggest. If I am right and traditional arguments for penal substitution are unworkable, there are still two alternatives open to the defender of penal substitution. One is to abandon penal substitution for a version of Anselmian satisfaction theory instead. This is a robust doctrine of atonement that delivers much of what penal substitution promises without some of the more problematic aspects of penal substitution. The other is to provide a different argument in favour of penal substitution. It seems to me that a robust doctrine of penal substitution can be salvaged, despite the foregoing, with a little help from Augustinian realism, the view according to which God constitutes humanity one metaphysical whole for the purposes of the imputation of sin. By extending the traditional use of this doctrine to encompass the atonement and union with Christ, a way might be found to salvage the doctrine of penal substitution. But providing such an argument is the work of another day.

Notes

1. See Simon Gathercole, "The Cross and Substitutionary Atonement," *Scottish Bulletin of Evangelical Theology* 21 (2003): 155.

2. To take just one example, J. I. Packer, in his Tyndale Lecture "What Did the Cross Achieve? The Logic of Penal Substitution," says that this doctrine marks out evangelicals in their belief that "Christ's death on the cross had the character of penal substitution, and that it was in virtue of this fact that it brought salvation to mankind" (Packer, "What Did the Cross Achieve? The Logic of Penal Substitution," *TynBul* 25 [1974]: 3–46; reprinted as an RTSF Booklet [Leicester: UCCF, 2002], 11). I shall cite this version of the lecture in what follows. The literature on penal substitution is considerable. For two other recent treatments of interest, see Christina A. Baxter, "The Cursed Beloved: A Reconsideration of Penal Substitution," in *Atonement Today*, ed. John Goldingay (London: SPCK, 1995), and Stephen R. Holmes, "Can Punishment Bring Peace? Penal Substitution Revisited," *SJT* 58, no. 1 (2005): 104–23.

3. There has been some recent discussion about the fact that certain models of the atonement, especially the penal substitution and satisfaction models, are intrinsically violent and should be set to one side for other models of the atonement which do not require violence as an intrinsic part of the model. However, this does not seem to me to be a serious criticism of these models of atonement. Any reflection upon the atonement has to deal with the fact that intrinsic in the atonement is the notion of violence being done to the person of Christ, even if only so that Christ may be seen to be an exemplar to human beings. It makes no sense to speak of Christian atonement without violence. One may as well speak of the work of Christ without a cross.

4. Packer, "What Did the Cross Achieve?" 35.

5. See Oliver D. Crisp, "Divine Retribution: A Defence," *Sophia* 42 (2003): 35–52.

6. Adapted from Marilyn McCord Adams, "Hell and the God of Justice," *Religious Studies* 11 (1974): 434. Paul Helm has pointed out to me that there

are other concepts of fairness one could apply to, such as "outcome" fairness. A fiscal system with graduated taxation is said to be fairer than one that lacks this. However, the three aspects of fairness mentioned by Adams will suffice for the present argument.

7. Louis Berkhof, *Systematic Theology* (1939; Edinburgh: Banner of Truth Trust, 1988), 375.

8. See Richard Swinburne, *Responsibility and Atonement* (Oxford: Oxford Univ. Press, 1989), 81–92 and ch. 10.

9. I think the term "penance" is unhelpful because of the theological baggage associated with it. But I shall not take issue with that here.

10. Steven Porter, "Rethinking the Logic of Penal Substitution," in *Philosophy of Religion: A Reader and Guide*, ed. William Lane Craig (Edinburgh: Edinburgh Univ. Press, 2002), 601–2.

11. I have argued this point in more detail in my "Divine Retribution: A Defence."

12. I do not claim that this reasoning about the status of the individual offended applies to relationships between creatures, only that it applies to the special case of divine-human relationships.

13. Swinburne claims that this infinite punishment thesis constitutes "exaggerated talk" and that allocating a moral value to sin is "somewhat arbitrary". This is a little rich coming from a philosopher whose use of Bayes' theorem to demonstrate the reasonableness of belief in God and the resurrection depends upon probabilistic values that are extremely difficult to quantify. In any case, Swinburne offers no substantive argument against the infinite punishment thesis. See *Responsibility and Atonement*, 154n10.

14. Turretin makes this point. See Francis Turretin, *Institutes of Elenctic Theology*, vol. 2, ed. James T. Dennison, trans. George Musgrave Giger Jr. (Phillipsburg, N.J.: P & R, 1994), t14.q10.418. But it seems that "absolute necessity" admits of the following conditional: "If there is to be forgiveness, then the satisfaction of divine justice is absolutely necessary." If so, then absolute necessity is embedded in a conditional of its own. But the point here has to do with whether God can put satisfaction to one side and forgive without justice being satisfied to the full, not the related point about whether satisfaction of divine justice is needed for forgiveness to be offered.

15. I will not pause to consider related questions such as whether all infinite punishment is equal punishment (argued for in my "Divine Retribu-

tion: A Defence") or the claim, made by Peter Geach, that God could mete out an infinite punishment for sin in a finite period. See Peter Geach, *Providence and Evil* (Cambridge: Cambridge Univ. Press, 1977), 148–49.

16. Swinburne, *Responsibility and Atonement*, 155.

17. L. W. Grensted, *A Short History of the Doctrine of the Atonement* (Manchester: Manchester Univ. Press, 1920), 216.

18. See Turretin, *Institutes of Elenctic Theology*, t14.q10.419.

19. Berkhof, *Systematic Theology*, 376.

20. William Shedd says this is called "acceptilation", but Alan Gomes points out that this is wrong. Acceptilation is the idea that an offended party received no payment of the debt owed by the offender, but that this is accepted as if it were paid in full. What is at issue here is acceptation: the partial payment of the debt owed, which is accepted as if the whole debt had been paid. See William G. T. Shedd, *Dogmatic Theology*, 3rd ed., ed. Alan Gomes (Phillipsburg, N.J.: P & R, 2003), 733n123.

21. This point is made in Charles Hodge's *Systematic Theology*, vol. 2, *Anthropology* (London: Thomas Nelson and Sons, 1874), 487. The difference between these two variations of this form of legal relaxation depends upon the way in which God accepts the penal substitution. In the first case, God decides to accept the inferior punishment. Here the substitute's satisfaction has an intrinsic worth, just not a worth equal to the satisfaction required for the crime committed. In the latter case, Christ's work does not have an intrinsic worth that makes it satisfactory; perhaps it is not satisfactory in the least, yet God graciously accepts it as if it were adequate or satisfactory. But both defend the idea that there is a relaxation in the fact that a substitute is able to atone for the sin of another and that this satisfaction is not equal to the culpability of the crime committed.

22. See Shedd, *Dogmatic Theology*, 123, and Hodge, *Systematic Theology*, 487. The first of these two views on legal relaxation is often attributed to Scotus and Grotius; the second, to those who defend a strong view of penal substitution, such as Owen or Turretin. (It does not particularly matter, for the sake of the present argument, whether these attributions are accurate. The point is these theologians are usually attributed with developing these two versions of legal relaxation with respect to the atonement.)

23. Berkhof, *Systematic Theology*, 377.

24. This is the scholastic distinction between the *reatus culpae* (liability to punishment) and *reatus poenae* (liability to guilt), the two aspects of original

guilt. I have discussed this elsewhere: see Oliver Crisp, "Scholastic Theology, Augustinian Realism and Original Guilt," *EuroJTh* 13 (2004): 17–28.

25. This raises a question about the justification of the sinner. How can someone who is still sinful and guilty for his sin be righteous in the sight of God? Presumably because the righteousness of Christ is imputed to the sinner, just as the liability to punishment of the sinner is imputed to Christ. So here too, it seems, God treats one person as if they were another, the sinner as if he were Christ. Space prevents the further development of this point.

26. Perhaps a version of Augustinian realism can be used to make sense of this way of thinking of the atonement. If God makes the elect and Christ one metaphysical entity for the purposes of atonement, then the sin and guilt of the elect could pass to Christ as a part of the whole entity, and Christ's righteousness could pass to the elect in a similar fashion. But this would require a sophisticated argument that I cannot pursue here. For more on this see Crisp, "Scholastic Theology, Augustinian Realism and Original Guilt."

27. John Calvin, *Institutes of the Christian Religion* 2.16.5, vol. 1, ed. John T. McNeill, trans. Ford Lewis Battles (Philadelphia: Westminster, 1960), 509–10.

28. Could the defender of penal substitution maintain that divine justice is inexorable whilst divine benevolence is not? Only if a moral agent "could have done otherwise" in a particular morally significant choice. For only then can it make sense to say that benevolence (whether human or divine) is not inexorable. This requires theological libertarianism. But according to theological determinism, this makes no sense because no moral agent could have done otherwise (presuming the determinist is a consistent determinist and applies this to all moral agents, God included). I am assuming that defenders of penal substitution in the Augustinian tradition have almost all taken this deterministic view. In which case, this libertarian manoeuvre is not open to them.

29. How is Christ's punishment an infinite punishment, if he suffers on the cross for a matter of only some hours? There are several possible responses to this. One, following Peter Geach, is to say that Christ is able to suffer an infinite punishment in a finite period, where time is an infinitely dense continuum. The other is to say that Christ's death is a death of infinite significance and intensity, since it is the death of the God-man.

chapter thirteen

towards a unified theory of the atonement

david t. williams

It is often noted that the New Testament does not explain the method of the atonement. Any explanation must remain at the level of a theory. This is not surprising: the same could well be said of a number of theological issues, such as the incarnation, which is then often understood in functional terms, or the Trinity, where the focus is on the revealed or "economic". It is even the case for the creation: the Bible clearly presents the fact that God created but leaves out what is for us the contentious issue of how. The later stress on ontology, which emanates from a more Greek way of thinking, is foreign to the Bible and could be said to have led the church away from the simple biblical emphasis. Nevertheless, we seem to be made in such a way that we can really accept something as true only if we can, at least to some extent, understand it, and this is certainly true of the atonement. It is, after all, incredible that salvation can occur, as Paul himself marvels (Rom. 5:8).

Even if it is not presented explicitly, advocates of the penal substitution theory hold that there is adequate witness to the idea in the New Testament. Certainly there is a long history of support for it, and it has been the dominant understanding in evangelical circles which have highly regarded the authority of Scripture.[1] But because it does remain a theory, and because there are a number of cogent objections that can be put to it, several other theories have been proposed. Notable among these is the so-called classic theory popularised by Gustav Aulén's *Christus Victor*.[2] This theory, he argued, has historical roots in the recapitulation model proposed by Irenaeus. Essentially, the belief is that a believer participates in the victory over sin and death that was achieved by Christ. Aulén held that penal substitution had usurped the ancient and rightful place that his theory should enjoy. This theory is indeed often overshadowed by the contrast between the penal substitutionary approach, sometimes referred to as objective, and a so-called subjective understanding which emphasizes that Christ's example motivates inner change in people.[3] In turn, these other presentations have been subject to objections, often emanating from advocates of the traditional understanding. It would be fair to say that no theory seems able to claim overwhelming support.

The symposium on the atonement held at London School of Theology in July 2005 demonstrated that evangelicals are not as united in their support for penal substitution as one might assume. Both support for and opposition to the theory were persuasively argued over the period of the conference, but no real consensus was achieved. Yet through the course of the event, speakers dropped hints that could be seen as a solution to the dilemma. The penal substitution theory is a valid understanding of the Bible, but only if understood as an aspect of a broader theory. By incorporating other aspects into it, one can provide answers to the objections made against the penal substitution theory.

This suggestion is not new. Probably reacting to the dominance of the penal substitution theory in his day, P. T. Forsyth expounded what he referred to as the "three-fold cord", especially citing 1 Corinthians 1:30.[4] He knew of the shortcomings of the alternatives, especially the subjective theory. He pointed out that the parable of the prodigal son, often held as an example of willingness to forgive without payment of a price, could not necessarily be understood in that sense. With good reason, he suggested that the errant son would likely have sold himself into slavery as his last hope.[5] In that case, the father would have had to pay the price of redemption in order to restore him legally. More recently, and more acceptably in evangelical circles, John Stott has also argued for a view of the atonement which comprises three main groups of theories: objective, subjective and classic.[6]

Theories of Atonement

The glory of the gospel is that God made a way of restoring humanity's relationship with himself that had been broken by sin; the wonder is that God did this without compromising his holiness. If he had ignored sin, or simply forgiven it, he would no longer be holy, as he would be condoning sin and having a relationship to what was sinful. Although God has "no pleasure in the death of the wicked" (Ezek. 33:11) but on the contrary "desires all men to be saved" (1 Tim. 2:4) and sees such love issue in forgiveness, he is unjust if he simply forgives without real atonement, as that would effectively say that offence against God may be permissible. The sin committed cannot just be forgotten but must be expiated. God cannot simply put the sin aside; it must be propitiated. Because an act cannot just be undone, the due penalty for sin has to be paid so that it can be justly cancelled. Sin, therefore, has to be removed from a person before salvation, wherein a relationship with God can be enacted. If the relationship of adoption as children of God (Rom. 8:15) is to happen, past sins have to be dealt with. The liberal appeal to love leaves out atonement.[7] There has to be salvation from sin as well as salvation to life, salvation from the negative to make possible salvation to the positive.

In the New Testament, just as in the Old, such atonement is understood to be achieved by sacrifice. Here the suffering and death of Christ is a sufficient sacrificial penalty for sin. Sin is expiated by means of the substitutionary sacrifice of Christ (here some prefer to speak of representation rather than substitution, but the essential idea is the same).[8] Jesus can therefore refer to his death as a "ransom for many" (Mark 10:45), the price he paid to release people from the burden and bondage of sin. He took the punishment for which Christians were liable, so that they could be forgiven, justified, declared righteous and thereby enjoy union with God in Christ: "For our sake he made him to be sin who knows no sin, that in him we might become the righteousness of God" (2 Cor. 5:21).

Because Christ is perfectly human, he can die as an appropriate sacrifice for the sins of the whole of humanity (1 John 2:2; 2 Cor. 5:19); because he is divine, his death is adequate for the sins of all. There is, then, no obstacle to establishing a relationship between believers and God, and where an offence sours that relationship, the death of Christ is continually effective to remove that offence and its effects (1 John 1:9).

Sacrificial imagery is common in the New Testament, notably in the book of Hebrews, but the idea of substitution is frequent elsewhere (e.g., Mark 10:45; Gal. 3:13). This is essential for the forgiveness of sins, for by means of what Anselm called the "amazing exchange", Christ received the punishment for the sins of the believers, while they receive the sinlessness of Christ and so are justified. This is one reason why Christ had to be fully human, not just to be a full substitute or representative for human beings but so that the imparted holiness is human, not angelic or of some other kind.[9]

This penal substitution theory is not without valid objections, despite its popularity in some sections of the church. Not least, it has been viewed as fundamentally unjust. The Socinians, for example, reacting to the Reformation understanding of justification, felt that it was immoral to transfer the punishment which was due to the sinner onto a party who was innocent.[10] Thus, although the theory was put forward in response to the justice of God, it was felt to be fundamentally unjust in itself. However, a view of salvation which sees it brought about by relationship with Christ, the key affirmation of the classic theory, immediately solves this problem, for just as husband and wife are often treated in law as one unit, so by virtue of the closeness of their relationship are Christ and the Christian also treated as one unit. Thus, it is not so much that punishment is transferred from one person to another in a substitution, or that one representative is punished instead of the rest, as it is that the unit as a whole bears the punishment due to the sin of the unit as a whole. Just as the Christian shares the life of Christ, so Christ shares the punishment of the Christian, both experiences are common. The union of the believer and Christ, as a union, is punished, and the believer lives eternally in union with Christ.[11] Then, on the other hand, the relationship with Christ enables new life through sharing in the resurrection of Christ from the dead. For Paul, the atonement is almost always linked not just to the cross but also to the resurrection.[12] Here, while the penal substitution theory has little place for the resurrection except as a proof that God had accepted the sacrifice of the cross, the classic theory unites them as two aspects of a process.[13]

Because of the union with Christ, it is possible for Paul to say that he makes up the sufferings of Christ and that he rejoices in sufferings (Col. 1:24); for him they are a common experience. Moreover, at the same time, a Christian in fact even keeps the law perfectly, but in Christ. It has been a tremendous Reformation principle that a Christian is declared righteous, rather than made righteous.[14] Generally, a distinction has been made in theology between this and sanctification, the process of actually becoming righteous after salvation. However, the word "justification" does mean the latter (Latin *justus facere*), and this is also made real by the union with Christ.

The fact that this is only a progress towards, and not an attainment of, holiness, is a problem with which all serious Christians wrestle. Knowledge of what is right does not lead to conformity to what is right. Luther went through agonies of spirit because he was unable to attain a righteous life, then went through agonies of body trying to suppress temptations, all to little avail. It was intensely liberative for him to realise that salvation did not have to be earned by attaining perfection, but was by grace. However, this immediately meant that although saved, justified and declared righteous, he still sinned. He knew that a Christian is *simul iustus et peccator*, "at once justified and a sinner".

This also means that human righteousness is in no way necessary for the relationship with Christ to occur. Although holiness and purity are essential, this is achieved by what Christ has done, not by human effort. After that relationship is established, a Christian can improve, but this is as a result of that relationship, never a cause of it. It is noteworthy here that in union with Christ, and therefore with his death, a Christian effectively dies (Rom. 7:4), so that the power of sin is broken. The Christian is thus enabled to live a life acceptable to God.

Nevertheless, the penal substitution theory, taken alone, does not give a strong motivation for a change in lifestyle. It may even produce the opposite, for as Paul had to argue in Romans 6 and 7, if forgiveness has been achieved, why change? Indeed, it could even be said that sin is good, so that more grace is received (Rom. 6:1)! Both the penal substitution and the classic theories – the objective theories – if seen alone, appear to view the atonement as something done almost apart from humanity. It seems to have little to do with the people for whom Christ died and rose. Again, it is often pointed out that a gift has to be appropriated, but there is a great desire within people to do something tangible so that they know that they are saved. What Christ did must be seen to affect the lives of believers. As Baillie points out, atonement is more than forgiveness.[15] Without at least a measure of repentance, a change in life, there is not really any reconciliation; without this, it becomes the "cheap grace" that Bonhoeffer so rightly rejected.

This lack is resolved by appreciating the need of *metanoia*, repentance, a change of life in response to the demand of the gospel. It is noteworthy that this was the content of Jesus' first preaching (Mark 1:15). This brings in the subjective aspect of atonement. But while the subjective theories of atonement presuppose a change towards or conformity with what is right, if taken alone, they give rise to two problems: how it is that such a lifestyle becomes possible while it seems not possible before this commitment, and how failings in the Christian life, particularly past sins, can be dealt with.

The first problem is one with which Paul wrestled. Knowledge of what was right did not lead to conformity with what was right. For him, as a Jew, the law was the source of that knowledge, but Paul's experience was that, far from leading to a good life, the law even led to the opposite effect as awareness of what was wrong led to the temptation to do it. This was resolved in two ways. First, as a Christian, he was not obligated to keep the law as he had been. This was no real solution, however, as even under no actual obligation, the law still indicated what God's desires are in principle. He knew what was right, what was expected of him, but seemed powerless to obey (Rom. 7:7ff.).

Second, complementing the loss of the need to keep the law because of union with the death of Christ, union with the life of Christ means that the power of the resurrection is also available to the Christian: "He who raised Christ Jesus from the dead will give life to your mortal bodies also through his spirit which dwells in you, if the Spirit of him who raised Jesus from the dead dwells in you" (Rom. 8:11). In other words, the Spirit who enables the relationship between Christ and the Christian, by virtue of his essential presence, also gives power over temptation and to do the works of God. It is the union with the victorious resurrection of Christ that is the means of that repentance, for it is the only way of empowering a lifestyle desired by God. Real obedience is possible only because of this union with Christ. Works are not the means of salvation but the result of the same union with Christ; they follow from and demonstrate the existence of the faith that unites the believer to God.

This clarifies the statement of James 2:14, that salvation is by works; otherwise it seems as if salvation is achieved by the action of the believer.[16] This mistaken belief was repeatedly repudiated by Paul (e.g., Eph. 2:8–9), Augustine, Luther, Calvin and many others, who strongly insisted that salvation is a gift of God and that the believer could not contribute to salvation. Indeed, the sacrifice to enable forgiveness is totally the action of God, not due to people. There is thus no hint of a salvation by human works.

Nevertheless, if the death of Christ fully dealt with sin, why is it that Christian experience is still one of sinning? As John points out, "if we say we have no sin, we deceive ourselves ... if we say we have not sinned, we make him a liar" (1 Jonn 1:8, 10). In a sense, sin after commitment to Christ is different from that committed before, as the latter was dealt with by sharing in the death of Christ. Once that death has occurred, sin is no longer relevant, for a dead person cannot be punished. However, once new life is possessed by relationship to Christ, death is in the past, and so that possibility is no longer valid. Nevertheless, sins must still be dealt with, as God is holy and the continued relationship cannot tolerate a lack of holiness.

Here, the death of Christ, and hence of the believer, is still a means of forgiveness. John writes, "He is the expiation for our sins, and not for ours only, but also for the sins of the whole world" (1 John 2:2). There is no need for further punishment. Nevertheless, this cannot be considered as automatic as before; John therefore notes the advocacy of Christ to the Father so that forgiveness may be applied.

It is the efficacy of the cross of Christ which enables forgiveness. This is an event for which the subjective theories often have little place except to see it as the culmination of a perfect life, an example to be followed in principle, and as an expression of perfect love. Yet it is hard to see why a perfect life had to end in such a way, hardly an attractive example to follow; on the contrary, it is readily seen as necessary if sins were really to be dealt with. Without this, past sins would remain and repentance would be ineffective for salvation.

At the same time, even the new life itself can be seen as the means of dealing with sins. Union with Christ enables obedience to prophetic demands. A dead body, when it is damaged, remains damaged and cannot be healed, but a live body will repair itself, depending upon the nature of the injury: "What is mortal is swallowed up by life" (2 Cor. 5:4). This means that open and deliberate sin, refusal to repent, would sever the relationship with Christ completely. Thus John distinguishes between sin which is mortal, and that which is not (1 John 5:16). This is also one instance of the corporate effect of the relationship with Christ. The Old Testament parallel is that the sacrificial system was effective only for the removal of ceremonial or accidental sin.[17] For deliberate sins, those committed "with a high hand" (Num. 15:30), the effect was the breaking of union with God and a cutting off from the Israelite nation. Specifically, dealing with past sins could not be effective without repentance. The point here is that it is the relationship with Christ that is at the heart of salvation; forgiveness enables but does not enact it. In the Old Testament, sacrifice was part of the covenant relationship, not prior to it. Although Robert Letham is trying to prove a very different point, he is very correct to observe that Christ saves *his people* from their sins (Matt. 1:21).[18]

A further objection to the penal substitution theory is that it appears to drive a wedge between Christ and his Father. The Father's desire is caricatured as a desire to punish, which is prevented only by the love of the Son. It was this problem which impressed Aulén, who therefore saw in the victory of the Son over death that the atonement must be the work of the entire Trinity. He took 2 Corinthians 5:19 as determinative: "God was in Christ reconciling the world to himself." Salvation was a work of the Trinity, resting on the union of the persons. This, incidentally, can be taken to mean that a doctrine of salvation likewise rests on union, which is in fact the emphasis particularly underlying the classic theory. It is evident that the difficulties of the penal substitution theory are then again resolved by the fact that a Christian is in union with Christ.

The classic theory thus relates to the unity of the Trinity. Traditional trinitarian theology, while concurring that all acts of God are acts of the whole Trinity, *opera Trinatis ad extra indivisa sunt*, usually includes an idea of appropriation, by which specific actions of God are attributed to specific persons. If this is applied to the atonement, forgiveness is a work of the Son, giving eternal life is a work of the Father (as is, in any case, stressed in the classic theory), and repentance is a work of the Spirit. A similar division can apply to the idea of time, in that forgiveness relates to the past, eternal life to the future, and change of life to the present.

Indeed, a small but significant point is that a combination of theories may be seen as theologically more satisfying in other ways as well. For example, the penal theory may well be criticised as excessively individualist, and so be balanced by the corporate emphasis of the classic theory, which can also bring a cosmic aspect to atonement,[19] a factor missing in the prescriptions for personal sins advanced by the other theories. Then the objective theories relate to God's transcendence, the subjective to his immanence, two poles which, as with other aspects, Christian theology has wanted to hold in tension.

These considerations support a theory of the atonement with three aspects: forgiveness, union and repentance, basically corresponding to the penal, the classic and the example theories. These were the three most common models in the early church.[20] Even if other theories have been put forward,[21] they can be treated as variants of the three basic ideas. To quote Letham, "The idea of satisfaction or penal substitution does not exclude other theories. It is compatible with the conquest theory and can also see subjective change occurring in human beings as a consequence of what Christ did on the cross."[22] This threefoldness can provide a powerful understanding of baptism (Rom. 6:1–4) as an outward sign of salvation. The Christian effectively dies with Christ, then rises with him into new life. It is due to an appreciation of resurrection that many Christians prefer the act of immersion, which clearly evokes being buried and raised, over that of sprinkling, which relates rather to cleansing from sin – a valid component of redemption, but hardly the whole matter. In addition, of course, immersion is a more effective washing! Baptism, then, not only signifies forgiveness and union with Christ but is a striking public commitment to a life of service in obedience to Christ. Similarly, the communion, while perhaps even more graphic as a reminder of the Christ's death, also demonstrates the essentiality of a full union with Christ for the continuance of the Christian life, and is done in obedience to his command.

An understanding of atonement is now more complete and self-consistent, but is it comprehensive? The number three is attractive and significant for Christians, but it does need to be explained how it is relevant to the idea of salvation. It is a fundamental number, as already observed, relating to time and the Trinity, but here the old understanding of Christ as prophet, priest and king can provide another threefold framework. Indeed, it has been commonly applied to the atonement.[23] In particular, Letham not only refers to the paradigm but uses it as a framework.[24] It is especially attractive to be able to relate the work of Christ in atonement directly to an understanding of his person.

A Word of Caution

There is an obvious attraction in a theological model, but anybody who uses one is in danger of forcing the evidence to fit the theory.[25] In particular, by widening the idea of atonement to include two other aspects beside the penal substitution model, the temptation can well be to restrict attention to just the three. Just as there are other facets of the person of Christ besides prophet, priest and king, so there other facets of his work. Nevertheless, other aspects can be subsumed under these three. Thus, for example, Douglas Hall, while acknowledging the long tradition of the threefold office, wants to note the existence of judge, and especially of steward; however, both of those are effectively kingly.[26]

No theory can be all-embracing, nor must it embrace every suggestion that has been made: it is quite possible that some ideas are plain wrong and should be omitted. Nevertheless, what this model does is to bring together the three most widely accepted understandings into a consistent framework which overcomes the shortcomings of each taken alone.

Jesus as Prophet, Priest and King

Part of the value of this understanding is that it is rooted deep in the Old Testament, as the figures of prophet, priest and king were the key figures of salvation in that context. Seeing Jesus as fulfilling these three roles in himself thus also unites the understandings of salvation in the two testaments.

The establishment of the offices of prophet, priest and king in the limited society of Israel was the means of relating each individual and the nation as a whole to God. However, even this system did not result in an ideal society. Part of the problem was the individuals who filled the Old Testament roles. The shortcomings of the kings hardly need comment. Indeed, it was because of their deficiencies that prophets were necessary to rebuke and correct them, and priests to atone for their misdeeds. The priests, despite their consecration, were fallible. The Old Testament records many priestly failings; the book of Hebrews records the shortcomings of the system, and the priests at the time of Jesus did not escape his censure. Even prophets were disobedient, as in the case of Jonah, and complained, as in the case of Jeremiah. Despite a close relationship to God, they were not infallible. Thus, while accepting the offices, Israel looked forward to their being enacted perfectly. They looked towards the coming of a perfect king (a second David), a perfect priest (a new Aaron), and a perfect prophet (a new Moses).

It was the coming of Christ that enabled the solution to become effective. He is the one who fulfils the Old Testament roles, performing them completely. The figures who occupied the various offices in the Old Testament may have been effective in themselves, at least to a degree, but the fact that they did fail pointed forward to the culmination of their roles in Christ.

Thus the expectation of a king, a fulfilment of the prophecy of an everlasting dynasty made to the paradigmatic king David (2 Sam. 7:12ff.), is realized in Christ. This prophecy has a dual fulfilment: first, there was a line of kings succeeding Solomon and culminating in Zedekiah, but at the same time the promise of an eternal dynasty is fulfilled in the eternal Christ, who is himself in that line.

Likewise, Deuteronomy 18 contains the prediction of a prophet who would be like Moses, the paradigmatic prophet (Deut. 34:10; Hos. 12:13).

This may be taken as a prediction of either a line of prophets or an eschatological prophet. The New Testament appears to accept both of these possibilities: John's gospel refers repeatedly to the latter expectation (e.g., John 1:21; 6:14; etc.), and the early preaching in Acts (3:22–23) can even bear both possibilities together. Both aspects are valid: there was indeed a line of prophets, but Jesus finally fulfilled the expectation.

Finally, although not such a prominent hope in the Old Testament, the expectation of a priest was present in some groups at the time of Jesus. Some suggest that the Qumran community expected two messiahs, a priestly one and a kingly one.[27] This priestly expectation may also be seen as realized in Christ, providing the background to the epistle to the Hebrews. The only difference, due to the Aaronic priesthood being restricted to the tribe of Levi, is that Jesus fulfilled the priestly expectation in the line of Melchizedek.

Although both the Old Testament and its development into Judaism generally kept the roles distinct, it is not surprising that these various expectations should be fulfilled in one person. Identification had already occurred to some extent in the rule of the high priests for a period after the return from exile (cf. Zech. 6:11). The rabbis also equated the priestly messiah with the prophet of Deuteronomy 18:18. Nevertheless, the usual expectation of the time was as at Qumran, where three figures were expected, but where they were definitely separate and even distinguished hierarchically.[28] The separation was due to the failings of each; however, if the roles were enacted more perfectly, combination within one individual would be possible.

Although Pannenberg and others are correct to observe that Christ never claimed any of the Old Testament roles of prophet, priest and king for himself,[29] the New Testament evidence for seeing Christ as the fulfilment of these roles is well known and has often been described. Modern treatments are to be found in Bruce Milne, Helmut Thielicke, Letham and in my own work.[30] These modern treatments can usually be traced back to Calvin, who has a brief description in his *Institutes*. However, the idea was not original to him, going back even to Eusebius. None of these would claim to be original, but rather they describe and bring together the relevant biblical material.

Thus, Jesus may be seen as legitimately filling and accepting each of the Old Testament roles, but also as more than a simple repetition of what went before. He is prophet, priest and king and, because of his divine nature, fulfils each role perfectly. It is also because of his Sonship that he can unite the roles; indeed, in Jesus, there are not three offices but one single office.

The Atonement as the Action of Prophet, Priest and King

The relationship of salvation, the adoption as children of God, cannot be achieved automatically but must be established. This will have two aspects: salvation requires both the removal of negative hindrances to, and at the same time the establishment of, the positive union with Christ. After all, it is possible to have contact between two parties but nevertheless no real relationship, such as when two have to live and work together, but an underlying problem continually affects the relationship. On the other hand, there may be no hindrance to relationship, but it has never been developed. Again, both aspects are vital: just as the Hebrew greeting *shalom* wishes the absence of a damaging hostility, it means at the same time a positive relationship of harmony. It is here that the work of Christ as prophet, priest and king becomes particularly relevant, because it enables both the removal of hindrances to relationship and gives a positive union with God in Christ.

In first-century Roman and Greek society, a childless couple would adopt a son in order to have an heir to whom they could pass on their name and property. However, a couple could not simply take over a child arbitrarily, but just as today, the process of adoption involved governmental and legal processes. It could not be done simply by the will of adopters or adopted but ultimately by the consent and action of the rulers of the state. Thus, there is a sense in which adoption is possible because Jesus has the role of king. He has the authority to adopt believers into this relationship with himself: "As my Father appointed a kingdom for me, so do I appoint for you that you may eat and drink at my table in my kingdom, and sit on thrones judging the twelve tribes of Israel" (Luke 22:29–30).

The kingly authority of Christ is perhaps seen most clearly in the resurrection, in which Christ was victorious as a king over the forces of sin and death, over "principalities and powers" (Col. 2:15). The apostolic preaching in the book of Acts stresses that in the resurrection, Christ has eternal life and has overcome death (Acts 2:31; 13:35ff.). Indeed, because of his divine nature, it was not possible for Christ to be held by the power of death (Acts 2:24). This is what he gives to Christians.

A king is not simply one with authority over his subjects, but exists and rules for their benefit. Because the king exists, life for the people is enhanced by their relationship to him. In any monarchic system, the actions and character of the king directly affect the people. If he is victorious, the people benefit; if he is defeated, so are the people. The pages of the Old Testament are full of the punishments suffered by the people because of the sins of the kings. Indeed, he is not so much over his people; rather, he embodies his people. Therefore, because Christ is king, he gives the benefit of eternal life to his people. Eternal life is not naturally a possession of mortal people, but only of God (1 Tim. 6:16). It becomes the possession of believers only in their union with Christ. Paul argues this in Romans 6: because Christians are united with Christ in his resurrection, and only because of that, they have eternal life: "For if we have united with him in a death like his, we shall certainly be united with him in a resurrection like his" (Rom. 6:5); "We believe that we shall also live with him. For we know that Christ being raised from the dead will never die again, death no longer has dominion over him" (Rom. 6:8–9).

In fact, because eternal life is Christ's by nature, a believer has eternal life immediately (John 3:36; 5:24). Although this will come to fruition in the eschatological resurrection, it is the possession of believers as soon as they enter into a relationship with Christ as king and have adoption as children of God. It is the Holy Spirit who enables this relationship. Jesus spoke of new life received by new birth and connected that with the work of the Spirit (John 3:5). This should not surprise us, as the fundamental role of the Spirit is enabling relationship. This follows from the Spirit's enabling of life itself, such as is seen elsewhere in the gift of life to Adam (Gen. 2:7, where the word often translated "breath" may also be rendered "spirit") or in Ezekiel's valley of dry bones (Ezek. 37:9).

Of course, a relationship to Christ as king is not simply one-sided; receiving its benefits involves a response. A king is not simply someone who gives the benefits of his rule to his subjects but one who governs and makes his kingdom run in an orderly way. His subjects obey him, and in this obedience comes order. Belonging to the kingdom involves conformity to the king. Thus, a relationship to Christ as king does not just give harmony with God but should result in harmony between people and with the environment.

Basically, salvation, union with Christ, should result in a changed lifestyle. Real union is possible only through the conformity of the life of a Christian to the will of God. It is possible only if there is agreement: "Can two walk together unless they agree?" (Amos 3:3). Such a change in lifestyle is the aim of the prophet, whose role is thus also essential in salvation. As with any prophet, Christ communicated the will of God not only by words and teaching but also by deeds, so that in imitation of Christ's obedience to his Father comes the obedience of his adopted children as well. This gives a role to Christ's life and ministry that neither the penal nor the classic theories can really provide.

Therefore, Christ as prophet points out the failings of the people by what he says and demands repentance and a lifestyle acceptable to God. Thankfully, the Christian is not in the position of ancient Israelites seeking to obey the words of the prophet, but is in union with Christ the king. From this union, the requirements of God are internalised to the Christian. This was indeed prophesied by Jeremiah: "I will put my law within them and I will write it upon their hearts; and I will be their God, and they will be my people" (Jer. 31:33).

On this basis, Paul can argue that Christians are not compelled outwardly to keep the law but that they please God by walking according to the Spirit (Rom. 8:4). In fact, this solves the basic problem where obedience is required by an external law only. In the Old Testament, people could obey the rulers according to the letter of the law but still be essentially disobedient. They could fulfil their religious obligations outwardly but not please God by so doing (Isa. 1:10–17). This was equally true in the time of Jesus, when at least some Pharisees, while meticulous in keeping every detail of the law and the tradition, yet displeased God.

In fact, the basic sin is not the transgression of a set of commands but a lack of relationship with God. It is only this, and not disobedience to law, that results in condemnation. Obedience to law comes only after the removal of that basic sin by the establishing of relationship: the Old Testament law was given as a result of the covenant between God and Israel. This means that the law was, and is, directly applicable only to Israel – to those in the covenant. Christians today, unless they are Jewish, are therefore not subject to it. They should generally obey it, particularly as it clearly reflects the will of God, but they are not saved by so doing. It is the relationship with God which brings salvation.

Particularly because obedience does not always come naturally to people, the internalisation of the requirements of God by the direct prophetic action of Christ to each believer through the Spirit ought to mean that the believer should be more obedient. Moreover, because life is made up of lots of individual circumstances, which can never be totally covered by a written code, the role of the prophet is essential in guiding in each circumstance.

It must be noted here that a prophet was not only one who received the message from God and was commanded to deliver it. He was also empowered to give that message. The prophets received the Spirit of God for that purpose, and Christ was enabled to obey God in all things in the same way. It follows that the prophetic demand for obedience that is received by the Christian is not an empty demand, but in the union with Christ, the Christian receives also the ability to obey what God commands. Just as two people will help each other as they work together, so the union with Christ enables the Christian. Christians are not alone in their struggle. There should be a gradual deepening of relationship and a growing agreement. This is generally known as sanctification, the increasing holiness of life that should be evident in Christians.

The necessity of Christlike obedience, if there is to be a real relationship with God and other people, heightens the basic problem of humanity. People do not naturally please God, and so are not naturally in a relationship with him. This means that if the relationship of adoption is to happen, there has to be salvation from sin as well as salvation to life. This involves the priestly role of Christ. This does not mean that the priestly work of Christ is limited to his death for us. He continues to represent us before God (Heb. 9:24), where he intercedes for us. In the ascended Christ's presence with God, we are represented in him before the Father.

It is therefore clear that salvation is multifaceted and involves each aspect of the office of Christ. First, sins must be forgiven, which is effected by the priestly death of Christ. But second, life is received by union with Christ, specifically with the eternal life which is his by his divine nature, manifested in his kingly victory over death in the resurrection (Acts 2:24). And third, union presupposes an obedience to the prophetic demands of Christ. Christ has not three offices but one, in which there are three roles. Letham quite correctly points out their interaction.[31] All three aspects are essential; none can be overlooked.

Finally, while the application of the model does enable a richer understanding of the means of atonement, it also lays the foundation for a solution to issues that have been extremely contentious in the modern church, such as, first, the extent of salvation and, second, the application of the salvation achieved by Christ that goes beyond the granting of eschatological eternal life. Space does not permit my dealing with these here, but I have done so in my earlier book, *The Office of Christ*.[32]

A Broader Salvation

Evangelical presentations of the gospel have frequently drawn criticism for being otherworldly and unduly eschatological – for dealing with life after death while having little to do with life in the present. One of the implications of the prophet-priest-king motif is that it meets this lack. If Christ is understood in terms of the threefold office, so should his followers be, especially as salvation is a union with Christ. Just as Christ is the agent of the Father in salvation to eternal life, so the church is his agent for other aspects of salvation. Indeed, the identification of believers in these three roles is clear in Scripture (e.g., "you are a royal priesthood ... that you may declare" [1 Peter 2:9]). Thus, their Christian action can be understood in this way too. I have elsewhere found the motif a powerful tool in this regard, indicating the way that Christians should act in applying salvation to the needs of the world.[33] Without being comprehensive, it may be applied in healing, in action against poverty and for the environment, and in many other ways, clarifying what are effective Christian approaches.

Perhaps one example can suffice: the salvation of the environment. First, human action for the world should indeed be kingly, reflecting the "dominion mandate" (Gen. 1:20). However, in keeping with the Old Testament model of kingship, such dominion cannot be absolute, since that sort of dominion is the prerogative of God alone. Rather, it is more akin to the derived power of a steward.[34] The king rules for the benefit of his people, not himself; this means that unnecessary exploitation should be curbed. A king is not so much over his subjects as in harmony with them. The world should not so much be a slave as a servant. On the other hand, kingly action should include the development of a world-affirming technology, as suggested in Ernest Schumacher's influential book *Small Is Beautiful*.[35] Technology need not be bad: it is God-given and can have wonderful results benefiting both humanity and the rest of the world.

Second, action for the world should be prophetic. The Old Testament role of prophet looked both to the future and to the present. This means that on the one hand, Christians ought to be aware of and publicize the future effects of present action. It is, incidentally, hardly correct to ignore the future on the grounds of God's expected re-creation! There is a prophetic demand for change in lifestyle. This demand for change would be strengthened by example, as was quite common for the prophets (e.g., Jeremiah 13). Hence, there is a need for a personal limitation of consumption and waste as far as is possible.

Third, action for the world should be priestly, seen as a sacrifice to God. Of course, the sacrifice of one person is barely effective without similar action by others who are made aware by prophetic action. Sacrifice in the priestly sense does have a positive side in that it is intended to do real good. Thus, to give a single example, trees can be bought and planted, in addition to our refraining from chopping others down. The action of the priest was to work with the material, affirming its value and integrating it with the spiritual.

Priestly action has another aspect as well. A priest is an intercessor and as such can ask God to act as creator and re-creator. This is an aspect of ministering on behalf of the environment to God. It incidentally follows that such priestly work should rest on personal harmony with the animals and inanimate creation. It is no accident that Francis of Assisi (and perhaps Daniel?) had such rapport with the animals and birds.

Seeing Christians, and ideally all humanity, as having a specific role to play in mediating between God and the world as prophet, priest and king gives a role to humanity which should result in the care for the environment. A conscious acceptance of the model, based on the Old Testament pattern, and awareness of the need to integrate the three roles as aspects of one, would go far to meet the challenges of a rapidly deteriorating ecosystem. At the same time, however, such care cannot come at the cost of reducing the Christian view of the special place of humanity in the created order. On the contrary, it in fact gives humanity an even greater dignity – indeed, as "little less than God" (Ps. 8:5).

The End of the Office

Just as the coming of Christ fulfilled and superseded the ministry of his Old Testament predecessors, so his resurrection and ascension marked a further change. The priestly sacrifice had been offered and was no longer necessary; his prophetic ministry had been finished, to be continued through Word and Spirit. Yet his kingship still waits for its full expression at the *parousia*. The offices continue until that time, in the church that he lived to inspire by his example, died to redeem, and rose to enliven. It was to achieve this type of church that Jesus came, acting as prophet, priest and king to restore humanity into more of that image of God in which they were created.

Notes

1. Louis Berkhof, for example, claims that penal substitution is the doctrine of the cross clearly taught by the Word of God (Berkhof, *Systematic Theology* [London: Banner of Truth Trust, 1958], 373–74. Likewise, J. I.

Packer calls it "a distinguishing mark of the worldwide evangelical fraternity" (Packer, "What Did the Cross Achieve? The Logic of Penal Substitution" [1975; Stirling: RTSF Monograph, 2002], 11).

2. Gustav Aulén, *Christus Victor: An Historical Study of the Three Main Types of the Idea of Atonement* (London: SPCK, 1931).

3. Berkhof, *Systematic Theology*, 384.

4. P. T. Forsyth, *The Work of Christ* (London: Hodder and Stoughton, 1910), 199.

5. Ibid., 110.

6. John R. W. Stott, *The Cross of Christ* (Leicester: IVP, 1986), 230. Likewise Bruce Milne, whose handbook of doctrine enjoys much favour as a basic evangelical text. See Bruce A, Milne, *Know the Truth: A Handbook of Christian Belief* (Leicester: IVP, 1982), 164–70.

7. Donald M. Baillie, *God Was in Christ: An Essay on Incarnation and Atonement* (London: Faber and Faber, 1956), 172.

8. Robert Letham, *The Work of Christ* (Leicester: IVP, 1993), 153.

9. Sinclair B. Ferguson, *The Holy Spirit* (Downers Grove, Ill.: IVP, 1996), 72. Incidentally, although the sinlessness of Christ has often been disputed in recent years, there is an adequate New Testament witness to it (e.g., Heb. 4:15).

10. Berkhof, *Systematic Theology*, 378.

11. Letham, *Work of Christ*, 131.

12. Baillie, *God Was in Christ*, 199.

13. Letham, *Work of Christ*, 151.

14. Ferguson, *The Holy Spirit*, 95.

15. Baillie, *God Was in Christ*, 171.

16. Letham, *Work of Christ*, 185.

17. Baillie, *God Was in Christ*, 175.

18. Letham, *Work of Christ*, 236.

19. Ibid., 163.

20. Ibid., 33.

21. Ibid., 159–60.

22. Ibid., 174.

23. For example, Berkhof, *Systematic Theology*, and Milne, *Know the Truth*.

24. Letham, *Work of Christ*.

25. In much of what follows, I am using material which I have worked out in more comprehensive detail in my book *The Office of Christ and Its*

Expression in the Church: Prophet, Priest, King (Lampeter: Edwin Mellen, 1997).

26. Douglas J. Hall, *The Steward: A Biblical Symbol Comes of Age*, rev. ed. (Grand Rapids: Eerdmans; New York: Friendship Press, 1990), 43.

27. M. C. Parsons, "Son and High Priest: A Study in the Christology of Hebrews," *EQ* 60, no. 2 (1988): 195–216.

28. Helmut Thielicke, *The Evangelical Faith*, vol. 2, *The Doctrines of God and of Christ* (Grand Rapids: Eerdmans, 1977), 358.

29. Letham, *Work of Christ*, 19.

30. Milne, *Know the Truth*, 150–51; Thielicke, *Evangelical Faith*, 342–43; Letham, *Work of Christ*; Williams, *Office of Christ*.

31. Letham, *Work of Christ*, 24.

32. Williams, *Office of Christ*, 168–91, 251ff.

33. Ibid., 251–52.

34. Hall, *The Steward*.

35. Ernest F. Schumacher, *Small Is Beautiful: A Study of Economics as If People Mattered* (London: Bland and Briggs, 1975).

historical
perspectives

chapter fourteen

bernard of clairvaux

theologian of the cross

tony lane

Introduction

Who Was Bernard?

Bernard was born of noble parentage in 1090 or 91 at Fontaines (near Dijon). He became a monk at age twenty-one, joining the recently founded abbey of Cîteaux. Three years later, he was appointed abbot of a new monastery at Clairvaux. Bernard went to Cîteaux to flee the world but in time became one of the most widely traveled and active leaders of the twelfth-century church. During the 1130s, he fought hard for Pope Innocent II against his rival, Pope Anacletus, eventually helping to secure Innocent's victory. After this, he was engaged in controversy with Peter Abelard, securing Abelard's condemnation at the Council of Sens in 1140 and thereafter by the pope. Bernard died in 1153. He was a brilliant writer, earning himself the title "mellifluous" or sweet as honey. It is because of his literary skills and his considerable spiritual insight that Bernard has proved to be a "man for all seasons", remaining popular in almost every generation.

In Bernard's time, the new scholastic approach to theology, pioneered by Anselm (d. 1109), was becoming established, and Bernard was drawn into controversy with Abelard, its greatest contemporary exponent. Bernard, by contrast, was the last great representative of the earlier medieval tradition of monastic theology. The contrast between these three figures is seen in their attitudes to the relation between faith and reason, with reference to the cross. Anselm maintained the traditional Augustinian programme of "faith seeking understanding" and applied this to the cross in his *Cur Deus Homo*. There he argued that the incarnation and the cross are reasonable because no other option was open to God. Abelard, by contrast, stated in the preface to his *Sic et Non* that "by doubting we come to enquire and by enquiring we reach truth." He applied this method to the cross and questioned aspects of the traditional teaching, especially the idea that Satan had any rights over sinful humanity. The approach of Bernard the mystical writer was very different – faith seeking experience. Unfortunately, his doctrine of the cross has never received the attention given to that of Anselm and Abelard.

Bernard's Doctrine of the Cross

Bernard refers repeatedly to the cross, and I have identified nearly seven hundred passages where he does so. While only a minority of these references contain sustained exposition of the theme, the fact that Bernard mentions it so often shows its importance for him. This is also seen in the richness of his vocabulary. He speaks repeatedly of Christ's death as a sacrifice bringing reconciliation and redemption. Through Christ's sacrifice, death and the devil were defeated, and we have been set free. Christ bore our punishment on the cross and paid our debt by his blood. He purged our sins and made peace between earth and heaven. And so on. That Bernard mentions these themes so frequently shows how fundamental and important they were for his theology. The longer explanations simply fill in the content that is intended by the briefer references.

Spurgeon once said of John Bunyan, prick him anywhere and his blood is bibline.[1] The same is true of Bernard. His writings are permeated by biblical citation and allusion. Conveniently, for our purposes, Bernard repeatedly uses the same passage to make the same point. Thus, for example, he repeatedly describes Christ on the cross as repaying what he had not stolen, each time using Psalm 69:4: "I am forced to restore what I did not steal." In this chapter, I will draw attention to the most important passages used by Bernard to expound the cross.

Though our topic is Bernard's teaching on the cross, it must not be supposed that he confined Christ's work of salvation to that event. His nativity was not effective for us without his death on the cross to pay the price of our redemption (Nat 1:8).[2] But equally, while the death of Christ delivers us from death, his life gives us a pattern of how to live (Tpl 11:18). Again, Bernard repeatedly cites Romans 4:25 to the effect that Christ was raised for our justification (e.g., SC

2:8). At his circumcision, Christ began to shed his blood for our salvation, since it was for our sins, not for his own, that he was circumcised (Circ 1:3).

While Bernard did not limit the salvific work of Christ to the cross, the latter was for him clearly central. Or was it? Here Bernard speaks with two voices. On the one hand, Jesus cannot be known except as hanging on a cross (Sent 3:74). This is Bernard's philosophy, to know Christ and him crucified, to view him on the cross as his Saviour (SC 43:4). He often cites 1 Corinthians 2:2 about resolving to know Christ and him crucified, sometimes adding "only" or "nothing but" (e.g., Tpl 6:12). But twice he goes on to state that knowing Christ and him crucified is for spiritual children and beasts (who feed on milk and hay, respectively) and is to be transcended by the spiritual adult (e.g., Tpl 6:12). Nineteen times he cites Paul's comment about glorying only in the cross of Christ (e.g., SC 25:8). Indeed, it is the mark of the true Christian to glory only in the cross (Ep 126:5). But here again, this is a stage to be left behind (Dil 4:12). Focusing on the sufferings of Christ is a stage that can be transcended through the Spirit (SC 20:7). This point is sometimes made by citing 2 Corinthians 5:16 together with John 6:63 (e.g., Tpl 6:12). The mystic can reach the point of viewing God face to face, which excludes the frailty of Christ's suffering humanity (SC 45:6). On this matter Bernard is torn between a biblical cross-centred piety and an Origenist mysticism.

There are two terms that come repeatedly in Bernard's account of the work of Christ. First, Christ is the redeemer. This is stated often, but by no means exclusively, with reference to his death on the cross. Christ has redeemed us from death and from Satan by restoring our relationship to the Father through his shed blood, which is the price of redemption (SC 20:3). In English, redemption has become a rather vague concept, but for Bernard the ideas of ransom and buying back are much more explicit. The second term is reconciliation, which like redemption is an all-embracing term and again is mentioned often, but by no means exclusively, with reference to the cross. While reconciliation means remission of sins, justification, redemption and liberation from the chains of the devil (Abael 8:20), the chief idea is that we have been reconciled to God the Father, which is possible only by Christ's sacrifice on the cross (7 Don SS 1–2).

Models

Both in the New Testament and in subsequent Christian history, different models have been used to expound the work of Christ. A typical list would be as follows: Christ as the second Adam; Christ as the teacher who brings moral influence; Christ the victor who defeats Satan and death; Christ who bore our sins on the cross. All of these models are found in Bernard, not isolated from one another but integrated into a coherent whole.

Christ as the Second Adam

Christ is the second Adam who recapitulates the first Adam, putting right what he made wrong. This is not Bernard's chief model, and because it places as much or more emphasis on the incarnation and the resurrection as on the cross, it is not featured much in this chapter. However, it is not completely lacking in his writings. It is found in the parallels between Adam and Christ, which we will discuss later. It is also found in the idea of the Great Exchange, often used by Bernard. The Son of God became man to make us sons of God (V Nat 1:2). He became poor that we might become rich (2 Cor. 8:9: e.g., Tpl 11:27). Christ was exiled from heaven to bring us back to heaven (Div 22:5). His filial obedience reversed the primal disobedience (Sent 2:4). He shared God's wrath with us so that we should share God's grace with him (Sent 3:119). He assumed the guilt of our sins, bestowing upon us his righteousness (Tpl 11:23).

Christ as Teacher and Moral Influence

Bernard is best known for his opposition to Abelard's subjective interpretation of the cross as the way in which God changes us. Before we turn to this opposition, we must note that Bernard was himself far from denying the subjective effects of the cross. God shows his love for us in Christ's dying for us as sinners (Rom. 5:8: e.g., Dil 5:15). From Christ's passion we should learn about his goodness (Epi 1:2).

This demonstration of love evokes a response on our part. Through his love shown on the cross, Christ demands, claims and wins our love (SC 20:2). Given his great love to us when we were so undeserving, he deserves our love in response (e.g., Dil 1:1), and it is shameful to look with ungrateful eyes on the Son of God dying for us (Ep 107:8). What can we do great enough to respond to such a great price paid for us (Sent 3:88)? Who is better entitled to my life than he who purchased eternal life for me at the cost of his own (Ep 143:3)? We are to love God because he created us – much more because he restored us by the death of his Son (Sent 3:113). Related to this, Bernard repeatedly draws a contrast between the ease with which God created the

world by a word and the great hardship with which Christ won our salvation
(e.g., Div 19:5). Salvation may be free for us, but it was costly for him (e.g.,
QH 14:3). When we see the great love with which Christ suffered for us,
we must obey God (Sent 3:106). Bernard recognises that a willing love is a
greater motivation than fear, reward or obligation (Ep 143:3).

The cross is a demonstration of the love of God and Christ, which
demands a response on our part. It is also portrayed as an example to be followed, and indeed, one reason why the cross was necessary was to set such an
example (e.g., Hum 3:7). Christ's death teaches us how to die, in the hope of
resurrection from the dead (Tpl 11:18).

So given Bernard's repeated teaching on the subjective effects of the cross,
what was his problem with Abelard? It was with his perception that Abelard
sought to reduce the cross to this only – that the whole reason for the incarnation was to teach us by word and example, and the whole reason for the
passion was to demonstrate and commend love (Abael 7:17; 8:22).[3] Bernard
quotes Abelard to the effect that our redemption is in fact the supreme love
produced in us through Christ's passion (Abael 9:24). Bernard's objection is
not that this teaching is untrue but that it is incomplete. He mocks Abelard's
idea that the chief function of the cross is to set us an example and a goal of
love. Did Christ really come to teach righteousness without bestowing it, to
demonstrate love without imparting it (Abael 7:17)? Bernard points out that
Abelard's view is based on a Pelagian understanding of the effects of Adam's
sin and of our ability as sinners to respond to a demonstration of love. Adam's
sin left us with more than an example to be followed and in fact made us sinful and mortal. Likewise, Christ brings us not just an example but liberation,
regeneration and life (Abael 9:23–24).

Christ as Victor over Satan and Death

For Bernard, reconciliation means, among other things, liberation from
the chains of the devil (Abael 8:20). This is a major theme for him. Christ has
defeated Satan (e.g., QH 14:8). He is the one who has conquered the enemy
and set the captives free (e.g., SC 13:5). With reference to Matthew 12:29
and Luke 11:21–22, Bernard repeatedly describes Christ as the one who has
bound the strong man and despoiled him, thus setting his captives free (e.g.,
Div 11:2). He has rescued us from the kingdom of darkness (Col. 1:13: e.g.,
SC 22:7), on the cross triumphing over the principalities and powers (Col.
2:15: e.g., Asc 2:1).

But Abelard objected to the idea that Satan has gained rights over humanity as a result of seducing Adam. If anything, Satan's act of seduction gives us rights of redress against him (Abael 5:11). Bernard mocks Abelard for setting himself up as a fifth evangelist with a new gospel (Abael 5:12). He points to many passages of Scripture that refer to Satan's dominion over fallen humanity. This domination is just, not because the devil willed or acted justly but because God justly allowed it, even though it was wickedly usurped (Abael 5:13–14). This is so because Satan's power comes from the guilt of our sins. Thus, by bearing our sins and paying the debt of death we owed, Christ justly freed us from Satan (Abael 6:15–16). Thus the falsehood of Peter (Abelard) is refuted by the gospel of Paul (the apostle): on the cross Christ despoiled the principalities and powers, bringing forgiveness of sins (Col. 2:13–15: Abael 6:15). Bernard's teaching about liberation from Satan is not separate from his teaching about Christ's death for our sins; rather, they are integrated into a coherent whole. Defeating the devil would not have been effective without a sacrifice for sin, since without that, we cannot be reconciled to God (7 Don SS 1).

Some of the early fathers held that Satan was tricked into accepting Christ in our place, not realising that he could not hold on to the sinless one, who was also God. Bernard continues this tradition and argues that Satan was fooled into laying hands on an innocent man, thus forfeiting his rights over humanity (Ann 2:3). Bernard often cites 1 Corinthians 2:8 for this (e.g., SC 28:11). The humanity of Christ was the trap by which Satan was tricked with a holy deception. He was tricked not merely into overstepping his rights but also into imposing punishment (death) upon the sinless one (Sent 3:70). By bringing about Christ's death, Satan enabled him to placate the Father, which we could not have achieved (e.g., SC 20:3).

Like that of the Fathers, Bernard's account of our rescue from Satan has been much criticised. Yet in its favour, we can note that it engages seriously with New Testament teaching about liberation from Satan. It does so using the vivid imagery of God deceiving Satan, but this is thoroughly integrated with the godward work of Christ.[4]

The defeat of Satan is closely connected with the defeat of death. Christ conquered death and hoodwinked Satan (e.g., SC 20:3). He destroyed Satan, who held the power of death (Heb. 2:14: e.g., Res 1:1). Christ destroyed both the devil's power and death (Sent 2:4), so we see death itself dead and death's author defeated (e.g., Dil 3:7). Before Christ's passion, the dead faced only the darkness of the grave (Ep 98:4), but the death of Christ has overcome death and put it to flight (Tpl 11:22). Christ's destruction of death (e.g., Nat 2:5) is not in isolation from the resurrection, since Christ conquered death by enduring it and rising again (Div 57:2). The death of Christ is the death of my death. How can I fail to live, for whom Life has died (Tpl 11:27)? Christ drank of death so that death would not consume humanity. Through his death, we get relief from our death (Sent 3:119). Bernard used the patristic fishhook analogy, but of death personified, rather than Satan (e.g., SC 26:11). Here again, the mythological imagery is integrated with the godward aspect of the cross. Sin is the cause of death, so by taking our punishment upon himself, and thus paying our debt, Christ provides the remedy for death, the consequence of sin (Tpl 11:20).

Christ Who Bore Our Sins on the Cross

On the cross, one bore the sins of all (Abael 6:15). Bernard expresses this truth in the language of various passages of Scripture. Christ bore the sins of many (Isa. 53:12: SC 67:5). He was delivered over to death for our sins (Rom. 4:25: e.g., SC 2:8), gave himself for them (Gal. 1:4: e.g., SC 68:3) and died for them (1 Cor. 15:3: Ep 462:8). The innocent one died for us (e.g., Sent 3:113), for the guilty (e.g., Tpl 11:23) and for sinners (Ep 462:8). The righteous one died for the unrighteous (1 Peter 3:18: e.g., Div 22:5), for the ungodly (Rom. 5:6: e.g., Div 40:5). He was numbered with transgressors (Isa. 53:12: e.g., SC 28:4) and bore our sins in his body (1 Peter 2:24: SC 28:12). He fixed our sins on the cross (Col. 2:14: e.g., SC 38:2) by taking them upon himself (Circ 2:1). Thus he made a purgation for sins (Heb. 1:3: e.g., Tpl 10:17) and by his passion most powerfully removed every kind of sin (Heb. 9:28: 4 HM 10).

Bernard describes this aspect of Christ's work in various ways. First, it is a sacrifice (e.g., Palm 3:3). Christ sacrificed himself for our sins (Sent 3:126:5). On the cross, he was both priest and victim (Sent 3:84). He offered himself as a victim, exposing himself to punishment (Palm 3:5). He is the holy victim, pleasing to God, for the reconciliation of us all (Pur 3:2). Indeed, it is only by this sacrifice that he is able to reconcile us to God. God smells the odour of Christ's sacrifice and accepts it (Epi var 4–5). As Christ's death is seen as a sacrifice, so is he seen as the sacrificial Lamb. He is the Lamb of God, who takes away the sins of the world (John 1:29: e.g., SC 28:11). He is the Paschal Lamb (1 Cor. 5:7: e.g., Res 1:13), of whose body no bone is broken (John 19:36: e.g., Div 6:3). He is the Lamb who slain (Rev. 5:6, 9, 12: e.g., 4 HM 5) and was led like a lamb to the slaughter (Isa. 53:7: e.g., SC 70:6).

Bernard refers frequently to the blood of Christ. As with the references to the Lamb, this also relates to the picture of Christ's death as a sacrifice. They are tied together in references to the blood of the Lamb (e.g., Circ 3:4) and to the precious blood of the Lamb (1 Peter 1:19: e.g., Sent 3:122). It is by his blood that he has redeemed us (e.g., SC 65:1), as is taught by Ephesians 1:7 (Abael 8:20), Hebrews 9:12 (e.g., Pur 3:2) and Revelation 5:9 (e.g., Sent 3:116). His blood is the price of our redemption (e.g., SC 20:3), and it is through the blood of Christ that we are justified (Rom. 3:24–25; 5:9: Abael 6:16; 8:20). We are washed from our sins by his blood (Rev. 1:5; e.g., Miss 3:14), because Christ's blood is more powerful than Abel's and proclaims forgiveness (Gen. 4:10; Heb. 12:24: e.g., Ann 1:4).

Less often, Bernard refers to the wounds of Christ. His wounds proclaim that God was in Christ reconciling the world to himself (2 Cor. 5:19: SC 61:4). We are healed by his wounds (Isa. 53:5: e.g., SC 25:8) and draw life from them (Ep 322:1). Bernard refers to the wounds of Christ especially in his teaching on assurance, which we'll discuss later.

Another theme, closely related to the idea of redemption, is Christ's paying the price for us. Christ is the one who repaid what he had not stolen, echoing Psalm 69:4 (e.g., Tpl 11:27). We have been bought at a price (1 Cor. 6:20; 7:23: e.g., Ep 239), and Christ has paid our debt for us (e.g., Tpl 11:20). Bernard refers repeatedly to the "price of redemption", a phrase taken from Psalm 49:7–8, and states that Christ's blood is the price of our redemption (e.g., SC 20:3). Christ acquired us by his blood (Acts 20:28: e.g., SC 68:4). In his passion (Epi 1:2), Christ gave himself (Sent 3:88), his life (e.g., SC 31:10) as the price of our salvation (Miss 4:8), indeed for the whole world (V Nat 3:10). It was man that owed the debt and a man who paid it, echoing Anselm (Abael 6:15). Christ's blood is the price of satisfaction to placate the Father (SC 22:7). Indeed, the blood of Christ is of greater value than the price for which we were sold into slavery to sin (e.g., Sent 3:122).

The ideas of a price to be paid and a debt to be repaid are prominent in Bernard's thought. But to whom were we indebted and to whom was the price paid? Bernard never answers that in so many words – any more than the New Testament does. But it is clear that nothing was offered to Satan. Satan loses his power over us because we have been reconciled with God and the punishment imposed by God (not Satan) is paid. Death is the consequence of sin, so by removing the cause, the consequence is eliminated and death is defeated.

The debt we owe is understood by Bernard as death, the punishment for sin. Christ provides the remedy for death by paying our debt, taking our punishment upon himself (e.g., Tpl 11:20). On the cross he accepted our punishment, the punishment of death (e.g., SC 11:7). He offered himself as a victim, exposing himself to punishment (Palm 3:5). The Lord laid on him our sins and the punishment for them (SC 28:3). Christ put on the garment of our curse (Gal. 3:13: SC 78:4). The cup that Jesus tasted on the cross but did not want to drink (Matt. 27:34) was the damnation of the wicked (Sent 2:131). Satan, the Deceiver, was deceived into imposing death, the punishment of sin, on the sinless one. The punishment of the innocent one outweighs the punishment due to the disobedient. The death that he did not need to suffer was imputed to sinners. The punishment inflicted on the innocent one brings absolution to the guilty (Sent 3:70). So through the cross, he dissolves our guilt, obliterates our disgrace and puts an end to our punishment (Sent 3:119).

Because of sin, we are separated from God and subject to death (Tpl 11:19). But Christ has, by his death, appeased the offended Father (SC 20:3). He is the holy victim, pleasing to God, for the reconciliation of us all (Pur 3:2). God smells the odour of his sacrifice and accepts it (Epi var 5). Christ's blood is the price of satisfaction to placate the Father (SC 22:7), and thus his death is the propitiation for our sins (1 John 2:2: e.g., Miss 3:14; 1 John 4:10: Sent 3:113). The Son of God brought grace and removed God's wrath; he shared God's wrath with us so that we should share God's grace with him (Sent 3:119). Although by nature we are children of wrath, through the redemption of Jesus Christ, we are made children of mercy. He has reconciled us to God by his death, delivering us from the just punishment due to us (Sent 3:127).

Bernard also refers to the death of Christ in terms of satisfaction. God found no way in his secret counsel to forgive guilt without a fitting satisfaction (Epi var 4). By dying for us, Christ made satisfaction for our sins (e.g., Tpl 11:23) and through this satisfaction brought reconciliation with God (SC 20:3). God may be exasperated by the horror of our villainy, but he is pacified by the sorrow of the satisfaction of his Son (Ep 462:8). On the cross, Christ thirsted for nothing but righteousness and exacted from himself a terrible satisfaction for our sins (Adv 4:7). This satisfaction is imputed to us (Abael 6:15).

Talk of satisfaction reminds one of Anselm's *Cur Deus Homo*, but the ideas are strikingly different. The idea of satisfying God's honour, central to Anselm, is absent from Bernard. It is God's justice, rather than his honour, that needs to be satisfied. This comes out clearly in two passages which echo Anselm's argument (Epi var 4–5; 7 Don SS 1–2). There is, as with Anselm, a link with the penitential system. Bernard does refer to the satisfaction that we might make for our sins (e.g., SC 4:2), although such references are rare compared with those to the satisfaction offered by Christ on the cross. There is no contradiction here in Bernard's thought, as he can insert a reference to our offering of penitential satisfaction in the context of discussing the satisfaction made by Christ on the cross (e.g., Div 42:5) and can urge us to follow Christ's example of offering satisfaction (Miss 1:8). Bernard is not saying that we can make a full satisfaction for our sins (Hum 5:18), as the debt we owe is too great to be repaid by our penitence (Div 22:7).

Bernard emphasises the completeness of Christ's work. He regularly cites Christ's affirmation that "it is accomplished" (John 19:30: e.g., SC 60:4). Christ will not die again (Rom. 6:9–10: e.g., SC 54:3; Heb 6:6: e.g., Div 28:2). The lost cannot be restored – is there another Christ or shall he be crucified again (Ep 54)? And yet, at the same time, Christ is again suffering and persecuted in his members (Ep 501). In the context of Middle Eastern geo-politics, Bernard can state that Christ goes to Jerusalem to be crucified again, echoing the apocryphal *Acts of Peter* (Ep 256:2).

Objections

The idea of Christ's bearing the punishment for our sins on the cross, and thus satisfying God's justice, has of course come under fire in our day. It was also questioned in Bernard's day by Abelard, in his *Exposition of Romans*. Why did Christ need to suffer and die for us, and how does his death bring justification and reconciliation? Should God not rather be more angered by the death of his Son? Surely the murder of Christ was a far greater sin than the theft of a mere apple! To whom was the blood of Christ paid as a ransom? To the one in whose power we were – God himself, not the devil. Abelard also questions the need for a ransom to be paid to God, who could simply forgive sin: "Indeed, how cruel and wicked it seems that anyone should demand the blood of an innocent person as the price for anything, or that it should in any way please him that an innocent man should be slain – still less that God should consider the death of his Son so agreeable that by it he should be reconciled to the whole world!"[5]

Bernard responds to these and similar charges both in his letter on the errors of Abelard (Abael) and in his other writings. He does so by pointing to the love of God, to the love of Christ and the voluntary nature of his sacrifice, to the relation between Adam and Christ and to the need for the cross.

For many today, it is simply scandalous that God should require punishment, whether from sinners themselves or from Christ in their stead. Bernard, by contrast, starts from the biblical presupposition that our sins justly merit punishment. By turning against God, we incur the punishment of separation from God and death. This is required by God's truthfulness (because of the promise made in Gen. 2:17) and by his justice (Tpl 11:19). Bernard saw the cross as reconciling the tension between God's mercy and his truth and justice. Truthfulness requires that we die, mercy that we rise again (e.g., Tpl 11:28). Again, God's kindness is not contrary to justice. Being infinitely just, he cannot leave offences against goodness unpunished (Hum 10:33). It is by mercy that God saves us, but this is not contrary to justice (Tpl 11:23). When Christ took our punishment upon himself, justice and peace kissed one another (e.g., Epi var 4–5). The classic text here is Psalm 85:10 (which speaks of mercy and truth meeting, justice and peace kissing), which is much cited by Bernard (e.g., Ann 1:9–14). He also cites, in this context, the statement of Psalm 25:10 that all the ways of the Lord are mercy and truth (e.g., Nat 3:3). Bernard often refers to the tension between mercy and truth or justice, apart from the allusions to these verses (e.g., Tpl 11:23).

Then, as today, some popular accounts of the atonement conveyed the impression of a harsh, vengeful Father whose anger and hatred of us is mollified only by the intervention of his Son. Such an account fails to bring out the love of God the Father and the way that the atonement is the unified work of all three members of the Trinity, an error into which Bernard does not fall. First, concerning the love of the Father, Bernard repeatedly cites a number of New Testament passages that highlight the priority of God's love, such as John 3:16 (e.g., Dil 1:1). It is God who shows his love for us in Christ's dying for us while we were sinners (Rom. 5:8: e.g., 4 HM 4). It is because God loved us that he sent his Son for us (1 John 4:10: e.g., SC 20:2). So great was his love that he did not spare his own Son (Rom. 8:32: e.g., SC 16:4).

But to talk of God's not sparing but sacrificing his own Son has led some today to invoke the charge of divine child abuse – as if Christ were a young child! This objection is met by the fact, which Bernard emphasises, that this was a cooperative venture with the Son playing a fully voluntary role. Not only did the Father not spare his Son, the Son also did not spare himself (4 HM 4) but gladly delivered himself up (Pent 2:7). This is a point Bernard makes repeatedly and in different ways. Christ's death was voluntary (e.g., SC 42:8), as is shown by Isaiah 53:7, which reads "because he willed it" in the Latin (e.g., Pur 3:2), and 53:12 (e.g., Miss 3:14). The will with which Christ submitted to the Father was the common will of the Father and the Son (Res 3:5). The Good Shepherd lays down his life for the sheep (John 10:11: SC 31:10), and Christ laid down his life of his own accord (John 10:17–18: e.g., Nat 2:5). Bernard often cites John 15:13, that there is no greater love than to lay down one's life for one's friends (e.g., Div 101). We know what love is because Christ laid down his life for us (1 John 3:16: e.g., Div 34:6).

There are two senses in which Christ voluntarily died for us. The first is that he was voluntarily obedient to the Father. This Bernard certainly affirms, repeatedly stating that Christ was obedient even to death on a cross (Phil. 2:8: e.g., Ep 541). Clearly there is some element of truth in this, as is seen in Jesus' subordination of his will to the Father in the garden of Gethsemane (e.g., Res 3:5). But this emphasis, on its own, remains vulnerable to the charge of divine child abuse since it could be taken to imply a voluntary but reluctant submission to the will of the Father. However, there is much more to it than this, and Bernard brings out the way in which Christ took the initiative. He loved me and gave himself for me (Gal. 2:20: e.g., Abael 9:25); he gave himself for our sins (Gal. 1:4: e.g., SC 68:3); he offered himself (Heb. 9:14: e.g., Pur 3:3). He judged my soul more precious than his own blood (Adv 3:6). Modifying 2 Corinthians 5:21, he speaks of Christ as the one who made *himself* sin for us (e.g., SC 25:9). Again, on the cross, Christ thirsted for nothing but righteousness and exacted from himself a terrible satisfaction for our sins (Adv 4:7). The death of Christ has the value it does only because it was freely offered, not violently forced (e.g., Tpl 11:20). Bernard says that Christ was compelled to undergo the ignominy of the cross and death by a voluntary coercion[6]—because of his filial obedience, because of our misery and because of the victory that would follow (Sent 2:4).

But, granted the unity of Father and Son, is this not merely an external legal transaction where we are concerned? Not for Bernard. One died for all, so all died (2 Cor. 5:14). It is not that one offended and another made satisfaction, because head and body together form or constitute one Christ. It was the head that suffered for the members, Christ for his body (Abael 6:15). (Many will understand this principle from their childhood, when one part of the body, not, in this case, the head, suffered punishment for the misdeeds of other parts.)

Bernard also uses another argument. He held to the Augustinian doctrine that it is through the sin of one man, Adam, that all people are counted as sinners, sharing his guilt, and actually constituted sinners because of the ensuing concupiscence or lust. Given that fact, how can one object to the idea that through the righteous deed of one man, Christ, we should be counted as righteous and indeed become righteous? Surely we would not want to say that Adam's sin has greater efficacy than Christ's death (e.g., Tpl 11:25). Just as the sin of Adam counts against me, so the righteousness of Christ restores me (Tpl 11:23). We lost our righteousness in Adam and receive from Christ an alien righteousness. We acquired an alien guilt from Adam, so why not an alien righteousness? Just as Adam made us sinners, Christ justifies us from sin (Abael 6:15–16). Few today hold to a full-blooded Augustinian doctrine of original sin, yet in a modified form, Bernard's argument is hard to evade. Only a dogmatic Pelagian would argue that human sin is *purely* a matter of individual choice. It is hard to deny the corporate sin of the race and hold that our individual choice of sin has nothing to do with the common human condition. Grant that there is a corporate dimension to sin, and the objection to the corporate dimension of salvation is gravely weakened.

Finally, Abelard questioned the need for the cross. To paraphrase, since God could have liberated us by a simple command, why all the blood and gore? Bernard's response is surprisingly low key. Who denies that there were all sorts of other ways that God could have redeemed us?[7] Perhaps the cross was the best way because Christ's sufferings are a warning to us (Abael 8:19). Again, "You ask, why by blood when he could have done it by a word? You ask him. It is permitted to me to know that it is so, not why it is so" (Abael 8:20). Here we see Bernard's attitude to the role of reason. Faith should lead us to worship and obedience, not to curiosity and speculation. But while this appears to lead him, in the controversy with Abelard, to deny that there is any inherent need for the cross, this is not his normal stance. In other contexts, he speaks differently. A wise physician would not use costly medicines if the cure could easily be effected without them (Nat 3:5). Redemption was costly, not because God did not choose another way but because none was suitable (QH 14:3). Defeating the devil would not have been effective without a sacrifice for sin, since without that, we cannot be reconciled to God (7 Don SS 1). God found no way in his secret counsel to forgive guilt without a fitting satisfaction (Epi var 4). Christ needed to suffer and die because unless a grain of wheat dies, it cannot bear fruit (John 12:24–25: SC 15:3). On the other hand, Bernard also stated that God could have rescued us without so much hardship but chose the way of the cross to cure us of ingratitude (SC 11:7), an answer that, as far as it goes, is not so far removed from Abelard's. (This was written about five years before the conflict with Abelard.) Again, one reason why the cross was necessary was to set an example for us to follow (e.g., Hum 3:7). How can we tie all of this together? *Can* we tie all of this together? Bernard seems to have been pulled in different directions by different concerns and seems not to give a clear answer to this question.

Outworking
Christ Won the Church

Bernard's outworking of his doctrine of the cross is expressed mostly in individual terms, but he also applies it to the church. Christ redeemed his unique bride from the yoke of the devil by his blood (Sent 3:112). He preferred the life of his body, the church, to that of his own body (e.g., Div 17:5). And, with a homely touch for the recipients of his letter, Christ preferred to die for Rievaulx Abbey than to lose it (Ep 92:1).

Justification

Christ is our righteousness (1 Cor. 1:30: e.g., 4 HM 13), and we are justified by his blood (Rom. 5:9) and that freely (Rom. 3:24–25; Abael 6:16; 8:20). Because of Christ's righteousness, we are justified by faith alone and have peace with God. His passion is our ultimate refuge, our unique remedy. Our only hope is for Christ's blood to cry out for us so we may be forgiven (SC 22:8). In particular, because of the cross, Christ's righteousness is imputed to us. Just as the sin of Adam counts against me, the righteousness of Christ restores me (Tpl 11:22–23). We lost our righteousness in Adam but receive from Christ an alien righteousness. He died for us, and the satisfaction that he made is imputed to us. Just as Adam brought guilt and made us sinners, so Christ's righteousness is granted to us (Abael 6:15–16). Clearly we have here an anticipation of the Protestant doctrine of justification, but this is only one side of Bernard's teaching, and there is more that points in a very different direction.[8]

Assurance of Salvation

Bernard applies the cross to those who are fearful of their salvation. Do we fear he will not forgive our sins? But he has fixed them to the cross with his own hands (SC 38:2). Assurance comes from the wounds of Christ (e.g., SC 61:3–4), and there is no greater cure for wounds of conscience than to meditate upon them (SC 62:7). It is there that we find peace of conscience when we sin gravely, for he was wounded for our transgressions (SC 61:3). If I have sinned greatly, I do not despair, because Christ sorrowed greatly for us. But such consolation should not mislead us into sinning more securely (Ep 462:8–9). Again, it should not be imagined from these few statements that Bernard held to a Protestant understanding of assurance.[9] Finally, Bernard's pastoral skill is seen in the way he applies the cross as medicine both for the overconfident and for the desperate. Those who are overconfident should, remembering that Christ suffered despite his innocence, be prepared to humble themselves and share in his sufferings; those who are desperate should remember that Christ suffered for the sake of sinners like them (Par 6).

Suffering with Christ

Today, too many argue that Christ suffered for us in order that we should not need to suffer. Bernard argues rather, as does the New Testament, that Christ suffered for us, and we are called to share his sufferings (e.g., QH 3:3), knowing we will also be glorified with him (e.g., Asc 6:4) as promised in Romans 8:17 (e.g., Res 1:16). Christ suffered for us not so that we need not suffer but so that we can bear our own cross (e.g., SC 21:2). Christ suffered and was obedient unto death, setting us an example to follow (e.g., 4 HM 11). As Christ, who is God, did not hesitate to die, so we should be ready to suffer for obedience (Hum 3:7). Unless we imitate Christ, we will not benefit from his passion (e.g., Dil 4:11). Suffering becomes sweet when we look back at Christ's passion (Sent 2:16). When we suffer something painful for Christ, we should do so with joy, as though drinking from a cup that he has given us (Sent 3:119).

Sanctification

For Bernard, the cross is not about how to find forgiveness while leading an unchanged life. Such a doctrine of cheap grace is far removed from his teaching. The cross has radical implications for Christian living. To some extent, this has been covered already when considering Christ as teacher and moral influence, but there are further implications. First, we are called to take up our cross and follow Christ (Matt. 10:38; Luke 14:27: e.g., Div 28:2). We are to deny ourselves and take up our cross (Matt. 16:24; Luke 9:23: e.g., Sent 3:94), though Bernard surprisingly never quotes the Lucan injunction to do this *daily*. Again, Christians are called to crucify the flesh (Gal. 5:24: e.g., SC 30:10), because the world is crucified to us (Gal. 6:14: e.g., Miss 4:10). Second, we are called to follow the Christ, who prayed "not my will but yours" (e.g., Res 3:3). Christ was obedient unto death so that we should no longer live under our own will (Ep 515). If Christ was obedient unto death, how can Christians free themselves from the yoke of obedience (Ep 87:2)? Third, Bernard argues from the purpose of the cross. Christ died for all so that all might live for him (2 Cor. 5:15: e.g., SC 41:6). He bore our sins so that we might die to sin and live to righteousness (1 Peter 2:24: e.g., Asc 6:3). Christ died to be our Lord (Rom. 14:9: e.g., SC 66:10). Finally, Bernard appeals to what one might call the psychological impact of the cross. If we think rightly of the Lord's passion, we should blush at the thought of following after sensual pleasures (Res 3:2). Because of the sweetness of Christ's passion, the flesh is no longer sweet to us (Div 29:4). We cannot glory in the cross and put our trust in money (Dil 4:11). The example of the cross should lead us to flee luxury (Ep 462:2).

Pastoral Application

In his letters especially, Bernard appeals to the cross. Most common is the reminder that this or that person is a brother for whom Christ died (Rom. 14:15: e.g., Ep 1:6; 1 Cor. 8:11: e.g., Ep 61). We should not deceive souls for whom Christ died (Ep 540). Bernard accuses people of seeking to destroy those who have been saved by the cross (e.g., Ep 2:4). We must remember how precious is the soul that can be redeemed only by the cross of Christ (e.g., Ep 54), so the cure of souls should not be entrusted to those with no regard for the blood shed by Christ (Ep 328). Pastors must give account to the Lamb of God, who died for the flock (Ep 62). Finally, those who oppose what Bernard sees as the will of God are described as enemies of the cross of Christ (Phil. 3:18: e.g., Ep 195:2).

Conclusion

Bernard's account of the cross is not flawless, but it has much to commend it. Unlike Anselm and Abelard, to whom so much attention is paid, he does not emphasise one model of the work of Christ to the detriment of others but rather integrates them into a whole. He is an able exponent of the historic Christian understanding of the cross.

Notes

This chapter was written as I was in the process of completing a book on this theme. Because of space limitations, I have here concentrated almost entirely on the primary literature. Also, I have generally cited only one passage for each point, though often there are many which could be cited. Those seeking more information should turn to the book.

1. C. H. Spurgeon, "The Last Words of Christ on the Cross," sermon delivered 15 October 1899, in *MTP* vol. 45, no. 2644 (London: Passmore and Alabaster, n.d.), 495.

2. References to the works of Bernard are inserted into the text, using the following abbreviations:

Abael: *Epistle on the Errors of Abelard*
Adv: *Sermon on the Advent*
Ann: *Sermon on the Annunciation*
Asc: *Sermon on the Ascension*
Circ: *Sermon on the Circumcision*
Dil: *Loving God*
Div: *Miscellaneous Sermon*
Ep: *Epistle*
Epi: *Sermon on the Epiphany*
Epi var: *Diverse Sermon on the Epiphany*
Hum: *The Steps of Humility and Pride*
Miss: *Sermon in Praise of the Virgin Mother*
Nat: *Sermon on the Nativity*
Palm: *Sermon on Palm Sunday*
Par: *Parable*
Pent: *Sermon on Pentecost*
Pur: *Sermon on the Purification of Mary*
QH: *Lenten Sermon on Psalm 91*
Res: *Sermon on the Resurrection*
SC: *Sermon on the Song of Songs*
Sent: *Sentences*
Tpl: *In Praise of the New Knighthood*
V Nat: *Sermon on Christmas Eve*
4 HM: *Sermon on Wednesday before Easter*
7 Don SS: *Sermon on the Seven Gifts of the Holy Spirit*

The original Latin text is found in J. Leclercq et al., eds., *Sancti Bernardi Opera*, 8 vols. (Rome: Editiones Cistercienses, 1957–77). The majority of works have been translated into English and many are found in the Cistercian Fathers series, published by Cistercian Publications (Kalamazoo, Mich.). Sometimes these translations are very loose where theological terms are concerned, so some of the points made in this chapter can be appreciated only by turning to the Latin. The paraphrases and translations of Bernard are my own, though not without reference to existing translations.

3. A false perception that can easily follow from reading his brief comments in his *Exposition of Romans* in isolation from the rest of his writings.

4. It can at least be said in Bernard's favour that he does not reduce this cosmic language to the idea that Christ has won victory over those political structures that fail to win the approval of the current left-liberal intelligentsia!

5. Peter Abelard, "Exposition of Romans 3:19–26," in *A Scholastic Miscellany: Anselm to Ockham*, ed. E. R. Fairweather (London: SCM, 1956), 282–83, much of which is cited in Abael 8:21–22.

6. Cf. Anselm, *Cur Deus Homo* 2:17.

7. Anselm's *Cur Deus Homo* does, of course, deny just that.

8. Cf. A. N. S. Lane, *Calvin and Bernard of Clairvaux* (Princeton: Princeton Theological Seminary, 1996), 47–71; Lane, "Bernard of Clairvaux: A Forerunner of John Calvin?" in *Bernardus Magister*, ed. J. R. Sommerfeldt (Kalamazoo: Cistercian, 1992), 533–45.

9. Lane, *Calvin and Bernard*, 64–68.

chapter fifteen

ransomed, healed, restored, forgiven

evangelical accounts of the atonement

stephen r. holmes

In this chapter, I intend to give an account of the history of British evangelical accounts of the atonement, with particular reference to penal substitution. I will attempt to argue for the following three theses:

1. Evangelical theologians and preachers have, with very few exceptions, wanted to insist on substitutionary doctrines of atonement but have ascribed far less importance to the question of whether substitution is expounded in penal terms.

2. Generally, evangelicals in Britain have held to penal substitution within a "many metaphors" view of the atonement: penal substitution is one way of speaking about the cross, and perhaps the most significant, but other ways are also valid. (This, it seems to me, is less true of American evangelicals.)

3. Penal theories were generally accepted without complaint or comment amongst evangelicals until about 1800; from that time on, there has been a constant undercurrent of complaint about penal theories, and so some explicit defences. I shall attempt here to highlight some possible causes of complaint.

Founding Fathers: The Eighteenth Century

Taking the 1730s as a starting point, we can take Joseph Butler's great *Analogy of Religion to the Constitution and Course of Nature* as a powerful example of the theological context into which evangelicalism was born. Butler defends penal substitution as normal and natural, arguing that "in the daily course of natural providence, it is appointed that innocent people should suffer for the faults of the guilty," and, therefore, "vicarious punishment is a providential appointment of every day's experience."[1] That Butler needed to make such an argument suggests the point was not universal, but that he was able to do so suggests it was not too controversial.

Moving to the founders of evangelicalism, we find that these were generally preachers and hymn writers, although some were reasonably able theologians. Jonathan Edwards alone can claim to be a thinker of the very first rank. I shall therefore begin with Edwards and dwell a little on the evidence provided by his work on the atonement.

Surprisingly, Edwards wrote only two sustained treatments of the mechanism of the atonement, although the issue is touched on many times in his writings. In a sermon series titled *A History of the Work of Redemption* (thirty sermons, all expounding Isa. 51:8!), Edwards argued the proposition that "from his incarnation to his resurrection, the purchase of redemption was made."[2] Note two things: redemption is the work of the years of incarnation, not just the hours of passion, and the controlling metaphor is mercantile: purchase. Penal language is present here, but in a fairly subsidiary role: Edwards makes the standard scholastic distinction of the two ends of Christ's work: satisfaction, or the paying of a debt, and merit, or the purchase of benefits.[3] These are both carried out throughout Christ's life, the one by the suffering and humiliation he underwent, and the other by the obedience he offered to the Father. Edwards spells out in some detail how different events of Christ's life meet these two ends, clearly intending to insist that the details of Christ's life, not just his death, are a part of the gospel story. The second purpose, merit, is almost always spoken of in terms of mercantile metaphors; the first, satisfaction, is sometimes described in penal terms, but more commonly it is again a purchase rather than a punishment.

The second sustained discussion is in an unpublished theological notebook, the *Miscellanies*.[4] This is a long discussion of patronage, offering an account of the rationality of a patron interceding on behalf of his client, transferring whatever favour or merit he might have to the client's account, and so on. Considering the saints as Christ's clients, Edwards offers an apologetic argument for the reasonableness of God's actions in the atonement.[5] There are also other strands within the corpus, notably a fairly Grotian discussion of God's need to inflict death somewhere because that was the penalty promised to Adam if the fruit was eaten.[6]

If one wished to make the case that penal substitution is central to the evangelical tradition, it would be possible to find several – many, even – statements from Edwards that speak of the atonement in straightforwardly penal terms. This was a way of discussing the atonement with which he was clearly familiar and towards which he felt no antipathy. However, merely to cite these statements would be a misreading of the evidence. Edwards in fact had many ways of speaking about the atonement, and penal substitution was not even the most significant. I read the account of patronage as an initial attempt[7] to argue for the rationality of the atonement: "it is not unreasonable" is a repeated phrase within this account. If this is a correct reading, then Edwards clearly did not even think that the penal tradition had particular explanatory power.[8]

Turning to the Wesleys,[9] there is again plenty of evidence that they simply and unreflectively accepted penal traditions of talking about the atonement. In a controversial text like *The Principles of a Methodist*, John Wesley can assume that this is a standard and recognisably orthodox way of discussing the atonement: Christ's role in justification is described there as "the satisfaction of God's justice by the offering his body [*sic*] and shedding his blood, 'and fulfilling the law of God perfectly' ".[10] Wesley asserts his impugned Christian orthodoxy by insisting that he believes in penal substitution.

However, if we look at *Hymns for the Use of People Called Methodists*, mostly written by Charles but edited and approved by John before publication, we find a plethora of atonement imagery and a repeated rejoicing in the substitutionary character of the atonement, in Christ's standing in our place, but a relative lack of any narrowly penal language. In part, this is no doubt due to the Wesleys' practice of being closely biblical in the imagery of their hymns, and so sacrificial language of blood turning aside wrath is far more prevalent than penal language of the transference of guilt.[11] In addition, we can find language of victory ("Jesus himself the stronger showed / and claimed me for his own" [hymn 90]), of healing ("Till Christ, descending from on high / Infected nature heal" [hymn 104]), and so on. Hymn 105 is perhaps of particular interest. It is in the section headed "For mourners convinced of sin" and offers seven stanzas of impassioned pleading for the gift of atonement, described in over a dozen different ways – healing, restoration, reclothing in holiness, the restoration of the *imago Dei*, the gift of riches to one who is poor and so on. None of the language is remotely penal.

There are certainly points in the hymns where the imagery is penal – most obviously, perhaps, in hymn 123, where the sixth stanza runs, "Guilty I stand before thy face / On me I feel thy wrath abide / 'Tis just the sentence should take place / 'Tis just – but Oh! thy Son hath died!" and the eighth, "For me I now believe he died / He made my every crime his own / Fully for me he satisfied / Father, well-pleased behold thy Son!" However, this is by no means the primary imagery of the hymnbook as a whole.

Turning finally to the *Forty-four Sermons*, we find that there is much more of a focus on penal imagery for the atonement, although it is not quite exclusive. Sermon 1, "Salvation by Faith," describes salvation in explicitly penal terms;[12] so does sermon 5, "Justification by Faith" ("for the sake of his well-beloved Son, of what he hath done and suffered for us, God now vouchsafes ... to remit the punishment due to our sins" [§8]), but the end of the latter sermon uses imagery that is more naturally read as sacrificial. The reason for this focus, I think, is that the core concept in these early sermons is righteousness and how it may be attained, and righteousness, at least as Wesley understood it, living before the new perspective on Paul, is a concept which lends itself to juridical metaphors. As with Edwards, then, there is clear textual evidence that both John and Charles were prepared to talk about the atonement in penal terms, but they were not restricted to this.

I do not pretend to have read every evangelical preacher or hymn writer of the eighteenth century, but I think this pattern is normal. Eighteenth-century evangelicals assumed the validity of talking of the atonement in penal substitutionary terms but were not limited to this way of talking or at all self-conscious about it: the idea that it might be difficult or controversial seems utterly foreign to them. For one last example, consider another Methodist, the saintly John Fletcher of Madeley. In a letter declining an appeal to intercede on behalf of a teenager who had been sentenced to hanging, Fletcher seizes the opportunity to intertwine an account of the penal justice under which the youngster is to be executed with imagery of the atonement, and so urges his client to "see [Jesus] bearing your curse, your shame, your punishment".[13] I will argue later that this coincidence of public penal violence and penal substitution is significant.

As I say, I think this pattern is normal. The first dissenting voice of which I am aware is Andrew Fuller, in 1799. Fuller set out to answer Tom Paine's argument that the Christian doctrine of redemption assumed an improper analogy between pecuniary and moral justice (the one relatively serious argument Paine offered in a fairly angry and ill-considered book).[14] In response, Fuller draws upon an edited publication of Edwards' attempts to make the atonement comprehensible in terms of clientage and patronage, and offers a long parable of his own concerning a king and his son.[15] The system implied by Fuller's parable is straightforwardly Grotian – penal without being substitutionary. There is no transfer of guilt, rather a forgiveness without cost and a claimed need that some method must be found to enable the king to demonstrate just how seriously he viewed the transgression.[16]

Abraham Booth accused Fuller of denying the Calvinistic doctrines of imputation and substitution, a charge to which Fuller responded in his *Three Conversations: Imputation, Substitution and Particular Redemption*,[17] and his *Six Letters to Dr Ryland*.[18] Here, Fuller argues for a transfer of the effects of guilt, rather than a transfer of guilt, because he believes guilt is not transferable.[19] The defence of penal substitution in an enlightened age was indeed going to depend in part on precisely the point Fuller lights upon, the question of the transference of guilt, but it is Hodge, not Fuller, who will offer a satisfying way through the problem.[20]

Radicals and Controversialists: 1800 – 1850

In the early years of the nineteenth century, many evangelicals continued to hold to penal substitutionary views. As far as I can tell from my small acquaintance with the voluminous works of Thomas Charles, the Welsh evangelical scene was relatively untroubled by controversy on this issue. Wilberforce, and others among the Clapham Sect, read very similarly to Wesley in talking about the gospel in a variety of terms, although perhaps with an emphasis on penal substitution.[21] In London, John Pye-Smith could defend a relatively traditional atonement doctrine in 1824, while at the same time developing surprisingly nuanced views on biblical inspiration in response to Lyall's new geology and to assaults on the orthodoxy of evangelical supporters of the British and Foreign Bible Society coming from Robert Haldane in Geneva.

However, the tenor of evangelical atonement theology changes significantly in the first half of the nineteenth century. Suddenly, there are many evangelicals who reject penal doctrines of atonement passionately. John McLeod Campbell's *The Nature of the Atonement* is perhaps the most famous single text, and although it was not published till 1856, Campbell claims that the book spells out the doctrines he was condemned for teaching twenty-five years before, and an examination of the privately published lithographed sermons from his Rhu period suggests that this claim is accurate.[22] Campbell was condemned, of course, for his claim that the extent of the atonement was not limited, but within that claim is an angry attack on penal substitutionary doctrines.[23] Campbell's rather idiosyncratic alternative proposal retains the vicarious or substitutionary character of the atonement: Jesus stands in our place and does all that needs doing on our behalf. It is not, however, penal in character: what Jesus does is offer a perfect confession of the rightness of the Father's estimation of our sinfulness.

Alongside Campbell are a number of other younger evangelical leaders offering similar criticisms around the same time: Edward Irving, Henry Drummond, Thomas Erskine of Linlathlen and so on. Let me briefly look at two of them. Irving displays his usual oratorical power and lack of tact in discussing penal ideas of the atonement in his third sermon on the incarnation.[24] They are no more than "bargain and barter" views that are unworthy of Christianity.[25] Instead, and building on his distinctive account of the incarnation, he offers a broadly physicalist doctrine of the atonement: Christ, in taking our sinful human nature, takes it finally to the grave and so destroys and re-creates human nature in himself.[26]

Erskine has several concerns about substitutionary theories of atonement, which are all now familiar: they are illogical, they are morally unworthy,[27] and they replace salvation from the power of sin in our lives with a purely forensic declaration of innocence, which has no power to transform or make holy.[28] In classical Reformation terms, Erskine was concerned that penal substitution taught a merely passive righteousness.[29] He certainly wanted to give an account of Christ's bearing the penalty for the sins of the world[30] but did not want that reduced to any account of individual substitution.[31]

There are, then, a number of evangelical leaders in the early nineteenth century who simply reject penal substitution. This rejection is by no means universal and should not be seen as such. Even into the second half of the century, so central a figure as Charles H. Spurgeon appears to hold views similar to the Wesleys on this: in his collection of writings and sermons on evangelism, *The Soul-Winner*, for example, we find energetic strictures against certain recent trends in doctrine (notably evolution and, predictably, baptismal regeneration) and against a vague and undefined modernism. Spurgeon is clearly concerned that the atonement be understood in vicarious or substitutionary terms; that the substitution be penal interests him not at all. Spurgeon can use penal language without any apparent consciousness that it might be controversial and can drift from this language to sacrificial or mercantile language without a thought.[32] Many faithful evangelicals proceeded as untroubled as Spurgeon about the questions, and the example of Spurgeon suggests someone holding such views could hardly be, on that account, regarded as irrelevant or marginal.

Nonetheless, if not universal, the turn presaged by Fuller and entered in full flow in the 1820s and 1830s is striking. Why should there be such a sudden and widespread rejection of a doctrine that was simply assumed two decades before? There was no doubt influence running from one writer to another, and one can, of course, find strong connections back to Thomas Chalmers from most of these figures, although I am not aware of any innovation in Chalmers' account of the atonement.[33] Again, we might look for evidence of the sharing of ideas within the Irvingite *Morning Watch*, Alexander Haldane's *Recorder*, and so on. It seems unlikely, however, that a doctrine that was uncritically accepted by seemingly every evangelical of a generation before should suddenly be found so widely difficult without reason. There is, so far as I can see, no new argument deployed by all these new doubters that was not seen by the elders. I suspect, instead, that cultural change made previously assumed positions suddenly, if not untenable, at least much more difficult.

Michel Foucault, in his seminal *Discipline and Punish*, contrasts the punishment of Damiens in 1757 – brutal and public, and described in the press with many pious improvements – with Faucher's ordered rules for a prison system, written eighty years later.[34] The pictures illustrate the shifting centre of gravity of European visions of criminal justice between 1750 and 1820, which Foucault explores at some length. It seems to me at least plausible to suggest that someone who accepted the earlier tradition of criminal justice, centred as it was on the public infliction of violence, would find it culturally easier to interpret the cross in terms of Jesus' bearing the punishment that was our due than someone who had been taught by cultural shifts to regard the earlier vision as barbaric. Foucault is, of course, very far from accepting the view that what is described here is a shift from barbarism to civilisation. The latter view is a different attempt to seize power over the bodies and minds of criminals – and, by extension, all members of society; it might even be a more successful one; it is in no sense more civilised, whatever that loaded word might mean. Crucially, for our purposes, the rhetoric justifying the earlier exercise of power was a rhetoric of desert and punishment; the rhetoric justifying the birth of the prison is a rhetoric of delinquency and rehabilitation. In Foucault's view, neither rhetoric is justified – both are disguised attempts to impose a hegemony.

It seems to me that Foucault's deconstruction of the suggestion that a purely rehabilitative view of penal policy is in some sense progressive or civilised is extremely important. Philosophical arguments as to why rehabilitation alone is not an adequate justification for punishment are well established. Nonetheless, even a familiarity with such arguments cannot quite get us past the notion that to punish for the sake of retribution is barbaric, a notion with little intellectual content but enormous rhetorical power. Foucault also shows how intimately the birth of the prison, and the rhetoric of rehabilitation, is connected to the new psychological technologies developing from the intellectual visions of the Enlightenment; if we accept this telling of the history, it might lend some support to the claim that the attack on penal substitution is part of the overall "liberal" attempt to align Christianity with a modernist intellectual context which is now collapsing.

I read, then, the discomfort with notions of penal substitution displayed by Fuller, Campbell, Irving and so on – and, of course, displayed far more nakedly by those, such as Newman,[35] who left the evangelical movement during this time – as a reaction to certain cultural themes concerning penal policy that were then becoming current. Beccaria had written *Dei delitti e delle pene* (*On Crimes and Punishments*) in 1764 and had been influential across Europe. It is therefore no surprise, I suppose, that a segment of British evangelicalism – given their common friendship with Chalmers, a culturally aware and engaged segment – should have found it more difficult to hold on to traditions of talk about the cross which seemed to borrow their understanding of penalty from the older cultural tradition.

Revival and Retreat: 1845 – 1920

Turning to the second half of the nineteenth century, the first major event is, of course, the founding of the Evangelical Alliance in 1846. I have not found any significant evidence that the birth pangs of the Alliance involved any significant debates over penal substitution. The vicarious or substitutionary character of the atonement was repeatedly stressed, but the sense that this had to be stressed in penal terms, rather than sacrificial or mercantile terms, is absent.[36] Consider, for example, T. R. Birks, who was honorary secretary of the Alliance for about two decades and the most considerable evangelical theologian of his day. In his *The Ways of God*,[37] Birks faced up to the fact that, whilst Christian piety still confessed the atonement, Christian intellect could offer no adequate reasons for holding to it.[38] He proposed to explain the doctrine in a way that would commend itself to the intelligent enquirer. This essentially involved him in a fairly drastic modification of traditional penal substitution. Christ, on Birks' account, is not a substitute so much as a representative: the idea of communal moral responsibility is one he develops at great length. Second, he rejects any notion that purely retributive punishment can be vicariously experienced; the punishment Christ undergoes is aimed at our reformation, and because of this, he can undergo it on our behalf.[39]

Continuing for a moment with the story of the EA, it is instructive to read the proceedings of both the golden and diamond jubilee conferences of the Alliance. The various addresses given to those conferences, particularly the one in 1907, routinely resort to a common rhetorical device, regardless of their subject. This involves pausing to give a free summary of the essentials of evangelical faith and affirming either one's commitment to it, the importance of the Alliance in promoting it, the pressing need of the world to hear it, or, most commonly, all three. Inevitably, whenever this is resorted to, the atonement is to the fore. Phrases used as part of this technique include, "His one all-sufficient sacrifice for human sin";[40] "A personal Saviour, Divine and human";[41] "Guilt is our obligation to suffer punishment for sin. And Christ bore that guilt";[42] "[A] deathless individual died for the sake of saving humanity from dying … a sinless individual became sin to save humanity from sinning."[43]

Alongside these brief summaries, we find two discourses by significant leaders more narrowly on the atonement. In 1896, F. B. Meyer offered a long meditation of Christ as the vine, which focused on horticultural images of life coming out of suffering.[44] He goes on to insist, however, that "you will miss infinitely the power of our Saviour's death, if you do not pass from the doctrine of substitution to incorporate with it the doctrine of identification."[45] Ten years later, James Orr has the platform and develops an argument about the unity of the Old and New Testaments which leads him to express the atonement solely in strongly sacrificial terms.[46] Precisely once in the two conferences is penal substitution unambiguously taught – sacrificial imagery is far more to the fore. I do not suppose for a moment that any one of these speakers would have denied the penal theory, but it was not the language they reached for, and not, apparently, the native language of the assembled Alliance.

I have already noted that so central a figure as Spurgeon could maintain what I take to be the classical evangelical position of an untroubled acceptance of penal substitution as one component of a broader atonement theology. The same might be said of James Denney at the turn of the century. In *The Death of Christ*,[47] Denney devotes considerable space and energy to defending the notion that the atonement was substitutionary: this is the emphasis of much of his most detailed exegetical work, and certainly of his most powerful rhetoric. He sometimes uses penal language to describe that substitution, and so clearly has no objection to the doctrine that is our interest, but probably more often he uses other metaphors. The same might be said of the great Birmingham Congregationalist R. W. Dale; Dale was perhaps more concerned with distortions of the penal theory, but assumed and defended its correctness, without being limited to that one way of expressing the doctrine.[48] He offers a careful discussion of different vindications of society's right to punish, defending simple retribution as the correct understanding,[49] and an account of how Christ can stand in the place of guilty humanity.[50]

At the same time, there is what seems to be a new theme within evangelical writings. For the first time, as far as I can see, we find writers insisting on penal substitution as the one and only correct way of talking about the atonement. The more famous, because more convincing, examples are American – Charles Hodge and R. L. Dabney. There are British equivalents, though. George Smeaton and T. J. Crawford – both Scots – each offer what we would now call a biblical theology of atonement, and both insist that the one truly biblical theology is penal substitution.[51] For Smeaton, "Jesus was visited with penal suffering ... as a representative, sinless in Himself, but sin-covered; loved as a Son, but condemned as the sin-bearer ... Thus God condemned sin in His flesh, and in consequence of this there is no condemnation to us."[52] For Crawford, quoting Hodge, justice is defined as "God's purpose to ... inflict ... penalty",[53] and Christ bears that penalty in our stead. This is vital: "if [the sufferings of Christ] were not penal, it does not appear in what way we could possibly regard them as satisfying divine justice, vindicating the broken law, displaying the evil of sin, or as furnishing a true substitute for the merited penalty of our transgressions."[54]

Finally, we must note the wider theological currents in the nineteenth century. The flawed historiography of Ritschl, von Harnack and their followers is not irrelevant for the development of evangelical critiques of penal substitution. The German liberal theologians wrote in an age and culture in which racial stereotyping was assumed, and they made full use of this unhappy mode of argument. Jewish religion, particularly its alleged emphasis on the wrath of God and the consequent need for some sort of magically propitiatory sacrifice, could be dismissed as "primitive" and "blood-thirsty"; the Roman development of atonement theory was held to be infected by some alleged legal mindset.[55] It is now, thankfully, less common to describe Jewish people as necessarily primitive; the equally ill-founded and equally racist assertion that the Romans somehow inevitably interpret all things through a legal lens is unfortunately still prevalent and regularly used as an explanation for the rise of penal theories of atonement.

In this period, then, the overall picture stabilises. Penal substitution remains an accepted doctrine for most evangelicals, but also a controversial one. Thoughtful evangelical theologians defend with energy the substitutionary character of the atonement and variously interpret that in penal or other categories. Only in Smeaton and Crawford do we find a pressed defence of the necessity of using penal terms as the real basis for any other language.

Decline and Defensiveness: 1920 – 1960

Evangelical and non-evangelical historians agree that there was a profound decline in evangelicalism in Britain in the first half of the twentieth century. David Bebbington puts the nadir in 1940;[56] Adrian Hastings locates it in the 1920s.[57] Ian Randall suggests the difference is due to differing estimates of what it is to be evangelical.[58] Certainly, Hastings restricts his interest to "conservative evangelicals", whereas Bebbington includes the briefly significant "liberal evangelicalism".[59] Regardless, it was clearly a difficult time for the movement; Anglo-Catholicism had the intellectual energy and, it seemed, the cultural superiority. In 1919, it appeared that penal substitution was suffering in the same way as evangelicalism: it was still around, but apparently only as a quaint historical hangover amongst the ill-educated. A letter in the press that year said as much, prompting a response from the leaders of the young Cambridge Intercollegiate Christian Union.[60] Writing a year later, historian of doctrine L. W. Grensted was able to assert that "[i]t would hardly be untrue to say that among reputable theologians the Penal theory is now extinct."[61] Quite delightfully, he felt able to offer a precise identification of its last adherent: "Philippi, who died in 1882". However, the rumours of demise were greatly exaggerated. It would be some years before another intellectually convincing defence was written by an evangelical, but as Grensted was writing, something new was happening in Germany. Emil Brunner's defence of penal substitution as central to the Christian doctrine of atonement in *The Mediator* is a major event.[62]

The declining influence of evangelicalism led to the creation of a number of new evangelical organisations. The Intervarsity Fellowship (IVF), which later became the Universities and Colleges Christian Fellowship (UCCF), almost uniquely amongst mainstream pan-evangelical movements, as far as I can see, did and still does specify that the atonement be understood in penal terms in its Doctrinal Basis: clause F of this text affirms "[r]edemption from the guilt, penalty and power of sin only through the sacrificial death once for all of our representative and substitute, Jesus Christ, the only mediator between God and man".[63] I would suggest, however, that it is not natural to read this clause as insisting that the atonement be understood in merely penal terms. Norman Grubb's recollection of a meeting to explore the possibility of reunion of UCCF with the more liberal Student Christian Movement in 1919 repeatedly suggests that the core phraseology then was "the atoning blood of the Lord Jesus Christ as central".[64] The evangelical scholarly society Tyndale Fellowship took on the IVF Basis when it was founded in 1944. The original 1948 Doctrinal Basis of what was then London Bible College asserted, "The substitutionary death of our Lord Jesus Christ, and His resurrection, as the only way of salvation from sin through faith".[65] The British Evangelical Council was formed in 1953 to unite more characteristically conservative evangelicals across the UK. Even so, like LBC, it apparently saw no reason to spell out a penal dimension in atonement: rather, its Basis of Faith affirmed simply Christ's "substitutionary and atoning death as a sacrifice for sin". The Evangelical Movement of Wales was at least as conservative as BEC, yet while affirming Jesus' "substitutionary, atoning death on the cross" and calling this death "a perfect oblation and satisfaction for our sins", its 1955 statement of doctrinal belief stops just short of explicit penal language in relation to the crucified Christ.[66]

For a further indication of what was going on in evangelical theology in the middle of the twentieth century, we can survey a run of a representative journal. The *Evangelical Quarterly* was reasonably established and mainstream by 1945, with Martyn Lloyd-Jones chairing its committee and F. F. Bruce as its assistant editor (he became editor in 1950). Over the next ten years, we find *EQ* charting the founding of Tyndale House[67] and witnessing publications from both established and new evangelical scholars. Amongst the younger writers offering contributions are Bruce himself, Leon Morris, Philip Hughes, T. F. Torrance and Jim Packer. When we look for discussion of the atonement here, we find two things: a series of writers pressing the point that all human discussions of the issue are necessarily limited and partial, and going on to discuss it in a variety of terms. John Baker, for instance, offers a series of "Meditations on the Cross" which assert this point and then discuss the cross in terms reminiscent of Campbell and Aulén.[68] Another writer, Alfred Marshall, asks the question "Did Christ Pay our Debts?" and makes the same apophatic point before answering no.[69] Francis Davidson, then principal of the Glasgow Bible Training Institute, counsels against discussing the mechanics of atonement in his exploration of "Evangelism for Today."[70]

Alongside this is a series of straightforward defences of the penal character of the atonement. In writing on "Sacrifice in the Epistle to the Hebrews," G. J. C. Marchant concludes, "The sacrifice of Christ on the cross, then, may be seen as ... cancelling the obligations of past transgressions."[71] Geoffrey Bromiley discusses "The Significance of Death in Relation to the Atonement" and asserts bluntly that "the death of Jesus Christ ... was an acceptance of the consequences of sin which involved a literal exacting of the penalty upon sin."[72] Ernest F. Kevan, then principal of London Bible College, offers a report of a discussion on some proposed dogmatic theses at the Tyndale Fellowship. The theses had proposed the formulation "He bore in His own human body, on our behalf and in our stead, right up to a criminal's death upon the shameful cross, the penalty and curse due to human sin." The modifications made to this in the discussion only strengthened the emphasis on penal substitution.[73] Finally, in 1952 there is a collection of papers, again originating in a Tyndale Fellowship meeting, on justification by faith, several of which touch tangentially on penal substitution and accept or support the doctrine.

For a final piece of evidence from this period, it is worth glancing at some comments from George Beasley-Murray. In his very first book, Beasley-Murray sought to wake evangelical Christians up to the importance of the resurrection, which he believed they had missed. In the introduction, he says, "Even Protestants, in their constructions of the doctrine of the cross, have left Christ on it and presumed that His saving work finishes with His death. The atonement is consequently explained in terms of a sacrifice on our behalf, a satisfaction of God's justice, a payment of our debt, a revelation of God's love, *and that is all.* It somehow seems to have been overlooked that the resurrection is an integral part of our Lord's work for us, so that salvation is essentially a deliverance from a living death in sin to a new life of righteousness in God."[74]

One can find, perhaps, isolated pieces of evidence for a hardening of the view that penal substitution is the one true way of understanding the cross during this period, but more common would seem to be a continued acceptance that this is an important and appropriate doctrine, alongside an awareness that no one pattern of teaching can adequately interpret the greatness of Jesus' work on our behalf.

New Perspectives and New Arguments: 1960 – 2004

Evangelicalism has, of course, been resurgent in Britain over the last generation, but the academic theological climate in which this resurgence has taken place has raised new questions over the tradition of talking about the atonement in penal substitutionary terms. Most significant, perhaps, has been the new perspective on Paul. If we should indeed understand first-century Palestinian Judaism in terms of a covenantal nomism, rather than a law-grace dichotomy, then it seems to me that just about every biblical argument for penal substitution suffers, except perhaps for those built on Isaiah 53. When I first wrote on this subject, I set myself the task of defending penal substitution on the assumption that it was nowhere taught in Scripture, because it seemed to me that such a defence was more helpful, and if only we know a bit of basic trinitarian theology and can think straight about notions of imputation, such a defence was easy. Even so, it is clear that the sort of biblical theological defence of penal substitution that Smeaton and Crawford offered is simply not possible if the new perspective is right, and evangelical accounts of atonement doctrine need to come to terms with that.

There is also a growing awareness in European and American theology of the changing cultural situation in which we work. Whether linked to the word "postmodern" or not, there is a widespread consciousness that the answers that were convincing two generations ago are no longer so convincing today. One facet of this has been the announcement that we are moving from a guilt-forgiveness culture to an honour-shame culture[75] and that this must change the way we preach the atonement. This intuition marks Joel Green and Mark Baker's influential critique of penal substitution, *Recovering the Scandal of the Cross*. It is also a feature of the study *Atonement for a "Sinless" Society* by Steve Chalke's co-author, Alan Mann.[76]

A couple of comments are perhaps relevant here. First, cultural shift is a long-term, confused and messy thing. Notions of shame, even directly connected to the atonement, have been around for some while,[77] and on the other hand, a glance at the tabloid press's response to Saddam Hussein, or to the death of Myra Hindley or Harold Shipman, suggests that they believe their readers still have a fairly strong belief in guilt and punishment. Second, we should perhaps note the psychoanalytic theories that suggest that guilt is a more adult response than shame.[78] I do not, of course, think we should take the claims of psychoanalysts at face value, but Freud is still a relatively important cultural interpreter for the modern West, so we should not ignore them either. Finally, even if we accept that the proposed shift is happening, we might consider whether it is not something that it is incumbent on us to oppose. On the standard anthropological telling, the two cultures converge in the situations where I did nothing and my peers do not think I did, or where I did something culturally inappropriate and my peers know about it. It is the other corners of the matrix where it makes a difference: if I did nothing but others believe I did something inappropriate, then in a guilt culture I may protest my innocence, whereas in a shame culture I am shamed by their false belief; on the other hand, if I have done something inappropriate and no one knows, then in a guilt culture I should still feel guilty, whereas in a shame culture I am not shamed.

If we view the development of the penal substitutionary tradition in historical context, we might acknowledge that it represented an appropriate theology of the cross for a culturally dominant colonial Europe, in which the practice of seeking to conceal oppressive outrages by further murder or oppression was routine. A penal theory of the atonement says to the colonialist who has murdered to conceal his exploitation that his guilt is not unknown or forgotten, however successful his cover-up might have been. In a shame culture, by contrast, such an oppressor stands in no need of atonement – nor does a child abuser who has prosecuted his abuse so successfully that the child is too scared to reveal it. No one, I presume, is pretending there is anything better about a shame culture than a guilt culture; they are merely attempting to describe a cultural shift and an appropriately missiologi-cal response. Given the sort of themes I have just been sketching, however, I wonder whether an equally significant missiological response might be to insist that the church be countercultural and continue to side with the voice-less, the oppressed, the abused and the silenced by talking very loudly about the continuing reality of guilt.

A third recent development which appears to have had a bearing on debates about penal substitution has been the long-overdue recovery of non-Christendom traditions of evangelicalism. The inspiration of John Howard Yoder and then Stanley Hauerwas, showing how the gospel might actually make a difference; the founding of the Anabaptist Network in Britain; and the increasing sense that comfortable accommodations between church and state, and indeed between church and culture, have come to an end have all combined to create what may be dubbed the post-Christendom movement. The novelty of this should not be overplayed – Independency has always been a significant part of the English Free Churches – but the Independents (and Baptists) were generally not pacifists. The rediscovery of continental Anabap-tism as an inspiration for evangelical Christianity, combined, no doubt, with certain cultural trends, has created a strong evangelical pacifist witness, which in turn has led to a questioning of the adequacy of atonement accounts that presuppose some sort of inner divine necessity for violence.

I would offer two brief comments in assessing all this. First, I have already given some indication of the extent to which I see atonement the-ologies being influenced by cultural assumptions. Given this, if a robust Christian ethic demands a reevaluation of attitudes to criminal justice, say, it should indeed have implications for atonement theology. To this extent, it seems to me that the recent critique levelled by Steve Chalke and others is important and valid. Second, I observe that the rewritings of the doctrine of atonement that come from this direction tend to make much reference to the "myth of redemptive violence". Although the phrase is Walter Wink's,[79] I presume that what lies behind it is an appropriation of René Girard's account of the undoing of primal violence in the gospel story.[80] Whatever one may think about Girard's proposal from an anthropological point of view, it is noticeable that he can make it work only through an extremely ambivalent attitude to the Old Testament,[81] a rejection of Hebrews and other later New Testament writings profoundly opposed to the gospel story,[82] and an effective denial of the deity of Christ. (On Girard's account,

Christ is divine in that he loves perfectly,[83] which is a remarkably anachronistic echo of nineteenth-century German liberalism.) Wink is aware of Girard's ambivalent attitude to the Scriptures but takes no notice of his christological problems.

Finally, let us consider some of the more recent defences of penal substitution. The most significant in British evangelicalism have been those offered by Jim Packer in his 1973 Tyndale Lecture[84] and by John Stott in his magisterial *The Cross of Christ*.[85] Perhaps as significant as the attempted defences is Packer's suggestion, endorsed by Stott even in his most recent writing, that penal substitutionary doctrines of the atonement are "a distinguishing mark of the world-wide evangelical fraternity".[86] Well, perhaps, but I have not found very much evidence that they have been particularly regarded this way within the history of British evangelical theology.

Conclusion

At the beginning, I stated three theses. They warrant review in the light of the evidence I have been examining.

1. Evangelical theologians and preachers have, with very few exceptions, wanted to insist on substitutionary doctrines of atonement but have ascribed far less importance to the question of whether substitution is expounded in penal terms. I hope this thesis is now obvious. With the exception of the UCCF, it is the position of all the major pan-evangelical doctrinal statements. One can find a few evangelical theologians who object to substitutionary language, and a few others who demand penal language, and I have tried to illustrate both positions. The mainstream, however, is as I have stated it.

2. Generally, evangelicals in Britain have held to penal substitution within a "many metaphors" view of the atonement: penal substitution is one way of speaking about the cross, and perhaps the most significant, but other ways are also valid. Again, I hope that has become obvious from my examples. In British terms, Smeaton and Crawford are out on a limb when they insist in the 1870s that the only way to talk about the atonement is in penal terms. Rightly or wrongly, British evangelicals historically have not believed this.

3. Penal theories were generally accepted without complaint or comment amongst evangelicals until about 1800; from that time on, there has been a constant undercurrent of complaint about penal theories, and so some explicit defences. This, it seems to me, is the most interesting point. The crucial shift, I believe, is the one Foucault describes: the move in criminal justice from public ritual violence to private psychological violence. This just makes a penal substitutionary metaphor less culturally plausible. Everything else, I think, depends on this. In recent years, it has been reinforced by trends in biblical studies and in culture. I suspect such cultural changes are why the current evangelical controversy on penal substitution is taking place.

So does this mean we are at liberty to give up on penal substitutionary accounts? It seems to me two things are at stake here. First is the question of the relationship of penal theories of the atonement to the biblical text. Whether penal substitution is a biblical model of the atonement, or a development of biblical models, is a question for others in this volume. If we take it as something found in the Scriptures, then we are not at liberty to set it aside from our reflections. But what if we conclude that it is not found in the Scriptures? This brings me to my second point: the history of the doctrine of the atonement is a history of developing models which build on or interpret the biblical data in ways that illuminate what is said in Scripture and are relevant to the culture, either by being culturally comprehensible or by being prophetic and challenging. I would claim that penal substitution once fitted this picture and that it therefore has a place in our theological reflections. Whether on this account it still has a place in our preaching depends on whether we find the model still culturally relevant, which might be a question of where precisely we minister and worship, and of the subcultural makeup of our congregation.

Notes

1. Joseph Butler, *The Analogy of Religion to the Constitution and Course of Nature* (London: RTS, n.d.), 224–25.

2. Jonathan Edwards, *The Works of Jonathan Edwards*, vol. 9, *A History of the Work of Redemption*, ed. John F. Wilson (New Haven: Yale Univ. Press, 1989), 295.

3. Ibid., 304.

4. Jonathan Edwards, *Miscellanies*, entries 1352, 1360.

5. The best discussion of this passage that I know of is an unpublished MA thesis submitted to King's College London by Edwin Tay in 2004.

6. This occurs several times in *Miscellanies*. See entries 1050–1100.

7. In the *Miscellanies*, Edwards played with thoughts that were not fully formed.

8. For a more detailed account of Edwards on the atonement, see my *God of Grace and God of Glory: An Account of the Theology of Jonathan Edwards* (Edinburgh: T & T Clark, 2000), 142–50.

9. I am conscious of the fact that conflating John and Charles like this is somewhat unfair, but it is, I think, acceptable for the texts which I am considering.

10. John Wesley, *The Works of John Wesley*, vol. 9, *The Methodist Societies*, ed. Rupert E. Davies (Nashville: Abingdon, 1989), 51. I suspect that the echo of the Eucharistic liturgy is deliberate.

11. See John Wesley, *The Works of John Wesley*, vol. 7, *A Collection of Hymns*, ed. Franz Hildebrandt and Oliver A. Beckerlegge (Oxford: Clarendon, 1983).

12. See sec. 2:3.

13. Quoted in Timothy Gorringe, *God's Just Vengeance: Crime, Violence and the Rhetoric of Salvation* (Cambridge: Cambridge Univ. Press, 1996), 3.

14. See Thomas Paine, *The Age of Reason* (London: Watts, n.d.), part 1, ch. 8.

15. Andrew Fuller, *The Gospel Its Own Witness* (1799), in *The Works of Andrew Fuller*, 3 vols. (Harrisonburg, Va.: Sprinkle, 1988), 2:74–84. See also Peter Morden, *Offering Christ to the World: Andrew Fuller (1754–1815) and the Revival of Eighteenth Century Particular Baptist Life* (Carlisle: Paternoster, 2003). Morden helpfully traces the development of Fuller's thought on this issue and the course of his controversy with Booth – see especially 84–97.

16. Morden, *Offering Christ*, usefully discusses both Fuller's use of the (Grotian) New England theologians who followed Edwards and how he departed from them on several significant points. See 93–97.

17. Fuller, *Works*, 2:680–98.

18. Ibid., 2:699–715.

19. See the first note on p. 705.

20. Hodge's distinction between two ideas both covered by the word "guilt" is, it seems to me, simply adequate to the task of answering this point. See *Systematic Theology* 2:466–67. It is perhaps worth noting that, in the course of preparing this paper, I had a class of final-year students who were very far from being uniformly evangelical or Reformed read Hodge, and they were agreed at the end of the seminar that Hodge's defence of his theory was logically coherent.

21. See particularly William Wilberforce, *A Practical View of the Prevailing Religious System of Professed Christians in the Higher Middle Classes in This Country, Contrasted with Real Christianity* (Glasgow: Collins, 1833).

22. I am grateful to Bob Walker for allowing me to see his copy of these sermons.

23. See J. McLeod Campbell, *The Nature of the Atonement*, with an introduction by James B. Torrance (Edinburgh: Handsel, 1996), 81–113.

24. Edward Irving, *The Doctrine of the Incarnation Opened, in Six Sermons*, in *The Collected Writings of Edward Irving*, 5 vols., ed. G. Carlyle (London: Alexander Strahan, 1865), 5:114–257.

25. Ibid., 146.

26. "All flesh now under Him as Lord ... He be, as it were, united unto all flesh, by virtue of what He did in flesh" (ibid., 5:151). See also Irving's sermon "Our Lord Jesus Christ" in *Collected Writings*, 4:335–49, particularly 341: "When the Son of God took flesh, He entered upon the travail of salvation; when He carried that flesh triumphant to the right hand of God, he finished the work."

27. Thomas Erskine of Linlathlen, *The Brazen Serpent; or, Life Coming through Death* (Edinburgh: Waugh and Innes, 1831), 36–39.

28. This is clear in various places in Erskine's *True and False Religion* (1874; Redlands, Calif.: Freeness Press, 1993). According to Geoffrey Rowell, Erskine in 1865 informed the Bishop of Argyll and the Isles that "false concepts of salvation were at the root of the substitutionary view of the Atonement." See Geoffrey Rowell, *Hell and the Victorians* (Oxford: Clarendon, 1974), 73n39.

29. Framed in these terms, the falseness of the accusation is immediately apparent. Whilst Luther at times appears weak on sanctification, it is clearly ridiculous to accuse the Reformers in general, who all worked with versions of penal substitution to a greater or lesser extent, of teaching a merely passive righteousness.

30. Erskine insists repeatedly on this point in *The Unconditional Freeness of the Gospel: In Two Essays* (Edinburgh: Waugh and Innes, 1831). He is similarly insistent in *An Essay on Faith* (Edinburgh: Waugh and Innes, 1822).

31. For more on Erskine's interesting theology of atonement, see T. F. Torrance, *Scottish Theology: From John Knox to John McLeod Campbell* (Edinburgh: T & T Clark, 1996), 263–85.

32. Charles H. Spurgeon, *The Soul-Winner; or, How to Lead Sinners to the Saviour* (London: Passmore and Alabaster, 1895). The point is general, but for an obvious example, see p. 276: "The Lord Jesus Christ was punished in our room, and we are no longer obnoxious to the wrath of God. Behold, the atoning sacrifice is slain."

33. Indeed, given that Chalmers made use of George Hill's *Lectures on Divinity* as a textbook, and Hill, while not unimpressed by Grotianism, taught fairly straightforward penal substitution, we may assume Chalmers was happy with it. For some account of the history, and some telling quotations from Hill's *Lectures*, see Torrance, *Scottish Theology*, 257–61.

34. Michel Foucault, *Discipline and Punish: The Birth of the Prison*, trans. Alan Sheridan (London: Penguin, 1977), 3–7.

35. John Henry Newman, *Lectures on Justification*, 303, cited in Carl Henry, "Justification: A Doctrine in Crisis," *JETS* 38 (March 1995): 60. For a discussion of Newman's rejection of penal substitution, see David Newsome, "Justification and Sanctification: Newman and the Evangelicals," *JTS* 15 (1964): 32–53.

36. See, for instance, Edward Bickersteth's summary of the gospel in 1846, at least as it is reported in John W. Ewing, *Goodly Fellowship: A Centenary Tribute to the Life and Work of the World's Evangelical Alliance 1846–1946* (London: Marshall, Morgan and Scott, 1946), 41. The 1846 Basis of the Alliance insisted on "the Incarnation of the Son of God; His work of Atonement for sinners, and His Mediatorial intercession and reign".

37. T. R. Birks, *The Ways of God; or, Thoughts on the Difficulties of Belief in Connexion with Providence and Redemption* (London: Seeley, Jackson and Halliday, 1863).

38. Birks' framing of the problem has a remarkably contemporary ring to it: "A provision for maintaining the rigour of justice, in which the fundamental idea of justice is set aside, does violence to the moral instincts of mankind. Yet this, it is often urged, is the very character of the orthodox

creed on the sacrifice of Christ and the penal suffering of the just and innocent in place of the unjust. To escape from the charge, not a few writers have carefully explained away the scriptural statements, so as to imply a merely exemplary character in our Lord's death, or a winning and attractive display of the Divine love, entirely devoid of any penal character. On the other hand, there have been those who, in recoiling from what they felt to be a dangerous heresy assailing the foundation of Christianity, have presented the Scripture truth in forms adapted rather to revolt the conscience, and repel thoughtful enquirers, than really to vindicate the wisdom and equity of the ways of God. For if moral merit or demerit, innocence or guilt — the most personal ideas in the whole range of human thought — are viewed as mere counters, like debentures or pieces of money, that may be transferred indifferently from hand to hand, with the sole condition that they retain a certain quantitative value, to secure so much reward or incur so much suffering, it is hard to resist the impression that the very foundations of moral suffering are subverted, and the deepest instincts of the purified conscience stifled and destroyed" (ibid., 119–20).

39. Ibid., 135.

40. G. S. Barrett, in G. S. Barrett, *Maintaining the Unity: Proceedings of the Eleventh International Conference and Diamond Jubilee Celebration of the Evangelical Alliance Held in London, July 1907* (London: Religious Tract Society, 1907), 17.

41. Giovanni Luzzi, in Barrett, *Maintaining the Unity*, 181.

42. Dinsdale T. Young, in Barrett, *Maintaining the Unity*, 243.

43. A. T. Pierson, in Barrett, *Maintaining the Unity*, 353.

44. In A. J. Arnold, ed., *Jubilee of the Evangelical Alliance* (London: John Shaw, 1897), 100–101.

45. Ibid., 101.

46. In Barrett, *Maintaining the Unity*, 147–48.

47. James Denney, *The Death of Christ* (London: Hodder and Stoughton, 1902).

48. See particularly R. W. Dale, *The Atonement: The Congregational Union Lecture for 1875* (London: Hodder and Stoughton, 1875). For an insightful commentary, drawing out both the essentially penal character of Dale's doctrine and the distortions he saw in some classical versions of penal substitution, see Colin E. Gunton, "Dale and the Atonement," in *The Cross and the City: Essays in Commemoration of Robert William Dale 1829–1895*,

ed. Clyde Binfield, supplement to the *Journal of the URC History Society* 6 (1999): 1–13.

49. Dale, *The Atonement*, 373–90.

50. Ibid., 401–30.

51. George Smeaton, *The Doctrine of the Atonement as Taught by Christ Himself* (Edinburgh: T & T Clark, 1871); Smeaton, *The Doctrine of the Atonement as Taught by the Apostles* (Edinburgh: T & T Clark, 1870); T. J. Crawford, *The Doctrine of Holy Scripture Respecting the Atonement* (Edinburgh: William Blackwood, 1871).

52. Smeaton, *Taught by the Apostles*, 177.

53. Crawford, *Doctrine of Holy Scripture*, 378.

54. Ibid., 185.

55. Albrecht Ritschl, *Die christliche Lehre von der Rechtfertigung und Versöhnung*, 3rd ed. (Bonn: Adolph Marcus, 1889); Adolph von Harnack, *History of Dogma*, vol. 7 (1899; New York: Dover, 1961).

56. David W. Bebbington, *Evangelicalism in Modern Britain: A History from the 1730s to the 1980s* (London: Routledge, 1989), 181–228.

57. Adrian Hastings, *A History of English Christianity, 1920–1990* (London: SCM, 1991), 199–203.

58. Ian Randall, *Evangelical Experiences: A Study in the Spirituality of English Evangelicalism, 1918–1939* (Carlisle: Paternoster, 1999).

59. On which see, for example, *Liberal Evangelicalism: An Interpretation by Members of the Church of England* (London: Hodder and Stoughton, 1923).

60. See Oliver R. Barclay, *Whatever Happened to the Jesus Lane Lot?* (Leicester: IVP, 1977), 86.

61. L. W. Grensted, *A Short History of the Doctrine of the Atonement* (Manchester: Manchester Univ. Press, 1920), 308.

62. Emil Brunner, *The Mediator: A Study of the Central Doctrine of the Christian Faith*, trans. Olive Wyon (London: Lutterworth, 1934), 455–74.

63. Earlier versions of this current text deployed slightly different wording but carried essentially the same theology with respect to the cross. See *For the Faith of the Gospel 1928–78: The IVF/UCCF Story* (Leicester: UCCF, 1978), 40.

64. See Barclay, *Whatever Happened?* 82.

65. Taken from Harold H. Rowden, *London Bible College: The First Twenty-five Years* (Worthing: Henry Walker, 1968), 18.

66. Although it does affirm that "sin pollutes and controls" humans and "renders them guilty in the sight of a holy God, and subject to the penalty which, in His wrath and condemnation, He has decreed against [them]". It then affirms Jesus' death as a "perfect oblation and satisfaction" for such sin.

67. See particularly F. F. Bruce, "The Tyndale Fellowship for Biblical Research," *EQ* 19 (1947): 52–61.

68. John Baker, "Meditations on the Cross," *EQ* 17 (1945): 161–68. Baker begins, "As there is no limit to the love of God, so there never can be human words able to exhaust the wealth of meaning in the Cross of Jesus Christ" (161). He then offers an account of vicarious repentance. See also Baker, "Meditations on the Cross," *EQ* 18 (1946): 161–68, which is a broadly *Christus Victor* account, and Baker, "Meditations on the Cross," *EQ* 20 (1948): 161–65, which again emphasises the victory motif.

69. Alfred Marshall, "Did Christ Pay our Debts?" *EQ* 23 (1951): 284–86.

70. Francis Davidson, "Evangelism for Today," *EQ* 27 (1945): 241–47. See particularly 245–46: "A frank admission that the atonement is beyond finite comprehension though not contrary to reason and not beyond faith will not belittle the preacher nor his message in the presence of the intellectuals ... the primitive preaching, the Kerygma of the New Testament, was a proclamation of salvation procured by Christ, and not an apologia of its meaning or method."

71. G. J. C. Marchant, "Sacrifice in the Epistle to the Hebrews," *EQ* 20 (1948): 196–210 (208).

72. Geoffrey Bromiley, "The Significance of Death in Relation to the Atonement," *EQ* 21 (1949): 122–32 (127).

73. Ernest F. Kevan, "The Person and Work of Christ," *EQ* 23 (1951): 213–18. The modified form was "He bore in His own human body, on our behalf and in our stead, right up to the death of the Cross, the penalty due to human sin" (214). The removal of "shameful" and "curse" suggests to me an intention to focus more narrowly on a penal account, although Kevan does not discuss these changes.

74. Quoted in Paul Beasley-Murray, *Fearless for Truth* (Carlisle: Paternoster, 2002), 39.

75. On which, see Stephen J. Patterson, *Beyond the Passion: Rethinking the Death and Life of Jesus* (Minneapolis: Augsburg Fortress, 2004). This distinction is made in anthropology at least as far back as E. R. Dodd's book

The Greeks and the Irrational (Berkeley: Univ. of California Press, 1951). It is developed in relation to Japan in various studies, perhaps beginning with R. Benedict, *The Chrysanthemum and the Sword* (London: RKP, 1967). Joel Green and Mark Baker relate it to Japanese culture in *Recovering the Scandal of the Cross: Atonement in New Testament and Contemporary Contexts* (Downers Grove, Ill.: IVP, 2000), 153–70.

76. Green and Baker, *Recovering the Scandal*, 153–70; Alan Mann, *Atonement for a "Sinless" Society* (Milton Keynes: Paternoster, 2005).

77. As I noted, it was a connection made in a thesis proposed to the Tyndale Fellowship, which I suspect is a relatively conservative association culturally as well as theologically, as far back as 1951. See n. 73.

78. This is implicit at least in Freud but made obvious in Erik H. Erikson, *Childhood and Society* (Harmondsworth: Penguin, 1965).

79. Walter Wink, *Engaging the Powers: Discernment and Resistance in a World of Domination* (Minneapolis: Fortress, 1992), 13–31.

80. See, variously, René Girard, *Violence and the Sacred*, trans. Patrick Gregory (Baltimore: Johns Hopkins Univ. Press, 1977); Girard, *Things Hidden Since the Foundation of the World: Research Undertaken in Collaboration with Jean-Michel Oughourlian and Guy Lefort*, trans. Stephen Bann and Michael Metteer (London: Athlone, 1987); Girard, *Job: Victim of His People* (London: Athlone, 1987); Girard, *The Scapegoat* (Baltimore: Johns Hopkins Univ. Press, 1986).

81. So, for example, *Things Hidden*, 157–58, where Girard agrees with Oughourlian's suggestion that in the Old Testament, "[t]he myths are worked through with a form of inspiration that runs counter to them, but they continue in being. The sacrifices are criticized, but they continue ... And even though he is presented in a less and less violent form, and becomes more and more benevolent, Yahweh is still the God to whom vengeance belongs. The notion of divine retribution is still alive." Wink is well aware of this: "Girard understands the Hebrew Bible as a long and laborious exodus out of the world of violence and sacred projections, an exodus plagued by many reversals and falling short of its goal" (*Engaging the Powers*, 146).

82. Girard, *Things Hidden*, 217–31. Again, Wink has grasped the point: "The earliest Christians were not able to sustain the intensity of this revelation, and dimmed it by confusing God's intention to reveal the scapegoating mechanism for what it was with the notion that God intended Jesus to die. This in turn led to their reinserting the new revelation into the scape-

goat theology: Jesus was sent by God to be the *last* scapegoat and to reconcile us, once and for all, to God (the Epistle to the Hebrews)" (*Engaging the Powers*, 148). Notice also Girard's suggestion that there is something deficient in the parable of the vineyard in Mark and Luke (*Things Hidden*, 188).

83. Girard, *Things Hidden*, 215 – 20.

84. J. I. Packer, "What Did the Cross Achieve? The Logic of Penal Substitution" (1975; Stirling: RTSF Monograph, 2002).

85. John Stott, *The Cross of Christ* (Leicester: IVP, 1986).

86. Packer, "What Did the Cross Achieve?" 11.

chapter sixteen

"live much under the shadow of the cross"

atonement and evangelical spirituality

ian randall

In 1789, Olaudah Equiano, an ex-slave, wrote about his story in what became a widely read book, titled *Interesting Narrative*. As a freed slave, he began to attend evangelical services. The result was that he had an instantaneous conversion, in which, as he put it, he "saw clearly, with the eye of faith, the crucified Saviour bleeding on the cross on Mount Calvary". This vision convinced him that he was "a great debtor ... to sovereign free grace".[1] This kind of testimony expresses the classic evangelical understanding of the place of the cross in the experience of conversion. Bruce Hindmarsh, in *The Evangelical Conversion Narrative*, shows how the testimonies of members of the Moravian movement which took shape in Central Europe in the early eighteenth century contained vivid descriptions of an apprehension of the atonement.[2] But the cross does not relate only to conversion. One of those influenced by the Moravians, John Wesley, although well known for his belief in "instantaneous" experience, also believed in a "gradual" work of God in the believer associated with the cross.[3] He spoke of what Christ did on the cross "for us" and what God does "in us".[4] Effects were corporate as well as individual. In *The Cross of Christ*, John Stott used the Moravians as an example of a community "comprehensively stimulated by the cross".[5] Early evangelicals had a vibrant, crucicentric spirituality.

Analysis of the shaping and outworking of evangelical experience has been increasing in recent years. Alister McGrath wrote *Roots That Refresh: A Celebration of Reformation Spirituality* in 1991, and he explored the topic of evangelical spirituality in a lecture in 1994.[6] By 2000, McGrath could write that, although resistance still remained within sections of evangelicalism to the word "spirituality", it had "gained virtually universal acceptance as the best means of designating the group of spiritual disciplines that focus on deepening the believer's relationship with God and enhancing the life of the Spirit".[7] It is still the case, however, when considering the cross of Christ, that much more attention is given by evangelicals to the theology of the atonement than to the cross in relation to spirituality. Indeed, Timothy George, in *For All the Saints: Evangelical Theology and Christian Spirituality*, speaks of a "deadly divorce" between theology and spirituality that has arisen in part because two realities, justification by faith alone and union with Christ, have not been seen as indissolubly bound together. They are bound together, he insists, in the cross.[8] This study explores the heart of evangelical spirituality – the cross – by looking at the contributions of some evangelical writers.

The Cross and Spirituality

In *The Message of the Cross*, Derek Tidball comments, "At the heart of evangelical spirituality lies the atoning work of Christ. The Christian life is viewed primarily as a life that finds its origin in the cross and is lived in grateful response to it and humble imitation of it."[9] Tidball's major study of the cross is very unusual if not unique in that it begins with spirituality rather than with the doctrine of the atonement. Yet this is true to the way in which evangelicals have understood the gospel. To embrace the saving gospel has not been seen primarily as an exercise in intellectual comprehension. At the same time, explanation is crucial. The Moravians called for both an experience and an understanding of the cross. In May 1738, when John Wesley famously felt his heart "strangely warmed", it was at a Moravian-led meeting in Aldersgate Street, London.[10] Wesley recorded, in cross-centred language, "I felt I did trust in Christ, Christ alone, for salvation; and an assurance was given me that He had taken away *my* sins, even *mine*, and saved *me* from the law of sin and death ... I then testified openly to all there what I now first felt in my heart."[11] The testimony explained the experience. August Spangenberg, perhaps the leading Moravian theologian, quoted from a Moravian *Exposition* of belief the following key passage: "All men are sinners, and cannot deliver themselves from this wretched condition: Jesus Christ is the One and Only Helper and Saviour.... All men must be directed straitway to HIM: Nothing is of any avail but his blood of atonement: He that finds forgiveness of sins in the blood of Jesus, has life and salvation, and can live holily as a child of God."[12] Later, John Newton, whose own experience of conversion was dramatic, referring to the *Exposition*, commented that "of all systems of divinity I am acquainted with, none seems in the main to accord more with my sentiments."[13]

If Europe saw a new crucicentric spiritual impetus in the eighteenth century, so did North America. Jonathan Edwards brought understanding and experience together, sometimes seeing this worked out in dramatic ways. Edwards was a primary shaper of evangelical spirituality. In his own phrase, in his *Religious Affections*, "holy affections" constituted a great part of true religion. "The Holy Scriptures," he asserted, "do everywhere place religion very much in the affections."[14] Yet for Edwards, evangelical spirituality was not to be defined simply as feelings. He insisted that "there must be light in the understanding, as well as an *affected* fervent heart."[15] Edwards asked how anyone who knew of the work of Christ on the cross could "be cold and heavy, insensible and regardless!" The cross is the focus. "Where," enquired Edwards, "are the exercises of our affections proper, if not here?"[16]

In the nineteenth century, evangelical preachers and writers returned to this theme, determined to present it afresh to their hearers and readers. In Birmingham, the Congregational minister R. W. Dale was concerned that one of the main reasons why people "do not trust in Christ to save them, is that they do not believe that there is anything from which they need to be saved". In the context of what Dale saw as a society regarding itself as "sinless" – a very different interpretation than that usually offered of Victorian society – he insisted on preaching salvation from sin. In his great work *The Atonement*, Dale argued for remission of sins through the cross not as a formality but as a "manifestation of the Divine mercy" to be received "with devout joy and immeasurable gratitude".[17] This was the experience of salvation, an experience which worked out in very practical ways. The same concern for the centrality of the atonement is seen in the preaching and writing of the Scottish Presbyterian James Denney, who spoke of those who might acknowledge that they had sinned but who did not see this as important since "God is gracious". Of course, Denney rejoined, "that is true, but not all the truth … it hides from those who speak so the unspeakable sacrifice, at the cost of which God's pardoning and reconciling love comes to mankind."[18]

Throughout the twentieth century, the works of both Dale and Denney continued to have an impact on the evangelical understanding of spiritual experience. Thus Martyn Lloyd-Jones recounted how in reading R. W. Dale's *The Atonement* and James Denney's *The Death of Christ*, he had found the real heart of the gospel and the key to the inner meaning of the Christian faith.[19] James Packer affirmed the importance of Denney's work for evangelical experience: "No one goes deeper than Denney in discerning the impact on thought and life of knowing that Christ on the cross died for my sins."[20] It is the cross that shapes evangelical spiritual experience.

Penalty and Power

To what extent, however, have those in the evangelical tradition seen penal substitution as integrally related to ongoing spiritual experience? A sampling of the literature on this subject should show how closely leaders in the evangelical tradition connected the two concepts.

The place of the cross in the spirituality of John Wesley is not always noted,[21] but it is a major theme in his preaching and thought. For him, the death of Christ involved penal suffering,[22] and salvation itself flows from the punishment of human guilt on the cross. Wesley also taught that Christ's work on the cross was a victory over sin and evil. The *Christus Victor* theme is taken up in three of his forty-four *Standard Sermons*. There has been a great deal of examination of Wesley's doctrine of sanctification, in particular his teaching about "entire sanctification"; it has not always been recognised, however, that for him the Spirit who sanctifies is the Spirit of the suffering and victorious Christ. From the cross flows both justification and sanctification.[23] In the first of his *Standard Sermons*, Wesley talks about Christ's "being made a curse for us", so that we can be "saved from guilt", but he sees more than this in the atonement. There is salvation from fear – "though not from the possibility of falling away from the grace of God" – and salvation from the power and guilt of sin: the person who has known the power of the cross does not commit "habitual sin" and does not engage in "wilful sin" but rather desires "the holy and perfect will of God".[24] It is crucial to note that for Wesley, it was a living faith in the substitutionary sacrifice of Christ that produced the power for inward and outward sanctity.

Although the Reformed tradition, as represented by Jonathan Edwards, is often contrasted sharply with the Wesleyan approach, there is much common ground. Like Wesley, Edwards stresses the gift of the Spirit as flowing from the atonement. For Edwards, believers were being drawn into the life of the triune God.[25] Pneumatologically speaking, this was a community of the Spirit, but at its heart was the atonement.[26]

James Packer also links spirituality to the cross. While Packer contends strongly that penal substitution is the "final and fundamental category for understanding the cross", he also argues that the direct benefits of the atonement – forgiveness and justification – are not the whole of our salvation. For Packer, as for Edwards, the "taproot of our entire salvation" is "our union with Christ himself by the Holy Spirit".[27] This is a profoundly experiential approach, linking penalty-taking with power. In Wesley, in Edwards, and later in Packer, we find reasoned portrayals of experience in relation to the atonement.

In Charles Haddon Spurgeon, we find soaring passion in sermons on the cross. In one of Spurgeon's early London sermons, he appeals to Christians: "And even you, ye Christians, when ye think that your Saviour died, should afflict your souls: ye should say, 'Alas! and did my Saviour bleed? / And did my Sov'reign die? / Would he devote that sacred head / For such a worm as I?' "[28] Much of the sermon had an evangelistic note, as was common with Spurgeon, but at the end he is concerned – and this was typical of Spurgeon – to stimulate believers to enter with exuberance into the blessings of the atonement.[29] The emphasis on spiritual joy is securely based, for Spurgeon, because it is an authentic response to believers' being accepted in Christ. R. W. Dale similarly argued that to see God in Christ enduring penal suffering produced "a cry of thanksgiving and worship".[30] Dale was deeply concerned to connect the atonement with the concrete realities of life, but the foundation was the reality of an actual atonement.[31]

One of the early influential books on the cross produced by the Inter-Varsity Fellowship was *Why the Cross?* by H. E. Guillebaud. Guillebaud supported penal substitution but opposed expressions like "God punished Christ." He saw the cross as "an outpouring of the love of God before which we can only worship". Guillebaud's aim was to deal with barriers to the acceptance of substitutionary atonement, and his hope was that what he had written would help people to "let themselves be gripped by the love of God in Christ, till all difficulties and objections melt away in the glory of the Cross".[32] For Guillebaud, explaining the cross was not only a theological exercise; the expectation was of a spiritual encounter. Leon Morris, writing in the 1960s, saw the cross as having rich, multidimensional effects on the daily life of the believer: "The great fact on which the New Testament insists is that the atonement is many-sided and therefore completely adequate for every need."[33] For these writers, penalty and power belong together.

To Appropriate a "Finished Work"

The language of the "finished work" of Christ is another way of describing what is foundational for evangelical spirituality. Alan Stibbs, arguing in the 1950s for the doctrine of penal substitution, emphasized the place of "the finished work of Christ" for assurance of salvation and quoted P. T. Forsyth, the outstanding Congregational theologian who developed his thinking about the atonement from the 1890s onwards.[34] Forsyth explained in *The Work of Christ* that personal transformation involves a spiritual experience lived in the light of the cross. Having argued that "Christ entered voluntarily into the pain and horror which is sin's penalty from God," he explored the realm of experience. Christ, he suggested, as he took the curse and judgment, "felt sin and its horror as only the holy could, as God did", and believers, as they "come under His Cross and near His heart", find that they are able to "rise to holiness"[35] as they "depend daily upon the continued energy of the crucified and risen One".[36] Writing about "Christian perfection", he suggested that the "very marrow" of evangelical faith and experience is that, as believers, "we are what redemption has made us."[37] The Christian life was one of dependence on what Christ did on the cross. The same themes are common in Spurgeon. For Spurgeon, a consequence of Christ's work was the overcoming of a range of evils in the world.[38] It is on the basis of an achieved reconciliation through Christ as substitute that the wider dislocation of the world can be healed.

Again, it is important to see that the Wesleyan holiness and the Reformed traditions are not as far apart in this area as might be thought. They share with each other, and with the Keswick holiness tradition, the belief that what has been done "once for all" has continuing effects in holy living. Wesley argued that the holiest people needed a prophet as guide, a priest to make even "perfect holiness" acceptable, and a king to supply continual holiness: "the most perfect ... need the blood of atonement."[39] The language of "perfect holiness" has not been Reformed usage, but a robust upholder of that tradition, J. C. Ryle, in his classic *Holiness*, shared a similar perspective on the ongoing nature of Christ's finished work. Initially, said Ryle, a Christian's faith "laid hold on the atonement of Christ and gave him hope". But as he grows in grace, he sees many more aspects of Christ. Ryle enumerates some of these aspects: "Substitute, Intercessor, Priest, Advocate, Physician, Shepherd, and Friend". All of these, he argues, "unfold themselves to a growing soul in an unspeakable manner".[40] Wesley and Ryle both outline profound experiences to be appropriated.

What about the spirituality of the Keswick Convention, which began in 1875 and which was hugely influential in shaping evangelical piety?[41] Evan Hopkins, the Anglican clergyman who did more than anyone else to give a framework and foundation for Keswick spirituality, was committed to moderate views of holiness. Thus, he emphatically denied the idea promulgated by some within the Wesleyan stream that there could be "eradication of sin". Rather, he saw the possibility of the "counteraction" of sin in the believer.[42] For Hopkins, this was a fruit of the cross. Spiritual experience was always, in Keswick teaching, related to Christ and what he had done. In 1913, Hopkins described how he was still sustained by the message of "the all-sufficiency of Christ" that he had first received in 1873.[43] Keswick spirituality has been another expression of a spirituality grounded in the finished work of Christ on the cross.[44]

Holy Love

Having seen in broad terms how evangelical spirituality is shaped by the cross, it is important to examine the way evangelical believers view the love of God in relation to the cross and to their experience, since this has been a source of debate. Such debate is not new.[45] As Howard Marshall notes elsewhere in this volume, a frequent criticism of penal substitution is that it teaches that because of the cross, God is prepared to abandon his wrath and forgive sinners. He comments that no responsible defenders of the doctrine take this point of view. On the contrary, evangelical leaders have been marked by their attempts to speak with great care about the atonement, seeking to avoid the danger of dividing Father and Son – the wrathful Father and the loving Son.

Several examples of the evangelical position Marshall describes may be highlighted. In the 1890s, F. B. Meyer, a Baptist minister who was the leading international representative of Keswick, wrote in standard evangelical terms of the need to "satisfy the claims of a broken law" through the cross. While Meyer never deviated from his belief in the substitutionary atonement of Christ, he portrayed increasingly the death of Christ as being "a tidal wave

out of the heart of God", rather than something which "pacified and mollified the Father's anger".[46] The focus in evangelicalism on the love of God may
also be seen in its hymns: far from evangelical spirituality being obsessed with
a wrathful God, the words of Isaac Watts in "When I Survey the Wondrous
Cross" about "love so amazing, so divine" have summed up for many evangelicals throughout the centuries their understanding of the cross as a reality
in spiritual experience.

As Watts' hymnody suggests, there was, among the early theological
shapers of evangelicalism, a common commitment to this theme. Jonathan
Edwards spoke of how the soul is "enlightened with a sense of the merciful
nature of God", as seen through the mediation of Christ.[47] Here is how
Edwards describes one stage in his own experience: "From about that time I
began to have a new kind of apprehension and ideas of Christ, and the work
of redemption, and the glorious way of salvation by him. An inward, sweet
sense of these things, at times, came into my heart."[48] D. G. Hart suggests
that for Edwards, and also for another eighteenth-century evangelist, Henry
Alline, a remarkable Free Will Baptist preacher in Canada's Maritime prov-
inces, "the experience of divine grace that transformed tortured and sorrow-
ridden souls into ones assured of God's love ... was the centrepiece of true
Christianity."[49]

Charles Spurgeon portrayed this love in graphic terms. Preaching in 1890
on Philippians chapter 2, he depicted the atonement and the response of
the believer in this way: "God can punish sin upon His own dear Son ...
One great gash opened the way to His heart." As Spurgeon presses home the
response, he speaks of asking for a life of obedience, self-denial and humility – but above all this love of God calls for a loving heart. Spurgeon commends George Herbert's poetry, "suffused with love for his dear Lord", and
suggests that if his hearers read the Scottish Presbyterian minister Robert
Murray McCheyne, they might hide their heads and say, "I am not worthy
to sing – 'Jesus, lover of my soul' for I do not return His love as I ought to
do."[50]

There were worries, however, that the spiritually vibrant presentation of the
cross that characterized Spurgeon was becoming less evident in evangelicalism
in the later nineteenth and early twentieth centuries.[51] P. T. Forsyth issued a
"blast of the trumpet" about the continual preaching of "God is Love" (1 John
4:8). This, he insisted, "is not the whole gospel". Forsyth spoke of "a kind of
consecration which would live close to the Father" but which did not always

take seriously enough aspects of the cross which he called "awful ... as full of judgment as of salvation". For Forsyth, true spirituality had to be shaped by love that was holy, or as he put it, "Love is not evangelical till it has dealt with holy law."[52] Forsyth averred that to be spiritual was "to answer God's manner of spirituality which you find in Jesus Christ and Him crucified". James Gordon comments that this was "a more muscular theology of God's love in which Forsyth took issue with the sentimental flabbiness of liberal theology, which, in his view, emptied the cross of offence, took wrath out of judgment and trivialized sin by removing its tragic consequences".[53] Others, like Forsyth, have insisted that the experience of God's love is cross-shaped. James Denney, commenting on Romans chapter 3, said that he knew of no "interpretation of Christ's death which enables us to regard it as a demonstration of love to sinners, if this vicarious or substitutionary character is denied".[54]

In the course of the twentieth century, Oswald Chambers, A. W. Tozer, Leon Morris and Eugene Peterson are among those who have recalled evangelicals to cross-shaped spirituality. Chambers, who became famous through his widely used devotional readings, *My Utmost for His Highest*, commented on the tendency "to evade being identified with the sufferings of Jesus Christ". He insisted that God's way was always the way of suffering, the way of the "long, long trail".[55] Tozer called evangelicals to reject the "new cross", offering "a jollier way of living", and to embrace the "old cross of sacrifice".[56] For Peterson, the spirituality that Jesus offers is "difficult, obedient and self-sacrificing".[57] Leon Morris, in *The Apostolic Preaching of the Cross*, pursues the theme of the true nature of divine love, as known in human experience. He writes, "There is a divine love, but it is not a careless sentimentality indifferent to the moral integrity of the loved ones. Rather it is a love which is a purifying fire, blazing against everything that hinders the loved ones from being the very best that they can be."[58] Holy love is transformative.

Response to Divine Self-Giving

What responses to the cross are found in evangelical spirituality? First there is worship. Derek Tidball, quoting from classic hymns used in evangelical worship, notes, "A multitude of hymns and songs about the cross testifies to its importance for spirituality."[59] In the eighteenth century, there were debates, sometimes bitter, between Calvinist and Arminian evangelicals. But Calvinists used Charles Wesley's hymn "O for a Thousand Tongues to

Sing," with its focus on Christ's redemption, as that which can break the power of cancelled sin, set the prisoner free and make the foulest clean.[60] Augustus Toplady's "Rock of Ages" became one of the most popular hymns among evangelicals on both sides of the Atlantic. Toplady was virulently anti-Arminian, but Methodists soon incorporated his hymn in their hymnbook, happy to sing of Christ's sacrifice as that which was "of Sin the double Cure", cleansing from "guilt and power".[61] In one of his sermons on the cross, Spurgeon exhorted his listeners, "The death of Christ ought to inspire you till you sing," and he quoted from a hymn beginning "Jesus, spotless Lamb of God".[62] Mark Noll summarizes the message of evangelical hymns as "Jesus Christ Saves Sinners."[63]

Connection with the cross is also made through Holy Communion. It is a common misconception that evangelicals have taken a low view of the Eucharist. In 1745, the Wesleys published *Hymns on the Lord's Supper*, which contained 166 items. As F. C. Gill notes, these are communion hymns which convey the depths and mystery of the Eucharist and which are intended to nourish spiritual experience.[64] This collection has a section titled "The Holy Eucharist as It Implies a Sacrifice." The theological significance is clear.[65] B. L. Manning highlights one hymn, "O Thou Eternal Victim, Slain," describing it as one of the greatest communion hymns written by Charles Wesley: a hymn about life by death and healing by blood.[66] John Wesley advocated frequent ("constant") communion.[67] The Moravians felt at communion that they were gathered into the passion of Christ, into the whole community of the faithful and into heavenly reality.[68] Spurgeon advocated and practised weekly communion. "We believe," he said in a sermon on the theology of communion, "that Jesus Christ spiritually comes to us and refreshes us, and in that sense we eat his flesh and drink his blood."[69] P. T. Forsyth similarly spoke of "Christ in a real presence giving anew His redemption".[70]

In evangelical devotion, as in the devotion of other Christian traditions, the cross is also a comfort in times of trouble. This is seen in the hymn "Just as I Am," written in 1835 by Charlotte Elliott.[71] She wrote it when she was – as a Christian – suffering from depression and doubt. Her aim was to write a hymn which focussed not on the contribution of human effort to spirituality but on divine acceptance through the cross.[72] This provides true comfort. Leon Morris adopted a similar approach in lectures he delivered in 1988 at Southern Baptist Seminary in Louisville, Kentucky. His lectures addressed a number of areas in human experience: the cross as the answer to futility, ignorance, loneliness, sickness and death, and selfishness. These were seen as relevant both to those seeking Christ and to those who were Christian disciples.[73]

On the subject of evangelical social ethics, a final observation may be made. Has the idea of penal substitution, applied so thoroughly by evangelicals to the matters of the inner life, produced a spirituality that has had "little room for the importance of ethical comportment"? This is the claim of Joel Green and Mark Baker. They continue, "It is also true that this particular way of portraying the significance of Jesus' death has had little voice in how we relate to one another in and outside of the church or in larger, social-ethical issues."[74] This is a remarkable statement, given that many of those considered in this essay were deeply committed to social change.[75] John Wesley published his *Thoughts on Slavery* in 1774, and his last letter was to William Wilberforce urging action against the "execrable villainy" of the slave trade. For Wesley, the campaign was a spiritual one in which Wilberforce needed divine help, otherwise he would be "worn out by the opposition of men and devils".[76] For Dale, writing in *The Atonement*, "Christian holiness is nothing else than a revelation of the inexhaustible energy of the holiness of Christ."[77] This included, for Dale, energy to achieve socio-political change. Nineteenth-century evangelicals such as Spurgeon and Dale spoke out forcefully on social and also political issues, local and national, that affected ordinary people. Spurgeon castigated British political leaders who were, as he saw it, bent on senseless wars, and asked, "How many of our weaker neighbours will have their houses burned and their fields ravaged by this Christian (?) nation?" Dale was especially interested in health and education and made connections between these issues and the challenge of dealing with the fundamental causes of poverty and crime.[78] Certainly there have been contrary voices, warning against social involvement, but they do not represent the mainstream of evangelical thinking since the early eighteenth century. Rather, the self-giving of God in the cross has been seen as calling for service to the world.

Conclusion

In this study, I have looked at the thinking of a number of influential evangelicals who have explored the theology of the cross and have asked how they approached the related issue of spiritual experience. For evangelicals, as Packer put it, theology must always be related to the activity of "trusting, loving, worshipping, obeying, serving and glorifying God".[79] This connection is abundantly evident in the writers and preachers examined. Charles Spurgeon regularly encouraged his hearers to understand and to respond to the atonement. "Try to understand, dear friends," Spurgeon said, "the greatness of the atonement. Live much under the shadow of the cross.... Feel that Christ's blood was shed for you, even for you. Never be satisfied till you have learned the mystery of the five wounds."[80] For a passionate articulation of evangelical crucicentric theology, perhaps Spurgeon is matched only by P. T. Forsyth. The preaching of "an atoning Christ and an atoning cross", Forsyth always insisted, was "the great message and experience of the Church". Yet even Forsyth argued that the way in which the atonement was explained might have to be adjusted in certain ways in order to communicate to the surrounding culture.[81]

It is this idea of adjustment which presents challenges. Today there is much more willingness than in the past among evangelicals to explore other Christian spiritual traditions. Derek Tidball has highlighted some of the dangers and also the opportunities for evangelical spirituality: "It is easy in today's world to come up with a hybrid spirituality which is no longer evangelical or to transform the evangelical tradition so much that it ceases to be evangelical. The challenge then is so to breathe life into tradition that it does, as it can, answer the deepest inner searches of the contemporary seeker."[82] Along with his call for the cultivation and outworking of a crucicentric evangelical spirituality, Tidball recognises the danger of "leaving Christ on the cross", thus failing to appreciate the significance of the incarnation, the resurrection and the day of Pentecost.[83] Yet surely Forsyth is right that if there is no cross, there is no Christ.[84] Fostering relationship with Christ, which is at the core of evangelical spirituality, means following the direction offered by Spurgeon: "Live much under the shadow of the cross."

Notes

1. Mark A. Noll, *The Rise of Evangelicalism* (Leicester: Apollos, 2004), 272.

2. D. B. Hindmarsh, *The Evangelical Conversion Narrative* (Oxford: Oxford Univ. Press, 2005), 177–80.

3. John Wesley, "Brief Thoughts on Christian Perfection," in *The Works of the Rev. John Wesley*, ed. T. Jackson, vol. 11, 3rd ed. (Kansas City, Mo.: Beacon Hill, 1978), 443.

4. John Wesley, "Justification by Faith," in *The Works of John Wesley*, ed. A. C. Outler, vol. 1, *Sermons I* (Nashville: Abingdon, 1984), 187; cf. M. E. Dieter et al., *Five Views of Sanctification* (Grand Rapids: Zondervan, 1987), 25.

5. John Stott, *The Cross of Christ* (Leicester: IVP, 1986), 293–94.

6. Alister E. McGrath, *Roots That Refresh: A Celebration of Reformation Spirituality* (London: Hodder and Stoughton, 1991); the 1993 lecture was significantly reproduced in Alister E. McGrath, *Evangelicalism and the Future of Christianity* (London: Hodder and Stoughton, 1988), ch. 5.

7. Alister E. McGrath, "Evangelical Theological Method," in *Evangelical Futures*, ed. J. G. Stackhouse Jr. (Grand Rapids: Baker, 2000), 21. By the time McGrath wrote these words, several fine books and booklets on evangelical spirituality had been written: J. M. Gordon, *Evangelical Spirituality* (London: SPCK, 1991); David K. Gillett, *Trust and Obey: Explorations in Evangelical Spirituality* (London: DLT, 1993); J. Tiller, *Puritan, Pietist, Pentecostalist* (Bramcote: Grove, 1982); P. Adam, *Roots of Contemporary Evangelical Spirituality* (Bramcote: Grove, 1988); J. C. P. Cockerton, *Essentials of Evangelical Spirituality* (Bramcote: Grove, 1994); more recently, P. Seddon, *Gospel and Sacrament: Reclaiming a Holistic Evangelical Spirituality* (Cambridge: Grove, 2004).

8. Timothy George, "Introduction," in Timothy George and Alister McGrath, *For All the Saints: Evangelical Theology and Christian Spirituality* (Louisville: Westminster John Knox, 2003), 4.

9. Derek Tidball, *The Message of the Cross* (Leicester: IVP, 2001), 21–22.

10. See H. McGonigle, *John Wesley and the Moravians* (Ilkeston: Moorleys / Wesley Fellowship, 1993).

11. W. R. Ward and R. P. Heitzenrater, eds., *The Works of John Wesley*, vol. 18 (Nashville: Abingdon, 1988), 249–50.

12. J. C. S. Mason, *The Moravian Church and the Missionary Awakening in England, 1760–1800* (Woodbridge: Boydell, 2001), 72. This is from August G. Spangenberg, *An Exposition of Christian Doctrine* (London, 1784).

13. Mason, *The Moravian Church*, 70, 73.

14. Jonathan Edwards, "A Treatise Concerning Religious Affections," in *The Works of Jonathan Edwards*, vol. 2, ed. J. E. Smith (New Haven: Yale Univ. Press, 1959), 102. For more on this theme see, B. Walton, *Jonathan Edwards, Religious Affections and the Puritan Analysis of True Piety, Spiritual Sensation and Heart Religion* (Lewiston, N.Y.: Edwin Mellen, 2002).

15. Edwards, "Religious Affections," 120.

16. Ibid., 123.

17. R. W. Dale, *The Atonement* (London: Congregational Union of England and Wales, 1897), 348–49.

18. James Denney, "In Him Dwelleth," unpublished sermon preached June 1885, cited in J. M. Gordon, *James Denney (1856–1917): An Intellectual and Contextual Biography* (Carlisle: Paternoster, 2006), 105.

19. I. H. Murray, *D. Martyn Lloyd-Jones: The First Forty Years 1899–1939* (Edinburgh: Banner of Truth Trust, 1982), 190–91. For more on Lloyd-Jones and evangelicalism, see J. Brencher, *Martyn Lloyd-Jones (1899–1981) and Twentieth-century Evangelicalism* (Carlisle: Paternoster, 2002).

20. J. I. Packer, "The Atonement in the Life of the Christian," in *The Glory of the Atonement*, ed. C. E. Hill and F. A. James III (Downers Grove, Ill.: IVP, 2004), 415.

21. It is missed in an otherwise helpful account in G. Mursell, *English Spirituality: From 1700 to the Present Day* (London: SPCK, 2001), 90–97.

22. H. Lindstrom, *Wesley and Sanctification* (London: Epworth, 1946), ch. 2; cf. Stephen Holmes elsewhere in this volume.

23. John Deschner, *Wesley's Christology* (Dallas: Southern Methodist Univ. Press, 1960), 116.

24. John Wesley, "Salvation by Faith," sermon preached 11 June 1738, in *Wesley's Standard Sermons*, ed. E. H. Sugden, vol. 1 (London: Epworth, 1921), 42–45. Wesley later modified some of his thinking about the believer and sin, but the central ideas remain.

25. Stephen R. Holmes, *God of Grace and God of Glory* (Edinburgh: T & T Clark, 2000), 149.

26. Robert Jenson makes Edwards' point this way: "the atonement worked by Jesus' life and death is achieved by such a community of him and us that if the Father loves the Son he must love us also" (Jenson, *America's Theologian* [New York: Oxford Univ. Press, 1988], 126).

27. Packer, "Atonement in the Life," 416–17. For a seminal treatment of penal substitution by Packer, see J. I. Packer, "What Did the Cross Achieve?" in *Celebrating the Saving Work of God: The Collected Shorter Writings of J. I. Packer*, vol. 1 (Carlisle: Paternoster, 1998), 85–123. Originally delivered as the Tyndale Biblical Theology Lecture in 1973.

28. Charles H. Spurgeon, "This Shall Be an Everlasting Statute Unto You, to Make an Atonement for the Children of Israel for All Their Sins Once a Year," sermon on Lev. 16:34 delivered 10 August 1856 at New Park Street Chapel, Southwark, *New Park Street Pulpit* 2:336.

29. Ibid.

30. Dale, *The Atonement*, 393–96.

31. As Stott puts it, "R. W. Dale's great book *The Atonement* was written in order to prove that Christ's death on the cross was objective before it could be subjective, and that 'unless the great Sacrifice is conceived under objective forms, the subjective power will be lost'" (*Cross of Christ*, 221).

32. H. E. Guillebaud, *Why the Cross?* 2nd ed. (London: Inter-Varsity Fellowship, 1946), 145, 185.

33. Leon Morris, *Glory in the Cross* (London: Hodder and Stoughton, 1966), 80–81.

34. P. T. Forsyth, *The Work of Christ* (London: Hodder and Stoughton, 1910). On Forsyth's understanding of the atonement, see T. Hart, "Morality, Atonement and the Death of Jesus: The Crucial Focus of Forsyth's Theology," in *Justice, the One and Only Mercy: Essays on the Life and Thought of Peter Taylor Forsyth*, ed. T. Hart (Edinburgh: T & T Clark, 1995), 16–36. See also A. M. Stibbs, "Justification by Faith: The Reinstatement of the Doctrine Today" (1958), in *Where Wrath and Mercy Meet: Proclaiming the Atonement Today*, ed. D. Peterson (Carlisle: Paternoster, 2001), 171; Stibbs, *The Finished Work of Christ* (London: Tyndale, 1954), 11, 39.

35. Forsyth, *Work of Christ*, 147, 159.

36. Ibid., 170.

37. P. T. Forsyth, *God the Holy Father* (1897; London: Independent Press, 1957), 111.

38. Gillett, *Trust and Obey*, 87; Charles H. Spurgeon, "The Three Hours' Darkness," sermon on Matt. 25:45 delivered 18 April 1886, *MTP* 32, 225–26.

39. John Wesley, "A Plain Account of Christian Perfection," in *The Works of John Wesley*, vol. 11, ed. Thomas Jackson (London, 1872), 417, 419.

40. J. C. Ryle, *Holiness* (London: James Clarke, 1952), 88–89.

41. D. W. Bebbington, *Evangelicalism in Modern Britain: A History from the 1730s to the 1980s* (London: Routledge, 1995), ch. 5.

42. Evan Hopkins, *The Christian's Pathway of Power*, March 1876, p. 41; A. Smellie, *Evan Henry Hopkins: A Memoir* (London: Marshall, 1921), 81.

43. *The Keswick Week* (1913), 122.

44. For more on the Calvinist, Wesleyan and Keswick strands in the nineteenth century, see D. W. Bebbington, *Holiness in Nineteenth-century England* (Carlisle: Paternoster, 2000).

45. One of the classic nineteenth-century books from within the Reformed tradition that questioned penal substitution was John McLeod

Campbell's *The Nature of the Atonement* (1856; Grand Rapids: Eerdmans, 1996).

46. F. B. Meyer, *At the Gates of the Dawn* (London: James Clarke, 1910), 74; Meyer, *The Soul's Wrestle with Doubt*, Little Books on the Devout Life (London, 1905), 50.

47. See J. Moody, *Jonathan Edwards and the Enlightenment: Knowing the Presence of God* (Lanham, Md.: University Press of America, 2005), 36–39.

48. Jonathan Edwards, "Personal Narrative," in *The Works of Jonathan Edwards*, vol. 16, ed. G. S. Claghorn (New Haven: Yale Univ. Press, 1998), 793.

49. D. G. Hart, "Jonathan Edwards and the Origins of Experimental Calvinism," in *The Legacy of Jonathan Edwards*, ed. D. G. Hart, S. M. Lucas and S. J. Nichols (Grand Rapids: Baker Academic, 2003), 164.

50. Charles H. Spurgeon, "Our Lord in the Valley of Humiliation," sermon on Phil. 2:8 delivered 5 June 1890, *MTP* 38: 535–37.

51. For a study of trends, see M. Hopkins, *Nonconformity's Romantic Generation* (Carlisle: Paternoster, 2004).

52. P. T. Forsyth, *God the Holy Father* (1897; London: Independent Press, 1957), 5.

53. Gordon, *Evangelical Spirituality*, 231–32.

54. James Denney, *The Death of Christ*, 2nd ed., including *The Atonement and the Modern Mind* (London: Hodder and Stoughton, 1911), 126.

55. Oswald Chambers, *My Utmost for His Highest* (London: Marshall, Morgan and Scott, 1927), 310.

56. A. W. Tozer, "The Old Cross and the New," in *Man: The Dwelling Place of God* (Camp Hill, Penn.: Christian Publications, 1966), 43.

57. Eugene H. Peterson, "Evangelical Spirituality," in *The Futures of Evangelicalism*, ed. Craig Bartholomew, Robin Parry and Andrew West (Leicester: IVP, 2003), 238.

58. Leon Morris, *The Apostolic Preaching of the Cross* (Grand Rapids: Eerdmans, 1988), 176.

59. Tidball, *Message of the Cross*, 21–22.

60. F. C. Gill, *Charles Wesley: The First Methodist* (London: Lutterworth, 1964), 72.

61. Noll, *Rise of Evangelicalism*, 268–69.

62. Charles H. Spurgeon, "Slaying the Sacrifice," sermon on Lev. 1:5 delivered 23 March 1884, *MTP* 30, no. 1772: 178–79.

63. Mark A. Noll, "Evangelicalism At Its Best," in *Where Shall My Wond'ring Soul Begin?* ed. Mark A. Noll and Ronald F. Thiemann (Grand Rapids: Eerdmans, 2000), 15.

64. Gill, *Charles Wesley*, 123.

65. J. C. Bowmer, *The Sacrament of the Lord's Supper in Early Methodism* (London: A. & C. Black, 1951), 181.

66. B. L. Manning, *The Hymns of Wesley and Watts* (London: Epworth, 1942), 126.

67. John Wesley, "The Duty of Constant Communion," in *The Works of John Wesley*, ed. A. C. Outler, vol. 3, *Sermons III* (Nashville: Abingdon, 1986), 430.

68. G. Stead, "Moravian Spirituality and Its Propagation in West Yorkshire during the Eighteenth-century Evangelical Revival," *EQ* 71, no. 3 (1999): 237; A. Freeman, "*Gemeine*: Count Nicholas von Zinzendorf's Understanding of the Church," *Brethren Life and Thought* 47, nos. 1–2 (2002): 9.

69. Charles H. Spurgeon, "The Witness of the Lord's Supper," sermon on 1 Cor. 11:26, *MTP* 59, no. 3338: 38.

70. P. T. Forsyth, *The Church and the Sacraments* (London: Independent Press, 1947), 176.

71. Gillett, *Trust and Obey*, 78, citing Julian's *Dictionary of Hymnology*.

72. For more, see F. W. Boreham, *A Late Lark Singing* (London: Epworth, 1945).

73. Leon Morris, *The Cross of Christ* (Grand Rapids: Eerdmans, 1988).

74. Joel B. Green and Mark D. Baker, *Recovering the Scandal of the Cross* (Downers Grove, Ill.: IVP, 2000), 31. See also 213–14.

75. For an introduction to these themes, see J. Wolffe, ed., *Evangelicals and Public Zeal* (London: SPCK, 1995).

76. J. Telford, ed., *The Letters of the Rev. John Wesley*, vol. 8 (1931; London: Epworth, 1960), 265.

77. Dale, *The Atonement*, 411–14.

78. For more on these developments, see D. W. Smith, *Transforming the World* (Carlisle: Paternoster, 1998); cf. Ian M. Randall, *What a Friend We Have in Jesus* (London: DLT, 2005), ch. 9.

79. J. I. Packer, "An Introduction to Systematic Spirituality," *Crux* 26, no. 1 (1990): 6.

80. Charles H. Spurgeon, "Wash Me, and I Shall Be Whiter Than Snow," sermon on Ps. 51:7 delivered 11 January 1866, *MTP* 57, no. 3278: 568.

81. P. T. Forsyth, *The Cruciality of the Cross* (London: Independent Press, 1909), 42–43.

82. Derek J. Tidball, *Who Are the Evangelicals?* (London: Marshall Pickering, 1994), 224–28.

83. Tidball, *Message of the Cross*, 27.

84. P. T. Forsyth, *The Soul of Prayer* (London: C. H. Kelly, 1916), 12.

contemporary
perspectives

chapter 17

the message of the cross is foolishness

atonement in womanist theology towards a black british perspective

lynnette j. mullings

Introduction

Three factors are fundamental to the life and worship of Black Majority Churches (BMCs) in Britain: the Bible, preaching and the cross. The Bible represents God's moral code for holy living and charts how God has continuously endeavoured to implement his plan for humankind since the beginning of time. Preaching is the Word of God in action, the Word come to life from page to pulpit, the means by which God's people can hear God's message delivered through his "anointed servant", the pastor, in a corporate setting. The cross represents salvation, the very reason for human existence. BMCs share the broader Protestant and evangelical emphasis that salvation comes only through acceptance of Christ's redeeming work on Calvary. However, they distinctively take this to be pivotal, not only for doctrine and evangelism but also for personal morality and discipleship.

Recent times have seen controversy rise within evangelicalism about the significance of Jesus' death on the cross, largely due to Steve Chalke and Alan Mann's book *The Lost Message of Jesus*.[1] Chalke and Mann argue that the radical kingdom message of Jesus has lost out through the centuries to a culturally captive paradigm that meets the needs of fewer and fewer people both within and beyond the church. They point out that a tension exists in which the church believes it is preaching "good news" while the wider public typically receives its message as "bad news".[2] In addition, Chalke and Mann assert there are countless churches filled with tired, disillusioned people struggling to live the Christian life – people whose weariness confirms that the liberating message of Jesus has been lost.[3] Furthermore, Chalke and Mann argue that within certain sections of the evangelical branch of the church, this has become not only central to the gospel but effectively the whole content of the gospel – a situation they regard as both unsatisfactory and damaging.[4] By contrast, Chalke and Mann propose that Jesus' death and resurrection *together* represent the most potent symbol of Christ's life-transforming message, that they are not different events but two interconnected scenes from the same drama of salvation.[5]

Chalke and Mann offer a much-needed challenge to rethink the message of Jesus in ways that speak relevantly to twenty-first-century social concerns, while honouring the inception of that message in first-century Palestine. Indeed, this refocusing of the gospel, and of the meaning of the cross in particular, has prompted me to reflect on my own church context.

I am a minister within the Wesleyan Holiness Church (WHC), a British evangelical Black Majority Church. Even though current statistics show an increase in membership after a period of decline,[6] there continues to be a leadership crisis within this denomination,[7] which will harm its health and effectiveness unless a new model of ministry and witness can be developed. In this context, I have observed a distinctive emphasis on preaching Christ crucified, but with little focus on the liberative action of God in raising Christ from the dead. In particular, there has been a dearth of preaching on the significance of that resurrection for contemporary social and political life. While Jesus is proclaimed in most BMCs as the one who took on human sin at its ultimate depth, and while BMC preachers typically stress this point through statements like, "It should have been us/you/me there," Chalke and Mann highlight the hope implicit in the whole event of crucifixion and resurrection for the poor, dispossessed and marginalised. In this, they echo the African-American theologian Jacquelyn Grant, who in 1993 suggested that the condition of Black people reflects the cross of Jesus, while his resurrection promises their liberation from oppression.[8]

Black British society faces significant problems, particularly in urban areas, where gang violence is on the increase, where Black-on-Black crime is prevalent, and where the selling, use and abuse of drugs is close to epidemic. Educational underachievement, unemployment and poverty also serve as hindrances to the

Black community's progress.[9] If this is the condition of Black British society, one might well ask how the Black Majority Churches' focus on the cross, and the function of that cross as a symbol of suffering, might prove truly liberative and empowering. Can the cross redeem such a community when so many feel unworthy to receive salvation because they are enmeshed in sin and despair and feel themselves to be so far from the moral standards they assume are necessary for participation in the life of the church? If Grant's statement is true that liberation comes more fully through resurrection, should not more emphasis be placed on this aspect of Jesus' mission in the world? Is the current balance right?

Applying Chalke and Mann's insights to the BMC context, I would suggest that the time has come for a reassessment of the cross which emphasises a more plural or "syncretic" approach to atonement theories.[10] This approach redresses the balance between death and resurrection, thus enabling a more transformative and progressive understanding of Black identity and a more enriching account of that identity with respect to wider society. More specifically, this reassessment will be developed in dialogue with important work on the atonement done recently by Womanist theologians. The Womanist perspective deserves serious attention, for as an intrinsically Black female approach, it provides distinct insights into this aspect of theological discourse. It is noteworthy that current Womanist thought on the atonement operates from a predominantly African-American perspective. As such, it represents an important challenge to engage critically with established interpretations as a means of formulating an understanding appropriate for the Black British context, where such approaches remain rare. Particular attention will be paid to developing a model of atonement theology relevant for BMCs, including the Wesleyan Holiness Church.

Defining Black Majority Churches

In his recent book, *Look What the Lord Has Done! An Exploration of Black Christian Faith in Britain*,[11] Mark Sturge defines a Black Majority Church as "a worshipping Christian community ... made up of more than 50 per cent of people from an African or African Caribbean heritage".[12] He proposes that this definition is more positive for Black Christians than terms like "Black Church" and "Black-led Church" because it shifts the focus from leaders to members. He argues that it thereby also provides a stronger basis for unity, presents opportunities for better pastoral support and local cooperation and has a positive psychological effect.[13] He goes on to name five identifiable segments that could be included in the overall designation Black Majority Church, each with its distinct origin and allegiances: (a) churches emerging from the African-Caribbean diaspora; (b) churches emerging from the African diaspora; (c) BMCs within historic denominations; (d) BMCs within the white Pentecostal denominations; and (e) African and Caribbean Spiritual churches.[14]

Sturge's attempt to redefine the demography of Black Christians in Britain serves as a corrective to previous profiles of the Black Christian community presented by white researchers, who sought to impose terms like "Black-led" and "Black Church" on this community.[15] In naming five identifiable segments within the Black Majority Church, Sturge nuances the taxonomy offered by Robert Beckford's *Dread and Pentecostal*.[16] Beckford similarly attempted to acknowledge the diversity of Black British church life by including denominations with traditional English backgrounds which had been populated by significant numbers of Black Christians. However, he still used the term "Black Church".[17] Here, I will refer to Black Majority Churches in the context of Sturge's understanding. It should be noted that African-Americans do not have the same issues with defining Black Majority Churches and use the term "Black Church" as a generic description of all African-American churches. Therefore, any reference made to Black Churches in this essay should be understood in the African-American context only.

Unexamined Faith verses Examined Faith

The need to revisit the theology of the cross at this time is of particular importance for BMCs. Delores Williams urges Black communities to "reflect upon the adage that an unexamined faith, like an unexamined life, is not worth living. Unexamined faith leads a people to be unconscious instruments of their own oppression and the oppression of others."[18] She adds that "an examined faith is a critical way of seeing that shows those things in a belief system that are life-threatening and life-taking. An examined faith inspires people to discard beliefs, images and symbols that have the potential to support scapegoating and destruction."[19] Williams reminds us to pause and draw breath while assessing why certain beliefs and practices are upheld and how they impact everyday lives and circumstances. However, for many in the BMCs and elsewhere, such critical examination is seen as destructive when applied to one's personal faith – a stripping away of long-cherished beliefs which leaves nothing behind. Indeed, many claim to prefer an unexamined faith to no faith at all. It is unfortunate that such views are held when, as Williams indicates, scholarly reflection has the potential to liberate new life.[20] An examined faith entails critical assessment of the very structures in which that faith is manifested, structures which might cause stagnation rather than collective progression.

Critical analysis is also necessary to ensure the relevance of doctrinal discourse for both individual and corporate contexts, the doctrine of the atonement being no exception. As Alan Richardson puts it, every age has a responsibility to refresh its interpretation of that central fact of history which is the life and ministry of Christ, for the essence of Christian religion is belief in a person rather than a system of ideas.[21] Hence, doctrines must be re-expressed and re-presented for every generation.[22] Richardson points out that although the facts of history do not alter, our account of their significance changes, develops and expands and, in the case of Jesus Christ, needs continual readjustment in the light of fuller knowledge and deeper experience.[23] So where the atonement is concerned, Richardson argues that we are free to construct our own theories as long as they are grounded in authentic forgiveness and liberation through Jesus Christ.[24] For Richardson, theory should be but an aid to practice: there is an "art" as well as a theory of atonement, and those who practise the art are best qualified to understand the theory, for Christian doctrines and theories about them are not abstractions removed from real life.[25] On this basis, the responsibility of the BMCs, as of other churches, is to revisit the theology of the cross in order to make new interpretations which are appropriate for the communities they serve.

In keeping with this approach, Chalke and Mann start by contextualising Jesus in his first-century situation and move on to recontextualise him for the present day.[26] This interaction between past and present horizons is also a feature of Womanist thought, but the temporal orientation is typically different. Here, Black women's lived experience is taken as the starting point for interaction with the biblical text and with historic doctrinal formulations. Theological understanding of a theme like the atonement is therefore deconstructed and reconstructed so as to bear relevance to Black women's contemporary circumstances. Thus socio-political issues of race, gender and class are prioritised in Womanist hermeneutics and are treated as critically significant for Black Churches and communities.

A Word on Womanist Theology

Over the past twenty years, Womanist theology has emerged as a Black feminist response to the inadequacy of Black theology in addressing the concerns of Black women, predominantly American. Although Black theology addressed issues of race and class that affected both men and women, it rarely spoke to the problems Black women faced on a daily basis with the "double jeopardy"[27] of being Black and female. Furthermore, it failed to bring into focus the "triple jeopardy"[28] faced by those who were Black, female and active in the church. Black theology has largely been written and promoted by Black male theologians. As such, it has been limited in its interaction with the experiences of ordinary Black women. It is not so much that Black women have not been subjects of concern in Black theology, or that Black men have not sometimes spoken eloquently on behalf of Black women.[29] Rather, as Jacquelyn Grant states, theological scholarship has not traditionally been seen as part of the woman's sphere.[30] If theology done only or predominantly by men serves to uphold the patriarchal structures of society, the liberative potential of Black theology is called into question.[31] In her assessment of the relationship of Womanist theology to Black theology, Kelly Delaine Brown Douglas points out the two-fold role of Black theology in the emergence of Womanist theology. First, by linking God to the Black experience, Black theology gave Black women access to systematic theological reflection. Second, by ignoring Black women's experience, Black theology forced Black women to develop their own theological perspective.[32] In other words, it became the right of Black women to name their own experience. This experience is largely one of survival and liberation in the face of racial, class and gender oppression.

The term "Womanist" was coined by the poet and novelist Alice Walker in her book *In Search of Our Mothers' Gardens*.[33] It is understood by Walker to come "from the Black folk expression of mothers to female children, 'You acting womanish,' i.e., like a woman. Usually referring to outrageous, audacious, courageous or *wilful* behavior."[34] It is also defined in relation to a woman who is all-embracing of life, particularly that pertaining to women's culture and values, even while her commitment is to the "survival and wholeness of entire people, male *and* female".[35] The term "Womanist" began to be used by Black female scholars in the 1980s as a means of entering into theological discourse while bringing attention to the marginalised voices of Black women and affirming their experience. The growing number of Womanist theologians who have contributed to the debate is significant. Jacquelyn Grant[36] and Kelly Delaine Brown Douglas,[37] whom we have mentioned already, as well as Delores S. Williams[38] and Katie Geneva Cannon,[39] are just a few of the names who have made important strides in revealing Black women's struggle to address the sexist attitudes they have endured from their male counterparts and in expounding the rich moral character of Black women's communal networks.

Atonement in Womanist Theology

Jesus and His Ministerial Vision

From the Black Christian perspective, Jesus is the one who is taken to identify most intensely with Black people's experience in general, and with Black women in particular.[40] Womanist scholars affirm this basic christocentricity but question whether certain theories of atonement prominent in Black preaching and teaching serve to affirm Christ's solidarity with Black people or have, in fact, detracted from such solidarity and thereby diluted the radical and liberative potential of the cross for Black Christian communities. The most radical reflections come from Delores Williams, who argues that there is nothing divine in the blood of the cross.[41] Williams contends that "the image of Jesus on the cross is the image of human sin in its most desecrated form."[42] In response to such desecration, Williams argues that the redemption that Jesus came to show was not through death but life – that is, through what she calls a "ministerial vision". This vision, says Williams, is focussed on righting relations between body (individual and community), mind (of humans and of tradition) and spirit.[43] For Williams, the fact that Jesus was crucified is the result of human evil trying to kill the ministerial vision. By contrast, the hope of an abundant life is met through the resurrection, which renders the ministerial vision victorious.[44] Williams contends that the classical theological concept of substitution, which she calls "surrogacy", was not part of Jesus' agenda. In her terms, he did not seek to become the substitute for humanity, for that suggests that God intends such surrogacy as a general moral good to be borne by others, including Black women. Since Williams views the crucifixion as an act of evil which produced malicious suffering, she rejects such an idea as ethically and theologically unsustainable.[45] Given the oppressive experiences of African-American women, Williams concludes that while Christian Black women cannot forget the cross, they cannot glorify it either, for to do so would be to glorify suffering and thereby falsely render *their* suffering, *their* oppression and *their* exploitation sacred.[46]

Clearly, Williams is critiquing both penal substitutionary and moral theories of atonement.[47] Within the penal substitutionary theory, the justice and grace of God are enacted through Christ's suffering: Christ bears the punishment for human sin as our substitute, thereby making it possible for God to forgive our sins while remaining consistent in both his wrath and his mercy (see Rom. 5:9–11; 2 Cor. 5:21; Gal. 3:13). At the same time, within the moral framework, Christ's death makes God's love supremely manifest, and its sacrificial power inspires us both to follow Christ and to act in sacrificial love towards others (John 3:16; Rom. 10:8–10; Eph. 2:4, 8).[48] However, by shifting focus from the suffering of Jesus on the cross to his broader ministerial vision, Williams suggests an alternative model of redemption – one defined by the fact that Jesus overcame death, rather than by the fact that he died.[49]

Redemption in Suffering?

If Williams is right to assert that redemption comes through life, not death, the long tradition in which Christian images of oppression are linked positively to Jesus' crucifixion must be questioned. In particular, the key issue raised by Williams' critique, as indeed by Chalke and Mann's in their context, is whether suffering can be redemptive. While this concern is larger and more complex than can be addressed within this essay, it is worth outlining some key reflections of other Womanist scholars in this area.

For many BMCs, the atonement is applied principally through exhortation to "bear the cross" – to endure the suffering experienced in daily life as a means of sharing in the sufferings of Christ (cf. Rom. 8:17). This is viewed as the Christian's duty, an obligation of discipleship which will lead to greater reward in eternity (Matt. 10:38; Luke 9:23; 14:27). The problem which arises here, however, is the specific nature of this suffering: does it entail any or all types of suffering, or only that inflicted by people upon one another? Does it include the suffering which results from "natural evil", as in floods, earthquakes, and the like, or only that suffering which is intentionally perpetrated by humans? Furthermore, is suffering something that we can be saved *in*, or only something that we need to be saved *from*?[50] This is the crux of the problem for Williams, who, in light of the outrageous oppression that Black men and women have endured, questions whether the brutality of Jesus' suffering on the cross has anything to teach us about redemption.[51]

Jacquelyn Grant powerfully reflects on Jesus in light of the struggle for liberation among African-Americans. She points out that in African-American women's understandings of Jesus, there are five key experiences, one of which she calls the experience of Jesus as "Co-sufferer".[52] By this, she means that just as Jesus suffered and was persecuted undeservedly, so African-Americans can identify with him as they suffer abuse and unjust punishment. JoAnne Marie Terrell takes up and expands this point in a challenging way. As harrowing and violent as it was, Terrell refuses to accept that Jesus' suffering was more brutal than the suffering that many other human beings have borne and still bear today.[53] Indeed, she sees this point as vital in the wider ethical and theological meaning of the cross: "If one buys the notion that Jesus is Emmanuel, God with us, one misses the point of the story entirely: that God identifies with us in all manner of suffering and does not seek to supersede us in suffering either in quantity or quality, but to persuade us to stop inflicting suffering, once and for all, and to assure us that whatever we suffer, however determined evil is against us, we can and will be redeemed."[54] Terrell's perspective poses a stark challenge to that majority Christian tradition which has represented Christ crucified as the ultimate image of human cruelty. Rather, it proposes that crucifixion is just one tool of oppression among many and stresses that thousands of people have suffered just as unjustly and horrifically, if not more. Terrell takes this view in light of her earlier writing, *Power in the Blood? The Cross in the African American Experience.* Here she sees Jesus' sacrificial act as the tragic, foreseeable result of his confrontation with evil.[55] Against this background, she suggests that "anyone's death has saving significance inasmuch as we learn continuously from the life that preceded it."[56] In response to Williams' claim that there is nothing divine in the blood of the cross, Terrell agrees that "there is nothing of God's *sanction* in violence."[57] However, she maintains that God shed his own blood in Christ; indeed, the fact that there must be something of God in the blood of the cross confirms for her the commonly held conviction of African-Americans attested by Jacquelyn Grant – that Jesus is indeed the "divine co-sufferer".[58]

As Terrell argues, to attribute nothing of God to Christ's shed blood devalues the ministerial vision to which Jesus himself was committed and in which he invited others to share. Moreover, in moving beyond the image of Jesus suffering on the cross, Terrell rightly emphasises that "the image of an empty cross signifies faith in the possibility of our own resurrection."[59] This point is also affirmed by Karen Baker-Fletcher, who sees in the empty cross a paradigm through which to negotiate our own commitment to life in all its abundance, not only for ourselves and our families but also for the wider communities to which we belong.[60]

Why Did Jesus Die?
Atonement in Perspective

For all their differences, there seems to be a clear overarching theme that links the work of the Womanist scholars we have been considering. The cross does not bear the whole story of atonement: indeed, Jesus' suffering and death are not to be glorified but treated as part of the tragic outcome of a life lived passionately for others, and particularly for those on the margins of society. In emphasising life rather than death, resurrection rather than crucifixion, there is an implicit rejection of those systemic factors which detract from life, such as injustice, oppression, persecution and abuse. This is the commitment that defined Jesus' life and ministry, and it is to this primary commitment that Womanist scholars like Dolores Williams, JoAnne Marie Terrell, Jacquelyn Grant and Karen Baker-Fletcher subscribe.

In a study of the gospel of Mark,[61] New Testament scholar Brian K. Blount suggests a liberational outlook which is in line with Womanist thought. Blount asserts that in Mark's narrative story, Jesus' message was essentially to preach the kingdom of God in transformative ways.[62] Blount takes the key practical outworking of this preaching to be Jesus' healings and exorcisms and sees these as most starkly challenging economic, political, cultic, legal and ethnic divisions.[63] Blount thus agrees with the Womanist theologians that the focus of Jesus' mission is not one of suffering. The suffering comes as a result of the kingdom preaching: it is much more a consequence than a purpose of Jesus' message. Hence, the disciples are called not to suffering but to interventionist preaching.[64] Blount asserts that in Mark, the cross is part of the writer's message but not the message's sole intent,[65] and like Williams, he sees the cross as a manifestly human activity.[66] In common with the Womanists, then, Blount challenges the status of the cross in the Christian tradition. The greater paradigm in his view is Mark's injunction to finish the gospel story by picking it up where Jesus left off. Indeed, Blount points out that this is exactly what Jesus called his disciples to do before he left them – to return in mission to Galilee, rather than to remain at the site, or in the mindset, of the cross.[67]

According to Rosetta Ross,[68] Jesus' passion can be viewed as a model for moral action based on two principles. First, moral teaching and action should consistently recognise the dignity of all people. Second, moral teaching and action should have the aim of bringing a positive quality of life to people, especially to the socially dispossessed.[69] This assessment captures the essence of the ministerial vision to which Jesus was committed, and this in turn goes to the heart of why he died.

Paving the Way: Towards a Black British Perspective

Given Richardson's point that we are free to construct our own theory of salvation as long as it is grounded in forgiveness and liberation in Christ, the Womanist approaches we have discussed offer rich resources for the Black

British context. My primary concern for my own church, and for BMCs in general, is that they are able to formulate a liberative hermeneutic that presents salvation in tangible terms. By this I mean taking a holistic view of Jesus' mission as a mission that promoted life, not death. If, from Williams' perspective, Jesus' ministerial vision was one of righting relations between body, mind and spirit, then the BMCs should seek to preach, teach and exercise this in visible and practical ways. Specifically, they are to *continue* preaching the story, changing people and circumstances in their communities so that they might more fully reflect Jesus' ministerial vision.[70]

The cross is a tool of oppression. As such, it challenges BMCs like my own to look at the many other tools used to oppress people today and to resist them in the name of Christ. To be fair, some BMCs are already responding to this challenge. The Bringing Hope Conference, held on May 26, 2004, in Birmingham, saw some three hundred delegates from across the BMC spectrum meet to formulate policies on tackling drugs, guns and gangs. Following the conference, a new project coordinator was appointed to implement these policies through key partnerships, all based on a training, resourcing and equipping programme targeted at areas most in need. Moreover, the Street Pastors initiative developed by Les Isaac of the Ascension Trust has grown significantly over the past few years. This encourages churches to become actively involved with young people on the streets at a time when most Christians are soundly asleep. It has proved highly effective in engaging those caught up in gang life.[71] Both of these initiatives are to be commended, but there is much more to be done, and it requires a concertedly collective approach. As Williams states, "Black people must either work together or go down together."[72]

I am not calling for a wholesale rejection of the classic Black Majority Church understanding of the cross. I would suggest, however, that serious engagement with the Womanist perspectives outlined here might encourage a more socially transformative understanding of atonement – one in which our traditional emphasis on being saved is turned outwards, so that we involve ourselves more explicitly in the processes of *saving* in tangible, boundary-breaking ways which go to the heart of what it means to be human.[73] Through a collective approach, BMCs can begin to tackle issues of social and economic poverty by creating programmes that will provide the relevant skills and training to help the unemployed back into work. Perhaps more importantly, we need to foster an entrepreneurial culture in which businesses are formed to catalyse a more economically vibrant Black community. In an education system which is failing so many Black children, efforts need to be redoubled in lobbying government to implement creative programmes of study that have already been tried and tested at the local level by local church groups and community organisations.[74]

These are just a few examples of ways in which BMCs can effect social, political and economic metamorphosis, as well as impact the spiritual sensibilities of the communities they serve. As Williams rightly points out, the church must reconceive itself not just as a religious centre but also as a marketplace, as both economic enabler and educational service provider.[75]

The same sort of transformation was illustrated at the Live 8 concert held on July 2, 2005, in Hyde Park, London. During the singer Madonna's performance, Birhan Woldu was invited onto the stage as a vivid demonstration of the hope that can arise from poverty and despair. Twenty years previously, she had been given barely ten minutes to live. Her father, heartbroken, had wrapped her tiny, emaciated body in a burial shroud and waited for her to die. Yet she had been saved by aid workers and now stood before thousands of people as a beautiful twenty-four-year-old Ethiopian woman. Her comment was telling: "The famine was devastating. The pain is still with me and I pray it will never happen again. I was one of the lucky ones – Live Aid saved my life."[76]

Such is the hope which BMCs and the church worldwide are called to engender. While insisting that the message of the cross is not foolishness, we must look beyond the grave to the resurrection, recognising that the very same power that raised Jesus from the dead can bring salvation to the most deprived and desperate people and to the most depressed communities.

Notes

1. Steve Chalke and Alan Mann, *The Lost Message of Jesus* (Grand Rapids: Zondervan, 2003).

2. Ibid., 42.

3. Ibid.

4. Ibid., 172.

5. Ibid., 174.

6. In 2006, the total membership recorded was 424, and for 2007, it is 501, whereas in 2004, the membership total was 394, and in 2005, it was 384. See the annual statistical reports in Conference Journals 2004, 2005, 2006 and 2007 of the Wesleyan Holiness Church, British Isles. The accuracy of these figures, however, cannot be relied upon due to inconsistencies in

local and district church reporting. See membership figures in Conference Journal 2003 against Conference Journal 2004.

7. See in Conference Journals 2006 and 2007 the reports of the district superintendent (DS), who lists ten out of the sixteen churches in the denomination in the UK under her care – an increase from seven as stated in the DS's report in Conference Journal 2003.

8. Jacquelyn Grant, "The Sin of Servanthood and the Deliverance of Discipleship," in *A Troubling in My Soul: Womanist Perspectives on Evil and Suffering*, ed. Emilie M. Townes (Maryknoll, N.Y.: Orbis, 1993), 199–218.

9. One indication of the seriousness of these trends is the ever-expanding work of the Council of Black-Led Churches and Birmingham Partnership for Change. This network continually brings to public attention the significant amount of work still needed to improve the educational and social welfare of Black young people.

10. JoAnne Marie Terrell emphasises that the church has developed no single doctrine or teaching on the atonement, only a number of theories that have different weight from communion to communion. She adds that Black Churches have long harmonised theories of atonement, in much the same way that Christian tradition harmonised synoptic and fourth gospel accounts of the life and ministry of Jesus. See her *Power in the Blood? The Cross in the African American Experience* (Maryknoll, N.Y.: Orbis, 1998), 107–8.

11. Mark Sturge, *Look What the Lord Has Done! An Exploration of Black Christian Faith in Britain* (Bletchley: Scripture Union, 2005).

12. Ibid., 31.

13. Ibid.

14. Ibid., 53.

15. For more on this point, see Arlington Trotman, "Black, Black-led or What?" in Sturge, *Look What the Lord Has Done!* 229. First published in Joel Edwards, ed., *Let's Praise Him Again: An African Caribbean Perspective on Worship* (Eastbourne: Kingsway, 1992).

16. Robert Beckford, *Dread and Pentecostal: A Political Theology for the Black Church in Britain* (London: SPCK, 2000).

17. Ibid., 3.

18. Delores S. Williams, "Straight Talk, Plain Talk: Womanist Words about Salvation in a Social Context," in *Embracing the Spirit: Womanist Perspectives on Hope, Salvation and Transformation*, ed. Emilie M. Townes (Maryknoll, N.Y.: Orbis, 1997), 99.

19. Ibid.

20. Mark Sturge makes a similar point. He argues that the future of the church depends on good leadership backed by excellent training, which in turn generates integrity in the handling of Scripture and the things of God. Sturge notes that BMCs have neglected taking part in theological debate and dialogue, usually out of the belief that to do so would be divisive. Yet he asserts that the art of debate is critical wherever Christians are called upon to contend for their faith in the media and in the public arena. See Sturge, *Look What the Lord Has Done!* 166.

21. Alan Richardson, *Creeds in the Making: A Short Introduction to the History of Christian Doctrine* (London: SCM, 1951).

22. Ibid., 11.

23. Ibid.

24. Ibid., 99–100.

25. Ibid., 112–13.

26. Chalke and Mann, *Lost Message of Jesus*, 16–17.

27. Francis Beale, "Double Jeopardy: To Be Black and Female," in *Black Theology: A Documentary History*, ed. James H. Cone and Gayraud Wilmore, vol. 1, *1966–1979*, 2nd ed. (Maryknoll, N.Y.: Orbis, 1993), 284–92.

28. Theressa Hoover, "Black Women and the Churches: Triple Jeopardy," in Cone and Wilmore, *Black Theology*, 293–303.

29. Two assumptions that Jacquelyn Grant discards as false in her essay "Black Theology and the Black Woman," in Cone and Wilmore, *Black Theology*, 325.

30. Ibid., 326.

31. Ibid.

32. Kelly Delaine Brown Douglas, "Womanist Theology: What Is Its Relationship to Black Theology?" in Cone and Wilmore, *Black Theology*, 292.

33. Alice Walker, *In Search of Our Mothers' Gardens: Womanist Prose* (London: Women's Press, 1984), xi.

34. Ibid.

35. Ibid.

36. Jacquelyn Grant, *White Women's Christ and Black Women's Jesus: Feminist Christology and Womanist Response* (Atlanta: Scholars Press, 1989).

37. Kelly Delaine Brown Douglas, *The Black Christ* (Maryknoll, N.Y.: Orbis, 1994).

38. Delores S. Williams, *Sisters in the Wilderness: The Challenge of Womanist God-Talk* (Maryknoll, N.Y.: Orbis, 1993).

39. Katie Geneva Cannon, *Black Womanist Ethics* (Atlanta: Scholars Press, 1988).

40. Jacquelyn Grant, "Womanist Theology: Black Women's Experience as a Source for Doing Theology, with Special Reference to Christology," in Cone and Wilmore, *Black Theology*, 281.

41. Williams, *Sisters in the Wilderness*, 167.

42. Ibid., 166.

43. Ibid., 164–65.

44. Ibid., 165.

45. Ibid., 167.

46. Ibid.

47. Elements of the penal and moral theories of atonement can be found in my own denomination's constitution. See article II of the Articles of Religion in *The Discipline of the Wesleyan Church 2000* (Indianapolis, Ind.: Wesleyan, 2001).

48. For a concise yet helpful treatment of the theories of the atonement, see Richardson, *Creeds in the Making*. For further reading, see Gustaf Aulén, *Christus Victor: An Historical Study of the Three Main Types of the Idea of Atonement* (London: SPCK, 1975).

49. For an outline of key ways in which Jesus is said to have shown humankind a vision of righting relations between body, mind and spirit, see Williams, *Sisters in the Wilderness*, 167.

50. For more on this distinction between salvation *in* suffering and salvation *from* suffering, see D. W. Amundsen, "Suffering," in *NDT*, 668.

51. Williams, *Sisters in the Wilderness*, 162.

52. The other four are Jesus as Equaliser, Jesus as Freedom, Jesus as Sustainer and Jesus as Liberator (Jacquelyn Grant, "Womanist Jesus and the Mutual Struggle for Liberation," in *The Recovery of Black Presence: An Interdisciplinary Exploration*, ed. Randall C. Bailey and Jacquelyn Grant (Nashville: Abingdon, 1995), 139–41.

53. JoAnne Marie Terrell, "What Manner of Love?" in *The Passion of the Lord: African American Reflections*, ed. James A. Noel and Matthew V. Johnson (Minneapolis: Fortress, 2005), 73–74.

54. Ibid., 74.

55. Terrell, *Power in the Blood?* 142

56. Ibid.

57. Ibid., 122.

58. Ibid., 124.

59. Ibid., 125.

60. Karen Baker-Fletcher writes, "With Christ we transform the cross into material for healing rather than destruction. The empty cross is a sign of resurrection, life, and hope" ("Womanist Passion," in Noel and Johnson, *Passion of the Lord*, 139).

61. Brian K. Blount, *Go Preach! Mark's Kingdom Message and the Black Church Today* (Maryknoll, N.Y.: Orbis, 1998).

62. Ibid., 8.

63. Ibid.

64. Ibid., 134.

65. Ibid., 191.

66. An activity which is distinct from Jesus' own baptism, transfiguration and resurrection (ibid.).

67. Ibid.

68. Rosetta E. Ross, "Passionate Living," in Noel and Johnson, *Passion of the Lord*, 145–59.

69. Ibid., 147–48.

70. Ibid., 152.

71. A view put forth strongly by Les Isaac himself at the Organising Congregations for Social Justice Conference held in London on 29 November 2003.

72. Williams, "Straight Talk, Plain Talk," 114.

73. A perspective which Blount advocates and which sees salvation as essentially acted out rather than being associated with a particular place or realm (*Go Preach!* 194).

74. Organisations such as 100 Black Men and Black Boys Can are making a significant impact in the lives of young Black boys through programmes of personal and educational development.

75. Williams, "Straight Talk, Plain Talk," 111–12.

76. Alexandra Williams, "Living Symbol of Hope," *Daily Mirror*, 4 July 2005, 3.

chapter 18

atonement in contemporary culture

christ, symbolic exchange and death

anna m. robbins

Allow me to begin this essay with a confession: I believe that penal substitution, rightly understood, is one of several appropriate lenses through which we attempt to understand the nature and work of the cross of Christ.[1] I believe that all of these lenses are important to construct the fullest possible understanding of the cross, recognising that our understanding is characterised both by the mysterious distance of God and the confidence that comes from encountering a God who discloses himself. Something significant of his self-disclosure is encapsulated in penal substitution concepts, which have been part of the church's witness consistently for two millennia. Regardless of how the doctrine has been misconstrued and mishandled over the history of the church, I am reluctant to relinquish my grasp of its premises.

However, as an apologist, I cannot resist offering a response to the notion that our contemporary, postmodern culture lacks the vocabulary to make the communication of the penal substitution model effective. Those espousing this notion have challenged us to focus on other models of the cross in order to reach our culture. I agree that we should make the fullest possible use of all the various models of the cross in our apologetic engagement of culture. The question is, Should penal substitution be one of them? Is it necessary for understanding Christ's work on the cross, or is it an embarrassing remnant of church history best left in modernity?[2] If penal substitution is more than a cultural manifestation that emerged in modernity, if it represents something true about God and his self-revelation, then its basic concepts must be communicable in the vocabulary of every culture, including the postmodern.[3]

The incarnational and apologetic risk lies in the challenge not to distort the atonement beyond its biblical basis and so lay another mere fragment of a map over the desert of the real; the challenge is to communicate in a world that is not completely my home without becoming lost within it.[4] And isn't that part of what the Christian life is all about, this side of glory? It is a biblical necessity to seek to communicate the gospel in Jerusalem and Judea and to the ends of the earth. Thus, the latter choice may be risky, but it is also biblically and missiologically necessary.

What I intend to do is engage in a philosophical and theological discussion, drawing particularly on the work of French social philosopher Jean Baudrillard to present a model of the cross in postmodern language. This may seem an absurd idea, since the postmodern, in theory, resists models and detailed codification.[5] Baudrillard's work is notoriously difficult to read, to understand, to interpret. Indeed, many of his ideas are incomprehensible, downright strange or even offensive. However, he is regarded as one of the most influential postmodern thinkers, and some of his cultural analysis is not only influential but also profound.[6] As I have reflected on Baudrillard's thought, I believe it has the potential to open our understanding of the atonement in postmodern language. This, I think, is more radically necessary than simply responding to the postmodern challenge through capitulation to its premises. More than that, I think Baudrillard's thought, insofar as it seduces rather than admits a theory of the cross at all, demands at least some significant elements of a penal substitutionary model of the cross.[7] So, in postmodern fashion, I will plunder just a few key ideas that will be important to my discussion.

Symbolic Exchange

For Baudrillard, along with other post-Marxist, post-Freudian theorists, the matter of symbolic exchange is important. The way that various thinkers portray the concept differs, but the idea is similar as it forms the basis of their cultural critique: human social relations depend on agreed exchanges between parties, based on perceived value. In primitive societies, this was a pure exchange, based on the value of need. The exchange took the form of objects or symbols that represented and remained connected to the real through the things they represented. This was not simply a commercial transaction but a social one that prevented the exchange from representing objects only.

But in modern and late modern society, the symbol is replaced by the sign. In a consumer culture, the sign becomes disconnected from the thing it represents as everything is commodified. Signs come not with social obligations but with price tags. They actually reverse the thing they are to represent. You think you bought something because of its usefulness to you, but you have, instead, been commodified by the commodity you purchased. In such a culture, even death is reversed and turned into a spectacle of life, as we gather the commodities of insurance plans, funeral arrangements and issues of social security around us like a sarcophagus against death.[8]

In late modernity, we are left with little other than a culture of sign exchange that is void of reality and meaning. We have moved beyond alienation to a place where reality is no longer perceptible. Alienation is impossible because we have lost the real. Baudrillard uses an old story by Borges to explain the disappearance of reality.[9] The real is like a territory that has had a map laid over it. The map hides the reality; more than that, the map comes to replace reality. When eventually the map itself starts to fade and crack, even that image of reality begins to fade. We are left in contemporary culture with nothing that is real apart from the image fading from a television screen just after the set has been switched off. Symbolic exchange critiques the commodification of social relations that occurs through sign exchange. Unlike sign exchange, "Symbolic exchange is ... radically opposed to the abstraction of economic and sign exchange. It is open-ended and it doesn't accumulate meanings (or profits) or alienate, because it doesn't split people from their identity or their social place by inserting them into the system of objects."[10]

Image and Alienation

This critique of culture is further represented in Baudrillard's orders of simulation. Simulation is what happens when signs are separated from the thing they represent, when an image of a thing becomes alienated from the thing in itself. The following pattern shows movement from an alienation of the real and its image to its complete separation, where alienation is not even possible as the real disappears behind the image:

1. The image reflects the real, but the real is deconstructed by the image.
2. The image masks the absence of reality: this is referred to as "abyssal vision", where the image has so deconstructed the real that the real begins to fold in on itself.

3. The image masks the absence of profound reality: copies (replicated images of the real) are no longer differentiated and the images have become the real.

4. The image reproduces itself as "hyperreality". Alienation between the image and the real is no longer possible, as the real has disappeared and been replaced by the self-replicating image.[11]

Perhaps the best way to access these ideas is to recount the transition from a myth to a spectre or spectrum that describes the nature and experience of human alienation. This is summarised by Baudrillard in *The Consumer Society*.[12] He tells the story of a film from the 1930s, *The Student of Prague*. It is a Faustian tale of a poor student who, through the manipulation of the devil, meets and falls in love with a rich, beautiful woman. As the student despairs of his ability to impress her with his humble means, the devil offers a deal: he will give the student a bundle of gold in exchange for his image in the mirror. The student agrees and all seems well. That is until, as Baudrillard puts it, the devil revives his image and puts it back into circulation.

The student occasionally meets his image and must manoeuvre strategically to avoid being seen together with it. But in time, the image hounds him and takes over his life. The image distorts his actions and makes them criminal; eventually he must hide, but his image pursues him, and he is without peace. He recognises that the only way out of his miserable state of affairs is to kill his image, which he does. However, in killing his image, he also kills himself. In the end, both are dead.

Like the character in the film, Baudrillard suggests that the student of Prague invites us to imagine a utopia where the alienation of the image and the person is overcome, albeit in death. However, unlike the film, he suggests that such reconciliation is now impossible, because death is now simply a means of sign exchange in a consumer society where everything is reversed. The myth of consumption, as our contemporary dominant myth, replaces the myth of utopia, where image and the real are reconciled in death. Because the image has become the real in a society of hyperreality, alienation is not possible, since alienation presupposes the internalisation of an external (morally other) reality. We merely gaze upon contemporary culture as a spectre and play its games. We cannot kill our image without killing ourselves. Reconciliation between the real and the image cannot be accomplished because the image is all there is. However, true to his existentialist influences, Baudrillard suggests that the only possible subversion of the consumer dynamic apart from the meaninglessness of unexpected violent death is suicide or suicidal action, such as the violence of protest, which meets death with death.[13] Reality is found only in the separation of life from death. One only ever refers to the other – reality is not found in either. They are lost in utopia.[14]

Baudrillard's analysis resonates with Marshall McLuhan's recollection of the Greek myth of Narcissus: "It is from the Greek word *narcosis*, or numbness. The youth Narcissus mistook his own reflection in the water for another person. This extension of himself by mirror numbed his perceptions until he became the servomechanism of his own extended or repeated image. The nymph Echo tried to win his love with fragments of his own speech, but in vain. He was numb. He had adapted to his extension of himself and had become a closed system."[15] McLuhan recognises that contrary to common misperception, Narcissus did not fall in love with *himself*; rather, he fell in love with his image. His image and words became separated, such that there was no alienation. His words no longer had power as they were replaced by the extension of his own image. McLuhan refers to the extension of the image or the separation of the image from the self as an "autoamputation" that prevents self-recognition. We become numbed and lost beyond alienation in our image-based consumer culture. If there is no alienation, we cannot hope for reconciliation. Like Narcissus, our words are forever separated from our image. Such a reflection helps us to grasp more clearly the direction of Baudrillard's discussion and encourages us to consider how it intersects with Christian theology, in particular, with an understanding of the atonement.

Beyond Alienation to Death

It is not difficult to see how Baudrillard's thoughts begin to have implications for the way we might understand the cross in postmodern culture. First, we can affirm that creation reflects God's image generally (e.g., Rom. 1:20) and that human beings bear the image of God particularly (Gen. 1:27; Rom. 8:29). But humans consistently deny their difference from God, not recognising that as bearers of God's image, they are alienated from him when they seek to exist independently of him.[16] Denying our difference and alienation from God, we begin to substitute ourselves for the real. As we replicate the image through our social activities, political organisations and in the media, it becomes a copy of a copy, and the image of God grows disconnected from the God it represents. In other words, humans as bearers of the image of God are disconnected from God himself. The image parades as the real thing, and humans become their own gods. As Nietzsche might put it, we have to become gods to make ourselves worthy of the deed of killing God.[17] As humans, we enter the desert of the real, where only fragments of the image remain. Perhaps most significantly, we offer the fragments of God's image in us as self-replicating gods, who reproduce themselves, creating a culture of the hyperreal that numbs us against any sense of being alienated from a creator God.

Biblically, we see this enacted in Adam and Eve, who allow the image to play as the real, as they aspire for the image of God in them to become as gods. Like the tragic hero of the Greek myth, Narcissus, they do not realise they have fallen in love with the image of God in them, rather than the God they reflect.[18] Similarly, on a collective level, the builders of the tower of Babel allow the image/imagination they have of God to become free-floating, disconnected from the real, and thus becoming a hyperreal god on its own. Indeed, on a social level, the numbness against alienation is exacerbated as one group replicates its own image as God and sets it up for worship by another group.[19]

The law was given to human beings, by God, as a response of grace to highlight the holy difference of God, as an assertion of his subjectivity, and offered as a touchstone of alienation. But this made possible only an external obedience. The spilling of blood, or death, through ritual sacrifice brought home for a moment the alienation of the image of God from the word of God, but it did not make it an enduring reality.

In the contemporary world, we see evidence of this in terms of individual spirituality that has turned the religious into little more than a commodity. Through new age products and therapies that seek escape from the real, we witness the replication of gods for purchase as sign exchange in a postmodern culture. We see evidence of the hyperreal collectively in terms of science, where the ecstatic hope of technology and genetic research, including cloning and development of artificial intelligence, may represent another way in which the copies of the image are becoming more real than the original God. The copies will be free of disease and defect, will be more intelligent than the most intelligent, and available at a price. All of this is God for sale, inoculating us against the alienation of the image from the real. This is the end of our alienation from God, and without alienation, there is no hope of reconciliation. Through the media, we have moved even beyond alienation of the human image from itself, and so us from each other. We are locked in hopeless isolation from one another, and from the real.[20]

This is the contemporary existential human predicament: we are creatures of nature who are bound to nature, and yet we bear the transcendent image of God.[21] The anxiety of the impending reality of the death of the image in us leads us towards two responses, which in biblical terms we may describe as sin. As the human image is replicated into a hyperreality on screen, some humans become inoculated against alienation from themselves and others, withdrawing into sensual retreat (numbness through being entranced by the image). Hence, we have the development of a massive entertainment industry, characterised by images on screens, pornography, gambling, video games and home shopping. We deny our alienation from others and abdicate responsibility for the other, preferring individual stimulation to social action.

On the other hand, some deny the contingent, alienated nature of the image of God in human beings, and the reality of its impending death, by imaging itself as God. We seek to extend the image by pretending that the image is the immortal real. Extending our power through economic and political domination of others, illusions about the extension of the image are manifested in the growth of multinational companies, globalisation, and the accrual of massive wealth and commercial power. For Baudrillard, such an extension of power is easily presented as a mask for the fact that we are actually powerless. In the anomie between life and death, we are not merely alienated from ourselves, from the rest of creation and from God. Rather, we are lost in the nothingness between life and death.

As Baudrillard states, "So it is with life and death in our current system: the price we pay for the 'reality' of this life, to live it as a positive value, is the ever-present phantasm of death. For us, defined as living beings, death is our imaginary. So all the disjunctions on which the different structures of the real are based ... have their archetype in the fundamental disjunction of life and death. This is why, in whatever field of 'reality', every separate term for which the other is its imaginary is haunted by the latter as *its own death*."[22] But in the work of the cross, Christ locates life and death again; he gives them a place, as he embodies the space between life and death, embracing both, and finding one in the other.[23]

A death is required in order to internalise our alienation as we are confronted afresh with our own death; it is only then that we can find a *topos* beyond utopia and heal the alienation of image and real. Our death is required by God, and deserved, because like Baudrillard's description of the student of Prague, we have sold ourselves to the devil by setting up God's image in opposition to him. The only way God can heal the breech is to kill the image that is masquerading as the real. But killing his image in us is insufficient because we have replicated ourselves into a hyperreality. Death is no reconciliation for us. We are not even able to grasp our alienation from God. So God knows that the only solution is to kill his real image. The only way to kill his real image is, in a sense, to kill himself. In killing himself, his own image, his image is reconciled to the real – we are reconciled to God, at least potentially. In a symbolic gift exchange, he dies in our place, and his righteousness before God is imputed to those who recognise their alienation from him and desire reconciliation to him.

For Baudrillard, "Only certain deaths, certain practices, escape this convertibility to consumer value: they alone are subversive, but do not often make the headlines."[24] Among these is suicide, and the suicidal. Violent death breaks into our sign exchange in a subversive way, as does active protest.[25] In a consumer society, death is only the symbol that reinforces our life. But Christ's death is a death of subversion. His self-giving (suicidal) and violent death confronts us with the reality of death that subverts the sarcophagus of death that surrounds us in contemporary culture. The security myth is confronted by terrorism, certainly. Yet long before terrorism shook our security, the reality of Christ's death brought home the possibility of our own as more than a self-replicating sign.

In a media society, Jesus is unique. He is the only true word (*logos*) and image (icon) of God.[26] He is Word and image held together in complete unity (John 1:1; Col. 1:15). In complete faithfulness to the Father, word and image remain integral to his existence. The temptation for Jesus to sell his image by turning it into an exchange commodity during his trial in the wilderness was overcome. In Christ, the desert of the real wells up to a spring of living water. And so God as love offers up himself as the word incarnate, the word imaged, knowing that in killing the perfect image, he will kill himself. In so doing, he takes our place and embraces the death we deserved as those who cause the image of God to masquerade as gods. In this sense, his death is both a demonstration and an achievement, as important for what it means for God as what it means for us.[27]

Christ confronts us collectively with human alienation from God as he enters into the vagaries of human history, internalising God in human experience and internalising, in a new way, the human image in himself. This makes our alienation from God possible. Moreover, he offers himself as the death that will offer means of reconciliation between the image and the real. We cannot pay this price ourselves, for we have become the hyperreal. If God kills us, he capitulates to the realm of sign exchange. With Baudrillard, we agree that a death is necessary, and *contra* Baudrillard, we believe a death is possible. If God in effect kills himself, death becomes reversible to life – not in the sense of commodity exchange but in the sense of gift exchange, where we are socially (not just individually) obligated, and where his satisfaction (as withdrawal from the consumer dynamic) is manifested. He requires a real image, his true image, to be killed in order for his holy justice to be satisfied. With such a death, he is satisfied, which places him outside the realm of the sign exchange of a consumer society. He demonstrates the reversibility of death in the resurrection, making possible a new, unalienated and real existence in us through our conversion and discipleship, where we follow him suicidally, putting death to self and taking on the authentic life of Christ (Matt. 16:24; Gal. 3:27).

Though the reversibility of death is vindicated in the resurrection, this death itself is victory, suicidal in its rebellion against a superficial system of sign exchange, making possible a real gift exchange. God's authentic image manifested in the incarnation reminds us of our alienation from God, the real image killed in place of our copies offers the only means of reconciliation; his righteousness, freely given, creates in us an obligation of response that does not arise from the exchange of commodified objects but arises from the relationships of the community of the Spirit. That which Baudrillard had deemed impossible is made possible: "The gestural place for a pointing to 'that' beyond 'this' is preserved. It lives in the irrepressibility of the counter-gift, the sacrifice, of the violence that makes sacred, which even the most thorough disenchanting the word cannot suppress."[28] In the words of another theologian, "If the fundamental human dilemma can be traced back to the original humans through whom sin and death entered into humanity so as to distort the divine image in humans and destroy the fragile spiritual bond between humans and their Creator God, then Christ is the answer: not just a theological and intellectual answer to a problem but an existential and spiritual reverse of the curse and the reconciliation of humanity to God."[29]

The atonement makes real alienation and its resolution possible.[30] It makes alienation possible through the incarnation, where the reality of another enters our moral space, and we have a sense of alienation from God. The self-giving sacrifice of Christ as the perfect image and word of God makes possible the internalisation of the law through the Spirit of Christ. In writing the word on our hearts as bearers of the image of God, the law of love is internalised, and we are invited to be aware constantly, in every moment, both of our alienation from God and our reconciliation to God, our alienation from society and creation, and the means of our reconciliation to community and creation through the Spirit, worked out in self-sacrificing discipleship.

Death to Self, Life in Christ

I believe what has been portrayed so far represents some aspects of a biblical substitutionary atonement in the language of Baudrillard. It offers not only a means of communicating the nature of the cross in postmodern idiom but a fresh appreciation of the cross as we see how communicable it is in these terms. It opens up our understanding of penal substitution in ways that offer us a deeper theological and spiritual appreciation of the atonement. Moreover, it carries with it significant implications for practical discipleship.[31]

To begin, we must recognise that in discipleship, we are invited to follow Christ in suicidal self-sacrifice (Luke 9:23). But we find ourselves caught up in Christ's reversal of death into life: for whoever loses their life "for my sake will find it" (Matt. 10:39). In penal substitution, God has given himself as the one to suffer a death to satisfy the Father and to provide the means of alienation and reconciliation for humanity. Such an exchange is truly gift exchange: it does not depend on use value and is more authentic than a sign because Jesus' life and teaching contradict the consumer mentality. It is a symbolic exchange within the Jewish cult system and brings with it an obligation. God, in exchanging the blood of his Son for ours, is the one to whom we are obliged to respond as subjects.

Baudrillard's notion of gift exchange applied to the cross challenges our individual interpretations of the cross because it locates us again in the social sphere, with obligations and responsibilities. Similarly, his notion of the subversive nature of the suicidal in protest gives us a political pastoral practice, which Vanhoozer has rightly called for.[32] But this response is not automatic. As Christians, we live within a culture that wreaks havoc with the symbolic exchange of the cross and risks turning it into a consumer sign. Indeed, it is often reduced to kitsch slogans on tea bags and mints, T-shirts, bracelets, even branded worship music. We play with the signs of the cross as though they exhaust the thing of its meaning. We use them as power over others and as means of extending life over death. We must accept responsibility for our obligation to respond to Christ's confrontation of death with death on our behalf.

Yet because the gift exchange of Christ is antithetical to consumer sign exchange, fewer and fewer people are able to grasp its significance. In the light of atonement, however, we find freedom through God's satisfaction. Through the death of Christ, he is satisfied, which places him, and potentially his body, outside of the commodifying culture. Substitutionary atonement offers a way of being integrated with God's purposes, and the possibility of freedom from bondage to a culture of consumption: if the Son shall make you free, you shall be free indeed (John 8:36). We are not surprised, then, to find ourselves out of step with culture in many ways. Nevertheless, we are not free from the obligation to live as the body of Christ in culture, reminding culture of its alienation from God and pointing culture towards the means of reconciliation to God.

We are left at this juncture with a choice – to communicate Christ as a value of sign exchange in consumerism or to pursue some other direction. To pursue the former means sacrificing any pretension to meaning or significance. The other choice is to attempt to shape our culture towards the possibility that symbolic exchange is still possible as part of human existence. Endeavours to speak of sin as shame and guilt attempt to do this sort of thing, but even those concepts require a social structure other than the one in which we presently exist. It would require a society that understands social obligation and community responsibility.

Our discipleship as Christians calls us to engage the process of shaping society as a precursor or pre-apologetic for presenting the gospel. There may be cultures that do not contain the categories of thought that would facilitate the presentation of the gospel. In such a case, it may be necessary to shape the culture so that it may develop the categories of thought that would allow the gospel to be presented clearly and allow people to consider the offer of the gospel in as free a manner as possible.

The question emerges, Can the symbols of real symbolic exchange – in other words, our lives in Christ – produce a different culture? Our apologetic and missional task does not only entail expressing the atonement in postmodern language. We must also find ways of challenging the very consumer structures of society so that suggestions of alienation from God do not seem so absurd, as they often do. One way that might occur is through the different life of holiness lived by the community of faith that highlights to the unreconciled the very fact of their alienation. In other words, through our actions that seek to live out our reconciled life in the world incarnationally, we demonstrate the life of Christ and raise the possibility that others might see him and become aware of their alienation from God (Matt. 5:16).

However, in order for people even to contemplate such notions, they may well need first to experience some measure of alienation and reconciliation between and within themselves. In a world of social divisions, there is a call for Christians to live out the real death of the atonement in laying down their lives in protest against injustice and alienation between human beings. In the words of one thinker, "If the world, as a matter of ideological fact, is separated into a real and fantasmatic realm, this can only be explained as the effect of an earthly split. That is: of a social division between ruler and ruled, exploiters and exploited, in which objectified human power is appropriated by the dominant and converted into power over its original producers. Salvation, correspondingly, is not just a matter of illumination and change of consciousness. The social relations of domination must themselves be overcome for the subjective side of alienation, the hell of human self-separation, to be redeemed."[33]

Vanhoozer's call to pastoral engagement is relevant here, as is Baudrillard's suggestion that protest subverts consumer culture. The potential for political, cultural involvement through protest is one way that the negative, dominating aspects of culture are challenged. Through protest, Christians may demonstrate their own satisfaction with sufficient resources that removes them from the cycle of dissatisfaction on which a consumer culture depends.[34] At the same time, protest offers the possibility to others that there may be a different way of being in the world. The cross demonstrates a justice that names evil for what it is and seeks reconciliation between human beings. To follow the way of the cross means becoming involved in the messiness of the world.

It is important to note that alienation and reconciliation extend not only to individuals and societies but also to creation. Nature too becomes a sign of the consumer culture, divided into good nature (dominated and a source of wealth) and bad nature (hostile and polluted).[35] But we discover in the work of the cross that God so loved the *cosmos* that he sacrificed his one and only Son. As creation bears the scars of alienation from its Creator in its very landscape, so it is able to groan in anticipation of its redemption in Christ. Christian discipleship in the world seeks to reconcile the divide between good and bad nature and treats the whole of the created world as one good, for which we are responsible. Involvement in issues of environmental preservation becomes an important part of what it means to have participated in a gift exchange with the Creator of nature.

We have hopefully caught just a glimpse of some possible implications of following through on a portrayal of the atonement in the language of Baudrillard. While we have not adopted his concepts without critique and selection, they have nonetheless allowed us to communicate some theological concepts that may at first appear alien to our dominant consumer culture. We have found that, contrary to those who insist that a penal substitutionary atonement is incommunicable in postmodern culture, the cross is communicable in every language. And we are not surprised that God has not left himself without witness in postmodern culture.

While the presentation here is less than complete, at least it opens a door to engagement with Baudrillard's concepts, which others may pursue more rigourously, with the purpose of demonstrating not only how Christian concepts are similar but also how they are unlike those employed by the gurus of postmodern culture. Through such explorations, we can at least conclude that in all that we do as disciples of Christ in a media-dominated, consumer culture, we are obligated to hold word and image together. In our proclamation and behaviour, we are to demonstrate the reconciliation that has been imputed to us through the righteousness of Christ. Though the reconciliation he effected lacks nothing, the symbolic exchange we engage when we receive the gift of salvation brings with it the obligation of response, as willing subjects who die to self and live for Christ in this world and the world to come, where even death is gain.

Notes

1. The postmodern appeal to non-violence challenges us to employ several models of the cross in presenting its meaning. Using several models prevents us from committing the violent offense of suggesting that there is one totalising metanarrative of the cross (something which some of us may fear more than others). At the same time, this very admission by consequence demands that others may not exclude penal substitution without committing a totalising violence on its proponents. Cf. Vanhoozer's first challenge in Kevin J. Vanhoozer, "The Atonement in Postmodernity: Guilt, Goats and Gifts," in *The Glory of the Atonement: Biblical, Historical and Practical Perspectives*, ed. Charles E. Hill and Frank A. James III (Downers Grove, Ill.: IVP, 2004), 370–71.

2. Indeed, I would suggest, with Robert Sherman, that the very claim that the model is immoral because it demands a penalty to be paid by an innocent party is itself an Enlightenment concept that drives a wedge between reason and revelation. Those who think they are being relevant postmoderns are sometimes simply capitulating to the pallid arguments of late modern liberalism, which has less rigour and credibility than what is usually labelled as either evangelical or postmodern theology. Cf. Robert Sherman, *King, Priest and Prophet: A Trinitarian Theology of Atonement* (London: T & T Clark, 2004).

3. I take "postmodern" to embody both the cultural conditions under which we live (postmodernity) and the philosophical influences that feed it and emerge from it (postmodernism). Often when Christians attempt to engage the postmodern, there is a discussion around very vague terms and assumptions about what "postmodern" means. It is difficult to find sustained discussion between theologians and postmodern philosophers despite the clear influence the latter have had on the former in recent days. Two possible exceptions are found in recent work by scholars such as Kevin Vanhoozer and Carl Raschke, and the body appears to be growing.

4. Marshall McLuhan highlights the tendency for the self to become lost within a visual culture. He contrasts the impact made on the sense by television's image fascination with that made by the word in Psalm 113. See Marshall McLuhan, *Understanding Media: The Extensions of Man* (London: Abacus, 1974), 55.

5. Such an activity may be described as enacting violence against Baudrillard's thought. However, according to its own parameters, the postmodern cannot raise such an accusation without enacting a violence of its own against my attempt.

6. Carl Raschke refers to him as "the doyen of postmodern cultural theory". See Carl Raschke, *The Next Reformation: Why Evangelicals Must Embrace Postmodernity* (Grand Rapids: Baker, 2004), 146.

7. For Baudrillard on seduction beyond alienation, see interview 3 in Baudrillard, *Baudrillard Live: Selected Interviews*, ed. Mike Gane (London and New York: Routledge, 1993).

8. Jean Baudrillard, *Symbolic Exchange and Death* (London: Sage, 1993), 177.

9. Jean Baudrillard, *Simulacra and Simulation*, trans. Sheila Faria Glaser (Ann Arbor: Univ. of Michigan Press, 1994), 1ff.

10. Chris Horrocks and Zoran Jevtic, *Introducing Baudrillard* (Cambridge: Icon, 1996), 33.

11. Baudrillard, *Symbolic Exchange and Death*, 72–73. The hyperreal is beyond representation. Cf. Jean Francois Lyotard's discussion of the separation of language from its meaning in his *The Postmodern Condition: A Report on Knowledge* (Manchester: Manchester Univ. Press, 1984).

12. Jean Baudrillard, *The Consumer Society: Myths and Structures* (London: Sage, 1998), 187ff.

13. Though in the world of the hyperreal even the violence of protest is reversed in the form of terrorism that threatens security which reverses into a process of affirming life (Baudrillard, *Symbolic Exchange and Death*, 37ff.).

14. Ibid., 133. This notion is akin to a Kierkegaardian-Heideggerian angst that stretches beyond Nietzsche's nothing to anomie.

15. McLuhan, *Understanding Media*, 51.

16. Cf. Rom. 3:23. All have sinned and fallen short of the glory of God – not lived up to the fullness of the image of God within.

17. Friedrich Nietzsche, *The Gay Science*, trans. Walter Kaufmann (New York: Vintage, 1974), 181–82.

18. Rom. 1:25. Humans tend to worship things God made – the image – rather than God himself.

19. I am drawing here on Reinhold Niebuhr's interpretation of sin as the corporate will to power. See, for example, Reinhold Niebuhr, *The Nature and Destiny of Man*, vol. 1, *Human Nature* (London: J. Nisbet, 1941).

20. Hence, for Baudrillard, alienation is no longer a possibility since there is no duel-relation in a consumer society. There is no symbolic exchange that carries with it a social obligation. According to Baudrillard, "We cannot speak of alienation here, for the subject is only alienated (like we are) when he internalises an abstract agency, issuing from the 'other world', as Nietzsche said – whether psychological (the ego and the ego-ideal), religious (God and the soul) or moral (conscience and the law) – an irreconcilable agency to which everything else is subordinated. Historically, then, alienation begins with the internalisation of the Master by the *emancipated* slave: there is no alienation as long as the *duel*-relation of the master and the slave lasts" (*Symbolic Exchange and Death*, 141).

21. For my analysis of sin as the retreat into sensuality and, conversely, the will to power, I am indebted to Niebuhr, *Nature and Destiny of Man*.

22. Baudrillard, *Symbolic Exchange and Death*, 133.

23. Like many existentialists, Baudrillard does identify the space between life and death as anxiety (or the vertigo of separation), which provides a touchstone for speaking of sin, since the Christian existentialist (Kierkegaard and Niebuhr included) often understands the anxiety between life and death as the initiator for sin as it seeks to deny its destiny of death (ibid., 142).

24. Ibid., 17.

25. Ibid., 176.

26. Cf. Oliver O'Donovan, "The Concept of Publicity," *Studies in Christian Ethics* 13, no. 1 (2000): 18–32.

27. Perhaps this presentation prevents the antagonism between Father and Son that so many find rightly reprehensible. God not only demands the obligations of the exchange to be fulfilled, but he meets the obligations himself.

28. Andrew Wernick, "Jean Baudrillard: Seducing God," *Post-Secular Philosophy: Between Theology and Philosophy*, ed. Phillip Blond (London: Routledge, 1998), 351–55.

29. Ray Anderson, *An Emergent Theology for Emerging Churches* (Downers Grove, Ill.: IVP, 2006), 54.

30. Vanhoozer demonstrates this in a different way through his "constructive proposal" ("The Atonement in Postmodernity," 396ff.).

31. In Baudrillard's language, rather than being objective recipients of the law, we are invited to respond to Christ's death on our behalf in order to internalise it. This makes us responsive subjects and does away with humanist and post-Hegelian "violent" ideas of God simply working through humanity for his own self-realisation: a philosophy which evangelicals have usually resisted and which Baudrillard has rejected.

32. Vanhoozer raises the challenge to offer a pastoral-political response to the postmodern. The reality test is often the best measure of the significance of a given theory (Vanhoozer, "The Atonement in Postmodernity," 372–73).

33. Wernick, "Jean Baudrillard," 349–50.

34. See Walter Brueggemann, *The Word That Redescribes the World*, ed. Patrick D. Miller (Minneapolis: Fortress, 2006), 114ff., 157ff.

35. Baudrillard, *The Consumer Society*, 100–101; Baudrillard, *Simulacra and Simulation*, 129ff.; cf. Horrocks and Jevtic, *Introducing Baudrillard*, 76–77.

penal substitution

a pastoral apologetic

derek tidball

To someone like myself, who was brought up to celebrate penal substitutionary atonement as a triumph of saving grace, the recent and increasing criticism of penal substitutionary atonement is somewhat bemusing. Once proclaimed as a positive symbol of freedom and forgiveness, the cross is now often viewed negatively and derided as a symbol of oppression and violence. The critics choose a distorted or crass version of penal substitution atonement (PSA) against which to mount their attacks, concluding that there is something inherent in PSA that makes it indefensible. In this chapter, I want to look at some of the criticisms that relate to our pastoral understanding of the cross, in the belief that much is lost if we abandon our belief in PSA.[1] Here the focus is not on a biblical defence but on a pastoral apologetic.

Three brief comments are necessary before proceeding. First, I do not believe that PSA is the only legitimate interpretation of the cross, or that it says all that needs to be said about the cross.[2] Second, I recognise that our attempts to articulate the gospel and theology take place in particular cultural contexts, and that our culture differs from the earlier cultures in which PSA was effectively forged and communicated. But I am not as convinced as some of its critics that PSA is incommunicable or irrelevant in today's culture. Third, many critics of PSA appear to have misunderstood the implications of its teaching, and as Hans Boersma has commented, "When an individual draws wrong inferences from a penal theory of the atonement, the error lies not with the penal theory but with the person drawing the mistaken conclusion."[3]

I have selected six issues that critics of PSA often raise as grounds for discarding it. In each case, the heading presents the positive statement for PSA before denying the negative.

It Terminates Guilt; It Does Not Perpetuate It

Some brought up in a strong evangelical tradition in which the preaching of the cross was essentially PSA testify that it led them to terrible insecurity, feeling not that they had been relieved of guilt but that they had been condemned to perpetual guilt.[4] PSA's view of the cross emphasises that men and women are rebels against their God, lawbreakers who have been found justly guilty and deserve punishment. Some hymns reinforce such a view with their talk of "Guilty, vile and helpless we"[5] or "Two wonders I confess – the wonder of his glorious love, and *my own worthlessness.*"[6] Such emphases leave some feeling not that "amazing grace" has "saved a wretch like me"[7] but that we remain wretches, undeserving of anything.

Hymn writer William Cowper, friend of John Newton, might be seen as an example of this. He was a man "acquainted with guilt" who possessed "a lacerated conscience, his mind tortured by a self-rejection which he saw as the mirror image of God's displeasure".[8] Some see his hymns as morbid and tormented. Yet in them he is struggling through the self-loathing he feels in order to discover that sinners have their guilt washed away and their guilty stains removed through the cross of Christ. This cross, he asserts, never loses its power.[9]

The more usual position that is a true and natural outworking of PSA is seen in Charles Simeon, who celebrated the fact that "I can transfer all my guilt to another! I will not bear them on my soul a moment longer."[10] A contemporary witness from a South London housing estate has equally grasped the significance of this. Talking of the guilt he experienced for the bad things he had done in life, Mark went on to talk of the relief from guilt the cross had brought. "The amazing thing about the cross was that the end of someone else started a new beginning for me. It's knowing that your sins are paid for, having assurance. It's freedom – from guilt. The guilt used to play over in my head but now I know I can come to the cross and confess it and Jesus will take it on himself."[11] A view of the cross in which another bears our guilt as our substitute, far from leaving sinners wallowing in guilt, is the only message that can assure them of freedom from it.

Today sin is treated lightly,[12] and so we may need to labour the seriousness and awfulness of sin in our teaching. Yet it is a travesty to use PSA to condemn rather than to minister forgiveness. To keep people imprisoned in guilt is to abuse it in the worst possible way. It is, ironically, to turn its message inside out and upside down. Without PSA, we will no longer be able to cry with any certainty, "Therefore, there is now no condemnation for those who are in Christ Jesus" (Rom. 8:1). Nor will we be able to assert that "it is for freedom that Christ has set us free" (Gal. 5:1) because he has dealt with the curse of the law that threatened to bring us down.

PSA may have the effect on sensitive consciences of encouraging an unwarranted feeling of self-loathing.[13] But this is only so in the hands of those who handle it coarsely or manipulatively. Those who speak of it must proclaim it as good news, not bad. The evident purpose of the hymns quoted above is to lead people to celebrate the freedom from guilt achieved by the cross, not to keep people entrapped in guilt.

Whether the sense of moral guilt before God in contemporary society is as strong as it once was is a valid question. Those who argue that it is not can make a persuasive case for their position and legitimately help us preach the gospel in a way that resonates more widely with contemporary culture. Shame rather than guilt might be the more dominant cultural currency today, as Alan Mann has argued.[11] Nonetheless, guilt is experienced by some and should not be dismissed too readily. Gary Jenkins, writing out of experience in ministry on a not-too-prosperous estate in London, says, "It remains common in pastoral ministry to encounter individuals who carry a deep burden of guilt often connected with the past." Many come, he reports, to confess their sins. When they unburden themselves in this way, he writes, "what they have wanted and have needed is forgiveness, the slate wiped clean, a removal of the condemnation they feel and a remedy for their deep feelings of guilt. They want to deal decisively and finally with those things from the past that continue to have such a hold over them in the present. They want it dealt with once and for all."[15] Who would wish to deny people such freedom by denying the legitimacy of the long-held PSA view of the cross?

Furthermore, whether people feel guilty is not the only issue. Whatever people feel, the question remains open as to what people are. Perhaps our preaching of the cross in contemporary society needs to lead people to an understanding of sin as wrongdoing before God that needs to be overcome, rather than assuming they will already know and agree with this. This understanding may be the discovery many make when they begin to grasp more fully the wonder of the gospel. If PSA is fundamental to God's revelation of his grace in Christ, as recorded in Scripture, and not merely the social construct of the Reformers, then we are obliged to speak of it and are in danger of denying others what God wants them to know. It may not seem initially to address the symptoms for which they seek a cure, but the deeper diagnosis of sin will prove a genuine pastoral kindness and lead to more complete healing. PSA, then, remains a vital and necessary way of speaking about the cross in contemporary society and, providing it is rightly taught, assures sinners that forgiveness and freedom from sin's penalties and consequences are theirs.

It Conquers Violence; It Does Not Glorify It

The most vocal critics have expressed the concern that PSA justifies violence. The cross, they say, portrays an angry God, in a horrific act of violence, punishing his Son for sins which he did not himself commit. Hence, the cross gives permission for the powerful to gain satisfaction by inflicting violence on the weak and presents the passive submission of the victim as an ideal to be imitated. Consequently, it is claimed, the cross justifies violent behaviour in every dimension of life: whether sanctioning the use of force in war, execution in the criminal justice system, domestic violence, or child abuse. The resort to violence is further justified by the belief that suffering is somehow redemptive and necessary for "salvation" to be achieved.

Many critics come from a feminist perspective and claim to have evidence of women and children suffering abuse at the hands of those who validate, or at least rationalize, their behaviour by reference to PSA. Joanne Carlson Brown and Rebecca Parker, for instance, speak for several in saying, "Divine child abuse is paraded as salvific and the child who suffers 'without even raising a voice' is lauded as the hope of the world."[16] Others from a different perspective raise the same unease. Timothy Gorringe relates the concern to the criminal justice system.[17] Still others, like Denny Weaver or Stuart Murray, question the link between church and power in Christendom and want to break the connection between redemption and violence.[18] The key issue, they say, is that wrongs should be righted, whereas the concern of PSA is that wrong should be punished. Their stand has implications for everything from family discipline, through penal policy, to international conflicts. Cynthia Crysdale may fairly be considered to summarise the concern: "Redemption comes to be understood (under Anselm's influence) as the requirement of a distant, omnipotent God for the satisfaction of his honour, God's mercy gets lost in the idealization of punishment and suffering, and God is seen as sadistic and bloodthirsty. Such a God *and the acceptance of our deserved punishment* become necessary in order for the message of salvation to mean anything."[19]

That some use the cross as justification for meting out violence on victims is undeniable. But there are four reasons why blaming PSA for this is highly questionable. First, whatever one's interpretation of atonement, it is unavoidable that the cross was a bloody and violent affair. Other interpretations of the cross do not lessen this fact.[20] The *Christus Victor* interpretation of atonement, supposedly the classic understanding of the atonement and advocated by some who embrace the non-violent tradition, seems logically to entail just as many problems from this view. From its perspective, Christ triumphs over all oppressing powers on the cross and releases those held in bondage to them by passive resistance. But the use of passive resistance is not ethically free from problems and may well be manipulatively used to exercise power. Certainly, the conflict and battle imagery inherent in *Christus Victor* implies militaristic and power motifs to which those who advocate it most would object. In a caricatured form, *Christus Victor* might be seen as a more powerful tool in the hands of Constantine and subsequent Christendom than PSA.[21] Removing PSA from our Christian vocabulary does not seem to solve the particular problem that these critics raise.

Second, PSA describes what God achieved in the cross of Christ. It does not present violence or punishment as anything more than a necessary evil which God took upon himself.[22] It does not claim to be a model for our dealing with one another and involves no justification for violence toward victims, willing or otherwise. As Boersma has pointed out, "Not all divine actions are to be imitated: We are not called upon to create the world or to pour out the Holy Spirit."[23] If PSA serves as a model for our behaviour, it does so by inviting us to bear wrongdoing and bring an end to it by exercising grace, as Ephesians 4:32 and a host of other Scriptures make clear.

Third, PSA is misunderstood if portrayed as an angry Father indulging his wrath at the expense of his unwilling and defenceless Son. The Son in question was not a young, passive and powerless child but a fully developed and intentional adult who worked in willing cooperation with his Father to secure the benefits of his death for others.[24] The term "child abuse" is misleading and inappropriate. As John Stott has written, "We must never make Christ the object of God's punishment or God the object of Christ's persuasion, for both God and Christ were subjects not objects, taking the initiative together to save sinners."[25]

Fourth, the connection between PSA and violent abuse or harsh penal policy is often asserted but not often demonstrated. However, other understandings of the cross explicitly do make a connection between passively enduring suffering and the violence borne by Jesus. Such a view is explicit and common in Catholic devotion and penitential practice, and even, for some years, was the justification for violent punishments being delivered in Catholic schools.[26] But there the view of atonement calls for an imitation of the suffering of Christ and is not connected with PSA.

It Personalizes Justice; It Does Not Depersonalize It

Critics of PSA often claim that it is a cold, forensic, impersonal or legalistic way of speaking about the cross, whereas issues of sin and salvation are essentially about a relationship between God and his creatures. PSA, it is said, exaggerates the role of the law and gives it an independent existence to which God himself is somehow subordinate. Sin as alienation and salvation as reconciliation are, it is sometimes claimed, more faithful to Scripture and more useful in contemporary culture. No one I know denies the importance of seeing alienation and reconciliation as key biblical concepts which resonate with the contemporary world. John Stott, an ardent advocate of PSA, certainly understood this when he wrote that reconciliation is "probably the most popular of the four [images] because it is the most personal".[27] The question is rather whether the critics' understanding of PSA is correct.

Justice is never, biblically speaking, an independent entity but always an expression of the character of a loving and holy God. It is a mistake to think of the moral law of God in terms of contemporary statute law, where a judge rules on behalf of an impersonal entity called the state and has no personal stake in the issues before him.

Brunner dealt with this issue in his work *The Mediator*. The moral law of the Bible, he argued, "is none other than the expression of the will of the Lawgiver, of the personal God".[28] It is, he wrote, "nothing in itself" but rather an expression of the Creator, who addresses his creatures personally, and an expression of "the One whose will is identical with Himself".[29] It is a manifestation of God's holy character, and therefore sin is seen as an offence against his holiness and an "infringement of his glory".[30] Later Brunner adds that it is also an expression of his love. God is opposed to that which destroys his creation and diminishes his creatures. "God is angry, because he is personal, because he is love."[31] Sinners have offended not some impersonal code but a personal God.

Brunner's critique has startling relevance for today. He noted that many sought to reject PSA because they believed it to espouse a primitive idea of punishment. As a result of the outworking of the Enlightenment, they sought to "swallow up" the idea of divine wrath in the idea of divine love. It was easy, he observed, to caricature PSA as if God were a bloodthirsty oriental monarch (as many continue to do). But so long as the church rejected PSA, it was, in reality, rejecting any idea of divine holiness and would continue to decline.[32] He believed that "the Cross is the only place where the loving, forgiving, merciful God is revealed in such a way that we perceive that His holiness and His love are equally infinite."[33]

PSA, far from dealing with the fact that people have broken some fixed and impersonal law, deals with the broken relationship people have with a personal God. The God who is alienated in this way is also, however, the God who himself provides an answer, as we shall see in the next section.

Some contemporary theologians wish to distance God from any direct involvement with the expression of wrath or judgment. They say the judgment we experience is the consequence of the way God has created the world, rather than the expression of his personal displeasure at sin.[34] Apart from the fact that this only places God one step removed from the judgment – the responsibility is still ultimately God's – this ironically depersonalizes the problem and solution, which is the very accusation levelled against those who hold to PSA. It is as if they are saying, "It's not God's fault; it's the system." Somehow they seem to want a personal solution (God's reconciliation through the cross) to an impersonal problem (our living out of joint with the way he made the world). But the biblical witness is that death is not natural; it is the wages of sin (Rom. 6:23), a response of divine judgment on human sin.[35] Correctly understood, PSA holds that both problem and solution are personal and relational, even if articulated in terms of law. PSA is a much more natural interpretation of the way the Bible consistently witnesses to God himself bringing judgment to bear on sinful people and nations.[36]

It Provides Satisfaction;
It Does Not Demand It

The wonderful good news of the cross, according to PSA, is that God himself meets the demands of justice and provides satisfaction for the law we have disobeyed. "The wages of sin is death, but the gift of God is eternal life in Christ Jesus our Lord" (Rom. 6:23). Why, then, do some speak of PSA as if God is making an unreasonable demand on us?

The caricature of PSA presents an angry God determined at all costs to get his way and "demanding" satisfaction for his broken law or offended honour. But the message of PSA is the reverse of this. It emphasises that nothing we can do can ever meet the demands of a holy God. As Augustus Toplady memorably put it,

> Not the labours of my hands
> Can fulfil Thy law's demands;
> Could my zeal no respite know,
> Could my tears for ever flow,
> All for sin could not atone:
> Thou must save and Thou alone.
> Nothing in my hand I bring,
> Simply to thy cross I cling;
> Naked come to Thee for dress;
> Helpless, look to Thee for grace;
> Foul, I to the fountain fly:
> Wash me, Saviour, or I die.[37]

It is impossible for us to render satisfaction, not least because we cannot undo what we have done. Consequently, God has himself freely provided satisfaction for us at his own expense. He demands nothing that he does not first provide.

Such a view significantly implies that all men and women approach God on the same level. None have any natural advantages or special privileges because they are more moral, live better, are more theologically literate, are more sophisticated, or have a particular spiritual background. Nor are any too distant, too immoral, too uneducated, nor too guilty to find salvation. Everyone is forgiven on the same free terms as everyone else. The price is not out of anyone's reach. To summarize Ephesians 2, *all* were dead in sin, *all* were deserving of God's wrath, but *all* may be made alive by grace, through faith, in Christ. Given this, no one can boast. Here is a gospel for *all*.

It Accomplishes Change; It Does Not Fictionalise It

The glory of the objective view of the atonement, especially in its penal substitutionary form, is that "something definite actually happened, something decisive that occurred *then* which affects things *now*."[38] Through the cross, a change took place that enables a change of relationship between God and sinful human beings and effects a change of status before God for repentant sinners. Contemporary theories of the atonement have become uncertain of this objective act of God and have emphasised instead the subjective appeal of the cross. Paul Fiddes, for example, argues that this subjective understanding is "basically the right orientation for our Christian thinking today" and presents the cross as "an event which has a unique degree of power to evoke and create a human response to the forgiving love of God".[39]

The move towards a subjective view is because the objective view, it is claimed, reduces the cross to a mere transaction that leaves sinners unchanged yet forgiven, merely because they have requested it. Two metaphors are frequently used in this regard, one financial and the other legal. Financially, the debt of sin is removed by a satisfactory payment being made by Christ in his death. Edward Irving spoke of this as "Stock Exchange divinity".[40] Sin, he legitimately argued, is not a separate entity from human beings and is therefore not a quantity to be weighed as if the cross is some "quasi-financial balancing act" in which God engages. Sin is relational and salvation must affect relationships too. Similarly, the metaphor of the courtroom is often mentioned as illustrating the problem with the objective view of PSA. Here a righteous judge declares a guilty person innocent because another has paid the penalty and borne the punishment in place of the person who is truly guilty. The guilty but pardoned person, it is argued, walks free from the courtroom without any change having taken place within and with no need for a lasting relationship with the judge. Indeed, some might even use it as an excuse to boast of their wrongdoing or to go on sinning in order that they might be forgiven again. This diminishes the work of Christ on the cross, it is said, to a legal fiction. Nothing has changed in reality. Only a subject view of atonement, it is said, which bears in upon the person and changes them from within can avoid "fictionalizing" the atonement.

Some evangelical preachers have sometimes crudely used this kind of metaphor, but their overzealous proclamation of the freedom from guilt that comes through the cross cannot be used to argue that PSA is inherently flawed. The objective view is defensible for a number of reasons. First, without the objective view, sinners are left uncertain whether they have returned to God sufficiently or responded adequately to his love. Sinners are left wondering whether they love God sufficiently to make the relationship secure. Only if God takes the initiative and fundamentally changes the basis for our relating to him can we be secure. Second, it is erroneous to speak of owing debts and being charged with an offence in a court as if they are not personal issues. Though today justice and debt may seem to be administered impersonally, most people caught up in the "system" do not view it as such. Some hardened individuals may treat lightly being on the wrong side of the law or the moneylender, but most do not. A jury system in determining justice is valued precisely because it is personal; it is about being tried by one's peers, not by a machine. Third, why would anyone want to prevent the wonderful freedom of the cross that is available to all, no matter what life they have led and how late their repentance? Did not Jesus assure the dying thief of his acceptance in paradise, once the thief had taken responsibility for his wrongdoing?[41] PSA requires people to take responsibility for their sin in order to benefit from forgiveness. Confession of sin is no mere ritual but a necessary ownership of guilt before that guilt is transferred. Fourth, although PSA may appear to permit people to "go on sinning" and not to change their way of life, the problem is hardly new. The problem is implicit in the doctrine of justification and the nature of grace itself, not a problem confined to PSA. It arose from the earliest days of the gospel and was fully addressed by the apostle Paul in his writings.

None would wish to deny the subjective element in atonement. God was making an appeal of love through the cross which should move a human being to respond and be reconciled to him. But that alone is not enough. Unless something happened, the appeal leaves one on uncertain ground. In P. T. Forsyth's words, "The feeble gospel preaches 'God is ready to forgive'; the mighty gospel preaches 'God has redeemed.'"[42]

Furthermore, if all God did was express his love for us, the moral objections to the cross become even more cogent, not less. I can understand why Father and Son in harmony should endure the cross to break the power and penalty of sin, to make a difference and effect salvation, but to do so only in the hope of wooing us back to him and of changing our attitude towards him makes the cross, already baffling, more puzzling still. I do not see how it solves the questions raised against PSA.

It Encourages Discipleship; It Does Not Marginalize It

Critics often claim PSA isolates the cross and disconnects it from the life and resurrection of Christ, making the first merely a necessary preliminary and the second a loosely attached appendix. PSA is also accused of having no implications for the ongoing life of discipleship which a believer is expected to live. The sinner is forgiven, as mentioned above, but so what? Steve Chalke, for example, has recently written that "penal substitution offers instant forgiveness without challenging basic day-to-day moral behaviour. It separates salvation from discipleship by disconnecting the way that Jesus lived from his saving work."[43] In focusing on this accusation, we ask, Does PSA marginalize the need for someone to live as a disciple of Christ in the world or does it encourage it?

The response of some to this accusation is to accept it, at least in part. Why should it be thought, they argue, that a particular view of atonement should answer every question or cover every base? PSA highlights certain aspects of the atonement, important and precious ones, without its having to say all there is to say about the cross. The teaching of Scripture regarding atonement is indeed many-sided. The criticism could equally be mounted against other theories, that they do not cover every aspect of atonement and discipleship.

This criticism against PSA is far from new. How does one hold on to free grace and justification without falling into the trap of antinomianism? Though there are many approaches to answer this question, the following approach is specific to the current debate over PSA.[44] PSA is not a superficial concept that exists in a vacuum. It emerges from a wider context and arises because of a doctrine of God that believes him to be holy and gracious, of law that is seen as good and wise, of sin that is serious and destructive in its effects, and of salvation that is celebrated as great and undeserved. Once we put it in this wider context, other things inevitably follow. In PSA we encounter a God who, while amazingly gracious, continues to be a God of holiness and requires that we be holy (1 Peter 1:13–22). PSA does not absolve us from a concern with issues of justice and right living but draws into a relationship with God, whose passionate concern they are. PSA tells us the demands of the law are met, but that law remains "holy, and the commandment is holy, righteous and good" (Rom. 7:12). Consequently, we are freed from the condemnation and penalty of the law in order that we might keep "the royal law" (James 2:8) "that brings freedom" (James 2:12). The emphasis on law in PSA shows us the need to live by it rather than ignore it. PSA treats sin most seriously and brings its awfulness into the sharpest focus. Although the good news of PSA is that sin is categorically forgiven, it does not thereby permit the recipient of forgiveness to treat sin lightly. The cross continues to stand as a symbol of sin's costly destructiveness, and those who grasp PSA will grasp that sin continues to be a horror to be avoided at all costs. They will flee sin and pursue righteousness. PSA tells us our salvation was achieved at the cost of the life of God's Son. Our freedom was "bought with a price", and as a result, we are not our own (1 Cor. 6:20) and will live to honour God and please him in our behaviour. PSA calls forth gratitude, a gratitude which is expressed by our living as disciples of Christ.

The charge that PSA marginalises discipleship, then, is not proven and arises only if it is presented in a narrow way, removed from its wider context. That context is essential if PSA is to make any sense or indeed have any coherence. The once-for-allness of forgiveness, of which PSA speaks, does not stand in contradiction with the ongoing process of discipleship, even if there may appear to be some tension between them. Properly understood, PSA leads to discipleship.

Conclusion

No formulation of the atonement is free from risk and caricature, including PSA. But to jettison it is to lose much. PSA is not only pastorally defensible but also pastorally indispensable. At heart, all theories of the atonement relate to our view of God, and to set PSA aside is to lose sight of a God who is wrathful because he is love. As Nigel Wright states, "The love of God is holy love and God manifests ultimate resistance to anything and everything which tends to destroy the creatures who are the objects of his love.... Divine wrath is therefore a manifestation of divine love. It is because he is the passionately loving God that is he provoked to righteous anger and indignation."[45] Without such anger, God would not love us but would be indifferent to us. Without such wrath, forgiveness would be trivialised.[46] Yet "mercy triumphs over judgment" (James 2:13) because the God who is angry is the God who provides an answer, at no cost to us, and appeases his wrath by his own self-giving in Christ, setting us free once and for all.

Notes

1. In writing this, I am greatly indebted to Dr Andrew Partington for his comments and to Simon Cragg, whose undergraduate dissertation explored this theme in 2006. This essay is dependent at a number of points on his unpublished work.

2. For my fuller views, see Derek Tidball, *The Message of the Cross* (Leicester and Downers Grove, Ill.: IVP, 2001).

3. Hans Boersma, "Eschatological Justice and the Cross: Violence and Penal Substitution," *Theology Today* 60 (2003): 188.

4. As one who was nurtured in this tradition, I have to say this was not my experience. Rather, the preaching of PSA led to the opposite and engendered a strong sense of God's love and acceptance of me, whatever I was guilty of.

5. "Man of Sorrows! Wondrous Name" by Philip Bliss.

6. "Beneath the Cross of Jesus" by Elizabeth Clephane. Italics mine.

7. "Amazing Grace!" by John Newton.

8. J. M. Gordon, *Evangelical Spirituality: From the Wesleys to John Stott* (London: SPCK, 1991), 74.

9. Ibid.

10. Cited in Tidball, *Message of the Cross*, 29.

11. Gary Jenkins, *In My Place: The Spirituality of Substitution*, Grove Books Spirituality Series 71 (Cambridge: Grove, 1999), 16.

12. We sometimes, I think, make too much of the way our contemporary culture treats sin lightly, as if this is unique. Sin was treated very lightly in the ancient world, but that did not deter the apostles from preaching and writing about it.

13. The negative reaction to PSA may have as much to do with the critics' psychological makeup as with questions of the doctrine's theological legitimacy. There is an issue to be explored here on the attraction between particular theories of the atonement and particular personality types, but this cannot be explored further in this paper and requires careful research that has not yet been satisfactorily undertaken.

14. Alan Mann, *Atonement for a "Sinless" Society* (Milton Keynes: Paternoster, 2005).

15. Jenkins, *In My Place*, 11.

16. Joanne Carlson Brown and Rebecca Parker, "For God So Loved the World?" in *Christianity, Patriarchy and Abuse*, ed. Joanne Carlson Brown and Carole R. Bohn (New York: Pilgrim, 1989), 2.

17. Timothy Gorringe, *God's Just Vengeance: Crime, Violence and the Rhetoric of Salvation* (Cambridge: Cambridge Univ. Press, 1996).

18. J. Denny Weaver, *The Nonviolent Atonement* (Grand Rapids: Eerdmans, 2001), and Stuart Murray, "Rethinking Atonement after Christendom," in *Consuming Passion: Why the Killing of Jesus Really Matters*, ed. Simon Barrow and Jonathan Bartley (London: Darton, Longman and Todd, 2005), 27–35.

19. Cynthia S. W. Crysdale, *Embracing Travail: Retrieving the Cross Today* (New York: Continuum, 1999), 115, quoted in Boersma, "Eschatological Justice," 187. Italics mine.

20. On the unavoidability of violence, see Hans Boersma, *Violence, Hospitality and the Cross* (Grand Rapids: Baker Academic, 2004), esp. ch. 1.

21. It would be interesting to analyse the language of the Bush administration with respect to justifying the Iraq war, where, I suspect, the idea of liberating people from Saddam Hussein's tyrannical regime (a *Christus Victor* approach) has been more prominent than the language of punishing Saddam Hussein for his evil (a PSA approach). The former, which led to horrific violence, was surely presented as the reason for the war even if the latter was subsequently played out in the courts.

22. The term "necessary evil" is not intended to distance God from the violence of the cross but is intended to stress the necessity of God's acting in this way in spite of the cost to himself. Boersma writes, "God's hospitality requires violence, just as his love necessitates wrath. This is not to say, of course, that God's violence and wrath are his essential attributes. God *is* love, not wrath; he *is* a God of hospitality, not a God of violence. There is an absolute primacy therefore of hospitality over violence" (Boersma, *Violence, Hospitality and the Cross*, 49). Perhaps one should note that 1 John 4:8 ("God is love") is balanced by 1 John 1:5 ("God is light"), both of which are essential attributes of God.

23. Boersma, "Eschatological Justice," 198.

24. In this respect, the sacrifice of Christ differs from the offering of Isaac in Genesis 22 and of the sacrificial offerings of tabernacle and temple, since these involved victims who were not fully conscious of their fate. Sin is, among other things, wilful wrongdoing, and only a person who is wilful can adequately substitute for wilful sinners. See Alec Motyer, *Isaiah*, Tyndale Old Testament Commentaries (Leicester: IVP, 1998), 336.

25. John Stott, *The Cross of Christ* (Leicester: IVP, 1986), 151.

26. Radio interview with Steve Gilhooley, whose story is told in Gilhooley, *The Pyjama Parade* (Edinburgh: Lomand, 2001).

27. Stott, *Cross of Christ*, 192.

28. Emile Brunner, *The Mediator: A Study of the Central Doctrine of the Christian Faith*, trans. Olive Wyon (London: Lutterworth, 1934), 459.

29. Ibid., 460.

30. Ibid., 462.

31. Ibid., 478. See also Boersma, *Violence, Hospitality and the Cross*, 48–49.

32. Sadly, the evidence suggests Brunner's forecast was true.

33. The paragraph is based on Brunner, *The Mediator*, 468–70. The quotation is from 470.

34. See, for example, Stephen Travis, "Christ as Bearer of Divine Judgment in Paul's Thought about the Atonement," in *Atonement Today: A Symposium at St John's College, Nottingham*, ed. John Goldingay (London: SPCK, 1995), 21–38. Ironically, this is a view espoused by C. H. Dodd in *The Epistle of Paul to the Romans* (1932; London: Collins, 1959), 47–50, which at the time was much opposed by evangelical scholars, such as Leon Morris, as an inadequate interpretation of the text. He spoke of God's wrath as anthropomorphic and argued that it should be understood as "an inevitable process of cause and effect in a moral universe".

35. Stott, *Cross of Christ*, 65.

36. Some critics of PSA are prepared to concede that in the Old Testament, God is spoken of as personally visiting people in judgment and expressing his wrath. The references to his doing so seem too numerous to avoid any other conclusion. Yet they say either that this is merely a naive and anthropomorphic way of speaking, necessary until more sophisticated theological language became available, or they take a Marcionite approach to the Old Testament and argue that it has been superseded by the New Testament, which shows a different view of God.

37. From "Rock of Ages."

38. Jenkins, *In My Place*, 8.

39. Paul Fiddes, *Past Event and Present Salvation: The Christian Idea of Atonement* (London: Darton, Longmann and Todd, 1989), 29.

40. For a discussion, see Colin E. Gunton, *The Actuality of Atonement: A Study of Metaphor, Rationality and the Christian Tradition* (Edinburgh: T & T Clark, 1988), 129–35.

41. Luke 23:39–43.

42. P. T. Forsyth, *The Cruciality of the Cross* (1907; Carlisle: Paternoster, 1997), 29.

43. Steve Chalke, "Redeeming the Cross from Death to Life," in Barrow and Bartley, *Consuming Passion*, 24. Chalke develops his argument by saying that it also leads to an individualistic, non-corporate view of salvation, "so it is no surprise that those who subscribe to this theory tend not to

be at the forefront of thinking about major socio-political issues confronting us" (24–25). This is certainly inaccurate historically. Eighteenth- and nineteenth-century evangelicals who held to PSA were at the forefront of any number of social movements, so there can be no automatic connection between cause and effect here. I doubt whether this claim could be substantiated from a contemporary viewpoint either, but I know of no reliable research that has been done to substantiate it either way. I accept that evangelicals who hold to PSA are certainly concerned about issues of personal morality, but I believe many of them are as concerned about issues of social morality. The cause of the difference may lie in their political understanding rather than their understanding of atonement.

44. I owe the direction of this thought to the contribution Dr Anna Robbins made to the atonement debate sponsored by the Evangelical Alliance and held on 7 October 2004 in London. In her so-far unpublished paper, she developed the importance of PSA for a Christian social ethic.

45. Nigel Wright, *The Radical Evangelical: Seeking a Place to Stand* (London: SPCK, 1996), 65.

46. Ibid.

We want to hear from you. Please send your comments about this book to us in care of zreview@zondervan.com. Thank you.